Main Melody Films

EDINBURGH STUDIES IN EAST ASIAN FILM
Series Editor: Margaret Hillenbrand

Available and forthcoming titles

Independent Chinese Documentary: Alternative Visions, Alternative Publics,
Dan Edwards

The Cinema of Ozu Yasujiro: Histories of the Everyday,
Woojeong Joo

Eclipsed Cinema: The Film Culture of Colonial Korea,
Dong Hoon Kim

Moving Figures: Class and Feeling in the Films of Jia Zhangke,
Corey Kai Nelson Schultz

Memory, Subjectivity and Independent Chinese Cinema,
Qi Wang

Hong Kong Neo-Noir,
Esther C. M. Yau and Tony Williams

'My' Self on Camera: First Person Documentary Practice in an Individualising China,
Kiki Tianqi Yu

Worldly Desires: Cosmopolitanism and Cinema in Hong Kong and Taiwan,
Brian Hu

Tanaka Kinuyo: Nation, Stardom and Female Subjectivity,
Irene González-López and Michael Smith

Killers, Clients and Kindred Spirits: The Taboo Cinema of Shohei Imamura,
David Desser and Lindsay Coleman

Sino-Enchantment: The Fantastic in Contemporary Chinese Cinemas,
Kenneth Chan and Andrew Stuckey

Hong Kong Cinema and Sinophone Transnationalisms,
TAN, See Kam

Main Melody Films: Hong Kong Directors in Mainland China,
Yiu-Wai Chu

www.edinburghuniversitypress.com/series/ESEAF

Main Melody Films

Hong Kong Directors in Mainland China

Yiu-Wai Chu

EDINBURGH
University Press

Edinburgh University Press is one of the leading university presses in the UK.
We publish academic books and journals in our selected subject areas across the
humanities and social sciences, combining cutting-edge scholarship with high editorial
and production values to produce academic works of lasting importance. For more
information visit our website: edinburghuniversitypress.com

Edinburgh University Press Ltd
The Tun – Holyrood Road
12(2f) Jackson's Entry
Edinburgh EH8 8PJ

Typeset in 10/13 Chaparral Pro by
IDSUK (DataConnection) Ltd, and
printed and bound in Great Britain

A CIP record for this book is available from the British Library

ISBN 978-1-4744-9386-4 (hardback)
ISBN 978-1-4744-9388-8 (webready PDF)
ISBN 978-1-4744-9389-5 (epub)

Contents

Acknowledgements   vi

A Note on Romanisation, Translation and Box Office Records   viii

Introduction: Main(land) Melody Films and Hong Kong Directors   1

1   How to Take Tiger Mountain? The Tsui Hark Model   29

2   Will Our Time Come? Ann Hui's Fallen City   54

3   Hong Kong Dreams in Mainland China: The Leap of Peter Chan   80

4   Founding an Army with Soft Power: Captain Andrew Lau   111

5   Stepping to the Fore: Dante Lam's Operation Trilogy   137

6   Underneath the Shock Waves: The (Un)told Stories of Herman Yau   163

7   Jumping on the Bandwagon: The Ensemble of Hong Kong
     Film Directors   189

Epilogue   213

Select Bibliography   236

Filmography   248

Glossary   259

Index   267

Acknowledgements

Most of this book was written during the time when Covid-19 completely turned day-to-day normality surreal. With the world at a stand-still, watching films at home became my major pastime. I understand that the main melody films discussed in this book were not very popular among the young Hong Kong audience. In an age of 'one world two capitalisms', however, it has become more and more acute to consider the future of Hong Kong cinema and the special administrative region per se in relation to the overall development of mainland China. Tracing the impact of Hong Kong directors on main melody films, this book aspires to make a modest contribution to this subject. Thanks to the distinctive position of Hong Kong in the new world order, this will hopefully shed light on related issues in other regions of the world too.

If there is an upside to the pandemic that made our lives topsy-turvy, it may be having more time to focus on writing. All chapters except some parts of the Introduction and Epilogue have not been published elsewhere. To publish a newly written monograph has become a luxury in Hong Kong tertiary institutions where research assessment exercises are heavily slanted towards so-called 'high impact' journal articles. Books serve a vital and even irreplaceable function, in my humble opinion, at least within the scope of the humanities.

This book began as a research project proposal. Although it did not get funding in the end (probably because of the taste of a reviewer), I must thank Kam Louie for his precious suggestions and comments on the project, without which this book could not have been shaped in a publishable manner. I would like to take this opportunity to thank him for bringing me to the University of Hong Kong, and Louise Edwards for giving me the chance to run the Hong Kong Studies Programme. It was from the bottom of my heart when I said in the job interview that it was an experience of a dream coming true for me. I must also thank Douglas Kerr and Elaine Yee Lin Ho for their kind support and guidance when I was trying to find my feet in a new environment. I miss the good old days when I had the privilege of working with them. Furthermore, I am grateful to the School of Chinese at the University of Hong Kong for giving me a small research grant, and the Faculty of Arts for a sabbatical leave to enable me to complete the writing.

My deep appreciation also goes to colleagues and friends who have helped me whether directly or indirectly in the process of completing this book: Chris Berry, Leonard Chan, Rey Chow, Po-shek Fu, Anthony Fung, Jeroen de Kloet and Shuk Man Leung. I owe special gratitude to Rey Chow whose academic writings I have admired for many years now. It was my great pleasure and honour to have the opportunity to work with her in a series of activities during her visits to the University of Hong Kong. I would also like to express special thanks to the series editor Margaret Hillenbrand and the team at Edinburgh University Press: Fiona Conn, Sam Johnson, Gillian Leslie, Caitlin Murphy, Fiona Screen and Richard Strachan. Preparation of the final manuscript became an enjoyable process with their professional advice and assistance. To Kin-Yuen Wong, teacher and friend, I have a long-standing debt. I dedicate this book to him as a belated retirement gift.

As always, I would like to conclude by recording my love for Nancy, Sebastian, Nathaniel, and our dear family members.

A Note on Romanisation, Translation and Box Office Records

Chinese names are generally romanised according to the style commonly used in Hong Kong, with English first names followed by Chinese surname (such as Ann Hui). For the sake of consistency, those without English first names are also romanised in the same way (such as Kar-Wai Wong), except those internationally known by other formats (such as Tsui Hark) or more commonly known by *pinyin* (such as Jin Yong). Names of mainland Chinese generally follow standard pinyin (such as Zhang Yimou) unless they have English first names (such as Jet Li). I have adopted the way other Chinese names have been transliterated by convention in Hong Kong, Taiwan and the mainland.

For film titles, I have used the corresponding English export titles.

All translations from Chinese materials are mine unless otherwise stated.

The box office records in mainland China are cited from <https://piaofang.maoyan.com/> and international box office records from <https://www.boxofficemojo.com/> unless otherwise stated.

Introduction: Main(land) Melody Films and Hong Kong Directors

National Rejuvenation

The Chinese dream of national rejuvenation, introduced by Xi Jinping at the start of his first term as General Secretary and President of the People's Republic of China (PRC) in 2012, remained the central theme of his speech delivered at the Nineteenth National Congress of the Chinese Communist Party (CCP) on 18 October 2017: 'our compatriots in Hong Kong and Macao will share both the historic responsibility of national rejuvenation and the pride of a strong and prosperous China'.[1] Xi also made it very clear that the development of Hong Kong and Macao would be closely tied to that of the mainland: 'We will continue to support Hong Kong and Macao in integrating their own development into the overall development of the country.'[2] In line with this, Xi underlined Beijing's policy to 'formulate and improve policies and measures to make it more convenient for people from Hong Kong to develop careers on the mainland'.[3] After the Nineteenth National Congress of the CCP, Beijing had plans to roll out new policies to integrate the Special Administrative Regions (SARs) into the mainland, and Hong Kong's reconfiguration would result in an increasingly marginal, minor position in Beijing's new blueprint. At a press conference during the Nineteenth National Congress, Zhang Hongsen, Deputy Director of the State Administration of Press, Publication, Radio, Film and Television (SAPPRFT), echoed Xi by saying that '[Xi] clearly pointed out the new direction for building stronger cultural self-confidence and helping socialist culture to flourish. The film industry will follow the guiding principles of the 19th CPC National Congress'.[4] Xi's pronouncements have since had a profound and unprecedented impact on cross-border collaborations. In this context, it is paramount for researchers to explore the relationship between Hong Kong's cultural industries and their mainland equivalents, thereby disclosing the ways in which their political economies interact.

It is against this critical backdrop that this book was conceived. As it builds on two of the author's previous books, it is necessary to recount some of the points made in those works in relation to this project. Firstly, *Lost in Transition* examined Hong Kong culture in the context of the rise of China, mapping its (dis)appearance after its reversion to China. As argued in the book, while Hong Kong's colonial history accounts for the special characteristics of its culture before 1997, its relation to China, the most swiftly developing economy in the world over the past decade, has introduced a paradigm shift. Hong Kong's relationship with the mainland has witnessed significant changes over the past ten years or so, which can be seen as the predicament and condition of imagining Hong Kong's future. The final pages of *Lost in Transition* consider whether the core values of Hong Kong might be not just lost but also found in transition.[5] *Found in Transition*, the sequel to *Lost in Transition*, further explored the (lost) momentum of Hong Kong culture, pointing to a new alternative Hong Kong imaginary – Hong Kong Studies as method – in the light of Hong Kong's changing relationship with both the world and China. After the twentieth anniversary of Hong Kong's reversion to China, a different theoretical perspective emerged, especially after heated controversies related to, among others, forced integration with mainland China and the fight for universal suffrage. Given the decline/demise of Hong Kong culture, such as cinema, popular music and television, it is not surprising that death has been one of the main themes of that culture. It was argued by way of conclusion in *Found in Transition* that with the increasing dependence of Hong Kong on mainland China in terms of not only politics but also economic and cultural markets, it will be ever more difficult for Hong Kong to inscribe its pluralities. It is thus necessary for Hong Kong Studies to rethink the inheritance and transmission of Hong Kong culture.[6]

It was also argued in *Lost in Transition* that the Chinese government had already officially expressed in the Eleventh Five-Year Plan (2006–10) its ambition to increase cultural influence through cultural development. The government pledged to adopt favourable policies to make full use of its resources to promote the influence and competitiveness of Chinese cultural products, from Confucian culture to Chinese popular cultures, which was a kind of 'charm offensive' – borrowing the term from Kam Louie – to win friends and influence in the world.[7] This has been Beijing's 'attraction' strategy to accumulate soft power, which is the key to the 'Beijing Consensus'.[8] Since then, China has been rising swiftly, and whether it is possible to export the China model – 'Chinese-style vertical democratic meritocracy'[9] – to other countries has become a hotly debated issue both inside and outside academic circles. No matter what one thinks, China has taken a proactive role in exporting this vaguely defined combination of authoritarian politics and state-guided capitalism through its One Belt One Road Initiative.

Departing from my previous work, which dealt with Hong Kong culture and studies in the age of China, this book proposes to explore a new dimension – the transmission and transformation of Hong Kong culture in the mainland – which will hopefully throw new light on the future development of Hong Kong Studies. While Beijing has become more proactive, if not tougher, in incorporating the SARs into the mainland, whether the plurality of Hong Kong culture and society will disappear or not is a key question to ask. At this particular juncture, the issue of integration with the mainland, whether Hong Kong likes it or not, has become a topic that is of the utmost importance for any consideration of the future of Hong Kong culture and the city per se. It was also argued in *Lost in Transition* that 'China has become a predicament as well as a condition for Hong Kong culture' in the age of China, especially after the signing of the Closer Economic Partnership Arrangement (CEPA) in 2003.[10] This has become even more acute for Hong Kong culture in the integration of the Greater Bay Area, which can be seen as incorporating Hong Kong and Macao's development into the overall development of the country.

When Xi Jinping asked the Hong Kong people to seize opportunities and 'compose new miracles under the Lion Rock' in his keynote speech delivered at a banquet attended by more than 300 elites from various sectors on the eve of the twentieth anniversary of Hong Kong's reversion to China, he cited the Cantopop song 'Creating Fate' (1984), originally sung by Alan Tam: 'A popular song in Hong Kong has this line: "Self-confidence is so important. Open up your mind and your dream will come true." We should have full confidence in ourselves, in Hong Kong and in our country.'[11] This rare reference to Cantopop and the use of the Cantonese slang 'don't miss the boat' did speak somewhat about the unique characteristics of Hong Kong culture and hence the importance of Hong Kong Studies. Ironically though, 'Creating Fate' (melody by Terence Tsoi and lyrics by Raymond Wong) was the theme song of a Hong Kong movie entitled *Heaven Can Help* (1984), directed by David Chiang. Indeed, Hong Kong culture cannot rely on heaven; to create its own fate, Hong Kong has to consider how to retain its own characteristics given its inevitable integration into the mainland. In this book, I aim to further explore this theme by going across the border to take on Hong Kong filmmakers' works that have affected both regions. Hong Kong filmmakers' increasing participation in 'main melody' (*zhuxuanlu*) films provides a good case study for this purpose, because it involves intricate cross-border dynamics that connect cultures to politics.

Chinese Main Melody Films and Their Transformations

Main melody films are not new to the mainland market. Simply put, they were derived from the musical term 'leitmotif', referring to 'state-sponsored', 'keynote' films with 'central themes'.[12] Best known as 'propaganda films' in the West, they had their roots in propaganda works that promoted certain ideas for and/or paid tribute to the nation, and in this sense the genre's history is as long as that of

Chinese cinema after 1949. While it is not easy to clearly define the different generations of early Chinese filmmakers, it is generally agreed that there were three generations before 1949: the first was comprised of its pioneers at the beginning of the twentieth century; the second developed the industry mainly with martial arts films in the 1920s; and the third 'Golden-age' generation won Chinese cinema international acclaim in the 1930s and 1940s.[13] During the early Mao years, the Fourth Generation of Chinese filmmakers focused on Soviet-inspired propagandist films, given the government's stranglehold on mass media. From 1949 to 1976, films were used to serve politics. During those thirty-odd years, films were not meaningfully different from propaganda explaining government policies and promoting patriotism. Shui Hua and Wang Bin's *The White-Haired Girl* (1950), Xie Jin's *The Red Detachment of Women* (1961) and Fu Chaowu, Sun Yongping and Yu Zhongying's *The Fiery Years* (1974), among others, were notable examples of propagandist films produced at that stage. In short, it had been 'three decades of propaganda-filled media' – as pointedly noted by Rey Chow – before the Fifth Generation directors won international attention again with award-winning films by Zhang Yimou and Chen Kaige in the 1980s.[14]

Owing to the open-door policy engineered by the then paramount leader Deng Xiaoping, who returned to the political arena after the downfall of the Gang of Four in 1976, the cultural industries in mainland China underwent significant changes in a decade of reforms when the capitalist energy of China was gradually released. Films such as *Mysterious Buddha* (1981), directed by Zhang Huaxun, and *The Shaolin Temple* (1982), directed by Zhang Xinyan, won commercial success, and Chen Kaige's *Yellow Earth* (1984) garnered international critical acclaim. When Chinese cinema became more market-oriented, it was necessary for the government to have tighter control over the industry. 'Post-Mao China, as the inheritor of the communist period of primitive accumulation and as a newcomer in the world market,' to cite Xudong Zhang, 'is giving rise to a nationalism that is new in the historical sense but which is creating a sense of déjà vu theoretically.'[15] It was in this special context that 'main melody films' entered the official lexicon in March 1987 when Teng Jinxian, the then Head of the National Film Bureau, called on studio managers to 'foreground main melody while encouraging diversity', and by 'main melody' he meant 'embodying patriotism, socialism, and collectivism; resolutely resisting money worship, hedonism, and excessive individualism; and unshakably opposing capitalism, and all corrupt, exploitative trends'.[16] It is therefore unsurprising that the 'diversity' noted by Teng could not but be subordinate to the main melody, since the term was actually used

> to define an official orientation of the Chinese film industry against the
> commercialization that had developed rapidly since the enactment of the

'reform and opening up' policy; the 'main melody' of the Chinese film industry should be uplifting films with didactic and pedagogical functions.[17]

In July 1987, the Central Government approved the founding of the Leading Group on Major Revolutionary and Historical Themes of Film and Television Creation, of which Ding Qiao was the group leader. *The Kunlun Column* (1988), co-directed by Hao Guang and Jing Mukui, *Baise Uprising* (1989), directed by Chen Jialin, and *The Birth of New China* (1989), co-directed by Li Qiankuan and Xiao Guiyun, were among the first batch of genuinely main melody films, which were also known as 'dedication movies' in commemoration of the fortieth anniversary of the founding of the PRC, that paid homage to the revolution and the CCP. When these 'dedications' ushered in the first stage of the development of Chinese main melody films, the Central Government tried using these films 'to advocate the "main theme of our time," market reform, especially since the June Fourth Tiananmen student demonstrations'.[18] From 1989 to 1995, only sixteen state-owned studios could make these kinds of movies, which were, expectedly, not much different from monotonous textbooks. In short, state media and funding bodies (such as the China Film Fund) worked closely together 'to produce films that are targeted at domestic and international markets, but promote views which are broadly compatible with the CCP's agenda of creating a pro-state vision of China as a powerful and culturally dynamic nation'.[19]

Early main melody films concentrated mainly on war and biographical events, with major revolutionary and historical themes holding patriotism, collectivism and socialism in esteem. *The Birth of New China*, among others, was a typical example of a Chinese main melody film. In the early 1990s, main melody films continued to be used to enhance the image of the Party (such as the *Decisive Engagement* trilogy [1991–1992], directed by Li Jun et al., and *The Creation of a World* [1991], directed by Li Xiepu to celebrate the seventieth anniversary of the founding of the CCP) and its leaders (such as *Mao Zedong and His Son* [1991], directed by Zhang Jinbiao, and *Zhou Enlai* [1992], directed by Ding Yinnan) in the aftermath of the political turmoil of the Tiananmen Incident. As Rui Zhang writes, 'To ensure these films fulfill this function, every aspect of the main melody film was monopolized by the state – from the recruitment of filmmakers to the exhibition of the films.'[20] Thanks to Beijing's protectionist policies and thus lack of foreign competition back then, these films were quite well received by the domestic audience. That said, in the so-called 'post-new era' after 1989, Beijing realised that 'it was imperative to reinforce state ideological apparatuses, and the film industry was one of the most important'.[21] According to Xie Mian and Zhang Yiwu, there was a major transformation of cultural production in the post-new era – after the new era of reform and opening up – as the Central Government began to see the importance of popular cultures in the marketisation of China's national economy.[22]

Hongmei Yu borrowed the accounts of Arif Dirlik and Chris Berry on post-socialism to describe 'an ideological map to read the ambiguities, contradictions, and uncertainties at the historical conjuncture of Mao's death and Deng's succession', foregrounding the importance of 'the radically different economic circumstances of post-1989 China', where the market effected 'a fundamental "genetic modification" that has led the country to postsocialism'.[23] It was in such a historical context that the then leader Jiang Zemin reiterated, in a 1994 speech on the direction of literature and art delivered at the National Conference on Propaganda Work, that main melody films should 'promote patriotism, socialism and collectivism and resolutely resist money-worship, hedonism and excessive individualism',[24] which 'marked the beginning of the massive production of main melody films' in three major categories: '(1) films focusing on revolutionary history; (2) biographical films of heroic characters, especially communist martyrs; and (3) films representing the achievements of the post-Mao political and economic reforms'.[25] Beginning in November 1994, the Chinese government 'adopted an independent accounting system by which 10 foreign blockbuster films, most of which were Hollywood movies, could enter the Chinese market each year',[26] arguably owing to the need to open the market and boost box-office income. The PRC State Education Commission also issued, in 1995, a list of 100 patriotic films that primary and secondary school students in China must watch, most of which 'critically depict China's invasion by the Great Powers or glorify CCP history'.[27] Thanks to the marketisation of Chinese cinema, changes could also be seen in the characters, subject matters and styles of main melody films in the mid-1990s:

> Although still functioning as mouthpieces of the government and propagating the government's new policies and heroic models, or simply legitimizing the status quo, the changing face of main melody films suggests a concurrent transformation in the Party art policy, specifically, a switch from the glorification of Party and state leaders to broader themes stressing common virtues such as patriotism, self-sacrifice, and loyalty.[28]

Besides Xie Jin's *The Opium War* (1997), which commemorated Hong Kong's reunion with China, there were also main melody films that were somewhat more loosely linked to patriotism towards the end of the twentieth century. To celebrate the fiftieth anniversary of the founding of the PRC in 1999, there were many dedications, including traditional main melody films such as *Flag of the Republic*, directed by Wang Jixing and Lei Xianhe, and *Roaring Across the Horizon*, directed by Chen Guoxing. During this time, there were also films that merged the main melody with commercial genres, such as *A Time to Remember*, directed by Ye Daying, and *Lover's Grief over the Yellow River*, directed by

Feng Xiaoning. The former was a revolutionary romance featuring Hong Kong superstar Leslie Cheung, and the latter was a war film about the CCP's Eighth Route Army's anti-Japanese battle during the Second World War packaged with the story of a female Chinese soldier and a grounded American pilot who was inspired by the noble spirit of the Chinese people. Despite the change of narrative strategies, as argued by Hongmei Yu, from 'representations of collective action' to 'a rising emphasis on the personal/individual perspective, which speaks directly to the ideological transformation of contemporary market-reform China', main melody films did not win much commercial success.[29] When 'profit incentives began to erode the main melody films in the second half of the 1990s',[30] as 'a unique cultural product of postsocialist China', main melody films still relied almost solely on government support for distribution and promotion: 'between 1995 and 2000, of the 80 to 100 movies produced each year, approximately 80 per cent could be considered main melody films' – they 'consumed huge resources yet accounted for few market profits'.[31]

A more radical change in Chinese main melody films had to wait until the new millennium. As China opened its market further after becoming a member of the World Trade Organization (WTO) on 11 December 2001, the quota of foreign movies on a revenue-sharing basis was raised from ten to twenty per annum. Owing to the change of the mediascape after entering the WTO, the State Administration of Radio, Film and Television (SARFT, later changed to the SAPPRFT in 2013) revised its policy in 2002 – it 'no longer insists on promoting only a top-down political message, but rather an image of China that is socio-culturally diversified yet politically "harmonious"'; despite this, more often than not, 'the domestic success of some main melody films is often artificially created by SAPPRFT's blackout system; that is, SAPPRFT sets aside a time period to show these films'.[32] In short, after the further opening of the market, 'the Chinese strategy', as astutely noted by Wendy Su, was 'to use money earned from Hollywood to promote "main melody" films'.[33] Main melody films began merging with the *dapian* (big pictures; high-concept blockbusters) blueprint, and '[w]ith its firm backing by China Film Group (CFG) and the State Administration of Radio, Film and Television (SARFT) and in its market control', as noted by Darrell Davis, Zhang Yimou's *Hero* (2002) 'was no less main melody than any main melody picture'.[34] While this 'quasi-main melody martial arts blockbuster' and 'China's first local blockbuster fully modeled on the contemporary Hollywood blockbuster'[35] stirred up controversies about its pro-establishment ideology, *Hero* successfully set an example for the blockbusterisation of the Chinese film industry. It found unprecedented success in terms of both box-office and critical acclaim, setting a then new record of RMB 250 million and winning a number of awards, including the Alfred Bauer Prize presented by the Berlin International Film Festival. Starring international film stars Jet Li, Zhang Ziyi, Tony Chiu-wai Leung and Maggie Cheung, *Hero* was an important watershed in the development of Chinese cinema in general and main melody films in particular. As pointed out by Zhang Hongsen, the then Deputy Director of the Film Bureau, it established

> a first model for Chinese blockbusters, and as the beginning of a new sort of film production, which ceased to break films down into attributes of main melody, commercial or art film, met the audience's aesthetic demands and made full use of cinema's commercial resources, including stars, technology, and modern management, showing that Chinese cinema had the potential to become a real soft power.[36]

On the one hand, *Hero* upheld the major theme of the importance of stability, and on the other, it appropriated 'the contemporary Hollywood blockbuster mode' that 'extended to finances and marketing'.[37]

Main Melody and/as Soft Power

Entering the age of *dapian*, the box office of mainland China grew swiftly and at an amazing speed. In this special context, 'the familiar boundaries – and contradictions – among art, politics and commerce have begun to break down', and Feng Xiaogang's *Assembly* (2007) can be seen as proof that main melody films made by mainstream directors successfully reached 'audiences less interested in overt political messages'.[38] However, as perceptively noted by Ying Zhu and Stanley Rosen, high-ranking film officials, unlike Feng 'who sees not only propaganda but apparently also art as out-of-date', still placed most emphasis on 'political messages' back then: the 'new kind of producer in China's new era', as highlighted by Jiang Ping, Vice President of the Film Bureau, in February 2007, must be 'politically sensitive, aesthetically sophisticated and have a flair for marketing'.[39] Thanks to the signing of the CEPA with the HKSAR, ever more mainland–Hong Kong co-productions, which were mostly blockbusters, were produced. When these co-productions attracted more and more Hong Kong film talents to the mainland market, the Chinese film industry also gradually accumulated the experience of producing blockbusters the Hollywood way. I have argued elsewhere that Chen Guofu and Gao Qunshu's *The Message* (2009) marked an important transformation in the production of Chinese blockbusters. This billion-dollar-budget spy *dapian* showcased Chinese cinema's ability to produce a commercial blockbuster without the co-productive contribution of Hong Kong filmmakers, which was a sign of things to come. In the words of Yu Dong, President of the Beijing Polybona Films Distribution Co. Ltd., '2009 marked a new beginning of an era dominated by mainland productions', and 'Hong Kong filmmakers are commissioned to produce films of mainland themes and stories'.[40] At that point, however, turning Party-themed main melody films (such as *Tie Ren* [2009], also known as *Iron Man*, a biopic about 'model' oil worker Wang Jinxi directed by Yin Li) into successful blockbusters was possible only with the help of the government – tickets 'bought up by the authorities on behalf of their staff'.[41] These were at most 'blockbusters with a government feel', so to speak. Notwithstanding, this was the predicament as well as the condition of 'Chinese Cinema with "Mainland Characteristics"',[42] and how to sing the main melody attractively in a commercial blockbuster remained an important question to explore.

The main melody not very overtly heard in *The Message* had to be sung loudly in *The Founding of a Republic* (2009), produced by the China Film Group Corporation and directed by its chairman, Han Sanping (co-directed with Huang Jianxin), given the latter's main theme of praising the nation. As apparent from the name, it was a typical dedication film paying homage to the sixtieth anniversary of the PRC. Utterly different from *The Birth of New China*, which was released twenty years before *The Founding of a Republic*, this main melody tribute was a commercial blockbuster. As rightly noted by Darrell Davis, 'with stars in every scene, high production values, and humanized portraits of leaders of the Guomindang, the CCP's historical enemy', this 'main melody film in the guise of a *dapian*' was the first of its kind to reach blockbuster status – not just in terms of production but also in box-office returns (earning RMB 420 million).[43] Han Sanping clearly spelt out the transformation of main melody in 'an era of entertainment for everyone':

> A good movie should be able to motivate audiences to purchase tickets. Therefore, *The Founding of a Republic* should operate from a commercialized approach, and its workflow should be integrated on a market-oriented basis . . . Those who can entertain the public well are the ones who gain recognition and support from the masses, as well as box office success and positive reception. Similarly, the ones who can entertain the people are the ones capable of educating and guiding the public in an imperceptible way.[44]

In other words, the 'enhanced main melody' that 'sought to marry the appeal of attractive, compelling characters with socialist ideology espoused by the Party'[45] began to lay more emphasis on the films' commercial attractiveness while conveying the central theme. The formula of 'main melody commercial blockbusters', as succinctly summed up by Zhang Jingwu, was to 'promote family and country feelings, entrust the spirit of the times, and at the same time win huge commercial success' by turning the 'main theme' into a hidden 'positive energy' without allowing the films to become crude propaganda.[46] The production quality of main melody films was henceforth upgraded in order to incite popular interest. Seeing 'the making of *The Founding* as both a necessity and an experiment, believing that it could become a model for future productions',[47] Han Sanping's bold experiment was successful, ushering main melody films into a new stage in the 2010s. As the playmaker of the commercialisation of main melody films, Han's statement demonstrated the initiative to entertain and educate the public at once. As *The Founding of a Republic* marked the beginning of a new era of Chinese main melody commercial blockbusters, it was a time when 'the familiar boundaries – and contradictions – among art, politics, and commerce have begun to break down, with films previously designated as "main melody" in China and "propaganda" films abroad successfully finding ways to stimulate audience interest'.[48] The subsequent episode, *Beginning of the Great Revival* (2011), also co-directed by Han Sanping and Huang Jianxin, continued to adopt the formula of 'enhanced main melody', pairing 'main melody official narratives with proven commercial expertise and global talent',[49] including a cast of leading film stars as key players in China's modern history, as well as cameo appearances by countless pop stars with an eye to commercial attractiveness.

Back in 1987, Paul Clark had already pointed out that 'films were a central tool in the remolding of socialist new citizens' in the eyes of Chinese leaders.[50] More than thirty years later, he reiterated that 'Beijing's rulers continue to invest films with such power, even as Chinese audiences have turned to other forms of entertainment and education in a media market that is very different from that of even three decades ago'.[51] As films and film festivals were seen as an ideal means to project China's image internationally, 'Chinese cultural authorities and many filmmakers still dream today of the magic blockbuster that will launch Chinese films to mass popularity in the United States and other Western countries'.[52] Unfortunately, however, 'in comparison with the rapid growth of Chinese films in the domestic market, the number of films exhibited overseas has increased relatively slowly'.[53] Worse still, Chinese main melody films have not been able to draw large domestic audiences (especially the younger generation), let alone overseas distributors. In 2010, the head-to-head clash between *Avatar* (2009), directed by James Cameron, and the state-backed Chinese *dapian Confucius* (2010), directed by Hu Mei, with Yun-Fat Chow as the male lead, further escalated the need for Chinese cinema to acquire soft power by going global. The immense popularity of the Hollywood blockbuster 'has created considerable challenges to state-sanctioned local films and to the CCP's ideological security in China'; meanwhile,

> as the Chinese economy ascends on the global stage, China also desires for more positive international image and greater international influence. Subsequently, the Party-state urged Chinese film and media industries to 'go global', to reach international audiences, and to help enhance China's soft power.[54]

The emphasis on soft power is closely related to China's 'going-out' policy in the new millennium.[55] The notion was introduced to China with the translation of Joseph Nye's *Bound to Lead* in 1992, but, as Kingsley Edney, Ying Zhu and Stanley Rosen have argued in the introduction to their *Soft Power with Chinese Characteristics*, although its use increased between 1994 and 2007, it did not jump markedly until 2008, after the then President Hu Jintao emphasised the increasing importance of promoting Chinese culture. The number of Chinese articles referencing soft power continued to rise until 2012, but in its subsequent decline, 'the concept had been incorporated into and become an important component of Xi Jinping's New China Dream discourse'.[56]

As mentioned above, Xi Jinping underscored the importance of national rejuvenation, and the country's soft power was a crucial yardstick for measuring China's place in the contemporary world. The conception of 'positive energy' in his new slogan of 2013 – 'Give full scope to the main melody; spread positive energy'[57] – should also be understood against the backdrop of national rejuvenation. It was no longer simple propaganda but also a way to accumulate soft power. On 15 October 2014, seventy-two years after Mao Zedong delivered his infamous 'Talks at the Yan'an Forum on Literature and Art' on 2 May 1942, Xi made a speech at the Beijing Forum on Literature and Art. After listening to the talks of seven representatives from the art and literature sector, he stressed that 'the literature and art undertaking is an important undertaking of the Party and the people, the literature and art battlefront is an important battlefront for the Party and the people'. (The seven representatives were Tie Ning [Chair of the China Federation of Literary and Art Circles and Chinese Writers Association], Shang Changrong [Chair of the China Theatre Association], Yan Su [Deputy Chair of the China Theatre Association and the Chinese Music Literature Association], Xu Jiang [Deputy Chair of the China Federation of Literary and Art Circles], Zhao Ruheng [Chair of the China Dancers Association], Ye Xin [Deputy Chair of the Chinese Writers Association] and Li Xuejian [Chair of the China Film Association]).[58] Admittedly, both talks emphasised the importance of socialist literature and art essentially as the people's literature and art, highlighting political rather than cultural significance. However, with patriotism still the main melody of literature and art creation, Xi further developed Mao's literary and art theory in the context of a new world order, as perceptively noted by Ning Wang:

> If we compare the two talks, we may easily find the marks of the time are very clear: in Mao, the national sense is more emphasized, while in Xi, the international and cosmopolitan significance of Chinese literature and art is particularly emphasized.[59]

When Joseph Nye, who coined the term 'soft power', discussed it in the current context of competition between China and America, he argued that 'public diplomacy in the form of soft power is more important than ever': 'In today's world the most compelling story transmitted and accelerated via cyberspace triumphs as the ability to disseminate the story and shape people's perceptions becomes ever more crucial.'[60] In this sense, if a main melody film continues to be 'a love letter written to our mother country',[61] the letter has to be beautifully composed, enhancing positive energy as well as accumulating soft power by attracting both domestic and foreign audiences.

Overall, the continuous marketisation of Chinese cinema means that main melody films have begun to pay more attention to commercial values. As convincingly argued by Xiaomei Chen, '[i]n a postsocialist state with "capitalist characteristics" such as the PRC, "propaganda" can no longer be simply dismissed as a monolithic, top-down, and meaningless practice characterized solely by censorship and suppression of freedom of expression in a totalitarian regime.'[62] The rise of Chinese soft power and changes in government policy in recent years have resulted in main melody films acquiring different meanings. In Xi Jinping's terms, 'main melody' is closely related to the conception of 'positive energy'. In other words, the primary concern is social impact, but at the same time commercial values are nonetheless important. To echo this, there has been a surge of blockbuster-commercialised main melody films. *Amazing China*, a 2018 Chinese documentary that praised China's achievements since Xi took power in 2012, is a related example. True to its name, it is an 'amazing' work. Chris Berry's point on the subject is worth citing here:

> [I]t is a form of propaganda in the pursuit of soft power . . . although the Communist Party of China is the power behind this, its attempt to win legitimacy in the eyes of its audience is based on quite similar values and styles of filmmaking to those used in the West.[63]

Commercialisation and marketisation have become an important strategy of main melody films. This matches perfectly with the themes of mainland–Hong Kong co-productions, through which Hong Kong directors have demonstrated their abilities to meet the criteria of marketability prevailing in mainland China.

Commercial Blockbusterisation and Hong Kong Directors

As Xi Jinping also stated at the Beijing Forum on Literature and Art in 2014, 'it cannot be denied that, in the area of literature and art creation, the phenomena that there is quantity but no quality, and there are "high plateaus" but no "high peaks" exist'.[64] Although Chinese cinema did enter a new stage of development after 2009, and *The Founding of a Republic* set the stage for main melody blockbusters, its commercialisation still had something to be desired. Against such a backdrop, Hong Kong directors had the chance to helm main melody blockbusters with an eye to enhancing their commercial competitiveness.[65] It is generally agreed among film critics that Tsui Hark's *The Taking of Tiger Mountain 3D* (2014) signalled a paradigm shift to commercial, high-concept main melody blockbusters. Based on one of the 'model' plays allowed during the Cultural Revolution, the film found a workable formula for an effective crossover of main melody films and commercial blockbusters. Actually, Miao Xiaotian, General Manager of the China Film Co-Production Corp, recognised the significant role that Hong Kong film talents played in boosting the industry in the mainland: 'In the past we focuse[d] mainly on art films. Through our collaboration with Hong Kong we understood the concept of commercial films, beginning to know how to attract the audience to our films.'[66] More importantly, Chinese films are still incapable of attracting foreign audiences, and only co-productions, according to Miao, are able to lure overseas markets. It is thus not surprising to see that on the list of the top 100 Chinese film directors, four of the top ten and thirteen of the top thirty were in one way or another related to Hong Kong. Of the top 100, a total of 35 were related to Hong Kong, positioned as follows:

4. Tsui Hark	41. Derek Yee
5. Stephen Chow	43. Sunny Luk and Longman Leung
8. Dante Lam	47. Edmond Pang
9. Raman Hui	50. Gordon Chan
15. Peter Chan	51. Raymond Yip
17. Kar-Wai Wong	52. Jeffrey Lau
20. Jing Wong	53. Benny Chan
21. Pou-Soi Cheang	65. Woo-Ping Yuen
22. Andrew Lau	66. Herman Yau
23. Daniel Lee	68. Teddy Chan
24. Stanley Tong	69. Stephen Fung
29. Wilson Yip	71. Tony Ching
30. Derek Kwok	77. Ann Hui
36. John Woo	78. Barbara Wong
37. Alan Mak	82. Ringo Lam
38. Felix Chong	88. Oxide Pang
39. Johnnie To	99. Derek Tsang[67]

According to a survey conducted by EntGroup, an independent third-party research company specialising in the entertainment industry in mainland China, the film market of mainland China is no longer dominated by major mainland directors such as Feng Xiaogang, Zhang Yimou and Chen Kaige. Hong Kong directors have exerted positive impacts on the diversification of film genres, which has contributed enormously to mainland China's box office.[68] Therefore, many top Hong Kong filmmakers have recently been commissioned to take the helm as directors in a series of main melody blockbusters, as more and more co-productions pay homage to national ideologies.

Mainland–Hong Kong co-productions have exerted a big influence on the function of cross-border collaborations for some time. Hong Kong cinema is seen as declining because of the rise of co-productions, especially after the CEPA was signed in 2003. Just three years after the implementation of the CEPA, Henry Fong, a senior Hong Kong actor-producer-director, lamented that '[f]rom now on Hong Kong cinema is Chinese cinema'.[69] As I have argued elsewhere, mainland–Hong Kong co-productions have since then been seen as an antidote to Hong Kong cinema, which has faced a swiftly shrinking market; however, it has turned out to be a *pharmakon* – both remedy and poison. Owing to various factors such as market considerations and (self-)censorship, the integration of Hong Kong cinema into the mainland has led to some scholars arguing that Hong Kong cinema has lost its special characteristics. However, at the same time, many Hong Kong filmmakers believe that the future of Hong Kong cinema lies in the mainland, given the enormous potential of its market. Whether the cure is worse than the disease, only time will tell, but it is evident that co-productions, as a model for the Hong Kong film industry, are not sustainable in the long run.[70] Notwithstanding, it is not surprising to see Hong Kong filmmakers going north to produce films in the mainland because of its huge market potential. For example, *The Mermaid* (2016), directed by Stephen Chow, one of the most representative icons of Hong Kong cinema in the 1990s, topped the mainland box office of co-productions with an eye-popping record RMB 3.391 billion, while the total box-office revenue of the local Hong Kong market was HK$55.24 million (RMB 46.07 million). The box-office figures spoke for themselves: it was perfectly understandable why Hong Kong filmmakers swarmed into the mainland market. Jing Wong is another good example, echoing the main melody from another angle. His *Chasing the Dragon* (2017), a reboot of his two crime classics *To Be Number One* (1991) and *Lee Rock* (1991), pinpointed the corruption of the Hong Kong police and their collusion with drug dealers back in the dark old days of the former British colony. Citing Hong Kong film critic Bono Lee, who said that mainland–Hong Kong co-productions have left local sensibility behind, Esther Yau shrewdly underlined the importance of 'post-Hong Kong cinema': 'all that is left is to seek out the "hidden currents" or traces of the preceding (read, more vibrant) Hong Kong cinema in the co-produced films'.[71] To this end, this book proposes to unearth the subtler interaction of mainland discourse and Hong Kong cinema after the top Hong Kong filmmakers went north to take charge of main melody blockbusters.

As noted by Zhang Hongsen, *Wolf Warrior 2* (2017) and *The Founding of an Army* (2017) are new exemplary mainstream movies, and the soft power of Chinese culture has significantly increased thanks to these main melody blockbusters.[72] (For example, *Wolf Warrior 2*, as noted by Chris Berry, 'seems to have initiated a whole new subgenre for Chinese cinema: the action-adventure overseas film'.[73]) Apparently, main melody blockbusters will be the main theme in Chinese cinema in the years to come, and Hong Kong filmmakers' participation in main melody films is a good topic through which the transmission and transformation of Hong Kong culture in mainland China can be examined. Interestingly, Teddy Chan's *Bodyguards and Assassins* (2009), which can be interpreted as a metaphor of the predicament faced by Hong Kong (the literal translation of the Chinese title is *A Besieged City in October*), can be seen as an early example of Hong Kong filmmakers' participation in main melody films in mainland China. To borrow the term from well-known Hong Kong director Peter Chan, it was a 'privately run' (as opposed to state-run) main melody film.[74] Since then, more and more Hong Kong directors have sung the main melody. Similar to *Bodyguards and Assassins*, Jackie Chan's *1911* (2011), also known as *Xinhai Revolution*, was a tribute to the 100th anniversary of the Xinhai Revolution. *The Soong Sisters*, directed by Mabel Cheung in 1997, a Hong Kong co-production about the wives of Sun Yat-sen and Chiang Kai-shek, was another early main melody film – at least in the loose sense of it – helmed by a Hong Kong director. Back then, however, the mainland still had a very precise understanding of the main melody, and thus Mabel Cheung was perhaps too pioneering in making a commercial main melody film at that juncture. It was a completely different story as the mainland market changed quickly and drastically, as mentioned above, in the new millennium. Since the advent of mainland–Hong Kong co-productions after the implementation of the CEPA, Hong Kong film directors started going north with an eye on the enormous potential of the mainland market – Tsui Hark, Peter Chan, Gordon Chan and the like shifted their bases to the mainland. Subsequently, more and more Hong Kong directors have been commissioned to make main melody blockbusters. In the eyes of Hong Kong audiences, 'the PRC has subsumed Hong Kong filmmakers to the national cause'.[75] As precisely summed up by Hong Kong film critic Matthew Cheng, the northbound Hong Kong directors can be categorised into three types:

> First, urban, petite bourgeoisie chic such as Peter Chan and Derek Tsang, who can skillfully capture city life in their films; second, Hollywood-style such as *The Taking of Tiger Mountain 3D*, using entertainment to dissolve politics; and third, humanistic touch such as *Our Time Will Come* (2017), focusing on the individuals but not the collective, examining how they survive their own epochs.[76]

Tsui Hark's *The Taking of Tiger Mountain 3D*, among others, is a very good example of how an established, famously commercial Hong Kong director made a main melody blockbuster based on one of the eight model plays allowed during the Chinese Cultural Revolution (the story is based on Qu Bo's 1957 novel *Tracks in the Snowy Forest*). Although Johnnie To made it clear in an interview that 'it is not possible to negotiate in between . . . if you wanted to make films in the mainland, you have to follow their rules',[77] his signature crime thriller shot entirely in the mainland, *Drug War* (2012), showed that he was able to zigzag creatively across the border by retaining, at least to a certain extent, his Hong Kong characteristics despite various limitations.[78] Tsui Hark's *The Taking of Tiger Mountain 3D* can, in a way, be seen as a similar case (for further details of this film, see Chapter 1). This can be attributed, at least in part, to Hong Kong filmmakers' experience of the northern venture.

The rest of the 2010s saw many main melody films directed by Hong Kong filmmakers, such as Dante Lam's *Operation Mekong* (2016), Oxide Pang's *My War* (2016), Andrew Lau's *The Founding of an Army*, Alan Mak and Anthony Pun's *Extraordinary Mission* (2017) and, above all, Dante Lam's record-breaking box-office hit (reportedly earning a total of RMB 3.4 billion) *Operation Red Sea* (2018), a Chinese anti-terrorism action film. In 2019, there were seven 'official' main melody films that commemorated the seventieth anniversary of the founding of the PRC, including *The Bugle from Gutian*, directed by Chen Li, *The Secret of China*, directed by Wang Jixing, *Chairman Mao 1949*, directed by Ning Haiqiang and Huang Jianxin, *The Bravest*, directed by Tony Chan, *My People, My Country* and *The Captain*, directed by Andrew Lau and *The Climbers*, directed by Daniel Lee. The latter three premiered in October, the month celebrating the anniversary of the founding of the PRC, as keynote films. Two of them (*The Captain* and *The Climbers*) were directed by Hong Kong filmmakers, which spoke volumes for the importance of Hong Kong directors in Chinese main melody commercial blockbusters.

In order to be entertaining, main melody blockbusters are designed according to mainstream standards and aesthetics. As one can observe in *Operation*

Red Sea, the rhythm and narrative perspectives followed those of commercial blockbusters, and the use of medium shots/close-ups and tight editing fulfilled the standards of commercial blockbusters. Traditional main melody films often adopted grand narratives, but with an eye to appealing to the mainstream market. More recent ones began using the narrative strategies of commercial blockbusters, focusing more on individual heroes in the main plots. *The Taking of Tiger Mountain 3D*, *Operation Mekong* and *Operation Red Sea*, among others, are good examples. Regarding characters, the heroes in recent main melody blockbusters were ordinary human beings. For example, the image of the revolutionary hero in *The Taking of Tiger Mountain 3D* was significantly different from those in traditional main melody films. Unlike the three 'stand-out' principles of sample plays, Tsui Hark shaped the protagonist as a round, ordinary, down-to-earth character, which is a good example of appealing to the general audience by deconstructing the stereotypes of flat heroic characters in traditional main melody films. Owing perhaps to their commercial backgrounds, Hong Kong directors tended to use young idols in their main melody films, such as Lin Gengxin in *The Taking of Tiger Mountain 3D* and Eddie Peng in *Operation Mekong*. Finally, one can also find in these main melody films interesting kinds of intertextual references,[79] such as the underlying links to Hong Kong kung-fu films in *Wolf Warrior 2* and *Bodyguards and Assassins* and those to police and gangster films in *Operation Mekong* and *Our Time Will Come*.

These examples of how Hong Kong filmmakers directed overt propaganda vehicles in their cross-border ventures had important implications for not only Chinese main melody films but also Hong Kong cinema. However, given the strict censorship system of mainland China, it would just be wishful thinking to claim that northbound Hong Kong filmmakers were engaged in the 'exchange of bargaining chips', 'enduring all disgrace and insult in order to accomplish their task' and acting as 'undercover cops'.[80] As Shuk-ting Kinnia Yau has argued, main melody films as traditionally understood 'have in recent years been charting a path to extinction due to the high degree of commercialization', as they 'have had to follow the pattern of *Wolf Warrior II*, putting effort into deifying the Chinese economy and military and gaining international attention'.[81] Notwithstanding this, 'the seesaw battle between political correctness and market reality' as evinced by new main melody films provided a precious opportunity for Hong Kong directors to develop their mainland ventures, which are excellent cases through which mainland–Hong Kong cross-border collaborations can be explored. As per Alain Badiou's stipulation that some films 'need to be critiqued because their reactionary dimension is not immediately obvious',[82] these main melody films, with their immediately obvious reactionary dimensions, may cast useful light on some other important issues.

Hong Kong Directors' Main(land) Melody

Given the space limitations of this book, I have chosen to focus on Chinese main melody films by Hong Kong directors in the 2010s, the decade of the commercialisation and blockbusterisation of this distinctive genre of Chinese cinema that had been unable until then to effectively reach the general audience. From 2011 to 2019, there were a total of 151 main melody films, raking in approximately RMB 36 billion at the box office.[83] As discussed above, the rise of China, its soft power and hence changes in related government policies have resulted in Chinese main melody films acquiring new meanings. Further outlined was how their transformation from political propaganda to commercial blockbusters attempted to win legitimacy based on quite similar values and styles of filmmaking to those used in the West. This introduction to the book has provided the theoretical backdrop against which the significance of Hong Kong filmmakers' participation in Chinese main melody blockbusters will be critically assessed. The subsequent chapters will look at different Chinese main melody projects helmed by Hong Kong directors in the 2010s. (In this book I use 'main(land) melody' to underscore Hong Kong directors' participation in main melody films in mainland China, whereas 'main melody' refers to the film genre in general.)

First of all, Chapter 1 will discuss Tsui Hark, once hailed as the 'Hong Kong Spielberg'. Marking the beginning of a new era of Chinese main melody commercial blockbusters, his epic action main melody film *The Taking of Tiger Mountain 3D*, based on one of the most well-known model works during the Cultural Revolution, enjoyed both box-office success and critical acclaim in the mainland. Although its box-office returns were abysmal in Hong Kong, Tsui was named Best Director for this film, not unsurprisingly, at both the Hong Kong Film Awards and the Hong Kong Film Critics Society Awards. This film is therefore an excellent example with which to explore the possible chemistry between Tsui Hark's model of filmmaking and the main(land) melody in cross-border collaborative projects. This chapter will first offer a brief account of Tsui's film career from Hong Kong to Hollywood and then to the mainland, before moving on to examine how the main melody film was inspired by his signature style of filmmaking. It will conclude by underlining the importance of the intertextual traces of the Tsui Hark model in this classic propaganda work.

Chapter 2 will examine the work of Ann Hui, similar to Tsui Hark, a key Hong Kong New Wave filmmaker who continues to be among the leading figures of Hong Kong cinema after four decades of filmmaking. Unlike Tsui, however, Hui is well known for her films featuring humanistic concerns and social awareness. In fact, she is among the most experienced Hong Kong directors to take part in mainland–Hong Kong co-productions. The two episodes of *The Romance* of *Book and Sword* and *Princess Fragrance* (1987), her rare martial arts films adapted from one of Jin Yong's masterpieces, are examples of early mainland–Hong Kong collaborations. After offering a brief account of Hui's films related to Hong Kong history, this chapter will look at *Our Time Will Come*, a mainland-financed film that reconsidered a less-known chapter in Hong Kong history: the unsung heroes who evacuated Chinese intellectuals from Hong Kong during the Japanese occupation. The chapter will then dwell on the (im)possibility of conveying messages in a main melody film situated in the fallen city of Hong Kong.

Chapter 3 will focus on Peter Chan, a director whose transnational career is typically 'Hong Kong' in nature: from local Hong Kong to Thailand, Hollywood and then to mainland China. The career of Peter Chan is in a sense a success story of a Hong Kong filmmaker, but his model of flexible identity, ironically, was closely intertwined with the waning of the distinctive characteristics of Hong Kong cinema as well as culture. As one of the forerunners to go north after the signing of the CEPA, Chan is very familiar with co-productions – such as *Perhaps Love* (2005) and *The Warlords* (2007). His *American Dreams in China* (2013), which successfully dramatised the ethos of a generation of China's youths, showed that he is good at merging a mainland theme into a mainstream film genre. This chapter will take on his more recent project, *Leap* (2020), a film about the legendary Chinese women's volleyball team, to further examine his ability to sing the main(land) melody in commercial genre films.

When Andrew Lau, who is most widely known for his crime film series *Young and Dangerous* (1996–1998) and *Infernal Affairs* trilogy (2002–3), co-directed with Alan Mak, was invited to helm *The Founding of an Army*, Hong Kong audiences must have been quite surprised. In commemoration of the ninetieth anniversary of the founding of the People's Liberation Army, this was arguably one of the most typical main melody films and as such had hard and fast rules to follow. Chapter 4 will investigate how the director famous for his crime films looked to turn *The Founding of an Army* into a commercial war film that aimed to both achieve a political goal and attract a broad audience. His subsequent project, *The Captain*, a disaster film dubbed the 'Chinese answer to *Sully*', will then be examined to show how Lau has contributed a new genre to main melody films.

In contrast to Andrew Lau, Dante Lam caught the mainland audiences' attention with a more predictable genre. Having won his fame with psycho-action thrillers like *The Stool Pigeon* (2010) and *That Demon Within* (2014), Dante Lam also tried to forge new ground with the sports-based dramas *Unbeatable* (2013) and *To the Fore* (2015). While the former, a story about a forty-eight-year-old disgraced former boxing champion, was praised by local critics as a film to cheer up the city of Hong Kong, the latter was not as well received. It was in fact *Operation Mekong* that brought Lam to the fore of Chinese cinema. His subsequent project, *Operation Red Sea*, the second in his *Operation* trilogy and reportedly one of the highest-grossing films in China, was a new kind of military-patriotic action film. Thanks to its astronomical budget and the support of the Chinese Navy, Lam managed to devise the bloodiest and most propulsive battle scenes ever allowed on mainland screens. Together with *The Rescue* (2020), the third film in the trilogy, Lam's *Operation* films paid contemporary tribute to China's military power. Based on the trajectory of Lam's career in Hong Kong, Chapter 5 will discuss how the Hong Kong director effectively developed this new genre of main melody films.

Chapter 6 will shift the emphasis to Herman Yau, whose film career seems to be different from the examples examined above. A director who remains very much central to the dwindling film industry in Hong Kong, he is one of the most efficient, versatile and productive directors in Hong Kong. Yau has long been considered a B-movie expert who has directed some cult horror classics, but more recently his high-concept crime thrillers, including *Shockwave* (2017) and *The White Storm 2: Drug Lords* (2019), have involved enormous production costs and amassed huge box-office totals, not only in Hong Kong but also in mainland China. His extraordinary ability to handle different themes, genres and budgets has made him stand out among his contemporaries. Moreover, his *The Woman Knight of Mirror Lake* (2011), a tribute to the Xin Hai Revolution, is actually a forerunner of cross-border main melody projects. This chapter will explore how Herman Yau, as a sure and quick marksman, shed light on a flexible model of Hong Kong filmmaking which has not been widely recognised and awarded.

Various Hong Kong directors have also joined the ensemble of main melody, including but not limited to John Woo's *The Crossing* (2014), Oxide Pang's *My War*, Alan Mak and Anthony Pun's *Extraordinary Mission*, Alan Mak's *Integrity* (2019), David Lam's anti-corruption *Storm* series (2014–19) and Tony Chan's *The Bravest*. These films are good examples of how Hong Kong filmmakers sang different main(land) melodies in their cross-border ventures. In addition, besides films with overt political undertones, there have also been works not so explicitly related to the main melody. Similar to mainstream genre films, the themes of these films, such as anti-drugs and anti-corruption, are actually in harmony with the main melody. While Johnnie To's *Drug War* is an earlier example of a cross-border crime film that echoed the main melody of anti-drug in the mainland, Jing Wong's *Chasing the Dragon* and its sequels (2017, 2019) pinpointed the corruption of the Hong Kong police and their collusion with drug dealers back in the British colonial days. All in all, Chapter 7 will examine different main melody projects of various Hong Kong directors, showing how they contributed different dimensions of entertainmentisation and blockbusterisation to main melody films.

I hope that the brief summary above has indicated that this book is not just about Chinese main melody films. It primarily focuses on Hong Kong directors' contributions to the development of such films, which dominated the Chinese film industry in the 2010s. Towards this end, it is necessary to trace the trajectories and analyse the styles of these Hong Kong directors before assessing their main melody projects. Great emphasis will, therefore, be placed on the films they made before they entered the mainland market. To wrap up the discussion, the Epilogue will re-examine the implications of Hong Kong filmmakers' participation in Chinese main melody films. Summarising the paradigm shift of mainland–Hong Kong cross-border cooperation in the cultural realm, it will then recapitulate the theoretical thrust of these examples, which will hopefully point towards a larger project on the transmission and transformation of Hong Kong culture in the mainland. Given the increasing importance of the Chinese film market at the time of the writing of this book, we can safely say that although alternative, local imaginaries in low- to mid-budget and independent productions are also important, it is necessary to envision the future of Hong Kong cinema in relation to the mainland market.

Some sections of this chapter have been published in *Global Media and China* 5:2 (June 2020): 109–23.

Notes

1. Xi Jinping, 'Secure a Decisive Victory in Building a Moderately Prosperous Society in All Respects and Strive for the Great Success of Socialism with Chinese Characteristics for a New Era', delivered at the Nineteenth National Congress of the Communist Party of China, 18 October 2017: <http://www.xinhuanet.com/english/download/ Xi_Jinping's_report_at_19th_CPC_National_Congress.pdf>; last accessed 1 May 2021.
2. Xi, 'Secure a Decisive Victory'.
3. Ibid.
4. 'Press Briefing on Promoting Ideological, Ethical and Cultural Progress', The State Council Information Office of the People's Republic of China, 21 October 2017: <http:// www.scio.gov.cn/32618/Document/1566419/1566419_1.htm>; last accessed 1 May 2021.
5. Yiu-Wai Chu, *Lost in Transition: Hong Kong Culture in the Age of China* (Albany: SUNY Press, 2013), 163–5.
6. Yiu-Wai Chu, *Found in Transition: Hong Kong Studies in the Age of China* (Albany: SUNY Press, 2018), 196–9.
7. Kam Louie, 'Confucius the Chameleon: Dubious Envoy for "Brand China"', *Boundary* 2:38 (Spring 2011): 77–100. See also Chu, *Lost in Transition*, 36–7.

8. Joshua Cooper Ramo, *The Beijing Consensus* (London: The Foreign Policy Centre, 2004).

9. Daniel A. Bell, *The China Model: Political Meritocracy and the Limits of Democracy* (Princeton: Princeton University Press, 2015), 180.

10. Chu, *Lost in Transition*, 112. For the development of mainland–Hong Kong co-productions, see, among others, Emilie Yeh and Shi-yan Chao, 'Policy and Creative Strategies: Hong Kong CEPA Films in the China Market', *International Journal of Cultural Policy*, published online 12 March 2018; Yin Hong 尹鴻 and He Mei 何美, 'Chinese Films after the Period of Co-production: The Historical Development of Mainland-HK Co-production in the Chinese Film Industry' (in Chinese) 〈走向後合拍時代的華語電影:中國內地與香港電影的合作/合拍歷程〉, *Communication and Society* 7 (January 2009): 31–60.

11. 'Full Text of Speech by President Xi Jinping at Welcome Dinner in HK', 1 July 2017: <http://www.chinadaily.com.cn/china/hk20threturn/2017-07/01/content_29958522.htm>; last accessed 1 May 2021. See also Tony Cheung, Peace Chiu and Ng Kang-chung, 'Chinese Slang and Famous Canto-pop Song Feature in Xi Jinping's Speech at Hong Kong Banquet', *South China Morning Post*, 30 June 2017.

12. 'State-sponsored', 'keynote' and 'central themes' are used to denote main melody films in the following, respectively: Jonathan Noble, '*Blind Shaft*: Performing the "Underground" on and beyond the Screen', in *Chinese Films in Focus II* (2nd ed.), ed. Chris Berry (London: British Film Institute, 2008), 37; Darrell William Davis, 'Marketization, Hollywood, Global China', *Modern Chinese Literature and Culture* 26:1 (Spring 2014): 201; and Xiaobing Tang, *Visual Culture in Contemporary China* (Cambridge: Cambridge University Press, 2015), 209.

13. Sheila Cornelius (with Ian Haydn Smith), *New Chinese Cinema: Challenging Representations* (London: Wallflower Press, 2002), 35.

14. Rey Chow, *Primitive Passions: Visuality, Sexuality, Ethnography, and Contemporary Chinese Cinema* (New York: Columbia University Press, 1995), 26. There have been different kinds of periodisations of Chinese main melody films. As this book focuses on main melody films helmed by Hong Kong directors, I will not dwell on a detailed analysis of the different stages of its development. Zhang Ying 張瑩 has offered a detailed account of main melody films in her *A Study of Main Melody Films since the New Period* (in Chinese) 《新時期以來主旋律電影研究》 (Shanghai: Sanlian, 2017); see the introduction and the first chapter for its definition and historical development.

15. Xudong Zhang, 'Nationalism, Mass Culture, and Intellectual Strategies in Post-Tiananmen China', in *Whither China?: Intellectual Politics in Contemporary China*, ed. Xudong Zhang (Durham, NC, and London: Duke University Press, 2001), 318.

16. Wendy Su, *China's Encounter with Global Hollywood: Cultural Policy and the Film Industry 1994–2013* (Lexington: University Press of Kentucky, 2016), 20–1.

17. Hongmei Yu, 'Visual Spectacular, Revolutionary Epic, and Personal Voice: The Narration of History in Chinese Main Melody Films', *Modern Chinese Literature and Culture* 25:2 (Fall 2013): 166.

18. Xiaomei Chen, *Staging Chinese Revolution: Theater, Film, and the Afterlives of Propaganda* (New York: Columbia University Press, 2017), 20.

19. Matthew D. Johnson, 'Censorship, Propaganda and Film Policy', in *The Chinese Cinema Book* (2nd ed.), ed. Song Hwee Lim and Julian Ward (London: Bloomsbury, 2020), 252.

20. Rui Zhang, *The Cinema of Feng Xiaogang: Commercialization and Censorship in Chinese Cinema after 1980* (Hong Kong: Hong Kong University Press, 2008), 40.

21. Su, *China's Encounter with Global Hollywood*, 21.

22. See Xie Mian and Zhang Yiwu, *Major Transformation: Cultural Studies of the Post-New Period* (in Chinese) 《大轉型: 後新時期文化研究》 (Heilongjiang Education Press, 1995); see also Xu Ben 徐賁, 'What Is the Post-New Period of China?' (in Chinese) 〈甚麼是中國的後新時期？〉, *Twenty-First Century Bimonthly* 36 (August 1996): 74–83.

23. Yu, 'Visual Spectacular, Revolutionary Epic, and Personal Voice', 170.

24. Su, *China's Encounter with Global Hollywood*, 20–1.

25. Yu, 'Visual Spectacular, Revolutionary Epic, and Personal Voice', 170; for further details, see Chris Berry, *Postsocialist Cinema in Post-Mao China: The Cultural Revolution after the Cultural Revolution* (New York and London: Routledge, 2004). According to Xudong Zhang, post-socialism is 'an intellectual liberation from the teleological historical determinism which, in the name of a rivalry between socialism and capitalism, tends to imprison the mind in a rigid and dogmatic notion of modernity defined by an earlier historical age (of imperialism, colonialism, the postcolonial nation-state, and socialist industrialization)'; Xudong Zhang, *Postsocialism and Cultural Politics: China in the Last Decade of the Twentieth Century* (Durham, NC, and London: Duke University Press, 2008), 12.

26. Shuk-ting Kinnia Yau, 'From *March of the Volunteers* to *Amazing Grace*: The Death of China's Main Melody Movie in the 21st Century', *Jump Cut* 59 (Fall 2019): <https://www.ejumpcut.org/currentissue/KinnieYauMainMelody/index.html>; last accessed 1 May 2021.

27. Ibid. 'Examples include *The Naval Battle of 1894* (Lin Nong; 1962), a narrative of the First Sino-Japanese War, *Guerrillas on the Plain* (Su Li and Wu Zhaodi; 1955), describing the Anti-Japanese War, *Liu Hulan* (Feng Bailu, 1950), portraying the Chinese Civil War, *Battle of Triangle Hill* (Sha Meng and Lin Shan; 1956) and *Heroic Sons and Daughters* (Wu Zhaodi; 1964), both depicting the Korean War (called in China the "War to Resist US Aggression and Aid Korea"). In the same year several film[s] premiered that mark the 50th anniversary of the end of the Anti-Japanese War, including *The July Seventh Incident* (Li Qiankuan and Xiao Guiyun, 1995), *Don't Cry, Nanking* Wu Ziniu; 1995), and *Black Sun: The Nanking Massacre* (Tun-fei Mou; 1995), all of which focus on anti-Japanese themes.'

28. Zhang, *The Cinema of Feng Xiaogang*, 70; see also Yomi Braester's succinct account of 'Mainstream Chinese cinema with Chinese characteristics' in 'Contemporary Mainstream PRC Cinema', Lim and Ward (ed.), *The Chinese Cinema Book*, 231–3. According to Braetser, 'Early "Main melody" productions operated on a business model unlike

that of the commercial mainstream: rather than relying on box-office revenues, they received generous government subsidies that allowed them to regularly exceed even the most expensive commercial productions.' (231)

29. Yu, 'Visual Spectacular, Revolutionary Epic, and Personal Voice', 168.
30. Ying Zhu, *Chinese Cinema during the Era of Reform: The Ingenuity of the System* (Westport, CT and London: Praeger, 2003), 154–5; 'In the mid-1990s, commercial entertainment films occupied 75 percent of the annual production output, main-melody films 20 percent and art films 5 percent.'
31. Su, *China's Encounter with Global Hollywood*, 21; the so-called 9550 Project was launched at the 1996 Changsha Film Work Conference, 'which required the major state owned film studios to produce fifty finely made main-melody movies during the ninth Five-Year Plan from 1996 to 2000, or ten films each year' (22).
32. Victor Fan, 'Poetics of Failure: Performing Humanism in the Chinese Blockbuster', in *Screening China's Soft Power*, ed. Paola Voci and Luo Hui (Abingdon and New York: Routledge, 2018), 61–2. 'The reform officially began in 2000 with Document 320 issued by the State Administration of Radio Film and Television and the Ministry of Culture. Between 2001 and 2005, the SARFT and the State Council promulgated several documents and supplementary regulations, which opened the gate for foreign and private capital to enter film production and theatre construction. The state especially encourages private capital to take an active role in boosting the film industry by removing many of the restrictions regarding ownership and operations. According to the Provisional Regulation of the Entry and Operation Qualification of Enterprises in the Film Industry co-released by SARFT and the Ministry of Commerce in 2004, private enterprises are encouraged to enter the film production sector with the Permit for Film Production issued by the SARFT, without necessarily affiliating with any state-owned enterprises.' Xiaofei Han, 'Production of Main Melody Film in Post-Socialist China: A Deconstruction of *Wolf Warrior 2*', in *The Political Economy of Local Cinema: A Critical Introduction*, ed. Anne Rajala, Daniel Lindblom and Matteo Stocchetti (Berlin: Peter Lang, 2020), 145.
33. Su, *China's Encounter with Global Hollywood*, 20. In other words, 'global Hollywood was harnessed to Chinese industrial and ideological ends'; Han, 'Production of Main Melody Film in Post-Socialist China', 144.
34. Davis, 'Marketization, Hollywood, Global China', 203; for an in-depth analysis of main melody and *dapian*, see 201–6.
35. Yu, 'Visual Spectacular, Revolutionary Epic, and Personal Voice', 191; Chris Berry and Mary Farquhar, *China on Screen: Cinema and Nation* (New York: Columbia University Press, 2006), 211.
36. Elena Meyer-Clement, *Party Hegemony and Entrepreneurial Power in China: Institutional Change in the Film and Music Industries* (London and New York: Routledge, 2015), 171.
37. Berry and Farquhar, *China on Screen*, 212.
38. Braester, 'Contemporary Mainstream PRC Cinema', 231.
39. Ying Zhu and Stanley Rosen, 'Introduction', in *Art, Politics, and Commerce in Chinese Cinema*, ed. Ying Zhu and Stanley Rosen (Hong Kong: Hong Kong University Press, 2010), 7.

40. Yu Dong, '2009: The Rise of Chinese Film Industry' (in Chinese) 〈2009 中國電影要發威〉, Chinafilm.com, 20 July 2009: <http://indus.chinafilm.com/200907/2054312.html>; last accessed 1 May 2021; Chu, *Found in Transition*, 117.

41. 'Blockbusters with a Government Feel', *Beijing Review*, China.org.cn, 30 June 2009: <http://www.bjreview.com.cn/movies/txt/2009-07/02/content_205010.htm>; last accessed 1 May 2021.

42. Zhu and Rosen, 'Introduction', 3.

43. Davis, 'Marketization, Hollywood, Global China', 205.

44. 'Testimonials by Directors of *The Founding of a Republic*', in *China Film Yearbook 2010*, ed. Qian Li (Beijing: China Film Press, 2010), 5–6.

45. Davis, 'Marketization, Hollywood, Global China', 202.

46. Jingwu Zhang, 'The Success and Stereotype of the Main Theme Commercial Blockbuster', Luju Bar, 23 November 2019: <https://lujuba.cc/en/106494.html>; last accessed 1 May 2021.

47. Tang, *Visual Culture in Contemporary China*, 205; for more details, see Chapter 5 'How (Not) to Watch a Chinese Blockbuster'.

48. Stanley Rosen, 'Film and Society in China: The Logic of the Market', in *A Companion to Chinese Cinema*, ed. Yingjin Zhang (Chichester: Wiley-Blackwell, 2012), 197; see also Zhu and Rosen, 'Introduction', 1–13.

49. Johnson, 'Censorship, Propaganda and Film Policy', 252.

50. Paul Clark, *Chinese Cinema: Culture and Politics since 1949* (Cambridge: Cambridge University Press, 1987), 56–8.

51. Paul Clark, 'Projecting Influence: Film and the Limits of Beijing's Soft Power', in *Screening China's Soft Power*, ed. Paola Voci and Luo Hui (Abingdon and New York: Routledge, 2018), 21.

52. Clark, 'Projecting Influence', 21.

53. Yanling Yang, 'Film Policy, the Chinese Government and Soft Power', *New Cinemas: Journal of Contemporary Film* 14:1 (April 2017): 84. 'Prior to 2006, less than 400 Chinese films were exhibited abroad; this then rose to over 450 annually, reaching a peak in 2013 when Chinese films were exhibited 951 times in 48 nations and regions.'

54. Frances Xiao-Feng Guo, 'China's Nationalism and Its Quest for Soft Power through Cinema', PhD thesis, University of Technology, Sydney, 2013, 28.

55. As argued by Yanling Yang, the 'tension between China's domestic political ideology, enforced by censorship, and its credibility on the international stage' has restricted the room 'for film genuinely to promote China's soft power'. Yang, 'Film Policy, the Chinese Government and Soft Power', 88. The author has provided a lucid account of the relationship between the 'Going-Out Policy' and China's soft power.

56. Kingsley Edney, Ying Zhu and Stanley Rosen, 'Introduction', in Edney, Zhu and Rosen (ed.), *Soft Power with Chinese Characteristics: China's Campaign for Hearts and Minds* (Oxford and New York: Routledge, 2020), 2–3; see also William A. Callahan, 'Identity and Security in China: The Negative Soft Power of the China Dream', *Politics* 35:3 (April 2015): 216–29; Ying Zhang refers to this as 'new main melody' in *A Study of Main Melody Films since the New Period*, which is closely related to soft power

and Xi's 'Chinese dream'; see Ying Zhang, *A Study of Main Melody Films since the New Period*, 238–56.

57. Chen, *Staging Chinese Revolution*, 21.

58. 'Xi Jinping's Talks at the Beijing Forum on Literature and Art', *China Copyright and Media*, 16 October 2014: <https://chinacopyrightandmedia.wordpress.com/2014/10/16/xi-jinpings-talks-at-the-beijing-forum-on-literature-and-art/>; last accessed 1 May 2021.

59. Ning Wang, '(Re)Constructing Neo-Confucianism in a "Glocalized" Context', in *Challenges of Globalization and Prospects for an Inter-civilizational World Order*, ed. Ino Rossi (Cham: Springer, 2020), 1011.

60. Joseph Nye, 'Foreword', in Edney, Zhu and Rosen (ed.), *Soft Power with Chinese Characteristics*.

61. Translated from the subtitle of the essay 'Looking Back at Thirty Years of Main Melody Films: A Love Letter Written to Our Home Country' (in Chinese) 〈回看主旋律電影三十年：寫給祖國的情書〉, 1 October 2019: <https://zhuanlan.zhihu.com/p/84925242>; last accessed 1 May 2021.

62. Chen, *Staging Chinese Revolution*, 1. See also Chris Berry et al., 'The State and Stakes of Chinese Cinemas Studies: A Roundtable Discussion', *Journal of Chinese Cinemas* 10:1 (2016): 67–86. In her *China's Encounter with Global Hollywood*, Su offered an in-depth account of how mainland and Hong Kong filmmakers have been working around marketisation and state censorship. *Staging China: New Theatres in the Twenty-First Century*, ed. Li Ruru (New York: Palgrave Macmillan, 2016) has some related discussions on 'main melody theatre'. Fan's *Screening China's Soft Power* also contains essays evaluating the rise of Chinese soft power from different perspectives.

63. Sarah Zheng, 'Xi Jinping Takes Leading Role in Hit Propaganda Film Extolling "Amazing" China', *South China Morning Post*, 4 March 2018.

64. 'Xi Jinping's Talks at the Beijing Forum on Literature and Art', *China Copyright and Media*, 16 October 2014: <https://chinacopyrightandmedia.wordpress.com/2014/10/16/xi-jinpings-talks-at-the-beijing-forum-on-literature-and-art/>; English translation of a summary published by Xinhua News Agency on 15 October 2014: <http://www.xinhuanet.com//politics/2014-10/15/c_1112840544.htm>; last accessed 1 May 2021.

65. For an informative account of the major stages of development of Chinese main melody films, see Cheng-Liang Lee 李政亮, *China: The Age of Chinese Blockbusters* (in Chinese) 《拆哪，中國的大片時代》 (Taipei: Azure Books, 2017), Chapter 2, and Yau, 'From *March of the Volunteers* to *Amazing Grace*'.

66. Jia Liudi 覃柳笛, 'Miao Xiaotian: Only Co-productions Can Lure Overseas Market' (in Chinese) 〈苗曉天：只有合拍片，才能走出去〉, *Oriental Outlook*, 16 July 2015: <https://kknews.cc/zh-hk/entertainment/48q25qg.html>; last accessed 1 May 2021.

67. For further details, see 'Top 100 Chinese Film Directors 2018' (in Chinese) 〈中國導演TOP 100權力榜〉, Sohu.com., 9 April 2018: <http://www.sohu.com/a/227648063_699621>; last accessed 1 May 2021.

68. Li Yizhuang 李以莊 and Xi Yue 席悅, 'Back to the Local: The New Age of Co-productions' (in Chinese) 〈回歸本土：新合拍片年代〉, *Bloomberg Businessweek* (Chinese Version), 14 February 2010: <http://read.bbwc.cn/askybl.html>; last accessed 1 May 2021.

69. 'Exclusive Interview with Henry Fong' 〈獨家對話方平〉 (in Chinese), *Sina Entertainment*, 18 June 2007: <http://ent.sina.com.cn/m/2007-06-18/20161602753.shtml>; last accessed 1 May 2021.

70. For more details, see Chu, *Found in Transition*, 117–20.

71. Esther C. M. Yau, 'Watchful Partners, Hidden Currents: Hong Kong Cinema Moving into the Mainland of China', in *A Companion to Hong Kong Cinema*, ed. Esther M. K. Cheung, Gina Marchetti and Esther C. M. Yau (Malden, MA: Wiley-Blackwell, 2015), 18; see also Bono Lee, 'The Possibility of China for Hong Kong Direction: The Transformation of Peter Chan's Identity', in *Peter Ho-Sun Chan: My Way*, ed. Cheuk-to Li (Hong Kong: Joint Publishing, 2012), 186–95.

72. Fan Xiang et al., 'Second Press Conference for the 19th National Congress of the Communist Party of China: China's Brand, Sound, and Image Increasingly Recognized', *Xin Min Evening News*, 20 October 2017.

73. Chris Berry, '*Wolf Warrior 2*: Imagining the Chinese Century', *Film Quarterly* 72(2), 2018: 42.

74. 'Peter Chan on *Bodyguards and Assassins*' 〈陳可辛談《十月圍城》〉 (in Chinese), *The Beijing News*, 19 December 2019.

75. Gary Bettinson, 'Yesterday Once More: Hong Kong-China Coproductions and the Myth of Mainlandization', *Journal of Chinese Cinemas* 14:1: (2020): 18.

76. Sin-Yee Choi 蔡倩怡, '*Our Time Will Come*: The Secret Message underneath the Main Melody' (in Chinese) 〈《明月幾時有》：主旋律暗渡陳倉〉, *MP Weekly*, 8 July 2017: <https://www.mpweekly.com/culture/明月幾時有-許鞍華-建軍大業-41950>; last accessed 1 May 2021.

77. Nga-Ting Wong, 'An Interview with Johnnie To and Patrick Yau: Johnnie To's *Three* on Fate in Troubled Times', *Ming Pao*, 8 July 2016.

78. Chu, *Found in Transition*, 132.

79. Wu Jing 吳靖, 'The Nirvana of *Wolf Warrior*: The Double Ensemble of Main Melody and Mainstream' (in Chinese) 〈《戰狼》涅槃：主旋律與主流的雙重合奏〉, *Film Criticism* 9 (2019): 46–8.

80. Yau, 'From *March of the Volunteers* to *Amazing Grace*'.

81. Ibid. It is true that '[s]uch consciousness of China as a "strong nation" has unavoidably intensified conflicts between China and Hong Kong as well as China and Taiwan, resulting in the failure of Main Melody movies to achieve the "united front" that figured so prominently among its priorities early in the new century. Main Melody movies have to the contrary even become the target of laughter and disdain by audiences in Hong Kong and Taiwan.'

82. Alain Badiou, *Cinema* (Cambridge: Polity, 2013), 10; for an informative account of Badiou's view on cinema, see Alex Ling, *Badiou and Cinema* (Edinburgh: Edinburgh University Press, 2011). I do not intend to dwell upon the complex and controversial

relationship between philosophy and cinema in this book; in addition to Badiou's *Cinema*, see, among others, Gilles Deleuze, *Cinema 1: The Movement Image* (Minneapolis: University of Minnesota Press, 1989) and *Cinema 2: The Time-Image* (Minneapolis: University of Minnesota Press, 1989), and Jacques Rancière, *Aesthetics and Its Discontents* (Cambridge and Malden, MA: Polity, 2009).

83. Chen Yuqi 陳玉琪, '*The Leap, Homeland* . . . Main Melody Films Becoming the Main Melody: Which One Will You Pick During the National Day Holiday? (in Chinese) 〈《奪冠》《家鄉》. . . . . . 主旋律電影成"主旋律"，國慶檔電影你選哪一部？〉, Chinese Business Net 中國經營網, 1 October 2020: <http://www.cb.com.cn/index/show/wzjx/cv/cv1337701580>; last accessed 1 May 2021; the total number depends on whether main melody films are strictly defined or not.

Chapter 1

How to Take Tiger Mountain?
The Tsui Hark Model

'Knowing very well there are tigers in the mountain, but still heading toward the tiger mountain.'

— Chinese proverb

Introduction

Fans of Tsui Hark – hailed as the 'Hong Kong Spielberg'[1] – must have been astonished when they found out that he was going to make *The Taking of Tiger Mountain 3D* (2014; hereafter, *Tiger Mountain*), which was based on one of the *yangbanxi* ('model works') classics approved during the Chinese Cultural Revolution. As one of Tsui's fans, I shared this feeling, although I was not unprepared. A great admirer of his early works, especially the nihilistic *Dangerous Encounters of the First Kind* (1980), I was struck by *All About Women* (2008), the so-called 'China's *Sex and the City*'. In this romantic comedy about three modern young women, the trendy, contemporary side of Beijing was foregrounded to such an extent that I almost thought it was commissioned by the tourism administration to promote the capital city to the world. It was with *All About Women* that I fully understood why Hong Kong filmmakers had left Hong Kong for mainland China to continue to develop their career in the co-production era after the signing of the CEPA in 2003. But for those who were enthralled by the distressed, restless Hong Kong in *Dangerous Encounters of the First Kind*, let alone the futuristic dystopia in *The Wicked City* (1992), written and produced by Tsui and directed by Peter Mak, *Tiger Mountain* was the last project they thought Tsui would take. It may have just been wishful thinking on their part though. The contents of the original model work did match well with Tsui's preference for the *wuxia* ('martial arts heroes') genre. Tsui once said in an interview: 'I have always been a fan of *wuxia* movies. They give us a refreshed view of what we had before, of the values and of the way we looked at life.'[2]

In addition, as Tsui's favourite theme of *jiang hu* ('river and lake': the world of martial artists in *wuxia* stories[3]) also nicely fit with the model work, it was not unreasonable that Tsui would want to turn *Tiger Mountain* – actually Qu Bo's novel *Tracks in the Snowy Forest* on which it was based – into a Hollywood-style action blockbuster.

It is now well known that Tsui wanted to make this film ever since he first saw the filmic version of the Peking Opera version of *Taking Tiger Mountain by Strategy* for the first time when he was working at a movie theatre in New York's Chinatown back in 1974.[4] The twenty-three-year-old was deeply impressed by 'its intriguing and seemingly unlikely link "between *jiang hu* and heroes of the [revolutionary] age".'[5] Forty years later, his own version premiered, which was clearly a dream finally accomplished. But a further question to explore is why it took so long for the film titan to realise this dream from his youth. As one of the most successful filmmakers in the history of Hong Kong cinema, he should have had all the necessary resources to shoot the film in the 1980s or the 1990s. One of the reasons behind this was, in my opinion, his reservations towards Hong Kong's reversion to China at that time. *Dangerous Encounters of the First Kind*, among others, was about a distraught generation of Hong Kong youngsters at a shaky juncture when the British started negotiating the future of their then colony with China. Moreover, as apparent in the 'fantastic conceptions of Hong Kong's post-1997 nightmare' in *The Wicked City*, as astutely noted by Michael Berry, the outcome of the handover could not but be catastrophic.[6] Not only Tsui but also many other Hong Kong filmmakers changed their opinions towards China, at least from a market point of view, in the new millennium, falling in love with a market that they had despised.[7] After his brief, unsuccessful venture in Hollywood (with the 1997 *Double Team* and the 1998 *Knock Off*), Tsui returned to Hong Kong to make *The Legend of Zu* (2001) – a '2.0' version of his monumental *Zu: Warriors from the Magic Mountain* (1983) – in collaboration with the China Film Coproduction Corporation. (I will come back to his career trajectory in the next section.)

Even if Tsui Hark had changed his view of the film industry, it still takes two to tango. Without the financial support and market of the mainland film industry, it would not have been possible for the grand imagination of his *wuxia* world to be realised. After Xi Jinping took power in 2012, national rejuvenation became the 'main melody', and, as clearly stated by Xi, a good main melody work had to appeal to the people, the experts and the market.[8] If Chinese cinema had entered a 'post-new era' ('the representation of the urban, the return to the everyday world, the divergence of film genres and the fusion of "art films" with genres'[9]) after 1989, as discussed in the Introduction, 2012 ushered in another era: 'Thought on Socialism with Chinese Characteristics for a New Era'. In other words, the primary concern was the social impact, but at the same time commercial values were nonetheless important. To echo this, there was a surge of commercialised main melody films. In this special context, a remake of *Tiger Mountain* would be a good choice to make ends meet: singing the main melody of the leadership of the Communist Party with a blockbuster that could attract the popular audience. But even so, there were many 'émigré directors'[10] – to borrow the term from Lisa Funnell – from whom the producers could have chosen to helm *Tiger Mountain*.

The producers of the film, leading mainland filmmakers Huang Jianxin and Yu Dong, who had taken proactive roles in mainland–Hong Kong co-productions, knew Hong Kong filmmaking extremely well. It must have been a very careful, prudent choice for them to invite Tsui to take the helm of this main melody film. In the end, the achievements of the film proved them right. Not only was the film a box-office hit that raked in RMB 883 million in mainland China (listed as the tenth most popular Chinese film of all time by the PRC box office in 2015), it also won accolades from critics in both the mainland and Hong Kong – Tsui was awarded Best Director at the 30th Golden Rooster Awards in mainland China, and he bagged the same award at the 35th Hong Kong Film Awards in Hong Kong. The film was even highly praised by China's state-run *Global Times*: 'Many moviegoers have been extremely curious how a Hong Kong director could remake such a mainland-centric red classic so well.'[11] Given the political tension between the mainland and Hong Kong, that was a rare and noteworthy achievement. As convincingly argued by Wendy Xie in her essay on Tsui's *Tiger Mountain*, 'the film undercuts the reverential Maoist revolutionary discourse inherent in the original source material by modeling on the *wuxia* (martial arts) paradigm', but she focused more on how 'Tsui [was] motivated by a desire to address the prevailing social climate of excessive commercialization and moral decay in contemporary China.'[12] The importance of Tsui's Hong Kong filmmaking experience has not yet been thoroughly evaluated. Meanwhile, Tsui's *Tiger Mountain* has displayed 'the dual identity of CEPA pictures, embracing a big mainland market while maintaining a Hong Kong imprint'.[13] Based on the (im)possibility of this imprint, I will endeavour to press harder on the issue in this chapter from the perspective of Tsui as a Hong Kong director commissioned to make a main(land) melody blockbuster. As clearly stated by Nansun Shi, veteran Hong Kong film producer and partner of Tsui Hark, 'Tsui said it was basically a James Bond story, the structure is *Mission Impossible*', and 'he considered how to do it for many years and when Huang Jianxin came on board as executive producer, he felt more comfortable. Hong Kong directors are really good at making these kinds of mission-based action films.'[14] Before I move on to explore the collaborative chemistry of *Tiger Mountain*, it is necessary to highlight the Tsui Hark model of filmmaking by providing a very brief account of his film career.

Trajectory of the Hong Kong Spielberg

Beginning his career with Hong Kong Television Broadcasting Limited (TVB) in 1977, Tsui Hark soon moved to the short-lived Commercial Television (CTV) and stole the limelight with his innovative treatment of *wuxia* drama in *Golden Dagger Romance* (1978). Shortly after CTV closed down in October 1978, Tsui had an opportunity to continue developing his directorial career in the film sector thanks to the success of his *wuxia* television experiment. He tried to perform a bolder experiment with his film debut, *The Butterfly Murders* (1979), which was considered a genre-mixing of *wuxia* and science fiction. Together with ground-breaking films by his contemporaries, such as Ho Yim's *The Extra* (1978), Ann Hui's *The Secret* (1979) and Alex Cheung's *Cops and Robbers* (1979), Tsui triggered the Hong Kong New Wave, which opened a new chapter in the history of Hong Kong cinema. I do not intend to dwell on *The Butterfly Murders* and Tsui's subsequent experimental and innovative projects *We're Going to Eat You* (1980) and *Dangerous Encounters of the First Kind*, which have been thoroughly discussed elsewhere. In short, these New Wave experiments were 'against tradition, against the system, against society', and in terms of film aesthetics they 'present[ed] the unpresentable'.[15] Tsui's talents were already widely acknowledged when he joined Cinema City, an up-and-coming film company founded by Dean Shek, Karl Maka and Raymond Wong. Cinema City's debut film *Laughing Time* (1980), directed by John Woo, who later became one of Hong Kong's world-class directors, was a comedy that paid tribute to Charlie Chaplin. It was therefore not surprising that Tsui's first collaborative project with Cinema City, *All the Wrong Clues* (1981), was utterly different in style from his previous works. Tsui's wit and gift for cinema, nonetheless, had shone through in this comedy. Despite 'gleefully lacking avant-garde elements or even a whiff of social commentary',[16] it gave birth to a new genre of cartoonish detective/spy comedy, and Tsui's talent was recognised by both the popular audience and film critics. It was not only his first box-office hit, it also won him the Best Director award – his first major award – at the 18th Golden Horse Film Festival in 1981.

Next, Tsui started a side project (which was in fact his major project), *Zu: Warriors from the Magic Mountain* (based on Huanzhu Louzhu's *wuxia* novel), with Golden Harvest, the then leading film company in the territory. Thanks to Golden Harvest's support, which boosted the budget to HK$13.5 million (an enormous sum back then), this new supernatural martial arts fantasy allowed Tsui to realise his *wuxia* dream with the building of huge, spectacular sets. He also invited a Hollywood special effects master to handle the special effects for his 'Hong Kong's version of *Star Wars*'.[17] I can still remember very clearly my jaw dropping to the ground when I first saw the film in a small cinema in Hong Kong back in 1983. The scene at the Chateau of Immortals, in which more than fifty fairies fly high to combat the demon-possessed protagonist, left me simply awestruck. Tsui's astonishing combination of martial arts, traditional wire-work choreography and state-of-the-art special effects was truly ground-breaking, raising the bar for excellence in special visual effects in Hong Kong films.[18] It was not just the technological breakthrough, the film also excelled in its 'delicate balance between handicraft and technology, traditional Eastern aesthetics and modern Western concepts'.[19] Despite this, the film was not a big success in the end, in terms either of box office takings or awards. Perhaps this was because Tsui and his film were too ahead of their time.

Tsui Hark continued to collaborate with Cinema City to make *Aces Go Places III* (1984) – the Hong Kong comedy version of James Bond and the third episode of Cinema City's signature New Year blockbuster – after his dream project, but he also started planning his own venture. He founded the Film Workshop Co. with his long-time partner Nansun Shi and released his producer debut (also as the director) *Shanghai Blues* in October 1984, a turbulent time in Hong Kong before the Sino-British Joint Declaration was signed in December of that year. Set in wartime Shanghai shortly before the Japanese occupation, the film was a 'mix of romantic naiveté, ironic sarcasm and cartoonish sophistication',[20] which was also in a sense bitterly cryptic for the Hong Kong people who were hopelessly worried about their future after 1997. The Film Workshop Co. gave Tsui the chance to develop into an all-round filmmaker: the Hong Kong Spielberg. As a producer, he changed the career of John Woo with the classic *A Better Tomorrow* (1986); Woo later became a world-class director with the Film Workshop Co.'s *A Better Tomorrow II* (1987) and *The Killer* (1989). He also turned Tony Ching into a top-tier director with the trilogy *A Chinese Ghost Story* (1987, 1990, 1991) (Tsui was the producer of all three films).[21] Of course, his directorial talent was not going to waste. Film critic David Denby called *Peking Opera Blues* (1986), which can be interpreted alongside *Shanghai Blues*,[22] 'a sensational piece of frivolous moviemaking – wild buffoonery carried to the borders of art':

> The first thing to be said about the teeming Hong Kong school of filmmaking – of which this movie, from most accounts, is the masterpiece – is that the directors and the audience have a completely different idea about action than we do. Action, in Hong Kong, has nothing to do with realism; action is rhythm and color – exuberant shenanigans, raised to the highest degree of excitement.[23]

In other words, action as rhythm and colour was one of Tsui's signatures. This could also be seen in his subsequent classics, the *Swordsman* series (1990, 1992, 1993) and the *Once Upon a Time in China* (the Chinese title is *Wong Fei Hung*, who was a martial arts master) series (1991, 1992, 1993, 1993, 1994). The first episode of the former was directed by the *wuxia* master King Hu, the second by Tony Ching, and the third was co-directed by Tony Ching and Raymond Lee. The signatures of the producer, Tsui Hark, were almost everywhere. All episodes except the fourth of the latter series were written, directed and produced by Tsui (the fourth episode was directed by Yuen Bun). These works by Tsui Hark have been extensively studied,[24] and I would just like to highlight two important themes here: *jiang hu* ('river and lake') and *luan si* ('turbulent time'). These recurring themes in almost all of Tsui's films were thoroughly developed in these two series. The Chinese title of *Swordsman*, adapted from Jin Yong's (aka Louis Cha) martial arts classic *The Smiling, Proud Wanderer*, actually included *jiang hu* – the literal translation of the Chinese title is 'smiling proudly in *jiang hu*'. Set in late nineteenth-century Canton, *Once Upon a Time in China* used the martial arts master Wong Fei Hung to sketch a period of turbulent times in modern Chinese history. It is important to remember that Tsui viewed history as fantasy, as fiction, and his *luan si* and *jiang hu* were deeply entwined. 'Once in *jiang hu*, one is not free to do what he wants', as a famous Chinese saying goes, but Tsui's obsession with *jiang hu* did not prevent him from doing what he wanted to do, so 'he changed the film *jiang hu* from the inside and has been mostly free to do what he wants'.[25] He was so dominating a filmmaker in the industry that even the grandmaster King Hu was shabbily treated when directing *Swordsman*. Tsui's films were often set in *luan si*, but he always managed chaos in turbulent times, so much so that 'controlled chaos' was considered 'Tsui's Evolution'.[26]

Smiling proudly in the *jiang hu* of Hong Kong cinema for many years, ironically, Tsui could not protect himself from the turbulence of Hong Kong shortly before its reversion to China. Because of numerous factors, including, among others, political anxiety, piracy and reconfigurations of the mediascape of Chinese popular cultures, Hong Kong cinema started declining quickly in the mid-1990s. At that juncture, however, established Hong Kong filmmakers found new opportunities in Hollywood. 'The cult discovery of John Woo and Tsui Hark', according to Poshek Fu and David Desser, led to the second American reception of Hong Kong action cinema in the late 1980s, and Western audiences began to understand that 'there was more to Tsui Hark than flying warriors'.[27] They were also fascinated by the impressive action sequences in their films, and thus John Woo, Tsui Hark and actors like Jackie Chan, Jet Li and Yun-Fat Chow were invited to leave the territory for Hollywood in the 1990s. As rightly noted by Stephen Teo, *The Blade* (1995) was a work marking 'some kind of turning point in Tsui's "local" career'.[28] Soon after the box-office as well as critical disappointment of this martial arts film directed, produced and co-written by Tsui, he decided to go to Hollywood. (*The Blade* is arguably one of the most undervalued works of Tsui Hark, which was 'spectacular' in a different sense – the dramatic close-ups, hysterical mood and lightning-fast shots redefined the possibilities of martial arts cinema.) It was unfortunate, however, that these Hong Kong directors had to start their Hollywood ventures with low-budget action movies. John Woo, Tsui Hark and Ringo Lam were all given the opportunity to work with Jean-Claude Van Damme, the Muscles from Brussels. In the end, arguably, only John Woo passed this initial stage successfully, moving on to *Face/Off* (1997) and *Mission: Impossible 2* (2000). After the far from successful *Double Team* and *Knock Off*, in which he simply did not have a chance to let his talent shine on the biggest stage of film production, Tsui ended his Hollywood trip prematurely and returned to Hong Kong. As argued by Lisa Morton, Tsui's incomplete project in Hollywood 'can probably be boiled down to three main obstructions':

> First, unlike much of Jackie Chan's work, Tsui's movies tend to be intensely Chinese in theme and design; second, whereas John Woo's films are almost entirely about men and male bonding, Tsui's female-driven and transgendered cinema is a tougher sell in Western culture; and third, in contrast to Wong Kar-Wai (who has directed just six features, only one of which – *Ashes of Time*, a martial arts epic – was a genre film), the Hollywood marketers simply cannot pigeonhole the prolific and versatile Tsui Hark.[29]

While I agree that it was difficult to pigeonhole the prolific and versatile Tsui, not all of Tsui's films could be described as female-driven and transgendered cinema. The main reason for his unsuccessful venture was that, as I surmise, Hollywood did not provide him with the chance to blend his emphasis on *jiang hu* and *luan si*, intensely Chinese and arguably untranslatable themes and designs, with his personal style informed by pulp fiction, comics and European art cinema. Van Damme was by no means close to representing *wuxia* in Tsui's filmic world. In 2002, Tsui released *Black Mask 2: City of Masks*, a sequel to Jet Li's 1996 film made for the American market, but by then the door of the mainland market had already been opened wide to Hong Kong filmmakers.

In the interim years at the turn of the millennium, Tsui released two films in 2001, both of which were ambitious projects designed to plough new ground for Hong Kong cinema. Tsui was the producer of *Master Q 2001* (2001), directed by Herman Yau. Adapted from a popular Hong Kong comic book series character, this film was the first-ever blend of live-action and 3D character animation in Chinese film history. As mentioned above, *The Legend of Zu* – the '2.0' version of *Zu: Warriors from the Magic Mountain* – was a collaborative project with the China Film Coproduction Corporation. Thanks to this collaboration, Tsui did have a generous budget for his special visual effects.

The advancement in technology also allowed him to achieve what was impossible back in 1983, but this was in a sense like the tail wagging the dog, as aptly underlined by Kin-yuen Wong:

> From a humanist viewpoint, the new *Legend of Zu* has many flaws simply because the characterization is thin, the thematic statement clichéd at best, the imported influence in its design is too obvious and perhaps too much digital composite technology is used for technology's sake. From a posthumanist perspective, however, Tsui Hark has done something unrivalled in the history of *wuda pian* ['martial arts films'].[30]

If *The Legend of Zu* was an effort to test the waters of the mainland market, the timing was not right. The audience was at that point captivated by *Crouching Tiger, Hidden Dragon* (2000), the Ang Lee-style, elegant rendition of *wuxia* romance. Again, perhaps because Tsui was much ahead of his time, the two films were not well received by the Hong Kong audience. Tsui's subsequent mainland–Hong Kong collaborative project was *Seven Swords* (2005), loosely adapted from a novel about the *wuxia* master Liang Yusheng. Arguably, this was, in Stephen Teo's term, an 'Eastern Western' influenced more by Akira Kurosawa's *Seven Samurai* (1954) and Sam Peckinpah's *The Wild Bunch* (1969).[31] In my view, this was not the best Tsui Hark film. His subsequent projects, *All about Women*, mentioned above, and *Missing* (2008) (not to mention the 2007 *Triangle*, jointly produced and directed by Tsui, Ringo Lam and Johnnie To), proved to be an unsuccessful detour.

Tsui's own time in China did not come until almost a decade after *The Legend of Zu*, when he released the martial arts suspense thriller *Detective Dee and the Mystery of the Phantom Flame* (2010; hereafter, *Detective Dee*). Selected to be released around the National Day holiday, *Detective Dee* (often dubbed 'the Chinese Sherlock Homes') was number six on a list of the top ten highest-grossing films in China in 2010.[32] Tsui then remade King Hu's *wuxia* classic *Dragon Gate Inn* (1967) in *Flying Swords of Dragon Gate* (2011), which was also a great success in the mainland market. At that juncture, the mainland audience started appreciating the beauty of *wuxia* meets special effects in Tsui's films, and this also captured international attention. Tsui was honoured with the Maverick Director award at the Rome Film Festival in 2013, and his *Detective Dee* sequel, *Young Detective Dee: Rise of the Sea Dragon 3D* (2013), was presented Out of Competition for its international premiere, screening after the Maverick Director award ceremony. It is significant (though not without irony to have his co-produced film screened after receiving the Maverick Director award) that this added extra colour to his already excellent résumé, making him the ideal director to be invited to take the helm of *Tiger Mountain*. All in all, the above can be summarised into a Tsui Hark model through which the film titan showcased his versatility as a filmmaker in his often avant-garde quests, with special emphasis on Chinese themes. 'A complete filmmaker who is well versed in every phase of the filmmaking process,' as perceptively stated by Sam Ho, 'Tsui the swordsman is one of the most important figures of the *jiang hu* that is Hong Kong cinema. He is at once a director, a producer, a professional service provider and a company boss.'[33]

Taking Tiger Mountain with Strategies

In fact, Tsui was not inexperienced in mainland–Hong Kong collaborations. In 1989, he was among the forerunners who went north to the mainland to shoot *A Terra-Cotta Warrior* (1990; aka *Fight and Love with a Terracotta Warrior*), produced by Tsui, directed by Tony Ching and starring Zhang Yimou and Gong Li. He also expressed clearly in an interview that 'there is no such thing as local and non-local', and that 'a director should not be bound by a city'.[34] As a main melody blockbuster based on a well-known model work, *Tiger Mountain* was certainly not a mission that could be easily accomplished. Determined to take the bull by the horns, the swordsman Tsui was really 'knowing very well there are tigers in the mountain, but still heading toward the tiger mountain'. As discussed in the previous section, Tsui's special liking for *jiang hu* and *luan si*, especially in the late-transitional period of Hong Kong, could not but be intensely human and, at the same time, sensitively political. Tan See Kam rightly maintained that there was 'a Chinese culturalism that maps a precarious and problematic relation to political China' in Tsui's filmmaking practices, which was seen as 'a mark of "Sinophone" filmmakers'; for example, the clever play with spoken and sung languages in the two Blues – *Shanghai Blues* and *Peking Opera Blues* – embodied 'a distinctive Sinophone flavor that gestures to the messy ensemble of heterogeneous formations in China and the Chinese diaspora and testifies to the fracturing of China and Chineseness'.[35] Apparently, it was unimaginable for a Sinophone – in the sense of its founder Shu-mei Shih – filmmaker to engage in a main(land) melody project based on a model work, paying homage to China and Chineseness. And, of course, it was equally, if not more, unimaginable for the Chinese authorities to allow a main melody film that testified to the fracturing of China and Chineseness. Therefore, Tsui's Sinophone mark, if it was still there, had to be self-erased upon entering Tiger Mountain.

Before exploring Tsui's revisions, it would be helpful to underscore his ambitious attempt to hybridise a new Chinese film genre. As noted in the previous section, Tsui had been mixing genres since his debut, *The Butterfly Murders*. Over the years, he also mixed and/or bent genres, especially in his films loosely adapted from *wuxia* novels by Huanzhu Louzhu, Jin Yong and Liang Yushen. For instance, his *Detective Dee* films were a 'transfiguring genre'.[36] It was therefore not surprising that he transformed *Tiger Mountain* into a sci-fi war adventure powered by advanced computer-generated imageries. When Tsui shared his insights into the making of this film with producer Huang Jianxin and actor Yang Yiwei at Tsinghua University in December 2014, both Huang and Tsui said that they were trying to make a typical genre movie specifically for the Chinese market, a film that would provoke social discussion, debate and interest.[37] In the meantime, as mentioned in the Introduction, Emilie Yueh-yu Yeh and Shi-yan Chao argued convincingly in their 'Policy and Creative Strategies: Hong Kong CEPA Films in the China Market' that Tsui's version still maintained a Hong Kong imprint. Based on their study of Tsui's CEPA pictures between 2004 and 2017, they scrutinised the contemporisation in Tsui's version via 'heroic positioning, technical polish, and narrative framing', noting that 'the striking feature about Tsui's remake is its soufflé of miscellaneous ingredients: CEPA policy, model opera, Hong Kong cinematic hyperbole, and Hollywood citations.'[38] Here, let me offer a brief, nuanced account of these aspects, with particular reference to key factors regarding the Tsui Hark model outlined in the previous sections.

Before moving on to discuss how Tsui took Tiger Mountain with his strategies, it is necessary to state that the model work was in fact not as firm and unchangeable as it sounded. First of all, Paul Clark has challenged the widely accepted (mis)conception of '800 million people watching 8 shows' during the Cultural Revolution.[39] The myth was constructed because these eight model works were, among other foreign films, the ones best remembered. Additionally, there were many versions of *Tiger Mountain* since it was first performed in August 1958 in Nanjing:

> From August 1958 to July 1970, *Tiger Mountain* developed from a modern *jingju* [Peking opera], "a delightful fruit of the Great Leap Forward", to a polished model for revolutionary literature and art, representing the culmination of the PRC's cultural reconstruction.[40]

Focusing on the film version, Chris Berry explored the 'red poetics' – colour, rhythm, music and other elements – of the 1970 film version of *Taking Tiger Mountain by Strategy* alongside two other model works – the films *Azalea Mountain* (1974) and *The Red Detachment of Women* (1971). As perceptively noted by Berry, 'we must acknowledge that the model works are hybrids [not quintessentially Chinese], and the particular combination of elements making up their hybridity played a strong role in making them so recognizable'.[41]

More importantly, since these hybridising processes were not identical, 'new meanings [were] attached to the poetics of the model works, including the film versions of the model works, by different audiences at different times'.[42] New meanings and styles were, of course, incorporated into Tsui's version, while adhering to the logic behind main(land) melodies: 'Make main melody films look good, and then use them to transmit the party's preferred values to audiences without them even noticing.'[43] Since his New Wave experiments, Tsui's films have long been well-known for their political overtones. Interestingly, his take on the main(land) melody was similar but at the same time different: similar in the sense that political values had to be transmitted unabashedly, but with underlying messages that were utterly different.

Model works, including the 1970 film version of *The Taking of Tiger Mountain*, had to obey the 'Theory of Three Prominences' (*san tuchu*): the first concerns highlighting the positive characters among all the characters in a work; the second states that heroic ones should be given prominence among the positive characters in a work; and the third specifies that the main heroic or central character should be highlighted most of all.[44] In addition, the protagonists and villains in model dramas should recycle the *yinyang* binary, as pointed out by Kirk Denton.[45] But since Tsui was aiming to make an entertaining film as much as, if not more than, to revive a red classic, the Theory of Three Prominences must also be combined with the 'three imperatives' of contemporary Chinese commercial cinema – 'thoughtful, artistic and enjoyable' according to Yeh and Chao.[46] Following Yeh and Chao's analysis, I will examine, in slightly rearranged order, the heroic positioning, technical polish and narrative framing of Tsui's version of *Tiger Mountain*.

First, it would be a romanticised understanding to think that a main melody film modelled on a red classic could deconstruct the Theory of Three Prominences. With his hands and feet tied, Tsui still nevertheless danced beautifully. Without violating the three prominences, Tsui's heroic positioning had to be thoughtful, artistic and enjoyable to befit commercial imperatives. Yang Zirong (portrayed by Zhang Hanyu) was the principal hero in the work. In a sense, Tsui put even more emphasis on the heroic character compared with the previous film versions (including the 1960 film version of *Tracks in the Snowy Forest* produced by August First Film Studio and directed by Liu Peiran). Adopting the typical characterisation of Tsui's own genre films, the protagonist Yang Zirong was highlighted (like Wong Fei Hung and Detective Dee) and turned into a 'hyperheroic' figure. Unlike the previous versions that emphasised the people (because of the theme of class struggle) and Yang as kind of a flat character, Tsui's adaptation focused less on the people and shaped Yang into a more complex character (as seen, for example, in his conflict with the team) which, in principle, was not allowed according to the Theory of Three Prominences. My sense is that this was achieved because Tsui tactfully juggled it with the hero-villain opposition, which, in other words, 'replaces the formalist and formulaic tendency of the red classics with melodramatic characterization' and 'restores Qu Bo's villains some of their vividness, a device to catch spectators' interest and enliven the conflict'.[47] In Tsui's Hollywood-style rendition, in which his spectacular action sequences and computer-generated effects were fully optimised, Yang looked more like Detective Dee, or even Ethan Hunt in *Mission Impossible*. Yang's less stereotypic character was compensated for and/or balanced by his sharp contrast with the villain Lord Hawk (portrayed by Tony Ka-fai Leung), who had a cartoonish hunchback and a nose like that of a hawk's beak. Similar to the perfectly righteous police captain Sun Honglei in *Drug War* (2012), Zhang Hanyu portrayed a flawless heroic character in stark contrast to the villains. That the bandit leader Lord Hawk was played by Hong Kong veteran actor Tony Ka-fai Leung may have been interpreted as a demonisation of Hong Kong, but as in the case of *Drug War*, this could also be seen as 'reverse extreme stereotypes', implying that when someone or something is too perfect to be true, it generally is not.[48] Furthermore, it was true that Tsui brought 'the model opera into a cosmopolitan, contemporary context' by 'treating the model opera the way model operas handled Peking opera: gestures of thoroughgoing renewal and contemporaneity',[49] but he treated Yang Zirong somewhat differently from other heroic characters, who were usually individual heroes. In Tsui's version, Yang entered the scene after fifteen minutes and the multi-character narrative did not centre on him alone.[50] Moreover, Tsui also highlighted the heroism of the People's Liberation Army (PLA), which was in conformity with other revolutionary narratives. The PLA, as argued by Nathan To, was 'flawlessly portrayed as noble, heroic, and brave', and 'the villains . . . instead depicted with an almost cartoon-like exaggeration of sinister insidiousness' in order to accentuate the PLA's heroism.[51] In this sense, the heroic positioning did not squarely counter the three prominences.

This can be further elaborated in regard to the narrative framing of the film. Unlike the mysterious action-adventure fantasy *Detective Dee*, in which 'Tsui Hark's signature Gothic plots repeatedly deliver sensationalist over-stimulations for the global cinema market long inured to violence and sex, or *guaililuanshen*' [strange and supernatural phenomena],[52] model works must more or less stick with a plot secondary to character. In order to make the all too well-known plot enjoyable, while also strategically advancing his signature controlled chaos and *wuxia*-style wicked plotting under the shell of revolutionary narrative, Tsui's version adopted 'narrative structures that operate like forms of one-up-manship', as underlined by Yeh and Chao:

Each feat or gag is a springboard for further permutations, not only by characters, but by setting, pace and scale. These kinds of intensifying action displays typify Tsui Hark's own training works ... Aerial and high-speed chases dominate the story, with Tsui Hark's signature gymnastic maneuvering, designed to elicit wonder and awe. These scenes recall theme parks and animation, juvenile appeals that wrest childlike amazement at amplified pyrotechnics. Another perspective is to bracket the revolutionary dogma of model opera, and attend to its own spectacle appeal.[53]

Without complex plot twists or subplots to captivate the audience, Tsui's 'thoughtful' version focused more on the 'artistic' dimension – the technical polish in the *mise-en-scène* and, more importantly, advanced CG-enhanced duel scenes dazzled by bombs, tanks and aircrafts. Tsui founded the first special effects house in Hong Kong after *Zu: Warriors from the Magic Mountain*, so it was right up his alley to package a Chinese story – be it fantasy or model work – with magical special effects. The generous budget of this main melody film, targeted at an enormous market, enabled his cinematic dream to be realised to a large extent.

King Hu's often-cited remark seems applicable to this film: 'If the plots are simple, the stylistics delivery will be even richer.'[54] But Tsui wanted to do something more: a meta-treatment of the plot with underlying intertextual tactics. In terms of genre-mixing, *Tiger Mountain* was successful. It was also true that imprints of Hong Kong cinema could be found in this commercialised main melody film based on a model work. Yeh and Chao's words nicely sum up Tsui's achievement: 'Through Tsui Hark, the revolutionary precepts of Tiger Mountain join with canonical Hollywood and world cinema. Genre is hybridized, and Tsui Hark's twentieth-century signatures in Hong Kong are revivified, using ultra kinetic, sensational, astonishing visual, and narrative effects.'[55] Insofar as this may have accounted for the film's recognition by the mainland Chinese audience and critics, a further discussion is needed to explore why the film was a total failure at the box office in Hong Kong,[56] while, surprisingly, Tsui was named Best Director at both the 34th Hong Kong Film Awards and the 22nd Hong Kong Film Critics Society Awards in 2015. Hong Kong film critics and scholars considered the SAPPRFT's attempt to repackage main melody films as martial arts or action blockbusters to be a sign of *daluhua* ('mainlandisation').[57] That the dystopian independent film *Ten Years* (2015) and the mid-budget crime thriller *Port of Call* (2015) were awarded Best Film at the two respective ceremonies did mean something: they paid tribute to the director Tsui Hark but not to the films he made. As rightly concluded by Yeh and Chao, 'it seems that Hong Kong commercial cinema has found a new pathway to continue its longevity' in a gigantic market, but 'that it now takes a model opera to resuscitate Hong Kong commercial cinema',[58] which is pointedly ironic; the Hong Kong cinema here is just a part of the Hong Kong model of filmmaking once applauded by audiences across the world. It is also a resuscitation of the commercial directorial skills of Hong Kong cinema in another market. While the Tsui Hark model is successful in mainland China, can Hong Kong cinema, or the Hong Kong model of filmmaking, survive beyond the mainland market?

Trace on Tiger Mountain: The Tactics of Taking

Tsui Hark would traditionally embed political messages in his films. This time, it was the other way round; he had to deploy his filmic spectacle to cover the partisan agenda of the model work in *Tiger Mountain*. In other words, instead of infusing political overtones into a Hong Kong film, he had to do the reverse: infuse a Hong Kong film into a blatantly political project. As discussed above, it was true that some Hong Kong imprints could still be found. But I would argue that they were only parts of the Tsui Hark model of filmmaking. When I discussed Tsui's narrative framing above, I did not go into the arguably most thoughtful aspect of the plot structure of *Tiger Mountain*: bookending the film with two sequences set in the present day. The story begins with a kind of prologue in which a Chinese immigrant, Jimmy (portrayed by Han Geng), watches the 1970 version of *Taking Tiger Mountain by Strategy* in New York in the present, followed by a transition to his origins in Northern China (which seems to be an autobiographical note of the director), where he imagines his own version of the fantasy story of Tiger Mountain. The film has two endings, the first a typical model play plot with poetic justice (i.e., Lord Hawk is shot and most of the bandits surrender), and the second an epilogue in which Jimmy returns to his grandmother's home in New York for Chinese New Year's Eve dinner. In the second ending, Jimmy's grandparents are actually characters in the film, and in the first ending, he imagines an alternative ending, which is powered by more computer-generated imageries, action and intense heroism. How to end a film is an art in itself,[59] and this was even more important in Tsui's project of entering Tiger Mountain. While it is not uncommon for films to have different endings in different versions (such as directors' cuts), mainland–Hong Kong co-productions often have two endings – 'one film, two versions' – because of different market demands and censorship. Tsui used the 'one version, two endings' here in his version of *Tiger Mountain*; of course, Tsui was not trying to 'draw a snake and add feet to it', as the saying goes. His mixing (turning) of revolutionary themes with (into) personal memory would have been forbidden during the Cultural Revolution, as collective values had to be upheld and practised at all times.

A straightforward explanation is that one ending would fulfil model play and main melody film requirements, whereas the other would appeal to commercial Hollywood-style standards. It is also reasonable to argue that the alternative ending was what Tsui wanted to use to conclude his film, but he was simply not in a position to make that call. The beauty of the endings lies exactly in their openness to very different, if not opposite, interpretations. On the one hand, the two modern-day sequences can be interpreted as stressing 'the debt owed by modern-day China to its PLA founders',[60] especially in the end credits that showcase pictures of real-life soldiers. In other words, the film aimed to promote Communist leadership and a singular notion of Chinese people to new genera-tions of Chinese, both domestic and diasporic, by framing the spectacular PLA story with contemporary international sequences:

> Jimmy immediately feels touched and inspired by his revolutionary vision of his grandfather and his army family. In tears, Jimmy creates for himself a poignant, joyful remembrance of what family truly means. Spectators, too, are invited to participate in this melodramatic sentiment. Diasporic ethnic Chinese in the West are also invited to re-discover cultural roots with a Chinese motherland that will protect and welcome us. Indeed, spec-tators are invited to adopt a prosthetic memory of the joys of Revolution, and amnesia of its brutal consequences.[61]

On the other hand, it can also be seen as Tsui's own playacting:

> ... the story of a director pretending to make a nationalist blockbuster which is based on the white-washed official history sold to the young people of China, but is actually a Trojan Horse critiquing their understanding of history ... You can only have one party if there is always a new enemy to fight, if there is always one more battle to win, if there is always one more mission to accept. It's when the missions are over that everyone settles down, and sends their children to American colleges so they can work for international companies and get rich, and that's when the problems start. The Communist Party's version of Chinese identity, Tsui seems to be saying, is only formed in opposition to an outside enemy, be they national enemies (the Japanese) or class enemies (Hawk's bandits).[62]

However, although a brief, brisk but measured voiceover at the beginning was provided, I am not sure whether the younger generation of diasporic and even domestic Chinese were sufficiently well versed in the historical background to appreciate the overtones, regardless of how the endings were decoded. So even though it may have been a Trojan horse, it was doubtful whether there were any soldiers inside. Likewise, it could also have been a Trojan horse to mobilise those Chinese who had settled in the West to find a new enemy and hence a new mission. Different audiences were entitled to have different interpretations. Simply put, when different audiences viewed Chinese (documentary) films, there was often 'an interesting divide between those who were supposedly "native informants" and those who had come to Chinese cinema as foreign observers', according to Rey Chow:

> On the side of the foreign observers, a tone of hesitancy and uncertainty, a need to defer judgement and to respect the more authoritative views of the natives was in the air. On the side of the native informants, the predominant tone was a mixture of anxiety and paranoia and, most of all, apprehension about the possibility of being orientalized and misunderstood.[63]

There was little doubt that mainland Chinese were the major target audience of the film. Despite the fact that *Tiger Mountain* premiered in Hong Kong in a post-Umbrella Movement[64] context on 14 May 2015, its box-office take of US$347,160 (~ RMB 273,840), compared with RMB 0.882 billion in mainland China, was abysmal for a blockbuster, so to argue that the film was not made for the mainland market made little sense. In a novel or film, a coda can be 'an overt meta-narrative task' assigned by its author, as Monica Spiridon explains: 'The Paratext enhances the meta-narrative potential of the Text itself, retrospectively pointing to a series of clues that the unobservant reader has probably ignored.'[65] In some mainland–Hong Kong co-productions, because ghosts were not allowed in the mainland film market, a meta-ending was used to attribute everything in the film to the illusion of the character(s). But apparently Tsui's paratext had a different task. Was Tsui trying to bring Hong Kong cinema to the mainland? Or was he simply commissioned to contribute his model of filmmaking to the commercialisation of main melody films? Even if he had been able to be a 'Sinophone' director, as argued by Tan See Kam, was he allowed to challenge Chineseness without violating revolutionary doctrines? I would argue that, unlike the strategic erasure (erased but still visible and legible) of Hong Kong traits in *Drug War*,[66] which may be seen as another kind of main melody film (i.e., anti-drug), it is the trace of *Tiger Mountain* that should be seen as the most important imprint of the Hong Kong model of filmmaking. For audiences who were familiar with Tsui's films, the intertextual trace was visible, leading them to the Tsui Hark model of filmmaking, and for those who were not familiar with his films, although the trace might not have been visible, it nonetheless remained. Equally important, as noted in the Introduction, *Tiger Mountain* was generally agreed to have successfully introduced a paradigm shift into commercial, high-concept main melody blockbusters, finding a workable formula for an effective crossover of main melody films and commercial blockbusters for Chinese cinema.

Turning a model work into a filmic spectacle was Tsui's strategy for taking Tiger Mountain, but this inevitably left a trace of Hong Kong cinema on the mountain as well. By following this trace, the strategy turned into a tactic that 'insinuates itself into the other's place, fragmentarily, without taking it over in its entirety, without being able to keep it at a distance', in the sense of Michel de Certeau: 'It has at its disposal no base where it can capitalize on its advantages, prepare its expansions, and secure independence with respect to circumstances.'[67] Insinuating itself into the other's place, the intertextual trace left by Tsui on Tiger Mountain is an often-neglected dimension to be explored. As noted in the previous sections, the filmic talent of the Hong Kong Spielberg has often been mentioned in the interpretations of Tiger Mountain. Had it not been for Tsui's exceptional résumé, he would not have been commissioned to take the helm of this main melody film. But one of the traces in this blockbuster was the intertextual references of not just visual effects, jiang hu and luan si, but also of the tactic in his lesser-known works that was actually, in my own view, inspired by The Raid (1991). Seen as the 'weakest of the Ching Siu-tung [Tony Ching]/Tsui Hark collaborations',[68] The Raid was a Hollywood-style action-adventure adaptation of the popular Hong Kong comic series Uncle Choi (the literal translation of the Chinese title) from the 1950s. Its main theme, interestingly, nicely fits with the main melody of the anti-Japanese invasion in recent mainland Chinese television dramas, and in this sense The Raid can be seen as a main melody forerunner. It was briefly mentioned in the introduction that Tsui wanted to make Tiger Mountain after he first saw a film version of the model work in 1974. When Xie Jin, one of the most prominent veteran Chinese filmmakers, asked him at a seminar in 1992 what he would like to film if he had an opportunity to do so in mainland China, his answer was, to the great surprise of everyone there, 'Taking the Tiger Mountain by Strategy'.[69] The Raid was perhaps a comforting replacement for his dream project, which could not be realised back then owing to the political climate of the then British colony and his own attitude towards the mainland as a market big enough to support the huge budget. That said, it is easy to understand that the storyline of The Raid was similar to that of Tiger Mountain.

Concluding Remarks

From The Butterfly Murders and Zu: Warriors from the Magic Mountain to the Detective Dee series, Tsui's genre-mixing fantasies were magically realist. That style was further hybridised with Tsui's typical comics-like storytelling, thanks to the original story on which the film was based. But the plot design was also modelled on *Tracks in the Snowy Forest*. In *The Raid*, Tony Ka-fai Leung (Lord Hawk) – an important figure that links the two films – also plays the villain role of Commander Masa, who runs a chemical weapons factory located in Japanese-held Manchuria. Uncle Choi (portrayed by Dean Shek, one of the founders of Cinema City and Tsui's long-time business partner) leads a team to demolish the factory. Closely analogous to the Hawk gang, the Japanese army plays the role of villain in this film set in the 1930s, a time when Puyi, the last Emperor of China, was chosen to be the 'Emperor' of the puppet state of Manchukuo established by Japan. As shrewdly noted by Hong Kong scriptwriter-cum-critic Jason Lam, the prototypes of some of the characters in *The Taking of Tiger Mountain 3D*, who were not present in *Tracks in the Snowy Forest*, could actually be traced to *The Raid*.[70] Unlike Tsui's later co-productions, *The Raid* did not have an enormous budget. This was perhaps the major reason why the visual effects, even benchmarked against the standards of the early 1990s, were not spectacular enough to turn Tsui's fantasy into a filmic spectacle. In terms of technological breakthroughs in Hong Kong filmmaking, it was not even close to *Zu: Warriors from the Magic Mountain*. As a Tsui Hark fan amazed by his 1983 masterpiece, I did not know how to appreciate the film when I first saw it. It was not until I watched *Tiger Mountain* that I realised, at long last, that without *The Raid* Tsui would not have made the film in that manner, leaving all traits of Hong Kong cinema in a main(land) melody film for his fans to trace. Similarly, there are allusions in *Detective Dee* 'to Tsui's golden-age milestones – most explicitly, *Zu: Warriors from the Magic Mountain*, *A Chinese Ghost Story* and *Once Upon a Time in China*', as pointedly underscored by Gary Bettinson: 'the local is now so deeply imbricated with mainland cinema as to almost subjugate it'.[71] I purposefully chose the term 'trace' – 'the mark of the absence of a presence, an always already absent present'[72] – to foreground the importance of tracing the Tsui Hark model of Hong Kong filmmaking; a text is to be understood by the trace of that other, which is forever absent, so to speak.

It was reported that when Tsui Hark told Xie Jin that he wanted to remake *Taking Tiger Mountain by Strategy*, Jackie Chan was also there, and he said that he would like to join him.[73] In Jackie Chan's plan, the year of the *Tiger Mountain* roll out would be 2010 (to be directed by Siu-Ming Tsui), but his project was aborted because of copyright issues. I do not doubt Jackie Chan's liking for the model work, as it was creatively adapted into the plot of his *Project A* back in 1983: the climactic scene emulated *Taking Tiger Mountain by Strategy* in its design to wipe out the bandits in their den. However, I have to say that, for me, it was fortunate that Tsui took the helm, otherwise the traces left on Tiger Mountain (by Jackie Chan) would have been very different (genuinely unappealing, to be frank), even though the action extravaganza's visual effects would have been more or less spectacular given the very handsome budget. In short, the traces of intertextual references between main melody films and Hong Kong genre films, especially Tsui's own, cannot be overlooked when following him to Tiger Mountain.

By way of conclusion, I would like to refer again to Rey Chow's interpretation of the works of the Fifth Generation directors in her seminal *Primitive Passions: Visuality, Sexuality, Ethnography, and Contemporary Chinese Cinema* to underscore the importance of tactics. In light of Edward Said's *Orientalism*, there have been critiques that have focused on Zhang Yimou and Chen Kaige as 'autoethnographies' and that have aimed to fulfil the desirous appetite of Western audiences. As argued in the Introduction, the fusion of the representation of Hong Kong and the main(land) melody can be interpreted as displaying a tactic. While *Tiger Mountain* may be seen as a display of tactics, the display itself also has to be considered. The film can be viewed as an example through which the Hong Kong reference can be traced with a concept related to erasure: 'catachresis'. With its root in Greek denoting 'misuse' or 'misapplication', this term was appropriated by Gayatri Spivak as a tactic of the colonised: 'a practice of resistance through an act of creative appropriation, a retooling of the rhetorical or institutional instruments of imperial oppression that turns those instruments back against their official owners'.[74] In line with Spivak's argument, this chapter has argued that whether *Tiger Mountain* was made only for the mainland audience or not, it was creatively appropriated to generate insights into Hong Kong (in China) Studies by highlighting the parenthetical. Let me end by paraphrasing Rey Chow's critical and incisive reading of Jia Zhangke:

> In an age when main melody films have become commercial blockbusters in Chinese cinema, Tsui's film astutely makes intertextual filmic display its central attraction. To this extent, the Hong Kong model of filmmaking is part of this display, arranged in accordance with self-conscious traces of his film trajectory . . . What Tsui's film makes explicit, then, is much less revolutionary discourse in the old-fashioned sense, with its acute problem of contending claims to 'the model work', as exemplified by the reception of *Taking Tiger Mountain with Strategies*. Rather, Tsui's work showcases the cultural politics of a new kind of conceptual project: a project of imagining mainland–Hong Kong collaboration not simply as a commercial task, a main(land) melody, or a self-erasure, but first and foremost as a display of different traces, a project that takes the very notion of 'main melody films' as its will to knowledge, its discursive force field.[75]

Notes

1. Richard Corliss, 'He Makes Movies Move, That's Why Tsui Hark Is the Hong Kong Spielberg', *Time*, 2 July 2001: <https://content.time.com/time/world/article/0,8599,2047487,00.html>; last accessed 1 May 2021.

2. 'Venice Rolls Out Red Carpet with Chinese Epic', *China Daily*, 1 September 2005.

3. The untranslatable notion of *jiang hu* is central to many Chinese works, especially *wuxia* literature and films. For a succinct explanation of this in relation to Tsui Hark, see Sam Ho, 'Introduction', in *The Swordsman and His Jiang Hu: Tsui Hark and Hong Kong Film*, ed. Sam Ho and Wai-leng Ho (Hong Kong: Hong Kong Film Archive, 2002), viii–ix.

4. Zhang Shihao 張世豪 and Liu Lanbo 劉藍博, 'Tsui Hark Held a Plan of Shooting *Taking Tiger Mountain by Strategy* for 40 years' (in Chinese) 〈徐克拍《智取威虎山》醞釀40年〉, *Chengdu Economic Daily*, 2 January 2015.

5. Hui Faye Xiao, *Youth Economy, Crisis, and Reinvention in Twenty-First-Century China: Morning Sun in the Tiny Times* (Abingdon and New York: Routledge, 2019), 120.

6. Michael Berry, *A History of Pain: Trauma in Modern Chinese Literature and Film* (New York: Columbia University Press, 2008), 371.

7. Yiu-Wai Chu, *Lost in Transition: Hong Kong Culture in the Age of China* (Albany: SUNY Press, 2013), 104–5; Takeshi Kaneshiro's words in *Perhaps Love* provide an apt description of the mixed feelings of many Hong Kong filmmakers: 'I fell in love with someone I despised.'

8. See 'Xi Jinping's Speech at the Seminar of Culture and Arts' (in Chinese) 〈習近平：在文藝工作座談會上的講話〉, *People's Daily*, 15 October 2015.

9. Xudong Zhang, *Chinese Modernism in the Era of Reforms: Cultural Fever, Avant-garde Fiction* (Durham, NC, and London: Duke University Press, 1997), 225.

10. Lisa Funnell, *Warrior Women: Gender, Race, and the Transnational Chinese Action Star* (Albany: SUNY Press, 2014), 104.

11. 'Golden Rooster Awards Recognize Chinese Blockbusters', *Global Times*, 20 September 2015.

12. 'What's Chairman Mao Got to Do with It? Nostalgia, Intertextuality and Reconstructing Revolutionary Myth in Tsui Hark's *The Taking of Tiger Mountain by Strategy*', *Cinéma & Cie* 30 (Spring 2018): 71–82.

13. Emilie Yueh-yu Yeh and Shi-yan Chao, 'Policy and Creative Strategies: Hong Kong CEPA Films in the China Market', *International Journal of Cultural Policy* 26(2), March 2020: 184–201.

14. Liz Shackleton, 'Nansun Shi Looks Back at Four Decades of Taking Chinese Films Overseas', *Screen Daily*, 21 October 2019: <https://www.screendaily.com/news/nansun-shi-looks-back-at-four-decades-of-taking-chinese-films-overseas/5143998.article>; last accessed 1 May 2021.

15. See, among others, Pak Tong Cheuk, *Hong Kong New Wave Cinema* (Bristol and Chicago: Intellect, 2008), 86–91. Also a Hong Kong New Wave director, Cheuk offers a comprehensive account of the Hong Kong New Wave in his doctoral-thesis-turned-book. See also Yiu-Wai Chu, 'Early Hong Kong New Wave Cinema: Presenting the

Unpresentable' (in Chinese) 〈表現不能表現的：早期香港新浪潮電影〉, in *Age of Hybridity: Cultural Identity, Gender, Everyday Life Practice, and Hong Kong Cinema of the 1970s* (in Chinese) 《雜嘜時代：文化身份、性別、日常生活實踐與香港電影1970s》, ed. Kwai-Cheung Lo 羅貴祥 and Eva Man 文潔華 (Hong Kong: Oxford University Press, 2005), 195–209.

16. Lisa Morton, *The Cinema of Tsui Hark* (Jefferson, NC: McFarland, 2001), 46.

17. Andrew Schroeder, *Tsui Hark's Zu: Warriors from the Magic Mountain* (Hong Kong: Hong Kong University Press, 2004), 1. 'Although Tsui admits in retrospect (on the DVD commentary) that he was, ultimately, not very pleased with by these effects, preferring the physicality and authenticity of on-set action, this collaboration between the two countries' formidable skill sets not only gave birth to a new era of Hong Kong visual effects but also worked to reinforce the themes of the film itself.' Louise Sheedy, '*Zu: Warriors from the Magic Mountain*', *Senses of Cinema* 58, March 2011: <https://sensesofcinema.com/2011/cteq/zu-warriors-from-the-magic-mountain/>; last accessed 1 May 2021.

18. Schroeder, *Tsui Hark's Zu*, Chapter 4. For an inspiring discussion of wire-work choreography in the context of the 'technologisation' of Hong Kong cinema, see Man-Fung Yip, *Martial Arts Cinema and Hong Kong Modernity: Aesthetics, Representation, Circulation* (Hong Kong: Hong Kong University Press, 2017), 186–90. For related information about the special effects of Tsui's works, see Wai-leng Ho, 'From the Local to the Virtual: On Special Effects', in *The Swordsman and His Jiang Hu*, 228–37.

19. Kar Law, Frank Bren and Sam Ho, *Hong Kong Cinema: A Cross-cultural View* (Lanham, MD, Toronto and Oxford: The Scarecrow Press, 2004), 286–7.

20. '*Shanghai Blues, Archival Gems: One Tale, Two Cinemas*', Hong Kong Film Archive (HKFA) Programme, 2020.

21. For a detailed account of Tsui Hark and Tony Ching's collaboration, see Howard Hampton, 'Double Trouble: Tsui Hark & Ching Siu-tung [Tony Ching]', in *Exile Cinema: Filmmakers at Work beyond Hollywood*, ed. Michael Atkinson (Albany: SUNY Press, 2008), 11–19.

22. Tan See Kam, *Tsui Hark's Peking Opera Blues* (Hong Kong: Hong Kong University Press, 2016), Act 3.

23. David Denby, 'The Peking Opera Blues Is the Masterpiece of the Teeming Hong Kong School of Filmmaking. You'd Be Crazy to Miss It', *New York Magazine*, 6 February 1989: 65.

24. See, for instance, Kwai-cheung Lo, 'Knocking Off Nationalism in Hong Kong Cinema: Woman and the Chinese "Thing" in Tsui Hark's Films', *Camera Obscura* 2:3 (December 2006): 37–61; Weijie Song, 'Cinematic Geography, Martial Arts Fantasy, and Tsui Hark's Wong Fei-hung Series', *Asian Cinema* 19:1 (Spring/Summer 2008): 123–42.

25. Ho, 'Introduction', ix.

26. Morton, *The Cinema of Tsui Hark*, 10.

27. Poshek Fu and David Desser, 'Introduction', *The Cinema of Hong Kong: History, Arts, Identity* (Cambridge: Cambridge University Press, 2000), 4; Michele Pierson, *Special Effects: Still in Search of Wonder* (New York: Columbia University Press, 2002), 161.

28. Stephen Teo, 'Tsui Hark: National Style and Polemic', in *At Full Speed: Hong Kong Cinema in a Borderless World*, ed. Esther C. M. Yau (Minneapolis and London: University of Minnesota Press, 2000), 144.

29. Morton, *The Cinema of Tsui Hark*, 1.

30. Kin-yuen Wong, 'Technoscience Culture, Embodiment and *"Wuda Pian"*', in *Hong Kong Connections: Transnational Imagination in Action Cinema*, ed. Meaghan Morris, Siu Leung Li and Stephen Ching-kiu Chan (Durham, NC, and London: Duke University Press, 2005), 285.

31. Stephen Teo, 'Akira Kurosawa, Sam Peckinpah, and the Action Concept of Eastern Westerns', in *A Companion to the Action Film*, ed. James Kendrick (Chichester: Wiley-Blackwell, 2019), 222–3.

32. Wing-fai Leung, *Multimedia Stardom in Hong Kong: Image, Performance and Identity* (Abingdon and New York: Routledge, 2015), 98.

33. Ho, 'Introduction', ix. See also Ho and Ho (eds), *The Swordsman and His Jiang Hu* for extended discussions of the relationship between Tsui Hark and the industry from different perspectives.

34. Cheung-Wai Hung 孔祥威, 'An Interview with Tsui Hark: There Is No Such Thing as Local and Non-local' (in Chinese) 〈「沒有本土不本土」〉, *01 Weekly*, 13 April 2017.

35. Tan, *Tsui Hark's Peking Opera Blues*, 19, 126.

36. Kenneth Chan, 'Tsui Hark's *Detective Dee* Films: Police Procedural Colludes with Supernatural-Martial Arts Cinema', in *Hong Kong Horror Cinema*, ed. Gary Bettinson and Daniel Martin (Edinburgh: Edinburgh University Press, 2019), 133–46.

37. 'Tsui Hark Revives China's Red Classic', *China Daily*, 24 December 2014.

38. Yeh and Chao, 'Policy and Creative Strategies', 196.

39. Paul Clark, *The Chinese Cultural Revolution: A History* (New York: Cambridge University Press, 2008), 26.

40. Xing Fan, *Staging Revolution: Artistry and Aesthetics in Model Beijing Opera during the Cultural Revolution* (Hong Kong: Hong Kong University Press, 2018), 94. For a highly detailed comparison of scene synopses and statistics of characters and languages of five versions (1958, 1964, 1967, 1969 and 1970) of the model work *Taking Tiger Mountain by Strategy*, see 80–9; for an account of the four issues emphasised by the creative team in the process of adaptation in the 1970 film version, see 94.

41. Chris Berry, 'Red Poetics: The Films of the Chinese Cultural Revolution Revolutionary Model Operas', in *The Poetics of Chinese Cinema*, ed. Gary Bettinson and James Udden (New York: Palgrave Macmillan, 2016), 33. Berry also offers a succinct account of the meanings of model works and different studies on *Taking Tiger Mountain by Strategy*; see 30–3.

42. Ibid., 49.

43. Zeng Yuli, 'China's Filmmakers Fine-Tune Patriotism for a New Generation', *Sixth Tone*, 13 December 2019: <https://www.sixthtone.com/news/1004833/chinas-filmmakers-fine-tune-patriotism-for-a-new-generation>; last accessed 1 May 2021.

44. Berry, 'Red Poetics', 36.

45. Kirk A. Denton, 'Model Drama as Myth: A Semiotic Analysis of "Taking Tiger Mountain by Strategy"', in *Drama in the People's Republic of China*, ed. Constantine Tung and Colin Mackerras (Albany: SUNY Press, 1987), 119–36.

46. Yeh and Chao, 'Policy and Creative Strategies', 199.

47. Ibid., 196–7.

48. Yiu-Wai Chu, *Found in Transition*, 140–1.

49. Yeh and Chao, 'Policy and Creative Strategies', 198.

50. Pierre Lam 皮亞, '*The Taking of Tiger Mountain 3D*: Tsui Hark's Masterpiece' (in Chinese), 〈智取威虎山3D：徐克拍出代表作〉, *Ming Pao*, 17 May 2015.

51. Nathan To, 'A Revolution for Memory: Reproductions of a Communist Utopia through Tsui Hark's *The Taking of Tiger Mountain* and Posters from the Cultural Revolution', *Frames Cinema Journal* 7 (June 2015): 8; the author also offers a meticulous reading of the use of cameras and old posters that convey the ideology and memory of a Communist utopia for a new generation increasingly distant from the Cultural Revolution era; see 8–16.

52. Sheng-mei Ma, 'Zen Keytsch: Mystery Handymen with Dragon Tattoos', in *Detecting Detection: International Perspectives on the Uses of a Plot*, ed. Peter Baker and Deborah Shaller (New York and London: Continuum International Publishing Group, 2012), 115–36.

53. Yeh and Chao, 'Policy and Creative Strategies', 198.

54. Stephen Teo, 'The Dao of King Hu', in *A Study of Hong Kong Cinema in the Seventies*, ed. Cheuk-to Li (Hong Kong: Hong Kong International Film Festival, 1984), 34.

55. Yeh and Chao, 'Policy and Creative Strategies', 198.

56. *The Taking of Tiger Mountain 3D* only received US$347,160 (~ RMB 273,840) in Hong Kong, which accounted for only 0.03% of the box-office total for the film; Yeh and Chao, 'Policy and Creative Strategies', 193.

57. Victor Fan, 'Poetics of Failure: Performing Humanism in the Chinese Blockbuster', in *Screening China's Soft Power*, ed. Paola Voci and Luo Hui (Abingdon and New York: Routledge, 2018), 61–2; see also Mirana Szeto, 'Sinophone Libidinal Economy in the Age of Neoliberalization and Mainlandization: Masculinities in Hong Kong SAR New Wave Cinema', in *Sinophone Cinemas*, ed. Audrey Yue and Olivia Khoo (Basingstoke: Palgrave Macmillan, 2014), 120–46.

58. Yeh and Chao, 'Policy and Creative Strategies', 199.

59. For a comprehensive account of Hollywood's strategies of endings, see Richard Neupert, *The End: Narration and Closure in the Cinema* (Detroit: Wayne State University Press, 1995).

60. Fionnuala Halligan, '*The Taking of Tiger Mountain*: Review', *Screen Daily*, 23 March 2015: <https://www.screendaily.com/reviews/the-taking-of-tiger-mountain-review/5085490.article>; last accessed 1 May 2021.

61. To, 'A Revolution for Memory', 16–17. 'Such attempts court transnational spectators to a utopian vision of China as "home" or motherland where one's cultural and ancestral roots can be recovered, and where histories can be (selectively) remembered.'

62. 'And in an ironic twist worthy of an opera, the very same young people who are being criticized are the ones who have bought the tickets that made this film a hit.' Grady Hendrix, 'Kaiju Shakedown: Taking Tiger Mountain', *Film Comment*, published by Film at Lincoln Center, January 2015: <https://www.filmcomment.com/blog/kaiju-shakedown-taking-tiger-mountain/>; last accessed 1 May 2021.

63. Rey Chow, 'China as Documentary: Some Basic Questions', in *The Poetics of Chinese Cinema*, 185.

64. The Umbrella Movement was a 79-day mass act of civil disobedience during which thousands of protesters occupied main roads across Hong Kong from September to December 2014. Known also as 'Occupy Central with Love and Peace', the movement was campaigning for 'genuine' universal suffrage without candidate screening. It was called the 'Umbrella Movement' because protesters used umbrellas to protect themselves.

65. Monica Spiridon, 'The (Meta)narrative Paratext: Coda as a Cunning Fictional Device', *Neohelicon* 37:1 (June 2010): 60.

66. Chu, *Found in Transition*, 132–47.

67. Michel de Certeau, *The Practice of Everyday Life* (Berkeley and Los Angeles: University of California Press, 1984), xix.

68. Morton, *The Cinema of Tsui Hark*, 179.

69. Xiao, *Youth Economy, Crisis, and Reinvention in Twenty-First-Century China*, 120.

70. For further details, see 'A Preliminary Inquiry into the Phenomena of Hong Kong Cinema 2015' (in Chinese) 〈2015港片現象初探〉, Hong Kong Film Critics Association, 6 June 2015: <https://www.filmcritics.org.hk/zh-hant/電影評論/座談會記錄/2015港片現象初探（上）>; last accessed 1 May 2021.

71. Gary Bettinson, 'Yesterday Once More: Hong Kong-China Coproductions and the Myth of Mainlandization,' *Journal of Chinese Cinemas* 14:1 (2020): 16–31.

72. Gayatri Spivak, 'Translator's Preface', in Jacques Derrida, *Of Grammatology*, Fortieth Anniversary Edition, trans. Gayatri Spivak (Baltimore: Johns Hopkins University Press, 2016), xxxvi.

73. For further details, see Yi Li 李毅, 'Jackie Chan on Tsui Hark's Version of *The Taking of Tiger Mountain*: I Already Did This 30 Years Ago' (in Chinese) 〈成龍談徐克版《智取威虎山》：我30年前就拍過〉, ifeng.com, 23 December 2013: <https://ent.ifeng.com/movie/news/hk/detail_2013_12/23/32382396_0.shtml>; last accessed 1 May 2021.

74. Stephen D. Moore, *Untold Tales from the Book of Revelation: Sex and Gender, Empire and Ecology* (Atlanta: SBL Press, 2014), 22; in other words, it is 'a process whereby the victims of colonialism and imperialism strategically recycle and redeploy facets of colonial or imperial culture or propaganda'.

75. This is paraphrased from Chow, 'China as Documentary', 200; the original reads: 'In an age when digital synchronicity has replaced temporal distinctions in the production of meanings, Jia's films astutely make hypermedial display their central attraction. To this extent, the Chinese voices, narratives and life stories are part of this display, arranged in accordance with self-conscious codes of global

medial literacy . . . What Jia's films make explicit, then, is much less documentary realism in the old-fashioned sense, with its acute problem of contending claims to "the real", as exemplified by the Chinese reception of Antonioni's film. Rather, Jia's works showcase the cultural politics of a new kind of conceptual project: a project of imagining modern China not simply as a land, a nation or a people, but first and foremost as medial information, a project that takes the very notion of "China as documentary" as its will to knowledge, its discursive force field.'

Chapter 2

Will Our Time Come? Ann Hui's Fallen City

'We can only hope through long lives / To share her charms across a thousand miles.'[1]

— Su Shi, 'Prelude to the Water Melody'

Introduction: Not a Simple Life

When Law Kar, veteran Hong Kong film critic, talked about the rise of Hong Kong New Wave cinema in 1979 and the directors associated with it, he cited Tsui Hark and Ann Hui as examples who 'have continued to play a significant role in its subsequent development'.[2] As arguably the most important wave of young film directors, and one which exerted the most profound impact on Hong Kong cinema, Hong Kong New Wave cinema was soon absorbed into the commercial mainstream system. Not many New Wave directors worked well with mainstream cinema, and in terms of a sustained impact on Hong Kong cinema across four decades after the New Wave, Tsui and Hui were the two most representative among them. However, while the two have continued to be productive up to the present, their styles are significantly different. Unlike Tsui, the 'Hong Kong Spielberg', Hui has worked 'on the edge of mainstream',[3] focusing more on low- to mid-budget productions. Moreover, she has rarely been involved in the screenwriting of her own works (except for *The Romance of Book and Sword* [1986], *As Time Goes By* [1997] and *The Postmodern Life of My Aunt* [2006]), and she did not begin producing her own works until *Ordinary Heroes* in 1999. Hui admitted that she is 'neither a stylist nor a cerebral auteur. She attaches far more importance to creative impulse than to viewer reception and the market.'[4] Therefore, Hui was considered a 'quiet, unflashy type' of 'jobbing director who takes finished scripts and works one assignment at a time', and she has been criticised by some 'as uneven or lacking an easily defined filmmaking style'.[5] It is not inaccurate to describe Hui in this way, and yet she has won more Best

Director awards than anyone else in the history of Hong Kong cinema. With just twenty-six films to her name up to 2018,[6] she has been named Best Director at the Hong Kong Film Awards six times (*Boat People* in 1983, *Summer Snow* in 1996, *The Way We Are* in 2009, *A Simple Life* in 2012, *The Golden Era* in 2015 and *Our Time Will Come* in 2017), which is a genuinely exceptional achievement. Besides numerous awards at different ceremonies, her Lifetime Achievement awards at the Hong Kong International Film Festival in 2012, the Asian Film Awards also in 2012 and the 2nd Malaysia International Film Festival in 2018 are particularly noteworthy. In recognition of her contributions to culture and society, the University of Hong Kong, her alma mater, conferred upon her the degree of Doctor of Social Sciences (*honoris causa*) in 2014. At the 77th Venice International Film Awards in 2020, she was the first female Hong Kong director honoured with a Golden Lion for lifetime achievement.

Born in Anshan (in Liaoning, China) in 1947, Hui moved with her family to Hong Kong when she was five. She was raised and educated in the then British colony, before attending the London Film School for further studies in 1972. After she returned to Hong Kong in 1975, she had the opportunity to work as an assistant to grandmaster King Hu.[7] Like Tsui Hark and many other Hong Kong New Wave directors, she started her career in the television sector, including Television Broadcasts Limited (TVB), Independent Commission Against Corruption (ICAC) and Radio Television Hong Kong (RTHK). Among the numerous television dramas that she directed, 'Boy from Vietnam' – a 1978 episode of RTHK's classic series *Below the Lion Rock* – was the most remarkable as it, together with Hui's later films *The Story of Woo Viet* (1981) and *Boat People*, became the director's famous Vietnam trilogy. Before these two films, she made her film directorial debut with *The Secret* (1979), a mystery thriller based on a then recent real-life murder case in Hong Kong. This pioneering Hong Kong New Wave film's innovative multi-perspectival narrative won her critical acclaim, but her next project, *The Spooky Bunch* (1980), was also widely recognised by critics. Both were chosen by the Hong Kong Film Archive, in 2011, as one of its 100 Must-See Hong Kong Movies. The subject matter and style of the ghost comedy *The Spooky Bunch* were utterly different from those of *The Secret*, showing that Hui was not just a 'jobbing director' but also an outstanding one who could do her job extremely well. Therefore, it is fair to say that Hui actually 'has little interest in personal style and focuses instead on subject matter, events and characters – and she is willing to adapt style and genre to fit'.[8] More proof of her preeminent directorial abilities was that the actors and actresses working with her often gave magical performances. Josephine Siao's Silver Bear for Best Actress at the 45th Berlin International Film Festival (for *Summer Snow*) and Deanie Ip's Best Actress awards at the

68th Venice Film Festival, the 15th Tallinn Black Nights Film Festival, the 6th Asian Film Awards and other award ceremonies (for *A Simple Life*) were two representative examples of this.

Hailed as the 'most celebrated director in Hong Kong film history',[9] Ann Hui's film career was hardly a simple life. It was therefore not unexpected that an outstanding Hong Kong director like Hui would be invited to direct a main melody film. Furthermore, Hui was among the first cohort of Hong Kong directors to collaborate with Chinese cinema in the 1980s. *Boat People*, her third film, was produced by Bluebird Film, a leftist Hong Kong-based film company, and was shot in Hainan, China. She accumulated considerable experience in filmmaking in mainland China through her works *The Romance of Book and Sword*, *My American Grandson* (1991) and *Eighteen Springs* (1997). After her first film fully financed by a mainland Chinese company, *Jade Goddess of Mercy* (2003), she made *The Postmodern Life of My Aunt* and *The Golden Era*, which primarily targeted the mainland market, and although *A Simple Life* was a co-production, it was a local story about an elderly maid in Hong Kong. It was therefore not surprising that Hui was interested in making the main melody film *Our Time Will Come* funded by China's Bona Film Group. The film, about Hong Kong guerrillas fighting against Japanese invaders during the Second World War, was branded by the investor as a work to commemorate the twentieth anniversary of Hong Kong's reversion to China. Hui explained in an interview why she wanted to make this film:

> The macro history of Hong Kong has long been my favourite theme. It was not meant to be made for the 20th anniversary of Hong Kong's reversion to China. When they said the film fit nicely with the anniversary, because it was about the contributions of Hong Kong people to the war, it was fine with me.[10]

In short, this history of mainland–Hong Kong co-productions may have been a bit exaggerated, but not Hui's contributions to the genre: 'Over these years, her own personal history is almost the history of Hong Kong co-productions.'[11]

Love for the Fallen City

As one of the most representative Hong Kong New Wave directors, Ann Hui experimented with different film languages in her early works. These experiments can be traced back to her television days. In 2009, the Hong Kong Film Archive showcased Hui's creative TV work in 'E-wave: The TV Films of Ann Hui & Ho Yim', in which her TV film works from five series were screened: *Dragon,*

Tiger, Panther: #6 (1976), *CID: Murder* (1976), two episodes of *Social Worker* –
'Boy' (1976) and 'Ah Sze' (1976) – all six episodes of the *ICAC* series, and three
episodes of the *Below the Lion Rock* series.[12] In fact, her TV works can often be
interpreted alongside her later films. The exile of 'Ah Sze' (portraying the female
protagonist's illegal migration from the mainland to Macau to Hong Kong), as
noted by Pak Tong Cheuk in his study of Hong Kong New Wave Cinema, 'became
the chief motif of many of Hui's subsequent films'.[13] Made in film stock, *Dragon,
Tiger, Panther: #6* was a revolutionary attempt in the Hong Kong television
industry at that time. Not only was it different from other video productions,
Hui also narrated the story from multiple perspectives – which was further
developed in her film debut *The Secret* – in which she provided plot threads with
no conclusive answers. The semi-documentary style *CID: Murder* was also eye-
opening for the television audience, and this style was skilfully refined in *Ordinary Heroes*, a film based on real-life Hong Kong social activists in the 1970s
and 1980s. Hui's humanistic concerns had shone through in the two episodes of
Social Worker, which presented lower-class life with touching delicacy. This acute
sensitivity to human suffering was at the heart of her *The Way We Are* and *Night
and Fog* (2009), two films set in Tin Shui Wai, an underprivileged district known
as the 'city of sadness' in Hong Kong. In 1977, Hui moved from TVB to ICAC,
where she directed her effort mainly to the anti-corruption television series
ICAC produced by the Community Relations Department. Thanks to the generous resources provided by ICAC, she managed to co-opt renowned screenwriters
Ho Yim and Joyce Chan and shot the series in film style. Hui's ability to handle
the police and gangster genre was apparent in this series and in the episodes
of TVB's *CID*, which, albeit somewhat differently, inspired her crime and killer
stories such as *The Story of Woo Viet* and *Zodiac Killers* (1991). As noted above,
her RTHK production – she moved to RTHK in 1978 – 'Boy from Vietnam' was
the first episode of her widely acclaimed Vietnam trilogy.[14]

As there could probably be a full-length study dedicated just to interpret-
ing Hui's New Wave career, I will not go much further here.[15] Rather, I will
focus on her works that are closely related to the city of Hong Kong. In a sense,
the Vietnam trilogy, especially *Boat People*, could be interpreted as a metaphor
of the future of Hong Kong – in the early 1980s, Hong Kong people started
worrying about their future after 1997. For the sake of brevity, I have chosen
to use *Love in a Fallen City* (1984) to illustrate her love for the 'fallen' city,
both then and now. Owing to her undergraduate training in literature, Hui
had taken a special liking to cinematic adaptations of literary works. *Love in a
Fallen City* was her first attempt to adapt a literary masterpiece, a short story
written by Eileen Chang, one of the greatest Chinese writers of the twentieth
century. Hui once said that among Chang's works, *Eighteen Springs* was her

first choice,[16] but as it was very difficult, if not impossible, to shoot the film in the mainland (*Eighteen Springs* is set in Shanghai) back then, she selected *Love in a Fallen City* given that its main setting was in Hong Kong. Another reason Hui picked this romance of two selfish people was arguably not the love but the fallen city. Hui and Chang were closely affiliated with the city of Hong Kong. When Chang was featured in the convocation newsletter of her alma mater, she was lauded as an important source of the cultural identity of the then British colony: 'Many of [HKU's] alumni, in particular acclaimed Chinese author Eileen Chang, have woven into the cultural fabric of this dynamic and ever-changing city by embarking on a journey that helped build the cultural heritage and identity of Hong Kong.'[17]

Combining contemporary sensibility with classical Chinese lyricism, Chang's untraditional love stories often offer cynical examinations of self-interest that frequently shape human relationships. Strictly speaking, *Love in a Fallen City* is less a romantic love story than a mind game between two selfish people. In the midst of turbulent times, ironically, the fall of the city helps the relationship between the protagonists, which begins with a trade rather than attraction and ends in marriage. The beautiful name of the story is simply misleading, intentionally though, because it is not love that made the city fall; the fall of the city 'forces' them to get married. The Repulse Bay Hotel on the southern side of Hong Kong Island, the main setting of the story, is where the couple play out their game of love. The original Repulse Bay Hotel, a grand colonial-style building built in 1920, became a famous Hong Kong landmark before it was demolished in 1982. With its wide veranda overlooking the world-famous beach, it was a fashionable meeting place for Sunday afternoon tea. One of the reasons Chang had her characters meet at the Repulse Bay Hotel is that it was a symbol of the cultural life of Hong Kong's upper class. (Unlike most Chinese writers, Chang was a fashionable woman with pioneering boldness, often described as a fashion 'maniac' and a *cheongsam* belle.)

However, since the hotel was demolished to make way for new luxury apartments in 1982, Hui wanted to build a 1:1 replica for the main setting of her film. This was not possible without the support of a large film company. Funded by Shaw Brothers, once a market leader in Hong Kong cinema, the film version of *Love in a Fallen City* had the resources to rebuild the hotel in Shaw's studio in Clear Water Bay. Paradoxically, as noted by a local film critic, because 'a Shaw Brothers production' was a double-edged sword, the director had to make 'all the compromises that implies'.[18] Hui's cinematic adaptation of the literary work swayed between art and commerce, and as she stated, '[t]o film critics it is not artistic enough, but to Miss Fong (Mona Fong, producer of the film) it is not commercial enough. In the end I am glad that I could lean more towards art'.[19]

Unfortunately, the film did not do well at the box office, nor did it convince film critics. As aptly put by the local screenwriter-cum-critic Ping-Hing Kam, it was 'a brave, bold failure'.[20] One of the major reasons behind this was, arguably, Hui's staunch faithfulness to the original, as 'the film version utilizes verbatim dialogues of the novel, which is rarely heard in Hong Kong cinema'.[21] Leo Ou-fan Lee, an understanding critic of Eileen Chang, also believed that Hui's film version failed to capture the feel of Eileen Chang's love story.[22] Hui herself believed that it was not a successful rendition of Eileen Chang's love classic, as the biggest thrust of *Love in a Fallen City* – that the fall of a city fulfilled the selfish wish of a couple – was best expressed in words, not as conveyed in the film: 'I could only present this as a wartime romance, and actually against that historical backdrop the irony could only be conceptually presented in words.'[23] (As astutely noted by Leo Lee, Eileen Chang, a cinephile, incorporated film elements into her novels, which had become one the most distinguishing characteristics of her style.[24]) The film's lack of success was not due to Hui's directorial skills either: 'Ann Hui has skillful directorial abilities, details from camera movements, scene transitions, guidance for actors, rhythm of editing, as well as framing, depth of field to sound effects are well executed with style.'[25] It seemed that the major reason behind the unsuccessful project was Hui's own paradox: she wanted to make a cinematic adaptation but she was not willing to give up her respect for literature, and perhaps more importantly, she was reluctant to present the fall of the city as a mere setting for a love story. This showed her strong commitment to the city.[26] I am not trying to claim that Hui's film version of *Love in a Fallen City* was a successful adaptation of one of Eileen Chang's masterpieces, but I would argue that as a film about Hong Kong, the director's special feelings towards the city were deeply felt. As Hui explained:

> One of the reasons Eileen Chang's *Love in a Fallen City* is immensely attractive to me is that it is set in the 1940s of Hong Kong. A director will get a kick out of making a film set in a historic era, while it is also a big challenge.[27]

The early 1980s was a chaotic time in Hong Kong's history, marked by a looming crisis in confidence brought about by the Sino-British negotiations over the future of Hong Kong after 1997. According to Hui, the film was completed in thirty-six days during the Sino-British negotiations,[28] so the release of *Love in a Fallen City* in 1984 (at the end of which the Sino-British Joint Declaration was officially signed) was not just timely but also pointedly metaphoric: it is reasonable to say that *Love in a Fallen City* could be seen as Hong Kong's collective anxiety towards reversion to China in 1997. If, as noted above, exile was the key motif in Hui's works over the years, the city of Hong Kong continued to be the place where she explored questions of home and diaspora: the fallen city in *The Golden Era* and *Our Time Will Come* in the 1930s and 1940s, and the falling city in *Starry Is the Night* (1988) and *Ordinary Heroes* in the 1980s and 1990s. Among her contemporaries, as she herself said at an academic seminar, she was the least familiar with politics, but she also made it clear that when directors shoot a film on social issues, they have their own comments.[29]

Out of Place, Out of Time

Ann Hui won critics' attention with her Vietnam trilogy, which arguably was about Hong Kong as much as about Vietnam. When she made the 'Boy from Vietnam' episode in 1978, the second wave of Vietnam refugees was acutely felt in Hong Kong. Hui showed her humanistic concerns about the refugees, but it was also a time when Hong Kong people started developing a stronger sense of local identity, and 'contributing to the formation of a Hong Kong identity was apparent threats from without', meaning the Vietnamese refugees.[30] Ironically, by the time *Boat People* was released in 1982, Hong Kong people had begun to fear that their future after 1997 would not be different from that of the Vietnamese refugees. *Boat People* turned a new page in Hui's film career, as it won international acclaim, but at the same time it was also an important chapter in the history of mainland–Hong Kong co-productions. Produced by Bluebird Film, which was masterminded by Xia Meng (aka Miranda Yang) who was hailed as 'The Great Wall Crown Princess' (i.e., the Great Wall Film Company, a leftist filmmaking operation with a close relationship with the mainland), the film was shot in Hainan because it was not possible for Hui to shoot it on location in Vietnam. The sensitive subject matter and the investor of the film stirred up heated controversies (e.g., it was shown Out of Competition at the Cannes Film Festival because of opposition from left-wing sympathisers), and it was banned in Taiwan, along with all of Hui's previous works, because it was shot in China.[31] It was also banned in China because it was 'seen as the first Hong Kong picture to address the phobia and anxiety of Hong Kong people about 1997'.[32] By virtue of the underlying message that touched the nerve of Hong Kong people, however, it enjoyed both box-office success and critical acclaim in Hong Kong, raking in five awards at the 2nd Hong Kong Film Awards and approximately HK$15 million at the Hong Kong box office. Hui's first experience of collaborating with Chinese filmmakers must have evoked mixed feelings. Not long after her unsuccessful *Love in a Fallen City* project, Hui was invited by Xia Meng, again, to spend several years in mainland China and make *The Romance of Book and Sword* with a predominantly mainland team, which was very rare in those days.[33] As perceptively noted by Ai-ling Wong, with the benefit of hindsight, the 1980s had already witnessed the dawning of mainland–Hong Kong co-productions, which China had purposefully developed.[34]

The film adaptation of Jin Yong's all-time martial arts classic was long enough to be divided into two parts: *The Romance of Book and Sword*, followed by *Princess Fragrance* released later in the same month. Despite being the only work that Jin Yong ever participated in regarding the screenplays of cinematic adaptations of his martial arts novels, the two episodes were much less well received than *Boat People* – 'big is the thunder but little is the rain', as the Chinese saying goes. One of the reasons was that Hui, albeit having been the assistant to the martial arts master King Hu, rarely handled this film genre. Another and perhaps more important reason was that it was difficult to adapt to the Chinese filmmaking system back then. Unlike *Boat People*, on which Hui worked mainly with a Hong Kong cast and production crew, *The Romance of Book and Sword* was almost entirely made by a mainland production team. After this, Hui was more comfortable shooting her films in the mainland. *My American Grandson* and *Eighteen Springs*, as mentioned above, were also shot mainly in Shanghai, but it was not until *Jade Goddess of Mercy* (2003) that Hui made her first work fully funded by a mainland film company. Adapted from the bestseller of the mainland writer Hai Yan, the film is about a policewoman who entangles herself in difficult choices between her career and three men in her life. Hui openly admitted that *Jade Goddess of Mercy* was a failure, mainly because she was not familiar with the development of the cultural industries in the mainland. She admitted that she did not know that *Jade Goddess of Mercy* was already a television adaptation, and she was also unaware of the extremely high television audience ratings in the mainland: 'In the end, when the two versions were compared, the audience [thought] that the film adaptation was less impressive.'[35] Perhaps it was because the mainland film industry had changed so much that it took Hui longer than expected to find her footing.

Hui's next mainland project, *The Postmodern Life of My Aunt*, starring her long-time partner, the megastar Yun-Fat Chow, and mainland screen diva Siqin Gaowa, was also hit-and-miss at best. Based on the novel bearing the same title written by the mainland author Yan Yan, about the life of a Shanghainese woman, this was, in a sense, a 'homecoming' journey for Hui – part of the film was shot in her birthplace, Anshan. Unfortunately, the mainland market was fascinated by high-concept blockbusters (by both mainland and Hong Kong directors) at that juncture, and Hui's style was simply not eye-catching enough to take the fancy of the mainland audience. For the Hong Kong audience, additionally, the satirical comedy was simply not the Ann Hui, or even the Yun-Fat Chow (as an ageing dandy in the film), they knew. Although the film tried crossing genres and stirring up reflections on life in post-Deng China,[36] it gave the impression that, in order to lure mainland viewers, it had to forfeit typical Hong Kong characteristics. To sum up her two mainland projects, Hui said that she began to understand that, unlike Tsui Hark and Peter Chan, she was not good at making a film simply using her own imagination. She preferred breathing life into her films, and since the sociocultural backgrounds of the stories in *Jade Goddess of Mercy* and *The Postmodern Life of My Aunt* were significantly different from those of Hong Kong, the city she knew best, the results were unconvincing both to herself and to her audience.

Hui's mainland venture did not end simply because of these two unconvincing attempts. Thanks to the reconfiguration of the mainland film market, there was a greater demand for films of different genres, and Hong Kong filmmakers were seen as an important means to diversify Chinese cinema.[37] This provided Hui with the chance to make a story she knew well: *A Simple Life*. The film was a co-production, but it was set in Hong Kong and was based on the real story of a film producer (portrayed by Andy Lau) and his elderly maid (portrayed by Deanie Ip). The film reportedly cost HK$12 million, but it bagged HK$28 million in Hong Kong and an unexpected RMB 68.19 million in the mainland market, a new box-office record for the veteran director.[38] What was even more remarkable was that this mainland–Hong Kong co-production won international as well as local Hong Kong acclaim, winning a 'grand slam' of major prizes at the 31st Hong Kong Film Academy Awards in 2012: Best Film, Best Director, Best Screenplay (Susan Chan), Best Actor (Andy Lau) and Best Actress (Deanie Ip) for only the second time in the history of Hong Kong cinema (the first was also for Hui's work, *Summer Snow*, at the 15th Hong Kong Film Academy Awards in 1996). Remarkably, in interviews conducted between 1996 and 1998, Hui said that it would be difficult for her to adapt to a new working environment and new colleagues, and thus she was not enthusiastic about developing her film career in a new market.[39] In the end, she did venture into co-productions, and it took her less than ten years to succeed in the mainland market, where she stumbled and tumbled several times before 1997.

By virtue of the success of *A Simple Life*, Hui had the opportunity to make *The Golden Era*, another literature-inspired film recounting the short but memorable life of the influential female Chinese writer Xiao Hong. In this biopic of Xiao Hong, Hui 'return[ed] to her interest in stories about the Republican Era and Japanese-occupied China',[40] which, perhaps more importantly, had subtle links to Hong Kong. This was an ambitious attempt at the cross-border imaginary, as Xiao Hong, born in Heilongjiang, Northeast China, spent the last two years of her life in Hong Kong before passing away in the occupied British colony in 1942. Among the numerous commentaries on *The Golden Era*, renowned Hong Kong novelist Kai-Cheung Dung's essay offered, in my view, the most understanding analysis of Xiao Hong as well as the film. Given the limited scope of this chapter, I will focus only on Dung's interpretation of the title of the film here. It was well known that the Chinese title of the film came from a letter Xiao Hong wrote to her lover, Xiao Jun, in 1936 during her sojourn in Tokyo: 'Free and comfortable, calm and leisurely, no economic pressure, this is really the golden era . . . living in a cage.'[41] This was freedom in a cage, and, as shrewdly noted by Dung, the 'cage' referred to not only the solitude of living alone in a foreign country but also her own isolation and alienation from the era, and 'out of place, out of time' was exactly the recurring theme of Xiao Hong's work:

> Now Ann Hui made *The Golden Era*, in which she completely captured the essence of Xiao Hong's work. In regard to our own era, inevitably and sadly, she had to suffer the same fate as Xiao Hong. The film cannot but become disharmonious, untimely, but a work true to Hui herself. Xiao Hong's 'golden era' is an ironic self-ridicule. Hui's pick of the title is perfect. Not only does this show her understanding of Xiao Hong, it also proves her overwhelming self-consciousness and confidence as a director sailing against the current.[42]

The Golden Era opens in Harbin and ends in Hong Kong, but Hui's journey continued in Hong Kong with her next project, *Our Time Will Come*.

Ordinary Heroes in Extraordinary Times

'Careful storytelling, meticulous contextualization of characters into the social fabric and specific locations, stylistic and intimate camerawork, and individual and emotional characterization', as succinctly noted by Lisa Odham Stokes and Rachel Braaten, 'all contribute to the personal becoming political in [Ann Hui's] work.'[43] Ka-Fai Yau crisply summarised the political in some of Ann Hui's films as follows:

> In *The Story of Woo Viet* and *The Boat People*, the political lies in the observer who is at once apart from and in the story; in *Ordinary Heroes*, the politics of missing has not just to do with the theme of missing, but also with what the film misses while tackling such a theme; in *Love in a Fallen City*, what is political is not just a crisis in history (the Japanese conquest of Hong Kong during the Second World War) that contributes to a love story, but also an adaptation of such a love story into an allegory of a later crisis in history (the handover of Hong Kong in 1997).[44]

Our Time Will Come was no exception. As noted in the introduction, it was seen as a main melody film as it was branded as a work to commemorate the twentieth anniversary of Hong Kong's reversion to China. But different from typical main melody films, such as Tsui Hark's *The Taking of Tiger Mountain 3D* (2014), it directed attention to ordinary people in the fallen city, in addition to the compulsory gunfights, martyrdom and patriotism. Similar to *Love in a Fallen City*, the story in *Our Time Will Come* is set in Hong Kong during the Japanese occupation, and the main plot line is about the underground anti-Japanese operations of the East River Column, masterminded by the Communist Party.[45] In this sense, the director sings the main(land) melody by extolling the Party's contributions to the anti-Japanese war as well as Hong Kong when it was a British colony. Furthermore, one of the main plot lines of the film recounts the evacuation of mainland literati, including the prominent Chinese writer Mao Dun, from Japanese-occupied Hong Kong to the mainland. In the film, as the literati safely leave Hong Kong, the Chinese patriotic 'Song of the Guerrillas' is played, in a scene that explicitly pays homage to the Party. It is also important to note that the female protagonist, Fang Lan (portrayed by Zhou Xun), based on a real-life primary school teacher, is a big fan of literature, and Mao Dun is one of her favourite writers. The film was typical Ann Hui, a director who was genuinely experienced in cinematic adaptations of literary works. In terms of an entertaining film experience, this main melody film (be that as it may), when compared with other blockbuster war films, was obviously less spectacular and the political narrative less overt. Despite a considerably bigger budget than those of Hui's other films, *Our Time Will Come* placed its emphasis much more on human relationships than on war scenes. As such, this film should be understood in relation to her earlier related works, especially those explicitly dealing with Hong Kong: *Love in a Fallen City*, *Starry Is the Night*, *Ordinary Heroes* and *The Golden Era*.

Besides *Love in a Fallen City* as discussed above, *Starry Is the Night* can also be read as a metaphor of Hong Kong's future after 1997, with an underlying message about social changes beneath the touching story of an ageing professor (portrayed by George Lam) and his former teaching assistant/lover (portrayed by Brigitte Lin), in which '[o]ne must tread through extremely sodden ground in the milieu of a romance genre to reach the gist of Ann Hui's real preoccupations: the momentum of history and politics interacting with personal lives.'[46] The two characters part company and meet again many years later, when Lin falls in love with Lam's son (portrayed by David Wu). Against the historical backdrops of the social movements of the 1970s and 1980s, including labour disputes and the Protect Diaoyu Islands Campaign, the film was perhaps the director's first unambiguous reflection on social changes in Hong Kong. *Ordinary Heroes*, without the romantic package of *Starry Is the Night*, tells the story of the relationship between two former social activists (portrayed by Kwan-ho Tse and Rachel Lee) who fought for the rights of the Yau Ma Tei boat people – not a coincidence, I suppose – and their mainland wives. Based on real-life characters, such as Rev. Franco Mella (portrayed by Anthony Chau-sang Wong), the film adopted a semi-documentary style to examine social activism in the 1970s and 1980s, and what had changed or not changed in the late 1990s, shortly after Hong Kong's reversion to China. When Hui talked about this film, she said that it was important to rekindle the passion of the (anonymous) heroes in the social movements of the 1970s and 1980s in order not to become cynical or nihilistic.[47] In short, to borrow the words of Vivian Lee, the film's 'political meanings' were to be found in the private realm of individual experiences.[48] In fact, both films juxtaposed the past and the present with a dualistic temporal framework, so Pak Tong Cheuk's remark on *Starry Is the Night* can also be applicable to *Ordinary Heroes*: 'If Ann Hui has been transformed by the social changes that have taken place over those twenty years to become more mature, then the character of Lin mirrors this process of maturation.'[49] In a similar sense, the use of flashbacks and other related film techniques in *Ordinary Heroes*, as incisively noted by Gina Marchetti in her analysis of the film, were used to underscore the gist of both films: 'The past and present link the personal and the political.'[50]

Our Time Will Come also linked the personal and the political to the past and the present. Hui plays a role in the film, interviewing an aged taxi driver (portrayed by Tony Ka-fai Leung in old-age makeup), who was an errand boy for an underground group, in the present day. The past and the present are linked by the pseudo-documentary interview that bookends the film (and also appears in between). That the film ends with a shot of modern Hong Kong's cityscape cannot be more unequivocal about this. Spanning almost eighty years, the film adopted a structure of temporality that was less complicated than that in *Starry Is the Night* and *Ordinary Heroes*. But the juxtaposition of past and present nonetheless exerted a meta-historical narrative function, which gave the feeling that Hui cared about the characters more than the history in this unemotional war film. Throughout her career, Hui has been interested in characters who, to cite Patricia Erens, 'find themselves exiles in a foreign land: Vietnamese in Hong Kong and the Philippines, Japanese in Vietnam, mainlanders in Hong Kong, Hong Kongers in England and Japan, Americans in China'.[51] The characters in *Our Time Will Come* find themselves exiled in their homeland, which is occupied by the Japanese. Similar to the characters in *Love in a Fallen City*, *Starry Is the Night*, *Ordinary Heroes* and even *The Golden Era*, ordinary people are trapped in an age of changes, in which they are forced to do something that they had not planned to do, whereas others choose to live with the consequences of their actions. In regard to the characters, *Our Time Will Come* explicitly echoed *Ordinary Heroes*. Hui said in an interview that she was deeply touched by the many ordinary heroes eclipsed by prominent figures when she read historical documents, and she was therefore interested in thinking how we, as ordinary people, could possibly imagine ourselves to be hero(in)es. Equally important, everyone who stands up against despotic rulers has something in common.[52] If cinema is 'first and foremost an art of the great figures in humanity in action', as noted by Alain Badiou,[53] Hui's films have been trying to shine the spotlight on the great ordinary people in humanity as well. That said, *Our Time Will Come* was distinctive because of its 'tone', according to the director herself:

> I finally came to know after forty years that a film is not a true reality. What you want to achieve is actually a kind of feeling, a tone. But this tone is not easily projected, because it has to emerge from concrete details . . . you have to know a lot, and process them with your imagination . . . My endeavor was to give my work a special tone, which the audience can feel after seeing my film. Now, *Our Time Will Come* is just the same. I think although it is a historical film, it is of utmost importance to find the right tone, so that the audience will have deep feelings. It is extremely difficult though . . . [And the tone that I wanted to establish in the film is] calmness in extraordinary times.[54]

To continue to live an ordinary life in extraordinary times has long been an important theme in Hui's works, as apparent in the titles, among others, *The Way We Are* and *A Simple Life*.[55] Food scenes are undeniably one of the most representative emblems of what Mirana Szeto called Hui's 'cinematics of everyday life'.[56] In *The Way We Are*, 'Hui's scenes of eating simple meals, shopping for groceries, opening and inhaling the aroma of durian and pomelo, or savoring the decadent sweetness of moon cakes', as underscored by Jing Jing Chang, 'become her concrete testimonials to the nuanced joys of daily life'; food and eating also played an important role in *A Simple Life*, especially in the detailed meal scenes.[57] Even in extraordinary times, food and eating continued to be important components of an ordinary life in Hui's films. For example, in *Love in a Fallen City*, when Fan Liuyuan (portrayed by Yun-fat Chow) and Bai Liusu (portrayed by Cora Miao) are having a meal at the Great China Shanghainese Restaurant, he says that he wants to take her to Malaya to go back to nature; and after the fall of the city, the couple treat the Indian 'princess' Saheiyini to oyster soup in their new home. Therefore, it was not surprising that Hui chose to include an elaborate scene of a wedding banquet in *Our Time Will Come*. 'To remain calm' and 'ordinary life goes on as normal' were the tones of Hui's unsentimental war film, which was untypical of main melody films. In his dialogue with Ann Hui, Hong Kong poet-cum-critic Chi-tak Chan aptly underlined *Our Time Will Come*'s focus on ordinary people, the female response to the grand historical narrative and, most pertinent to my discussion here, Tony Ka-fai Leung's not very articulate retelling of history. Despite his first-hand experience of the historical event and time period, Leung's character does not seem to be talking about this very much. 'This kind of historical storytelling – in a far from open manner – downplays the importance of the historical incident. I think this is very "Hong Kong": not many Hong Kong people would claim loudly that they had a heroic past.'[58] This was also untypical of main melody films.

Ann Hui was not Tsui Hark. She was not interested in emulating the style of his main(land) melody films either. Unlike *The Taking of Tiger Mountain 3D*, which boasts spectacular, flamboyant fight scenes with state-of-the-art computer graphics, the innovativeness of the atypical war film *Our Time Will Come* lay in the director's humanistic concerns. Lim-Chung Man, who won the Best Art Direction award at the 37th Hong Kong Film Awards for *Our Time Will Come*, said in an interview that Ann Hui refused to use CG in post-production to enhance the setting of old Hong Kong, as she insisted on placing the emphasis on the people and their stories.[59] Hui once made it clear in an interview that she was not interested in history or politics:

> After *Boat People*, I was deemed a social-minded and political filmmaker. This reputation [became] even more pronounced after *Ordinary Heroes*. I find all these accolades very strange indeed. I am really a fuddle-headed person. I don't know much about geography, history. To me, history is like myth. I would research the topic, though. I like venturing into the unknown. Actually, I don't know much about politics, and I don't care for it either.[60]

In her own opinion, her best films were concerned with people, not history or politics: 'I think those works that are generally considered to be my best films are dramas about people like *Summer Snow* and *Boat People*, which I think I am most comfortable with.'[61] That said, as stressed by Ann Hui in *Keep Rolling* (2021), a touching documentary about her directed by Lim-Chung Man, she is very committed to Hong Kong, and what she can do best is to keep making films for and about the city. David Bordwell's inspiring phrase regarding *The Way We Are* – 'Modest doesn't mean unambitious'[62] – could also be perfectly applied to *Our Time Will Come*. Hui's ambition was to set a tone for her story in which ordinary people, herself included, survive extraordinary times.

The Best Kept Secret?

Although the director paid heed to ordinary heroes in the fallen city of Hong Kong in *Our Time Will Come*, her film did stir up controversies when it premiered in Hong Kong in 2017. One of the major reasons, besides being branded as a main melody film, was that the cast was heavily slanted towards mainland stars. The female protagonist, among others, was played by the mainland leading actress Zhou Xun, whose dialogue was dubbed into Cantonese in the Hong Kong version. In fact, dubbing had not been uncommon in Hui's earlier works, such as with Brigitte Lin in *Starry Is the Night*, Jacklyn Wu in *Eighteen Springs* and Kang-sheng Li in *Ordinary Heroes* (these Taiwanese stars are not native speakers of Cantonese), but in a time of heated mainland–Hong Kong conflicts, as noted by Karen Fong, Zhou Xun's 'lead role in an assertively local story might also seem a painful reminder of China's subsuming of Hong Kong's once dynamic cinema (and global influence more generally)'.[63] In the meantime, some critics, especially Hui's fans, maintained that it would not be doing the director justice if *Our Time Will Come* were simply considered propaganda. In general, they argued that Hui was actually doing a Hong Kong-style variation of the main(land) melody.[64] For example, the phrase 'see you again after victory', heard several times in the film, could be interpreted as referring to not only the anti-Japanese war but also Hong Kong's own social movements. The Chinese title, besides symbols such as umbrellas in the film, also sounded cryptic to those who knew the language and literary allusion.

The Chinese title of *Our Time Will Come* is very poetic: 'How long has the bright moon existed?'[65] (This line may also be read as 'when will the bright moon appear?') According to Ann Hui, the Chinese title came from the screenwriter Kei-Ping Ho (the English title was chosen by Nansun Shi), and it sounded hopeful to her:

> Personally I feel that natural sceneries such as the sun, moon and stars in the film are symbols of eternity, signifying hope. In dire straits, that may sound ironic, but at the same time it also offers hope to people as the bright moon will finally appear.[66]

'How long has the bright moon existed?' is the first line of the Song Dynasty poet Su Shi's masterpiece 'Prelude to the Water Melody'. In the film, 'Prelude to the Water Melody' is recited by the Japanese Colonel Yamaguchi (portrayed by Masatoshi Nagase), who is a big fan of Chinese poetry. Interestingly, the original Chinese version of 'How long has the bright moon existed?' is best read in Cantonese, as the term *jishi* ('what time') is not commonly used in Putonghua. Some Hong Kong fans therefore understood the film as having a secret message underneath the poetic title.[67] That may have been just wishful thinking on the part of Hui's fans, as she made it clear in an interview: 'Starting from *The Secret*, I seldom pick the titles of my films . . . Few if any titles were my own.'[68] Moreover, Deanie Ip, who openly supported the Umbrella Movement, was also commonly seen as a 'local' dimension in the main melody film. If so, however, this was hardly a secret at all. *Our Time Will Come* was scheduled to be the opening film of the Shanghai International Film Festival in 2017, but it was withdrawn from this slot shortly before commencement of the event. Hui did not make any explicit comments on the reason for this, but it was generally reported that it was due to Deanie Ip. She was therefore erased from all promotional materials in the mainland market, although she won the Best Supporting Actress award at the 37th Hong Kong Film Awards with her truly outstanding performance in this film. The film had even been interpreted as a 'pseudo-main melody' film, and together with its pseudo-documentary narrative and the ending scene of modern Hong Kong, the message could be understood in a 'two negatives make a positive' manner.[69] But I am afraid that would have been just a hallucination, as not only Deanie Ip but also the film would have been banned had the film been considered by the mainland authority as having hidden messages.

In light of this understanding, even if Ann Hui was trying to convey messages besides the main melody, she was not trying to 'pretend to be paving a path to advance while sneaking through another secret passage', as the Chinese saying goes. Obviously, not every film has to be interpreted in relation to social issues, and Matthew Cheng's remark offered a fair analysis of *Our Time Will Come*: 'It may just be the critics' own wishful thinking to interpret the work from the perspective of Hong Kong, and to stress the subjectivity of Hong Kong.'[70] Instead of narrowing our view of it, an examination from another perspective would be helpful. In Jessica Siu-Yin Yeung's reading of *The Golden Era* and *Our Time Will Come*, 'Hui's struggle and mastery of using allegory to reclaim the discursive rights to narrating Hong Kong history through a fragmentary mode of storytelling' provides a platform for further discussion of the latter's relation to Hong Kong.[71] It has been argued by Yeung that 'Hui embeds an allegory within another in *Our Time Will Come*', and the allegorical essay 'Dusk' (1934), written by Mao Dun, who stayed with his wife in the female protagonist's place before leaving for the mainland, is recited three times 'to allegorize revolution and hope' in the film.[72] The allegory had a double reference to both the characters' and the audiences' respective times, and the important point to note is that it was by no means a national allegory:

> Under state suppression of cinematic expression, Hui's *The Golden Era* and *Our Time Will Come* allegorize the geopolitics of post-handover Hong Kong. The two films allegorize with fragmentary narratives, the mix of realist and fictional elements, the biographization of ordinary hero(in)es, open endings, and the themes of rescue, resistance, and revolution. Allegorical cinema

compels Hong Kong filmmakers to be more creative in their storytelling, so as to negotiate delicate interactions between nationalism, localism, self-censorship, and art.[73]

This reminds me of Aijaz Ahmad's critique of Fredric Jameson's argument that all third-world texts have to be read as 'national allegories'.[74] Jameson's division of the globe into three worlds is no longer applicable, for sure, but his strategic use of 'all third-world texts' to produce a theory of third-world literature is noteworthy here. Given the emphasis of this chapter, I am not going to dwell on a discussion of the debates in question but would rather use Imre Szeman's 'Who's Afraid of National Allegory?' to highlight one point. When Szeman used the concept of national allegory to point to 'a number of things about how we should think about postcolonial or third-world texts in the context of the period of decolonization and globalization', the most important in regard to our discussion here would be this one:

> ... what needs to be considered is the conditions of possibility for the practice of writing literature in these regions, for it is only in this way that we can understand the precise and complicated ways in which this older, imported 'technology' participates in the task of cultural revolution that is so important to third-world societies.[75]

In this context, to paraphrase, the conditions of possibility for the practice of Hong Kong filmmakers in Chinese cinema need to be considered, for it is only in this way that we can understand the precise and complicated ways in which they participate in main(land) melody films, which is so important to Hong Kong cinema. Hope is not to be understood as a national allegory but, in the special context of *Our Time Will Come* as a main melody film, the theme is, paradoxically, hopelessly entwined with Chineseness. Fortunately, Ann Hui has been able to make ends meet over the years. As noted by Josephine Siao, who started working with Hui in *The Spooky Bunch* forty years ago, 'William Chang [renowned production designer, costume designer and film editor] said a director is like God, and Ho Yim said like a dog; Ann Hui can achieve a good balance between the two.'[76]

Concluding Remarks

In his 'Always Herself, Always Hong Kong', Cheuk-to Li, Curator of Hong Kong Film and Media at M+ Museum, succinctly summarised Ann Hui's contributions to not just cinema but also to the city of Hong Kong:

Ann Hui has moved continuously between the commercial and the artistic, between genre films and literary adaptations, and between mainstream work and marginal production, always seeking a way forward in the gaps and crevices. One could argue that this flexibility and persistence also characterise Hong Kong. In that sense, calling Ann Hui the most Hong Kong of Hong Kong directors would hardly be an exaggeration.[77]

Even though Hui believed that the box-office failure of *Love in a Fallen City* 'initiated her commercial decline',[78] she kept her commitment to herself as well as to her city. *Eighteen Springs*, *The Golden Age* and *The First Incense Burner* (2021) showed her untiring interest in cinematic adaptation of literature, whereas *Ordinary Heroes*, *The Way We Are* and *Night and Fog* evinced her unrelenting concerns about the falling city. It was thus not a sheer coincidence that Hui decided to make *Our Time Will Come*, a film set in the fallen city of Hong Kong during the Second World War. In terms of the box office, *Our Time Will Come* did quite well in the mainland, grossing almost RMB 65 million, slightly less than *A Simple Life* but more than *The Golden Era*. However, its box-office performance of HK$1.82 million in Hong Kong was miserable, just about six per cent of that of *A Simple Life*. In terms of awards, *Our Time Will Come* won Best Picture, Best Director, Best Supporting Actress, Best Original Film Score and Best Art Direction at the 37th Hong Kong Film Awards, but nothing significant in the mainland. Shuk-ting Kinnia Yau's point is worth noting here: 'For a "main melody" film, such an achievement is rare in the context of Hong Kong', and its popularity could be attributed to the fact that 'Hong Kong film critics have nevertheless generally viewed *Our Time Will Come* as a "failed" main melody film, given that Ann Hui excised nearly all "red" elements from the movie'.[79] That its critical acclaim came from its being a 'failed' main melody film sounds like a zero sum game. In addition, as noted above, the film did embody the compulsory main melody themes, and the director did not dare to excise them all. While Hong Kong critics interpreted the film as a 'failed' main melody work, mainland officials saw it as a success. *China Film News*, masterminded by the China Film Administration, published an essay two days after *Our Time Will Come* premiered, praising the film as an admirable effort to turn the genuine kinship and friendship and the pure but helpless love among ordinary Hong Kong people into burning patriotism. It also commended the use of language, citing 'see you again after victory' as an example.[80]

Mainland film scholars have foregrounded Hui's style of using ordinary people to subvert the narrative mode of traditional Chinese war films, and Tony Ka-fai Leung was seen as a creative attempt to use an ordinary perspective to record this special chapter of Hong Kong history as part of the overall anti-Japanese war of China.[81] It is apparent here that the mainland media was also trying to appropriate Ann Hui's typical film style and humanistic concerns, turning them into vehicles to carry main melody messages. In this sense, *Our Time Will Come* can be seen as a practice through which the conditions of possibility for the work of Hong Kong filmmakers in Chinese cinema can be considered. Well known as a veteran director working 'at the margin of mainstream', Ann Hui has practised different styles in different films.[82] As perceptively summed up by Law Kar, over the years, Hui has been good at handling 'small stories', but not grand narratives,[83] or at shattering grand narratives into small stories. It is her humanistic concerns, not filmic style, that have remained unchanged over the years:

> Hui's first concern seems to be human beings in all their complexity, and the difficulty of human relationships. Her cinematic techniques are always marshaled to furthering this philosophy. Over and over again Hui's films seem to warn against trying to impose ready-made solutions on life's complex problems.[84]

It was not a secret that the cultural politics of diasporic identity in Hui's semi-autobiographical film *Song of the Exile* (1990) squarely dealt with Chineseness: 'Less Chinese and yet more China-centric than Aiko [Japanese living in China], both mother and daughter [Hueyin] reveal the contingency of Chineseness that underlies the crisis of identity.'[85] I fully understand Hong Kong fans' wish to decode *Our Time Will Come* in a way that would let the fallen city's imaginaries surface. As I see it, Mei-Ting Li has offered an inspiring account of the film as not an attempt to 'sneak through another secret passage' to smuggle in her own message: in *Our Time Will Come*, 'Hong Kong is *de facto* the main melody'.[86] I agree with most of her analysis of the film, including the conclusion that Tony Ka-fai Leung, who has 'taken' the role of Lord Hawk [in *The Taking of the Tiger Mountain 3D*], narrates the story in a subjective way and takes this chapter of anti-Japanese history, which belongs to Hong Kong history, back from Chinese history: 'In the end some chose to leave (including Fang Lan who departed later), but those who stayed in Hong Kong naturally undertake the Hong Kong now.'[87] It is not wrong to claim, in my opinion, that Hong Kong is the main melody in *Our Time Will Come*, but it is necessary to note the other aspects of the main melody, such as rhythm and harmony, which might (or even must) entangle themselves with Chineseness. More pertinently, Elaine Yee-lin Ho argued, in her discerning explanation of how the Chineseness of Hui's films has been mediated by a Hong Kong vantage point, that

> [i]n configuring cinema as critical practice, Hui's optic frequently turns to the forms of inherited Chinese cultural life as they endure in Hong Kong

and to Chinese history framed by Hong Kong's location on the temporal and spatial edge of two empires.[88]

My sense is that to see the film as a Trojan horse might simply be fantasising. It is true that 'Hui skates a fine line' in this main(land) melody film, but, as shrewdly noted by Karen Fong, she 'astutely fulfills the expectations of her mainland financing while still upholding local identity', and 'covert operations and a canny ability to negotiate seemingly contradictory purposes have long been central to Hong Kong success'.[89] In *Our Time Will Come*, Ann Hui – 'always herself, always Hong Kong' – remained calm, to borrow her own idea about the tone of the film, and continued to do what she does well: keep rolling and tell a story about ordinary people in extraordinary times. This evinces the love for her city and its cinema. It was therefore not unexpected that when she was honoured by the Venice International Film Festival with the Golden Lion Lifetime Achievement Award in 2020, she highlighted the importance of Hong Kong in her acceptance speech:

> Above all, here, I would like to revert this honour back to Hong Kong, the city where I grew up. It has given me an education and a scholarship to study in London. It has given me my life experiences, and my chances to work and find fulfillment. I treasure even my sufferings there and all those crazy cool people. And now I will go home and try to help the younger filmmakers so that they will also get life achievement prizes in the future. Long live cinema.[90]

As 'a struggle against the impure world' and 'a collection of precious victories', as reminded by Badiou, cinema instructs us to uphold that 'the worst of worlds shouldn't cause despair', and Hui continues to show us the 'lesson of hope' that 'something can happen even though the worst may prevail'.[91] 'Prelude to the Water Melody' ends with the poet's best wishes: 'We can only hope through long lives/ To share her charms across a thousand miles'. It is also the director's best wishes to her beloved city and its cinema.

Notes

1. English translation Ronald C. Egan, *Word, Image, and Deed in the Life of Su Shi* (Cambridge, MA, and London: Harvard University Press, 1994), 346.
2. Law Kar, 'An Overview of Hong Kong's New Wave Cinema', in *At Full Speed: Hong Kong Cinema in a Borderless World*, ed. Esther C. M. Yau (Minneapolis and London: University of Minnesota Press, 2000), 31.
3. Esther M. K. Cheung, Gina Marchetti and Tan See Kam, 'Interview with Ann Hui: On the Edge of Mainstream', in *Hong Kong Screenscapes: From the New Wave to the*

Digital Frontier, ed. Esther M. K. Cheung, Gina Marchetti and Tan See Kam (Hong Kong: Hong Kong University Press, 2011), 68.

4. Cheuk-to Li, 'Always Herself, Always Hong Kong', *M+ Screenings: The Film Life of Ann Hui*, 8–16 December 2018: <https://www.westkowloon.hk/en/whats-on/current-forthcoming/m-screenings-the-film-life-of-ann-hui/chapter/curatorial-statement-2569>; last accessed 1 May 2021.

5. Patrick Frater, 'Ann Hui: Asian Filmmaker of the Year Quietly Built Hefty Resume', *Variety*, 3 October 2014: <https://variety.com/2014/film/asia/ann-hui-asian-filmmaker-year-busan1201317988-1201317988/>; last accessed 1 May 2021.

6. See *Ann Hui: Forty* (in Chinese) 《許鞍華：電影四十》, ed. Cecilia Wong 卓男 and Stephanie Ng 吳月華 (Hong Kong: Joint Publishing Co., 2018), 8; for brief synopses of her twenty-six films, see 346–59.

7. For a detailed account of Ann Hui's biographical information and academic training, see 'Hui, Ann: Critical Biography', *Hong Kong Women Filmmakers*: <https://hkwomenfilmmakers.wordpress.com/hui-ann-2/>; last accessed 1 May 2021.

8. Frater, 'Ann Hui: Asian Filmmaker of the Year Quietly Built Hefty Resume'.

9. Edmund Lee, 'Ann Hui, Most Celebrated Director in Hong Kong Film History, Turns 70', *South China Morning Post*, 21 May 2017.

10. Gillian Jin 金其琪, 'Ann Hui: Seventy Years of Diaspora' (in Chinese) 〈導演許鞍華七十年流徙〉, *Blogger World*, 246 (30 June 2017): <http://blog.sina.com.cn/s/blog_5f0b84100102x2il.html>; last accessed 1 May 2021.

11. Ibid.

12. 'HK Film Archive to Screen TV Films by Ann Hui and Ho Yim', Hong Kong Government Press Release, 9 February 2009: <https://www.info.gov.hk/gia/general/200902/09/P200902090205.htm>; last accessed 1 May 2021.

13. Pak Tong Cheuk, *Hong Kong New Wave Cinema (1978–2000)* (Bristol and Chicago: Intellect, 2008), 55–6.

14. For a brief account of Hui's TV works, see, among others, Yiu-Wai Chu 朱耀偉, *The (Post)Youth Age of Hong Kong Popular Culture* (in Chinese) 《香港流行文化的(後)青春歲月》 (Hong Kong: Chung Hwa, 2019), 43–4.

15. See, for instance, Cheuk, *Hong Kong New Wave Cinema*, 53–81.

16. Carole Hoyan 何杏楓, 'On the Cinematic Adaptation of Ann Hui's *Love in a Fallen City*' (in Chinese) 〈論許鞍華《傾城之戀》的電影改編〉, in *Rereading Eileen Chang* (in Chinese) 《再讀張愛玲》, ed. Joseph Lau劉紹銘, Ping-kwan Leung 梁秉鈞 and Zidong Xu 許子東 (Hong Kong: Oxford University Press, 2002), 119; for additional background of the film version, see William Tay 鄭樹森, 'Commentary' (in Chinese) 〈講評〉, in *Rereading Eileen Chang*, 127–9. See also, Po-Wai Kwong 鄺保威, *Ann Hui Talking about Ann Hui* (in Chinese) 《許鞍華說許鞍華》 (Hong Kong: Po-Wai Kwong, 1998), 73.

17. 'Eileen Chang: A Hong Kong Legend', Cover Story, *The University of Hong Kong Convocation Newsletter*, Fall 2007: 10.

18. Alan Stanbrook, 'Under Western Eyes: An Occidental View of Hong Kong Cinema', in *Hong Kong Cinema in the Eighties: A Comparative Study with Western Cinema*, ed.

Fifteenth Hong Kong International Film Festival (Hong Kong: Urban Council of Hong Kong, 1991), 48.

19. 'From *Love without End* to *Lust, Caution*' (in Chinese) 〈從《不了情》到《色戒》〉, *New Times Weekly*, 27 (17 September 2006); see also Lau, Leung and Xu, *Rereading Eileen Chang*, 62–171.

20. Ping-Hing Kam 金炳興, 'A Brave, Bold Attempt' (in Chinese) 〈一次勇敢而大膽的嘗試〉, *Film Biweekly* 142 (1984): 46–7.

21. Kei Shek 石琪, *Hong Kong Cinema: New Wave* (in Chinese) 《香港電影新浪潮》 (Shanghai: Fudan University Press, 2006), 49.

22. Leo Ou-fan Lee 李歐梵, *Fin de siècle Murmur* (in Chinese)《世紀末囈語》(Hong Kong: Oxford University Press, 2001), 442.

23. 'Why Do We Love Watching Ann Hui?' (in Chinese) 〈我們為什麼愛看許鞍華？〉, *Read 01*, 2 November 2016: <https://read01.com/zh-hk/zn4jLo.html#.XmXRKqg-zY2w>; last accessed 1 May 2021.

24. Leo Ou-Fan Lee, *Shanghai Modern: The Flowering of a New Urban Culture in China, 1930–1945* (Cambridge, MA: Harvard University Press, 1999), 271–2.

25. Sen Ma 馬森, *Film China Dream* (in Chinese) 《電影中國夢》(Taipei: Showwe Information Co. Ltd., 2016), 220.

26. 'Why Do We Love Watching Ann Hui?'

27. Ann Hui, 'On *Love in a Fallen City*' (in Chinese) 〈談「傾城之戀」〉, *Ming Pao*, 3 August 1984, Jinsong Xin 辛金順, *Silent Voices: Essays on Sinophone Literature* (in Chinese) 《秘響交音: 華語語系文學論集》 (Taipei: Independent & Unique, 2012), 16.

28. Hoyan, 'On the Cinematic Adaptation of Ann Hui's *Love in a Fallen City*', 96.

29. 'Ann Hui and Her Hong Kong', a seminar co-hosted by Ann Hui and Mary Wong at Hong Kong Lingnan University, 3 November 2014: <https://commons.ln.edu.hk/videos/23/>; last accessed 1 May 2021.

30. Gordon Mathews, Eric Ma and Tai-lok Lui, *Hong Kong, China: Learning to Belong to a Nation* (London and New York: Routledge, 2008), 37.

31. Patricia Erens, 'The Film Work of Ann Hui', in *The Cinema of Hong Kong: History, Arts, Identity*, ed. Poshek Fu and David Desser (Cambridge: Cambridge University Press, 2000), 184.

32. Stephen Teo, *Hong Kong Cinema: The Extra Dimension* (London: British Film Institute, 1997), 214.

33. 'To the surprise of many people, Ann Hui went to mainland China in the mid-80s to spend several years inside the country where she was born, staying there to produce *Romance of Book and Sword*, a two-part film about which critics made many political interpretations.' Lo Wai Luk, 'A Child without a Mother, An Adult without a Motherland: A Study of Ann Hui's Films', in *Hong Kong New Wave: Twenty Years After*, ed. 23rd Hong Kong International Film Festival (Hong Kong: Provisional Urban Council of Hong Kong, 1999), 68.

34. Ai-ling Wong, 'Blue Bird Indulge Me Please and Spy a Little Glance: The Film Journey of Ann Hui' (in Chinese) 〈青鳥殷勤為探看：許鞍華的電影之旅〉, in Wong and Ng, *Ann Hui: Forty*, 32.

35. Jin, 'Ann Hui: Seventy Years of Diaspora'.
36. See, for instance, Gina Marchetti, 'Gender Politics and Neoliberalism in China: Ann Hui's *The Postmodern Life of My Aunt*', *Visual Anthropology* 22:2–3 (2009): 123–40.
37. Li Yizhuang 李以莊 and Xi Yue 席悅, 'Back to the Local: The New Age of Co-productions' (in Chinese) 〈回歸本土：新合拍片年代〉, *Bloomberg Businessweek* (Chinese Version), 14 February 2010.
38. The mainland box-office takes for *Jade Goddess of Mercy* and *The Postmodern Life of My Aunt* were only RMB 5 million and 6.64 million, respectively; Esther C. M. Yau, 'Watchful Partners, Hidden Currents: Hong Kong Cinema Moving into the Mainland of China', in *A Companion to Hong Kong Cinema*, ed. Esther M. K. Cheung, Gina Marchetti and Esther C. M. Yau (Malden, MA: Wiley-Blackwell, 2015), 27.
39. Kwong, *Ann Hui Talking about Ann Hu*, 86.
40. For an informative account of *The Golden Era* in relation to world cinema and soft power, see Gina Marchetti, 'The Feminine Touch: Chinese Soft Power Politics and Hong Kong Women Filmmakers', in *Screening China's Soft Power*, ed. Paola Voci and Luo Hui (Abingdon and New York: Routledge, 2018), 232–43.
41. Translated from *Historical Materials of New Literature* (in Chinese)《新文學史料》, 4–5 (Beijing: People's Literature Press, 1979), 283.
42. Kai-Cheung Dung, 'Xiao Hong's Golden Era, Our Golden Era' (in Chinese) 〈蕭紅的黃金時代，我們的黃金時代〉, *Ming Pao*, 24 September 2014.
43. Lisa Odham Stokes and Rachel Braaten, *Historical Dictionary of Hong Kong Cinema* (Lanham, MD: Rowman and Littlefield, 2020), 203.
44. Ka-Fai Yau, 'Looking Back at Ann Hui's Cinema of the Political', *Modern Chinese Literature and Culture* 19:2 (Fall 2007): 144.
45. For an elaborated account of the East River Column, see Sui-jeung Chan, *East River Column Hong Kong Guerrillas in the Second World War and After* (Hong Kong: Hong Kong University Press, 2009).
46. *The China Factor in Hong Kong Cinema*, ed. Fourteenth Hong Kong International Film Festival (Hong Kong: Urban Council of Hong Kong, 1990), 147.
47. See 'Ann Hui and Her Hong Kong'.
48. Vivian Lee, *Hong Kong Cinema Since 1997: The Post-Nostalgic Imagination* (Basingstoke: Palgrave Macmillan, 2009), 279–80.
49. Cheuk, *Hong Kong New Wave Cinema*, 66; see also Lo Wai Luk, 'A Child without a Mother, An Adult without a Motherland', 68.
50. Gina Marchetti, *Citing China: Politics, Postmodernism, and World Cinema* (Honolulu: University of Hawaii Press, 2018), 93.
51. Erens, 'The Film Work of Ann Hui', 179.
52. Nic Wong, 'Stars Accompanying the Bright Moon: An Interview with Ann Hui and Ivana Wong' (in Chinese) 〈繁星伴明月：許鞍華、王菀之〉, *Jet Magazine* 179 (July 2017): <https://jet.my-magazine.me/article/detail/interview/9613>; last accessed 1 May 2021.
53. Alain Badiou, *Cinema* (Cambridge: Polity, 2013), 239.
54. Wei-Chen Chen 陳韋臻, 'Tone of the Era: Who Can Name It? Ann Hui and *Our Time Will Come*' (in Chinese) 〈時代的調子，誰能命名：許鞍華與《明月幾時有》〉,

Funscreen 603 (15 July 2017): <http://www.funscreen.com.tw/headline.asp?H_No=665>; last accessed 1 May 2021.

55. For a further discussion of ordinary life in *The Way We Are* and *Our Time Will Come*, see Hui's interview: Ding Xiongfei 丁雄飛, 'Ann Hui on Films, Shanghai and *The First Incense Burner*' (in Chinese) 〈許鞍華談電影談上海談《第一爐香》〉, *Shanghai Book Review*, 13 October 2018.

56. Mirana M. Szeto, 'Ann Hui at the Margin of Mainstream Hong Kong Cinema', in *Hong Kong Screenscapes: From the New Wave to the Digital Frontier*, 53–4.

57. See, for instance, Jing Jing Chang, 'Ann Hui's Tin Shui Wai Diptych: The Flashback and Feminist Perception in Post-Handover Hong Kong', *Quarterly Review of Film and Video* 33:8 (2016): 722–42; Antonio D. Sison, *The Sacred Foodways of Film: Theological Servings in 11 Food Films* (Eugene, OR: Pickwick, 2016), 66–90.

58. '*Our Time Will Come*: A Dialogue between Ann Hui and Mit Chan [aka Chi-tak Chan]' (in Chinese) 〈《明月幾時有》許鞍華、陳滅對談〉, *Initium Media*, 25 July 2017: <https://theinitium.com/article/20170725-culture-dialogue-xuanhuachenmie/>; last accessed 1 May 2021.

59. For details, see 'Lim-Chung Man: Never Forget Why She Started Making Films' (in Chinese) 〈文念中：堅守拍電影的初心〉, in Wong and Ng, *Ann Hui: Forty*, 286–7.

60. Cheung, Marchetti and Tan, 'Interview with Ann Hu'.

61. Michael Berry, 'Ann Hui: Living through Film', in *Speaking in Images: Interviews with Contemporary Chinese Filmmakers*, ed. Michael Berry (New York: Columbia University Press, 2005), 433.

62. David Bordwell, 'Modest Doesn't Mean Unambitious', David Bordwell's Website on Cinema, 30 May 2008: <http://www.davidbordwell.net/blog/2008/03/30/modest-doesnt-mean-unambitious/>; last accessed 1 May 2021.

63. Karen Fang, 'Ann Hui's *Our Time Will Come* and Christopher Nolan's *Dunkirk*', *CHA Journal*, 9 November 2017: <https://chajournal.blog/2017/11/09/our-time-will-come-and-dunkirk/>; last accessed 1 May 2021.

64. See Ben Au, 'Red Co-productions? Don't Underestimate Ann Hui' (in Chinese) 〈紅色合拍片？別太小看許鞍華〉, *HK01*, 12 July 2017: <https://www.hk01.com/社會新聞/104168/明月幾時有-影評-紅色合拍片-別太小看許鞍華>; Ping-ting Chan 陳娉婷, 'Hong Kong-style Variation beneath a Red Co-production: Ann Hui Did Not Forget Hong Kong' (in Chinese) 〈紅色合拍片下的港式變奏：許鞍華沒有忘記香港〉, *The News Lens*, 16 July 2017: <https://www.thenewslens.com/feature/hk-movies-newwave/73590>; Pony, 'From *As Time Goes By* to *Our Time Will Come*: Ann Hui's "Reunion"' (in Chinese) 〈從《去日苦多》到《明月幾時有》：許鞍華的「團」與「圓」〉, *Funscreen 604*, 22 July 2017: <http://www.funscreen.com.tw/review.asp?RV_id=2119>; all last accessed 1 May 2021.

65. English translation Egan, *Word, Image, and Deed in the Life of Su Shi*, 346.

66. Wong, 'Stars Accompanying the Bright Moon'.

67. This is one of the examples: Sin-Yee Choi 蔡倩怡, '*Our Time Will Come*: The Secret Message underneath the Main Melody' (in Chinese) 〈《明月幾時有》：主旋律暗渡陳倉〉, *MP Weekly*, 8 July 2017: <https://www.mpweekly.com/culture/明月幾時有-許鞍華-建軍大業-41950>; last accessed 1 May 2021.

68. According to Ann Hui, the Chinese titles of *The Spooky Bunch* was selected by Josephine Siao (producer and female lead), *The Story of Woo Viet* by Alfred Cheung (screenwriter) and *Boat People* by Jin Yong; Chen, 'Tone of the Era'.

69. See '*Our Time Will Come*: A Pseudo-Main Melody Film in the High Altitude' (in Chinese) 〈明月幾時有：高處不勝寒的偽主旋律電影〉, *Sparrow Watching Movies Film Review*, 8 July 2017: <https://cheercut.com/our-time-will-come/>; last accessed 1 May 2021.

70. Quoted in Choi, 'Our Time Will Come'.

71. Jessica Siu-Yin Yeung, 'Ann Hui's Allegorical Cinema', in *Cultural Conflict in Hong Kong: Angles on a Coherent Imaginary*, ed. Jason Polley, Vinton Poon and Lian-Hee Wee (Singapore: Palgrave Macmillan, 2018), 91.

72. Ibid., 98–9.

73. Ibid., 99.

74. Fredric Jameson, 'Third-World Literature in the Era of Multinational Capitalism', *Social Text* 15 (Autumn 1986): 65–88; Aijaz Ahmad, 'Jameson's Rhetoric of Otherness and the "National Allegory"', *Social Text* 17 (Fall 1987): 3–25.

75. Imre Szeman, 'Who's Afraid of National Allegory?', in *On Jameson: From Postmodernism to Globalization*, ed. Caren Irr and Ian Buchanan (Albany: SUNY Press, 2006), 198.

76. Josephine Siao, quoted in the documentary *Keep Rolling*.

77. Li, 'Always Herself, Always Hong Kong'.

78. Daniel O'Brien, *Spooky Encounters: A Gwailo's Guide to Hong Kong Horror* (Manchester: Headpress, 2003), 176.

79. Shuk-ting Kinnia Yau, 'From *March of the Volunteers* to *Amazing Grace*: The Death of China's Main Melody Movie in the 21st Century', *Jump Cut: A Review of Contemporary Media* 59 (Fall 2019), <https://www.ejumpcut.org/currentissue/KinnieYauMainMelody/text.html>; last accessed 1 May 2021.

80. 'Making a Good Start in Summer: *Our Time Will Come* Ranks Top This Year in Terms of Audience Satisfaction' (in Chinese) 〈暑期檔「開門紅」，《明月幾時有》觀眾滿意度居年內首位〉, *China Film News*, 3 July 2017, <https://kknews.cc/entertainment/e8ng4m4.html>; last accessed 1 May 2021.

81. Chen Xuguang 陳旭光 and Tien Yizhou 田亦洲, 'New Era of Chinese Cinema: New Configurations, New Norms and New Aesthetic Constructions' (in Chinese) 〈中國電影新時代：新格局、新規範與新美學建構〉, *Commentaries on Literature and Art* 1 (2018): 74–84.

82. Szeto, 'Ann Hui at the Margin of Mainstream Hong Kong Cinema', 51.

83. Law Kar, 'Reading and Describing Ann Hui Closely' (in Chinese) 〈細讀細說許鞍華〉, in *Ann Hui: Forty*, 20–1.

84. Erens, 'The Film Work of Ann Hui', 192.

85. Audrey Yue, *Ann Hui's Song of the Exile* (Hong Kong: Hong Kong University Press, 2010), 63.

86. Mei-Ting Li李薇婷, '*Our Time Will Come*: Hong Kong Is the Main Melody' (in Chinese) 〈《明月幾時有》：香港就是主旋律〉, *Cinezen*, 11 July 2017: <https://www.cinezen.hk/?p=7713>; last accessed 1 May 2021.

87. Ibid.
88. Elaine Yee-lin Ho, 'Women on the Edges of Hong Kong Modernity: The Films of Ann Hui', in *At Full Speed: Hong Kong Cinema in a Borderless World*, 178. Ho provides a meticulous account of the implications of memory in Hui's work in this essay; see 177–206.
89. Fang, 'Ann Hui's *Our Time Will Come* and Christopher Nolan's *Dunkirk*'.
90. From the closing ceremony of the Venice Film Festival 2020: <https://www.youtube.com/watch?v=zULGYIUOzWI>; last accessed 1 May 2021.
91. Badiou, *Cinema*, 231–2.

Chapter 3

Hong Kong Dreams in Mainland China: The Leap of Peter Chan

'I don't put on acts. I am what I act.'

— Peter Chan, *Leap*

Introduction

Peter Chan is arguably the Hong Kong director who is the most sensitive to the diasporic experience. Born in Hong Kong, where his father, Tung-Man Chan, was a director and producer, he moved to Thailand with his family at the age of twelve, and then went to Los Angeles where he studied film.[1] While spending six years of his adolescence in Thailand, he watched many European films – not Hollywood productions because Thailand was anti-America at that time – which deeply influenced him later in his film career. In 1983, when he was still studying in Los Angeles, he went back to Hong Kong for the summer and was recruited as an interpreter for John Woo's film *Heroes Shed No Tears* (1986). (The film was completed in 1983 but did not premier until 1986, owing to contract issues between John Woo and the producer, Golden Harvest.) Because the film was shot in Thailand, they needed an interpreter who could speak Cantonese, Thai and English. He was supposed to return to college after that summer job, but this was destined to be 'a trip of no return':

> The film production got postponed and last [sic] until Christmas. So I decided to work on another picture for a year. It was a movie in Barcelona with Jackie Chan and Sammo Hung. Then I went to Yugoslavia to work on another Jackie Chan's [sic] movie. So one picture became two pictures, became three pictures.[2]

Having accumulated filmmaking experience in different capacities from the films he had worked on, including, among others, Jackie Chan's *Wheels on Meals*

(1984), *The Protector* (1985), *Armour of God* (1987) and *News Attack* (1989),[3] Peter Chan soon had the chance to make his directorial debut, *Alan and Eric: Between Hello and Goodbye* (1991; hereafter abbreviated as *Alan and Eric*), thanks to the support of Eric Tsang, friend, collaborator and *Bo Le* (a person who is able to discover talents and understand their worth). His debut was well received by both Hong Kong audiences and critics (it won the Best Film award at the Hong Kong Film Directors' Guild Awards), acquiring the momentum needed to further pursue his career in the film industry.

After co-founding the United Filmmakers Organization (UFO) with Eric Tsang and others in 1992, Chan later became one of the most representative directors and filmmakers in Hong Kong in the 1990s. In need of the support of a major film company, the UFO merged with Golden Harvest in 1996, signalling the end of its highly creative, glorious but short-lived era. According to his father Tung-Man Chan, although some UFO productions made a lot of money, others did not do well at the box office. As the company could not make ends meet, it was taken over by Golden Harvest, and Peter Chan began to look into other possibilities to further develop his film career.[4] Because Hollywood had a keen interest in Hong Kong cinema in the mid- to late 1990s, Peter Chan was invited to work with DreamWorks and directed *The Love Letter* (1999), followed by a brief venture in Asia. He co-founded Applause Pictures in 2000 and focused on pan-Asian film productions,[5] including the ghost horror anthology *Three* (2002), which he co-directed with Thai director Nonzee Nimibutr and Korean director Jee-woon Kim (Chan's episode was 'Going Home'). Not unlike those of Tsui Hark and other Hong Kong directors, his Hollywood venture fell below expectations, and although his pan-Asian project was indeed creative and pioneering, unfortunately it was not successful, in commercial terms at least. This was perhaps due to the swiftly changing mediascape in Asia impacted by the rise of Chinese cinema at that juncture. In the midst of a reconfigured Chinese film industry, Chan did not 'go home' and 'embark on localised Hong Kong production', because that was 'not only unsustainable given the modest size of the region's domestic market, but also undesirable for a filmmaker pledged to pan-Asian and international film production'.[6] As the Chinese film market opened its door wider to Hong Kong filmmakers after the signing of the CEPA in 2003, the adaptable and quick-thinking Chan was fast to react and moved his base to the mainland to start his co-production career with *Perhaps Love* (2005). In 2008, he founded We Pictures, 'a new breed of film company set to transform the outlook of Chinese language cinema'.[7] In the subsequent year, he collaborated with mainland Chinese producer Huang Jianxin, setting up the new Beijing-based production company Cinema Popular with Polybona International – the market leader of mainland–Hong Kong co-production distribution in China – as the mainland market was increasingly dominated by China-based investors and producers.

I have argued elsewhere that Peter Chan's trajectory can be seen as exemplary of a fluid, flexible mode of Hong Kong filmmaking.[8] His understanding of Hong Kong cinema is itself flexible and fluid, as he noted in a seminar organised by the Hong Kong International Film & TV Market (FILMART) in 2006:

> I think it's a very narrow-minded concept to think that a Hong Kong film needs to take place in Hong Kong, and needs to have an all Hong Kong cast and crew, and needs to be in the Cantonese language. I'm actually quite disappointed at people who have been talking like this, especially Hong Kong critics and fellow filmmakers.[9]

Although *Perhaps Love* and the subsequent *The Warlords* (2007), co-directed with Raymond Yip, won Chan critical acclaim, the films failed to make a profit due to their enormous budgets. For example, it was reported that the male lead, Jet Li, received US$13 million (RMB 100 million) for his appearance in *The Warlords* out of a US$40 million budget,[10] so even after bagging US$42.9 million at the box office, it was not profitable at all. Back then, period films were the mainstream in co-productions because there were fewer censorship restrictions (and fewer sensitive contemporary issues), and therefore martial arts and historical war films dominated the scene. Hong Kong directors such as Tsui Hark and John Woo might have taken to this like ducks to water, but for a director who excelled at transnational, metropolitan sensibility, this was simply sailing against the wind. Chan's next mainland project, *Dragon* (2011), a *wuxia* film starring the then rising megastar Donnie Yen, failed to impress – as per Peter Chan's high standards – once again, despite his truly creative handling of the martial arts genre. Thanks to the reconfigured industry in mainland China after 2009, more film genres were needed, and Chan managed to impress with his *American Dreams in China* (2013), in which his transnational imaginary fit perfectly with a new generation of Chinese who had had the opportunity to develop their careers in America. The film won him the Best Director and Best Film titles at the 29th Golden Rooster Awards in China, which was a token of recognition in the mainland market. His next project, *Dearest* (2014), starring Zhao Wei, bagged three major accolades, including Best Film, Best Director and Best Actress, at the Huading Awards. After almost a decade, Chan had his feet firmly planted in the mainland market. According to Peng Kan, Research and Development Director of the Beijing-based consultancy Legend Media, Hong Kong films had been integrated into another film industry, larger in scale, and he cited Peter Chan and Tsui Hark as two examples of successfully making the transition into the mainland market.[11]

Almost a Hong Kong Story

Championed as 'Asia's most versatile filmmaker who can develop quality films with strong commercial appeal . . . Chan is more than a Hong Kong filmmaker.'[12] His filmmaking model, as exemplified by the transformation from UFO to Applause Pictures and then We Pictures, has indeed been flexible, and in this regard, it is typically Hong Kong in nature. After *Comrades, Almost a Love Story* (1996; hereafter abbreviated as *Comrades*), however, Chan took on new challenges beyond Hong Kong. He understood the changing rules of the game very well: 'cross-border film co-production has become the dominant mode of Hong Kong film production', as he candidly put it in an interview in 2013, which was 'a shift from "made in Hong Kong" to "made by Hong Kong"'.[13] His films during that time, albeit creative and transnational, no longer squarely explored the local social context of Hong Kong. Many UFO films that he directed and produced in the 1990s were truly innovative Hong Kong imaginaries in the late-transitional period shortly before the handover. Chan became more than a Hong Kong filmmaker, but he was first very Hong Kong. In this section, I will examine the Hong Kong stories in his films, with special emphasis on *Alan and Eric* and *Comrades*.

Alan and Eric, starring Alan Tam and Eric Tsang, is a banal story about two best friends who, since a young age, are in love with the same woman, probably paying homage to François Truffaut's New Wave love triangle classic *Jules and Jim* (1962). In the film, although Eric feels affection for Olive (portrayed by Maggie Cheung), he does not think that he is good enough for her. Alan Tam, one of the most popular singers in the history of Cantopop, was still in his heyday when the film was made. In the film, the outlooks of the handsome idol and the comedian Tsang are indeed very different, and their close friendship forms the tension in the story. Olive falls in love with Alan, who later becomes a successful singer, while Eric's chicken farm business in Hong Kong has failed, so he decides to leave and sails around the world. As time passes, Alan and Olive's relationship hits a rough spot, and Eric tries to keep them together, while fortuitously expressing his love for Olive. Later, the three meet again in San Francisco, where Alan learns that Eric's days are numbered because of a serious illness. However, Eric makes it clear that he would be truly happy to see his best friend marry the woman he himself loves. Towards the end, Alan and Eric live out their childhood dream – the former as Sinbad and the latter as a pirate – sailing together with Olive to Treasure Island, the man-made island in the middle of San Francisco Bay. In the film, they finally find Treasure Island in San Francisco, and, as well said by Eric, their adventure is a de facto 'treasure hunt' as they search for what they lost over the past ten or so years.[14] The literal translation of the Chinese title,

A Tale of Two Cities – probably inspired by Charles Dickens's classic – is a more apt description of the theme of the journey from Hong Kong to San Francisco in the film: adventuring for one's love, friendship and, above all, dream.

Notwithstanding the dramatic tension in the triangular relationship, the otherwise hackneyed love film stood out from other Hong Kong cinematic romances with its transnational, diasporic imaginary, which became almost a signature of Chan's later films. Similar to the director's personal experience, the protagonists do not mind moving from one place to another in order to chase after their dreams. Whether Sinbad's adventures were Peter Chan's own childhood dream or not I cannot tell, but it is safe to say that he had embarked on a diasporic adventure, from Hong Kong to Thailand to Los Angeles and then back to Hong Kong, to chase after his own dream of cinema. At that time, his Treasure Island was in Hong Kong.

The diaspora issue in *Alan and Eric*[15] resonated with the social fluctuations in Hong Kong in the early 1990s, a time when quite a number of its residents had left the territory in the aftermath of the June Fourth Incident in 1989. Insofar as *Alan and Eric*, as argued by Thomas Shin in his essay collected in the book *Peter Ho-sun Chan: My Way*, embodied 'mixed feelings towards circumstances and destiny, with a type of self-pity that is typical among Hong Kongers',[16] Hong Kong was the place of Alan and Eric's childhood memories, without the social issues that the city was actually experiencing at that particular juncture. Unlike Ann Hui, who often foregrounded the city's historical and social backdrop in her love stories, such as in *Love in a Fallen City* (1984) and *Starry Is the Night* (1988), Chan had no interest in political overtones. The all-time classic 'Moon River' – the song young Alan sings in a singing competition in *Alan and Eric* – was used to subtly link the episodes into a coherent theme. Not only does the song inspire young Alan and Eric to become dream makers, it also echoes the life force of diasporic drifters, as found in Johnny Mercer's lyrics: 'Two drifters off to see the world; there's such a lot of world to see'. The theme song of *Alan and Eric*, 'Dearest Love in My Life', sung by Alan Tam, is a good example of this. While the lyrics echo the underlying theme of the love story ('Even if we part company one day, I will miss you, I really miss you. I don't mind waiting idiotically, waiting to find the dearest love in my life in the end'), the song itself is a typical Cantopop romantic ballad that has nothing to do with adventure, dreams and/or the city. The romantic ballad is the most popular genre of Cantopop, which is still the voice of the city. In this sense, the song as well as the film, albeit socially indifferent, are very Hong Kong. It was this part of Hong Kong that Peter Chan's debut and later films evinced.

Chan's two subsequent projects, *He Ain't Heavy, He's My Father* (1993) and *Tom, Dick and Hairy* (1993), were co-directed with UFO collaborator Chi-ngai

Lee. The former is a nostalgic reboot of the 1960 Cantonese film classic *My Intimate Partners*, and the latter an urban romantic comedy. Both were good attempts, but Chan's career-defining work is definitely *He's a Woman, She's a Man* (1994), starring the legendary Leslie Cheung. The Chinese title of the film was borrowed verbatim from the Chinese title of Audrey Hepburn's *Roman Holiday* (1953), which means 'aristocrats' in Chinese. It was perhaps no coincidence that 'Moon River' was chosen for *Alan and Eric*, as the song was first sung by Audrey Hepburn in her 1961 classic *Breakfast at Tiffany's*. *He's a Woman, She's a Man* is a perfect example of Peter Chan's elegantly adroit presentation of stylised scenes of the lives of celebrities and urban professionals through glamorous costumes and settings.[17] The cast in the sequel, *Who's the Woman, Who's the Man* (1996), also featured the Cantopop diva Anita Mui, and the film was even more classy (almost flamboyant) but all too calculated. However, these works, also based on triangular relationships, were related less to the diasporic experience than to cross-dressing, sexual orientation and the voluptuous life of Hong Kong in the late-transitional period before its reversion to China.

The year 1996 had very special meaning for Chan's film career in Hong Kong. He released three films in this penultimate year of British colonial Hong Kong – *Who's the Woman, Who's the Man*, *The Age of Miracles* and *Comrades*. *The Age of Miracles* was an ambitious attempt to deal with the theme of death, which prompted critics to say that Chan was trying to be the 'Hong Kong Spielberg'. Chan squarely tackled the theme of life and death, as well as the hot issue of immigration among Hong Kongers before the handover. Yet, despite his admirable ambition, the film was not very well received. One of the reasons was that it was shown during the Lunar New Year, and death is taboo for Chinese during that time of the year. But the more important reason, as noted by Shu Kei, was that, without Spielberg's (occasional) childlike innocence, the film was too rehearsed. The emotive scenes were simply too calculated to be actually touching, so to speak.[18] In short, the meticulously calculated, well-rehearsed style of Peter Chan fit nicely with *Who's the Woman, Who's the Man*, but it did not work well with the subject matter of *The Age of Miracles*. In the context of my emphasis on Chan's diasporic experience in his Hong Kong story, I will now move on to examine *Comrades*, which was another shrewd treatment of the Chinese diasporic experience in an increasingly global era.

Comrades may have reminded audiences of the couple fated for each other across time in Claude Lelouch's *And Now My Love* (1975). In the film, this 'almost a love story' begins in 1986, when Xiaojun (portrayed by Leon Lai) and Li Qiao (portrayed by Maggie Cheung) move from the mainland (Tianjin and Guangzhou, respectively) to Hong Kong, where they meet, fall in love and separate, and then to New York where they are reunited by chance. The triangular relationship in *Alan and Eric* becomes quadrilateral in *Comrades*: Lai has a fiancée (portrayed by Kristy Yang) in the mainland who joins him later in Hong Kong, and Cheung has taken up with a gang boss (portrayed by Eric Tsang), with whom she leaves Hong Kong to flee his enemies. *Comrades* premiered just a year before the handover, and by 1997, the notion of Chineseness was made poignant: 'Hong Kongese/Chinese identity becomes a mobile, deterritorialized, transnational, and changing mechanism';[19] not only were Hong Kongers seeking to flee the territory before the handover, the city was also seen by many mainlanders as a way station along their diasporic journey to overseas countries. Thanks to the perfect combination of the social background, the theme of drifting and the director's masterful handling, the film bagged nine awards at the 16th Hong Kong Film Awards in 1997, including Best Picture, Best Director, Best Actress, Best Supporting Actor, Best Screenplay, Best Cinematography, Best Art Direction, Best Costume Design and Best Original Music Score. It was also a commercial success: the record HK$15 million at the box office was decent for an 'arts and letters' film. As Rey Chow has already offered a penetrating, gripping account of the film in 'By Way of Mass Commodities: Love in *Comrades, Almost a Love Story*',[20] I will just highlight two important points related to my discussion here: transnational imagination and Peter Chan's Hong Kong.

Regarding transnational imagination, Peter Chan showcased, once again, his ingenious use of popular songs in his love stories. The Chinese title of *Comrades – Tian Mi Mi –* was the all-time hit Mandarin song of Taiwanese superstar Teresa Teng (Deng Lijun in pinyin), who was so popular in Chinese communities across the world, including the not-yet-fully-open mainland China, that she was nicknamed "Little Deng" as she shared the same family name with the then Chinese leader Deng Xiaoping: 'Deng the leader ruled by day, but Deng the singer ruled by night.'[21] As astutely noted by Rey Chow, the two protagonists 'love and find each other again in "Teresa Teng"': 'Theirs is a special kind of love story: their hearts are connected not so much on their own as through the fetishized commodity, through their lingering mutual devotion to (and consumption of) a celebrity performer's lowbrow pop songs.'[22] In the film, the song itself and Teresa Teng the singer are used as an imaginary link between not only the two protagonists but also the shared experiences of all diasporic Chinese. 'The transnational, pan-Chinese love songs of Teresa Teng, rather than the Chinese national anthem and revolutionary songs of mainland China, create an emotional cohesiveness among diasporic Chinese.'[23] The protagonists fall in love after selling Teresa Teng's cassette tapes at a Chinese New Year market in Hong Kong, and they are brought back together in New York after the news of Teng's demise is broadcast on television. As perceptively noted by Kwai-cheung Lo, 'Teng's song first appears nondiegetically when

Xiaojun is giving a bike ride to Li Qiao on the busy streets of Hong Kong', and '[t]his inscription of a different space in the local site of Hong Kong could be interpreted as the desire of homeless Chinese to construct their own sense of locality.'[24] The song therefore functioned not just to string together complex relations but also to portray the diasporic experience, placing 'the romantic encounter in the broader context of the multiplicity of the Chinese diasporic experience'.[25]

The protagonists, together with countless new mainland immigrants, moved to the former British colony for their 'Hong Kong Dream', which was actually about capitalism, not the place itself: 'This migration should be understood not simply in geographical terms but also in political-economic terms, as a migration from communism to capitalism.'[26] During the ten years of historical backdrop in *Comrades*, Hong Kong was still seen by many as a place of opportunities for wealth mobility. As aptly put by Michael Curtin, the visits to the ATM (automatic teller machine) in the film 'convey an almost erotic relationship that seems to displace all other forms of interpersonal connection'.[27] In this sense, Hong Kong is both the ATM and the capitalism it symbolises; no one stays at an ATM after removing their money. On the topic of Hong Kong, Kwai-cheung Lo also noted an important point about *Comrades*:

> Asked if he originally intended to make a film about Hong Kong – born residents who have emigrated, Peter Chan said he was really talking about 'the rootlessness of the Chinese as a people, and of their continuing search for a new home'.[28]

This sums up the director's understanding of Hong Kong and Chineseness. Almost a Hong Kong story, Chan's short-lived UFO adventure ended after *Comrades*. It was understandable that for a fluid, adaptable filmmaker like Chan, the change of sovereignty and the decline of Hong Kong cinema (because of piracy, the handover and the subsequent Asian financial crisis) would set him off on a new journey to continue to find his own dream of cinema. The city of Hong Kong in Chan's film career was, parallel to that of Lai's and Cheung's in *Comrades*, more a means than an end. In a 2002 interview, Peter Chan explained why Hong Kong films had declined, touching on an issue about the Hong Kong story:

> I think the reason Hong Kong films have declined in popularity is that Hong Kong people are still looking for stories to tell. They don't have stories to tell right now because they have yet to ascertain their true identity. That will take some time – a few years, maybe even a decade.[29]

In response to this issue, Prasenjit Duara rightly claimed that 'the people of Hong Kong apparently managed to steer away from this sense of crisis', as they began to take 'their destiny into their own hands during the first decade of the twenty-first century': 'A strong sense of local commitment has been revealed not only in the successive waves of protests to enhance democratic participation but also through engagement to protect and conserve historical sites and places of community memory.'[30] However, during this time, Peter Chan had already left the Hong Kong film industry for greener pastures, although he still produced some Hong Kong films, such as *Golden Chicken* (2002). Therefore, if I may paraphrase the title of Chan's film, his was almost a Hong Kong story – 'not quite, not complete, not the real thing'.[31]

In Love with a New Market

In the 1990s, established Hong Kong directors and actors were lured to Hollywood. As succinctly put by Yingchi Chu:

> It has always been a strategy of the Hong Kong film industry to expand its market through Hollywood. Before 1997 the emphasis had been mainly on Hong Kong's investment in Hollywood products. In contrast, the post-1997 era has seen a steady increase in the exchange of film talents and investments. Not only is there a growing number of Hong Kong filmmakers working in Hollywood and Hong Kong, as for instance John Woo, Ringo Lam, Tsui Hark, Ronny Yu, Stanley Tong, Kirk Wong, Peter Chan, Chow Yun-fat and Michelle Yeoh, but Hollywood has likewise shown a notable interest in funding and producing Hong Kong films.[32]

All of the examples above, except for Peter Chan, were largely involved in action films because Hollywood was most interested in this signature genre of Hong Kong cinema. This made evident that Peter Chan was believed to be a director who could present another dimension of Hong Kong cinema to the audience in the West. The distinctiveness of Chan, paradoxically, proved to be a serious limitation to his Hollywood venture, which ended after *The Love Letter*, his collaborative project with DreamWorks. It was true that he 'did not find the corporate culture suitable for his career',[33] but, perhaps more importantly, most Hong Kong directors had experienced a frustrating spell in Hollywood, and it was even more difficult for him to hit the fancy of Western audiences with a romantic comedy.

Peter Chan showed his pioneering vision once again by advancing his film career in Asia before the Asian wave in Hollywood conceded in the new millennium. The mission of Applause Pictures, the company Chan co-founded in 2000, was to 'fashion a pan-Asian cinema palatable to global, Americanist tastes', and Hong Kong was urged to 'take the lead in Asia to organize other industries ... to produce an Asian cinema'; Applause Pictures also had 'a deracinated battle-plan': 'The people who are portrayed in the movies that strike Americans as very Chinese, such as martial arts films, are not real people.'[34] Even though Applause Pictures did manage to 'line up production crews in Hong Kong, Japan, and South Korea' and 'develop a production network with counterparts in Thailand and Singapore', and its representative series *The Eye* and *Three* – the cast and crew of which were pan-Asian – achieved considerable market success,[35] Chan found that the mainland market that had just begun opening its door wider to Hong Kong filmmakers was more attractive, as his ambition needed a bigger market to achieve success. Meanwhile, Hong Kong cinema had lost its appeal in Hollywood, rendering the pan-Asian venture unsuccessful. Applause Picture's branding and visibility were eventually enhanced by its horror films, which won both recognition and film awards. As pointed out by Ben-huat Chua, '[t]oo big and too tempting to be ignored, Applause decided to enter the China market', but unfortunately the company 'had to abandon its strengths in the horror and eroticism genres, as horror and "spirits" films were banned in China until 2008', switching its centre of attention 'to undertake big budget blockbuster films, with capital injected from mainland Chinese film enterprises'.[36]

Peter Chan tested the water with his blockbuster musical *Perhaps Love*, and I have argued elsewhere that Takeshi Kaneshiro's words in the film – 'I fell in love with someone I despised' – could be borrowed to provide an apt description of the mixed feelings of many Hong Kong filmmakers.[37] Falling in love with a market too big to despise, Hong Kong filmmakers started swarming north in the 2000s. There were commercial reasons, of course, but speaking of one of his reasons for making *Perhaps Love*, Chan also made it clear that he did this for Hong Kong cinema: 'We're making this film to appeal to a bigger audience, so that Hong Kong film, or the spirit of Hong Kong film, does not die.'[38] *Perhaps Love* won six awards at the 25th Hong Kong Film Awards in 2006: Best Actress, Best Art Direction, Best Cinematography, Best Costume Make Up Design, Best Original Film Score and Best Original Film Song, but lost to Johnnie To and his *Election* (2005) in the major awards – Best Director and Best Film. Interestingly, as implied by the English title, Johnnie To's signature triad thriller was an allegorical reference to the election system in Hong Kong, with the Basic Law promising to move towards universal suffrage in due course. Back then, moreover, To was still seen as the 'last flag of Hong Kong cinema' who had not totally turned towards the mainland market.[39] Against this background, it was easy to understand why *Perhaps Love* did not win Best Director and Best Film. (It did win the Best Director award for Chan at the 43rd Golden Horse Awards in

Taiwan.) Peter Chan seemed to be quite satisfied with *Perhaps Love*, as he spoke highly about it compared with his film *Comrades*. On the face of it, *Comrades* adopted an austere style, but actually, as Chan confessed, it was a very highly calculated, 'sugar-coated' Hollywood-style film, as seen with the purposefully positive characters played by Leon Lai and Maggie Cheung. Although *Perhaps Love* looked like a Hollywood musical film, it was much truer to reality in terms of characterisation (as seen with the character of Zhou Xun, who was selfishly interested in her own career).[40] However, although it was exemplary of Applause Pictures and its 'largely successful tactic for financing, producing, and market-ing films', '*Perhaps Love* certainly does not push the same critical buttons of Hong Kong/Chinese identity that *Comrades* does', as rightly noted by G. Andrew Stuckey.[41] In a sense, the success of *Perhaps Love* marked its own failure (at least in Hong Kong), because of its deracinated battle plan mentioned above: 'the erasure of one's identity ... serves as an emblem of the pan-Asian cinematic trajectory towards a deracinated "universality"'.[42] 'Pan-Asian production is not just an economic strategy,' as noted by Stephen Teo in his perceptive account of *Perhaps Love* in the light of pan-Asian-ness, 'but something that reaches deeper into the recesses of identity, the global and the national.'[43]

The next mainland–Hong Kong co-production helmed by Peter Chan was *The Warlords*, with a superstar-studded cast that included, among others, Jet Li, Andy Lau and Takeshi Kaneshiro. Set in the Qing Dynasty during the Taiping Rebellion, the war epic followed the major trend of co-produced period dramas during the 2000s. The shift from pan-Asian-ness to Chineseness helped the film achieve more success in Chinese film markets. It did well at the box office (US$42.9 million) and swept up eight awards at the 27th Hong Kong Film Awards in 2008, including Best Film, Best Director and Best Actor. It was also named Best Feature Film and won the Best Director award for Chan at the 45th Golden Horse Awards. *The Warlords*, despite not being a profitable project due to the sky-high salaries of the superstars, marked a watershed in the history of mainland–Hong Kong co-productions, usher-ing Hong Kong cinema into the era of Chinese cinema. Let me quote what I wrote on the subject:

> When he [Peter Chan] gave his award acceptance speech for Best Director Award at the 45th Golden Horse Film Festival and Awards, he thanked the audience for supporting Chinese cinema. Perhaps by mere coincidence, in the excerpt of *Warlords* edited for the ceremony, the protagonist Jet Li cried: 'My soldiers die only on the battlefield but not of starvation!'[44]

Jet Li's outcry echoed the sad situation lamented by Peter Chan in an inter-view regarding the Hong Kong film industry at that juncture: 'a third of our labour was cut off' because of the shrinking market and exodus of investors, and 'everyone's career in the industry seemed vulnerable, both in terms of the pressures against quality production and the disappearance of jobs.'[45] In short, to borrow Chan's own words,

> *The Warlords* was about the corporate world and our lives nowadays. What if we have certain ideals and it turns out you can only achieve it at the expense of sacrificing your brothers, but those ideals are for the bigger good for humanity?[46]

The Warlords did prove Peter Chan's versatility, showcasing his ability to make a period war film, which was not typical of his style. As the predominance of period martial arts films in mainland–Hong Kong co-productions continued, Chan moved on to his next project, *Dragon*, whose eponymous Chinese title was *Wu Xia*. Chan said that he had long been a fan of *wuxia* films, but since 'it's such an established and even drained genre, there's very little room for original-ity left', which was why he had not yet made one. When he decided to finally embark on a *wuxia* project, it was with a mission to revitalise this genre:

> What we usually see is the choreography; we see how flashy it is, or how fan-tastical it can be. But all those seemingly fantastical moves can be explained in terms of physics. For example, I like to think about how does light body skill work, or acupuncture points, or the impact of a punch. How much physical damage would it do to our internal organs? How do people die from these injuries? It's all a mystery; no one would question it. Of course I can't explain all of it, otherwise I'd be a martial arts expert, but I'd like to find an explanation in a logical and medical way, in terms of physics or mechanics.[47]

While the visual-driven *Dragon*, the first film by Chan to be chosen as a Cannes official selection, was neither his typical dialogue-driven nor character-driven film, it did bring something fresh to the *wuxia* genre: 'a new direction with a minute visual analysis of the anatomy and physiology of the martial arts body'.[48] It was a shame that despite Chan's innovation, *Dragon* was not as successful as his two previous projects, not only in the mainland but also in Hong Kong, as can be seen in Table 3.1.[49]

The market percentage of *Dragon* in Hong Kong dropped significantly, and in terms of the box office, was just less than one-third of that for *The Warlords*. Nevertheless, this did not deal a significant blow to the highly adaptable direc-tor who liked adventures. As noted in the Introduction, the reconfiguration of the mainland film market resulted in a greater demand for films of different

Table 3.1   Box-office revenues for Peter Chan's films

Year	Film Title	Country	Box-office Revenue in Mainland China (RMB) (Market Percentage)	Box-office Revenue in Hong Kong (HK$/RMB) (Market Percentage)	Annual Box-office Ranking for All Films
2005	*Perhaps Love*	China/CEPA	¥30,077,000 (67.18%)	$14,130,000/ ¥14,695,200 (32.82%)	13
2007	*The Warlords*	China/CEPA	¥195,489,000 (88.34%)	$27,490,000/ ¥25,807,612 (11.66%)	2
2011	*Dragon*	China/CEPA	¥170,216,000 (96.36%)	$7,810,000/ ¥6,429,973 (3.64%)	–
2013	*American Dreams in China*	China/CEPA	¥539,260,000 (99.28%)	$4,897,014/ ¥3,898,023 (0.72%)	7
2014	*The Dearest*	China/CEPA	¥345,067,000 (99.95%)	$234,651/ ¥189,095 (0.05%)	–

genres, and Hong Kong filmmakers were seen as an important means to diversify Chinese cinema.[50] It was in this context that Peter Chan tried something new, though equally as transitional and diasporic as *Comrades* – to bring the American Dream to China.

Going back to the issue of transnational migration at which he was most adept, Chan forfeited his pan-Asian mission and instead made a film palatable to global, Americanist tastes, *American Dreams in China*, but which had little in the way of marketability outside mainland China.[51] Resolute in his aim at hitting the swiftly growing mainland film market, Chan decided to revive the American Dream in China. In this story, which begins with three mainland Chinese students dreaming of studying in America in the 1980s, the migration experience is no longer unidirectional. *American Dreams in China* and *Comrades* are similar and different at the same time: similar in the sense that Leon Lai, Huang Xiaoming, Deng Chao and David Tong all have a dream of adventure, but different in that the latter three do not need Hong Kong as a way station anymore. Hong Kong is no longer necessary for this Chinese success story, as evidenced by the fact that the box office in Hong Kong only accounted for a mere 0.72 per cent of the film's revenue (according to Box Office Mojo). Dubbed 'the Chinese *Social Network*', the film is loosely based on the real story of New Oriental, one of the most well-known education companies in China. In the film, only Deng Chao is able to move to America in the end. Staying put in China, Huang and Tong start an English tutoring business called New Dream, joined later by the disillusioned Deng who returns to China. Their business becomes so successful that the company is listed on the American stock market, but the trio's relationship turns sour. Chan's meticulously calculated plot highlights select memories of Chinese college students' idealism and adventurous spirit in the 1980s, while effectively avoiding sensitive issues (which some may consider self-censorship), such as the June Fourth Incident. Apparently, he is interested much less in history than in writing a new Chinese success story (the film paid tribute to successful Chinese entrepreneurs in its end credits[52]) in the midst of social changes:

> People feel that the 'American Dream' must belong to America, but America's economy is already saturated . . . the American Dream was what happened in America in the last century . . . but now this 'American Dream' is taking place in China every day.[53]

All in all, the film is 'about Chinese nationals' rootedness in China and their willful return from overseas'.[54]

Despite the highly calculated shift of emphasis from diaspora to home, however, the film was not convincing in the eyes of mainland critics: 'What is curious about Chan's description, however, is the unquestioning characterization of China's present in terms of America's past. This was perhaps why several critics in China found the film lacking inspiration for constructing a more Chinese-specific dream.'[55] Peter Chan's 'homecoming' project, albeit unsuccessful in convincing Chinese, let alone Hong Kong, critics, became his highest-grossing film at the box office (see Table 3.1). '*American Dreams in China* proves Chan has a handle on what he needs to do to get a coveted mainland release, but it also hints at a one or the other creative process.'[56] The commercial success of this project provided Chan with 'a degree of leverage with SARFT, possibly accounting for the script censors' leniency toward *Dearest*, Chan's subsequent project about China's child abduction crisis'.[57] More importantly, it enabled him to continue to search for his own Treasure Island in China. As *Dearest*, based on a true story of child abduction, which was a serious social problem in China, is not closely related to my emphasis on transnational imaginary and how it informed the director's main(land) melody projects, I will now move on to Chan's new take on sports films, an innovative rendition of an old genre.[58]

Chinese Women's Volleyball Spirit: Peter Chan's *Leap*

Peter Chan's successful relocation of the American Dream to China perfectly echoed the main melody of the Chinese Dream. It was therefore not unexpected that he would direct main(land) melody films, but it was rather surprising that he would opt to do a sports film. After the post-production of the biopic *Li Na*, based on the story of the world-class Chinese tennis player, the shooting of which was reportedly completed in February 2019, We Pictures officially announced the project *Chinese Women's Volleyball* (2020), later retitled as *Leap*, in April 2019.[59] It was reported that Chan started this ambitious project based on the legendary Chinese women's volleyball teams – which won the world title and Olympic gold medal in 1981 and 2016, respectively – in October 2018. He recalled in an interview that he was contacted by 'the China Film Administration, the country's top sector regulator, to ask him to helm the project', and although he was not a sports fan, 'he was impressed about a Chinese women's volleyball team's competition in Bangkok in late 1970s when he was still a high school student in Thailand'.[60]

Sports films are often entangled with propaganda. For example, *Olympia*, the four-hour film about the 1936 Berlin Olympics, was seen as a propaganda film rather than a sports film because the producer and director Leni Riefenstahl was linked to the Nazi Party.[61] The use of sports films as propaganda in China also has a long history. One of the most commercially successful Chinese silent films of the 1930s was *Queen of Sports* (1934) – probably the first Chinese biographical sports film – the female protagonist of which was a gifted young athlete from a rich family.[62] Masterminded by the representative Leftist director Sun Yu, the film is one of 'the best representatives of the left-wing cinema movement'.[63] In fact, one year before this, a documentary film about the Mukden Incident and the Japanese occupation of Shenyang in Northeast China was screened at the Fifth National Games held in Nanjing to boost anti-Japanese morale, which proved to be very effective: 'All of the athletes were touched by this film, and while viewing it they shouted "Fight with the Japanese invaders" and "Get back the lost land of the Northeast provinces".'[64] After the founding of the PRC, films were also used in connection with sports. A documentary film entitled *Long Live Youth* was made about the First National Games of the People's Republic of China held in Beijing in 1959, and was used to 'celebrate China's 10 years' achievement in sport after the founding of the PRC'.[65] Since then, it has been common practice to use documentary films to record and promote sports. Besides documentaries, there have also been Chinese feature films with sports themes over the years. One of the best examples is *Woman Basketball Player No. 5* (1957), directed and written by Xie Jin who won fame with this film and became one of the most well-known directors in China.

Regarding Chinese volleyball, while *The Volleyball Flower* (1980), directed by Lu Jianhua and produced by the Changchun Film Group Corporation, was generally a drama about Chinese women's volleyball, *The Drive to Win* (1981), directed by Zhang Nuanxin and produced by the Youth Film Studio of Beijing Film Academy, put more emphasis on the team aspects of the sport. The film, which focused primarily on the female football player Sha Ou, who contributed everything to the national volleyball team, won the Special Jury Award at the 2nd Golden Rooster Awards. After China lost the 1978 Asian Games volleyball final to Japan, Sha Ou retired because of a serious injury. Later she re-joined the team as coach and helped them win the World Championship in 1981, which was the PRC's first-ever title in any of the three major ball games (i.e., football, basketball and volleyball). A documentary film entitled *Fight Hard: The Champion's Story of Chinese Women's Volleyball Team* (1982), directed by Zhang Yitong, Shen Jie and Li Hanjun, was also made to commemorate their unprecedented achievement. The Chinese women's volleyball team became immensely popular in the whole country (e.g., team player Zhou Xiaolan, alongside renowned film star Gong Xue, graced the cover of the March 1982 issue of *Popular Movies*, the then best-selling film magazine in China). Subsequently, thanks to the outstanding performances by Chinese sports teams at international competitions, quite a number of sports films were produced, but they were unabashedly propagandist:

> [P]opular patriotic slogans of the time, like 'win honour for the country', are overstated and what is also stressed in these sports films are that encouragement and support from the Party are the key to the final victory of the team.[66]

In the year that Beijing hosted the Olympics, the film *The One Man Olympics* (2008), directed by Hou Yong and based on the real story of eminent sprinter Liu Changchun, who was the only Chinese representative at the 1932 Los Angeles Olympics, was released. Although the quality of filmmaking was much improved, this was still not a marketable film made for the popular audience. In other words, Chinese sports films to that point were not commercially attractive.[67]

In the 2010s, because of the change of government policies in the name of soft power, the Chinese film industry tried hard to diversify its products to attract audiences not only locally but also globally. In 2015, Dante Lam made a bold attempt with *To the Fore*, a film about competitive cycling, starring idol actors Eddie Peng, Shawn Dou and Si-won Choi. However, it only recorded RMB 0.145 billion at the box office, which was miserably low compared to the RMB 3.671 billion for his signature main(land) melody blockbuster *Operation Red Sea*

(2018) (for more details, see Chapter 5). The audience was caught by surprise when Peter Chan announced his new film project on the tennis star Li Na in 2015. It was even more unexpected that he started another project about the Chinese women's volleyball team before the Li Na film was released. *Leap* was completed quickly and was scheduled to be launched during the Lunar New Year in 2020, but was rescheduled due to the COVID-19 coronavirus outbreak. The main melody reverberated in the special arrangement of the two sports blockbusters. Although *Leap* did not hit Chinese screens until one week before National Day on 25 September 2020, I include it here because the film was Peter Chan's own 'leap' into the mainland market. It was not only a blockbusterisation of main melody films but also a trailblazing commercialisation of the sports film genre in Chinese cinema.

Unfortunately, *Leap* was doubly hit before its premiere, not only by Covid-19 but also by a copyright issue. The Chinese Volleyball Association issued an official announcement on 16 January 2020 stating that without prior approval, the team had been commercially exploited: in the name of promoting the national women's volleyball team, some businessmen had infringed on the rights of the team and its players.[68] Former coach Chen Zhonghe lodged a complaint, as reported by *Yangtze Evening News* on 8 January 2020, stating that the film was 'exploitative and defamatory' – 'They've infringed my name, image and reputation' – and, more importantly, the film's producers were 'trying to cash in on the success of the women's volleyball team': 'We played not for fame or money, but for our country ... We definitely won't allow film companies to make money through the propaganda of the Chinese women's volleyball team.'[69] The title of the film was subsequently changed to *Leap* (in Chinese, the literal translation is 'Snatching Victory'). Interestingly though, promotional materials kept the original title 'Chinese Women's Volleyball' after 'Leap' by adding a reminder, if not disclaimer, that it was the 'original title'. The whole saga reminded me of Herman Yau's *The Woman Knight of Mirror Lake* (2011), the making of which involved a complicated issue of 'censorship' in the context of Chinese-style socialism (for more details, see Chapter 6). *Leap* was a similar if different case evincing this kind of peculiar style of censorship.

Besides the scene that outraged Chen Zhonghe (reportedly, it was the snatching of a chicken leg from a canteen worker), some scenes were presumably cut, as evidenced by the fragmented plot in the middle of the film. The story of the final version begins in 1979, shortly after the open-door policy launched by Deng Xiaoping. It was a time of historic change as Chinese people began to see the world again, a critical juncture at which China desperately needed something to boost its self-esteem as a newcomer to the world community. The first part of the film focuses on the preparation work before the 1981 World Championship, in which the Chinese women's volleyball team showcased its world-famous spirit to beat Japan in the final. Another important match in the film is the quarter-final against Brazil, the host country, at the Rio de Janeiro Olympics in 2016. With Lang Ping, the mainstay of the 1981 championship team, as head coach, the Chinese women's volleyball team refound its typical fighting spirit to beat Brazil, the reigning Olympic champions, and then moved on to bag the gold medal. The film was supposed to narrate the ups and downs of the team during these decades, but owing to the scope and, more probably, Chen Zhonghe's complaint, the ups and downs are instead summarised by a match that took place in between the two finals of 1981 and 2016. The match between China and the United States in 2008 was a showdown between Lang Ping and Chen Zhonghe, who were the head coaches of the US and Chinese women's volleyball teams, respectively, at the Beijing Olympics.

It was rather unfortunate that the relationship, if not conflict, between Lang Ping and Chen Zhonghe was not fully developed in the final version, owing perhaps to the complaint. Some of the dialogue was changed and redubbed, as can be observed from the mismatch between the words spoken and the lips forming the words. With Chen Zhonghe as head coach, the Chinese women's volleyball team's gold medal after a hard-fought battle with Russia at the 2004 Athens Olympics was glaringly marginalised in the film. Huang Bo (supposedly in the role of Chen Zhonghe in the film) does sing the Minnan song 'Fighting to Win' in the film, which plays a more important role than the ending song 'River of Life' sung by Faye Wong and Na Ying, but it is the song, not the character, that the director emphasises. The copyright issue also forced the production team to erase almost all of the names of the coaches (including Chen Zhonghe) and players (Lang Ping's teammates became anonymous). It was in odd, stark contrast to the team that won the 2016 Olympics: most of the gold medallists were played by real players, including Zhu Ting, Hui Ruoqi and Zhang Changning (except for Wei Qiuyue, who was pregnant at the time of shooting, and thus her role was played by another volleyball player, Yao Di). It was indeed strange for the main characters to remain anonymous in a film touted as the real story of the Chinese women's volleyball team, and the volleyball matches were recreated so seriously and professionally that they looked like authentic footage. The audience, especially those who knew about the legendary 1981–6 team, must have been amazed when they saw Lang Ping's cancer-stricken teammate – supposedly Chen Zhaoti – persuade her to take charge of the national team before passing away (her name was not even mentioned at the funeral).

Despite the controversy, *Leap* effectively fulfilled its mission as a main melody blockbuster. It raked in a total of RMB 836 million, ranking third in National Day films (behind *My People, My Homeland* and *Jiang Ziya*) and fifth in 2020, a year heavily impacted by Covid-19. It was a remarkable achievement for a pioneering endeavour to develop a new genre. Paying blatant tribute to the country at the very beginning of the film, Peter Chan did not mind reminding the audience that it was a main melody film about how the Chinese women's volleyball team won fame for the country. Back then, China had just opened its door to the world, but was still lagging well behind other modern countries in terms of economic development. The first world title of the Chinese women's volleyball team cheered the whole country up in that special context. The Chinese women's volleyball spirit has since then become a byword for perseverance and, more importantly, patriotism. The news hit headlines in newspapers across the country, as underlined by *People's Daily* in its front-page commentary: 'Emulate the Women's Volleyball Team, Revitalize the Chinese Civilization: China Won', '[I]nspired by the Chinese women's volleyball spirit, the modernization [of our country] could certainly be achieved.'[70] However, *Leap* was not just about the sport, nor was it simply propaganda. There was no denying that the Chinese women's volleyball spirit was the key source of pride of the Chinese people in the 1980s, during which time the national team consecutively won major world titles between 1981 and 1986: one Olympic title (1984), two World Cup titles (1981 and 1985) and two World Championship titles (1982 and 1986). It was and still is the only Chinese team to have won a world title of the three major ball games.

Over the years, there have been a number of terms typically used in connection with Chinese women's volleyball on social media site Weibo and in the state-run *People's Daily* as per the report by NetEase's Data Blog: 'struggle, championship, study, and motherland'.[71] Peter Chan said in an interview that he and his production team made references to the 1981 film *The Drive to Win*, which was about the first major world title of the Chinese women's volleyball team.[72] It was not about the production but the aura of the time presented in the film. Tough training and strong determination may bring success in sports games like volleyball, but they do not count much in the production of commercial blockbusters. In the early 1980s, China simply did not have the resources to produce commercially attractive movies. The Chinese women's volleyball spirit did shine through in *The Drive to Win*, but in terms of legitimacy in the eyes of the world audience, it was not until the new millennium that Chinese cinema gradually achieved similar values and styles of filmmaking to those adopted in the West. Peter Chan explained how he was inspired by the spirit of the Chinese women's volleyball team when he had to face difficulties and challenges, such as when casting real athletes as actors and trying to re-enact the classic volleyball matches:

> Every time I wanted to give up, I thought of coach Lang Ping's words: 'The spirit of the women's volleyball team is not to win the championship, but to

fight tooth and nail even though they know they may fail.' This is a film with a sense of mission.[73]

This sense of mission, as I see it, was not only singing the main(land) melody of patriotism, but also singing it in a way that could draw a large audience.

Lang Ping and/as Gong Li: China – World – China

As the story unfolded, it gave the impression that Peter Chan was shooting a biopic of Lang Ping, as she was the only character who had used her real name in the first part of the film. Had this been the case, however, Peter Chan would have delved more into the inner conflicts of Lang Ping in her later career, when she coached the arch-rival United States team to beat China and finally won a silver medal at the 2008 Beijing Olympics. Notwithstanding its heavy emphasis on Lang Ping and her development from player to coach, it was much less a biopic than a film about the eras behind the different stages of her career. Nor was *Leap* meant to be a documentary about the success story of the Chinese women's volleyball team, although the director did invest heavily in re-presenting the matches as real footage. Casting Lydia Bai, the daughter of Lang Ping, as the young 'iron hammer' may have given the impression that the director actually wanted to emphasise inheritance and transmission. Huang Bo's catchphrase – 'We really did not have anything back then, but we did have something in our hearts' – reminded the young volleyball players and the audience that it was the spirit of fighting to win that mattered. In the 2010s, China had undoubtedly changed so much that it was no longer the country that desperately wanted to win the world's attention in the 1980s. Tough training, strong determination and the spirit of fighting to win has faded with the rise of China during the past three decades.

Peter Chan made it very clear that he did not intend to shoot *Leap* merely as a sports film, as he wanted to deal more with characters in the midst of social changes: he was well aware that the passage of time was the major characteristic of his signature movies, although he did not understand clearly why.[74] In this sense, *Leap* embodied the main melody mission to highlight patriotism through the spirit of the Chinese women's volleyball team, but at the same time it was about the changes in China and the world over the past few decades. Pointing his camera at the squabble between the two generations of players on the 2016 Olympic team, Chan showed that it was difficult, if not impossible, to pass the same 1980s spirit down to the new generation, let alone inspire them with it. The reforms made by Lang Ping after she resumed the post of head coach were also mentioned in the film, but just in passing, which was far from to sufficient

to cultivate dramatic tension in a mainstream commercial film. One may interpret this as a result of the complaint made by Chen Zhonghe and the statement
issued by the Chinese Volleyball Association, but the dramatic tension was arguably not the most distinguishing characteristic of Peter Chan's films. Similar to
American Dreams in China and even *Comrades*, he was trying to make ends meet
by highlighting the period of Chinese society's reform and opening up, during
which the country as well as the world witnessed so many dramatic changes.
Towards this end, his own mission of conveying the changing values of people
was accomplished by Lang Ping, Gong Li and himself, who all shared a similar
experience of travelling back to China from the world.

As mentioned above, *Leap* focused so much on Lang Ping that it almost gave
the impression that it was a biopic about the most well-known Chinese wom-
en's volleyball player in history. However, the internal conflicts of this complex
character, who had led the arch-rival US team to beat her own country on home
soil in 2008, were not duly emphasised. The characterisation of Lang Ping was
slanted much more towards the formation and transformation of the Chinese
women's volleyball spirit. Perhaps one of the most qualified persons to say so,
Lang Ping once stated clearly that the Chinese women's volleyball spirit was not
simply about winning: 'Sometimes we know very well that we cannot win, but we
still continue to fight with all our might.'[75] In the film, Lang Ping keeps asking her
players before the showdown with Brazil in the 2016 Olympics why they want
to play volleyball. Back in the late 1970s, the answer would certainly have been
for the country. However, the generation of players in 2016 did not quite know
how to answer, and the irony was all the more pointed as they ended up hitting
Brazil hard. After being pressed by Lang Ping, Zhu Ting, who played a similar
hammer role on the team, bursts out shouting that she wants to be Lang Ping.
Later, Lang Ping calms Zhu Ting, advising her not to emulate her as the most
important thing is to be oneself. This must have sounded familiar to Hollywood
film audiences: from the country to the team to the role model to oneself. Despite
this, inadequate dramatic tension was cultivated in the film. Yet Chan was not
incapable of cultivating such tension, if his proven track record of handling characters in his directorial debut *Alan and Eric* is anything to go by. 'After watching
and shooting a lot of films, one would think when everything in a film looks to be
positive, which are too good to be true, they are generally not,' as Chan confessed,
and so he wanted to treat the interaction between Lang Ping and Zhu Ting, two
generations of iron hammers, like an ESPN documentary, and other scenes with
real players were also treated in a similar way.[76] In this sense, it was not simply a
biopic of Lang Ping but rather Lang Ping's personal experience from China to the
US and back to China that was the key in the latter part of the film, presenting
a transformation of the Chinese women's volleyball spirit through her own life.

The casting of Gong Li as Lang Ping was, of course, a market-oriented consideration, but at the same time it was also a shrewd strategy as the two women shared a similar life trajectory, albeit in different fields. It may not be an exaggeration to say that Gong Li is a Lang Ping in the film sector, as explained by Chan in an interview with Tencent:

> She has the same status in the film circle as Lang Ping in the sports. They both started their careers in the 1980s, the first to go abroad and become international stars, and then becoming a great influence to Chinese women everywhere.[77]

Shining brightly through the camera of Zhang Yimou in their debut *Red Sorghum* in 1987, Gong Li quickly rose to fame after the film won Chinese cinema's first Golden Bear award at the 38th Berlin International Film Festival. Their collaboration continued to attract the limelight with *Ju Dou* (1990), *Raise the Red Lantern* (1991), *The Story of Qiu Ju* (1992), *To Live* (1994) and *Shanghai Triad* (1995). Gong Li had also worked with Chen Kaige, another world-acclaimed Fifth Generation director, in *Farewell My Concubine* (1993), *Temptress Moon* (1996) and *The Emperor and the Assassin* (1998). Most of these were award-winning projects, which brought Chinese cinema to the attention of the world, at least in terms of critical acclaim. It is therefore fair to say that Gong Li, 'at least for foreign audiences, became the face of Fifth Generation Chinese cinema'.[78] Gong Li's 'performances are tied to themes of national identity in a modernizing China',[79] but she also eyed the commercial film market by shifting part of her emphasis to Hong Kong cinema in the 1990s, which was still in its heyday, in scattered, highly commercial projects such as the typical Stephen Chow comedies *God of Gamblers II: Back to Shanghai* (1991) and *Flirting Scholar* (1993). In Wayne Wang's *Chinese Box* (1997), a US production about Hong Kong's handover to China, she first caught the attention of mainstream audiences in the West. After her collaborative projects with Kar-Wai Wong in *2046* (2004) and *Eros: The Hand* (2004), she ventured to Hollywood, establishing herself there with the popular movies *Memoirs of a Geisha* (2005), *Miami Vice* (2006) and *Hannibal Rising* (2007). Interestingly, she reunited with Zhang Yimou in his *Curse of the Golden Flower* in 2006, the year she also starred in Michael Mann's Hollywood crime thriller *Miami Vice*. Her role as a Japanese in *Memoirs of a Geisha* had already stirred up heated controversies among Chinese audiences, and her sex scenes, albeit shortened for the Chinese cinema, were reported as 'controversial' by the Chinese media.[80] Notwithstanding the difference in nature, this reminded me of the 2008 showdown between the women's volleyball teams of China and the US in Beijing, when Lang Ping was slammed by some Chinese fans as a 'traitor'.

As Huang Bo mentioned in *Leap*, he decided to withdraw his application and let Lang Ping take the position of head coach because he thought that he did not have the 'global' experience that Lang Ping had. It is not difficult for an outstanding experienced actress like Gong Li (who won the Best Actress award at the Venice International Film Festival with *The Story of Qiu Ju* back in 1992) to play Lang Ping, but it was her similar experience that resonated most productively in the role. My sense is that the latter half of the film was more attractive because of Gong Li playing Lang Ping, as underneath the Chinese women's volleyball spirit there were resonances that made the film more complex, with a richer narrative than other main melody films. In the film, Lang Ping (and actually Gong Li as well) remarked at a press conference,

> I was once asked by a journalist why Chinese people put so much emphasis on winning or losing in a volleyball game, I answered: 'Because emotionally we are still not strong enough. One day we became strong enough emotionally, we will be able to take that easy.'

Had it not been said by Lang Ping, and had the role not been played by an actress such as Gong Li, this would have been much less convincing. Apparently, Lang Ping, Gong Li and Peter Chan himself became emotionally strong enough to take up their respective roles.

Concluding Remarks

It was not surprising that Peter Chan was among the Hong Kong filmmakers commissioned to participate in main(land) melody projects, but it was quite unexpected that he chose a biopic film about Li Na in order to do so (the project began in 2015, and shooting started in 2018). Always one to carve out a new path, Chan chose not just to jump on the bandwagon but also to help pull it with a different genre of main melody film: the sports film. That Chan decided to do sports films, a genre that was not well developed in the mainland market, was indeed a trailblazing endeavour. When asked why he chose the sports film genre and *Li Na*, Chan answered as follows:

> It's not just tennis, but also how she represents a whole generation. The people born in the 1980s really make up a critical mass in China. And I think it's time to have a story about somebody from that post-80s generation that reflects the changing landscape of China today. The sensibilities of the post-80s generation are very different from traditional Chinese values. China is a very collective society, and everything is less about self and more on

the group, more on the society and the country. Here we have the post-80s, which is very much a 'me' generation. In that sense she's very, very different from all the characters that we've been dealing with in *American Dreams in China* and *Dearest*. Li has a very strong personality, and you could not confine her to a group, because she definitely would stand out and be very visible anywhere you put her. It's very typical of the younger Chinese. They don't like to conform.[81]

Here Chan made a very valid argument about self and group, but perhaps although *Li Na* resonated with the main melody as a Chinese success story, it was the collective, not the individual, that should be highlighted in mainland China. In the end, *Leap* premiered before *Li Na*, but in a sense, it was actually an excellent chance for the audience to have a decades-spanning look at the accomplishments of not just the Chinese women's volleyball team but also Peter Chan himself.

Similar to the Chinese women's volleyball team, Chan also went through ups and downs, from *Alan and Eric* to *Leap*, and his experience in collaborative projects enabled him to understand the operational logic of main melody blockbusters. 'The career of Peter Chan in a sense told an exemplary story of the success of the Hong Kong mode of flexible identity, which, ironically, also sounded the death knell for Hong Kong cinema,' as I have argued elsewhere using *Perhaps Love* and *Warlords* as examples.[82] It was an exaggeration to sound the 'death knell' for Hong Kong cinema. Although established filmmakers like Peter Chan left the Hong Kong market for greener pastures, Hong Kong cinema did not die, albeit it is still striving hard to find a new direction. Actually, Peter Chan understood the predicament of Hong Kong very well: 'We've always had the benefit in the past of being China's middleman to the world. That's where we made all the money. But when China doesn't need a middleman anymore, we're in trouble.'[83] However, even though this may be true in terms of commerce, the case seems a bit different in regard to filmmaking, if not other cultural and creative industries. When he spoke of his reasons for making *Perhaps Love*, Chan said, 'We're making this film to appeal to a bigger audience, so that Hong Kong film, or the spirit of Hong Kong film, does not die'; and, according to him, it would be foolish to only 'make films in Cantonese on the streets of Hong Kong without expanding it to the world'.[84] Be that as it may, Hong Kong cinema was not restricted to the streets of its territory during its heyday, although the films did speak Cantonese. While I respectfully disagree with him on this point, I must say that his films really appealed to a bigger audience. For Peter Chan, to borrow Darrell Davis and Emilie Yueh-yu Yeh's point, pan-Asian film is more than creative teamwork, but really 'a collaboration of different markets by trying to break through the market barrier, the culture barriers, and the language barriers so [that] we have enough population to sustain a healthy industry'.[85]

That was the reason Chan shifted to Hollywood and pan-Asian productions, but in the end, he found enough population to sustain a healthy industry in the mainland market. Almost fifteen years after *Perhaps Love*, Peter Chan demonstrated that his mode of flexible identity could contribute enormously to the reconfiguration of Chinese main melody blockbusters in the 2010s. His exceptional ability to make ends meet – main melody, complaints, censorship, market, his own mission and so on – is beautifully showcased in *Leap*.[86] That film broke new ground for Chinese main melody blockbusters, showing that sports-themed films have enormous potential in the mainland market.

There were different restrictions for Hong Kong directors moving to a different market, be it Hollywood or mainland China. Peter Chan seemed to be more willing or able to adapt to the environment of mainland China. Regarding his experience in Hollywood, in an interview after *Dearest* had its world premiere at the Venice Film Festival, he stated firmly: 'I would try not to work there again, unless I can absolutely call the shots.'[87] Talking about his mainland projects, 'the "serious" film director – more so than topflight matinee idols – is venerated both by the mainland critical firmament and by the market itself, whose passionate film culture accords auteurs a level of reverence and loyalty rare in Hong Kong.'[88] It is indeed easier said than done. Peter Chan has been able to put this into practice because he thoroughly understands the rules of the game:

'SARFT can make us censor as much as they want during the script-approval process, but that doesn't mean we have to shoot their version of the script. The film is going to be censored again anyway, at the distribution-approval stage. So, I still shoot the things they ask me to remove from the script.' Often, Chan insists, these initially expurgated scenes survive the final cut, though not without some jockeying with the postproduction censors . . . Postproduction censorship brings a fresh set of obstacles, but filmmakers once again safeguard artistic freedom by tactical means. The judicious director haggles over weighted compromises. '[The censors] may tell you to change eight things [in the director's cut],' says Peter Chan. 'You can't fight them on all eight points [but] you can fight for the two or three things that you really care about.'[89]

Perhaps equally important, Chan has been able to work well with mainland film workers, thanks to his meticulous attention to individuals. He takes crew members' cultural and linguistic backgrounds seriously, knowing very well that, among other things, the careful use of language is an essential part of a production's social formation.[90] Gary Bettinson's point that 'PRC proscriptions are best seen as galvanizing, not thwarting, creativity' may not be fair to all Hong Kong directors in the mainland market, but I do agree that it is applicable to Peter Chan.[91] Let me conclude by citing Chan again: 'Life is full of restrictions.'[92] He has been able to remain creative despite these restrictions.

Notes

1. For Peter Chan's short bio, see the website of We Pictures, We Distribution: <http://www.wepictures.com/en/about-peterchan.php>; last accessed 1 May 2021.

2. Thomas Podvin, 'Conversations with Peter Chan Ho Sun', *Hong Kong Cinemagic*, 27 October 2008: <http://www.hkcinemagic.com/en/page.asp?aid=291&page=1>; last accessed 1 May 2021.

3. According to Chan, his major career change came with *News Attack*, of which he was the producer. After that, he set his goal to become a director. See Michael Berry, *Speaking in Images: Interview with Contemporary Chinese Filmmakers* (New York: Columbia University Press, 2005), 489.

4. Tung-man Chan, 'UFO: Once-famous in 1993' 〈93 UFO公司曾經風光一時〉, *World Journal Thailand*, 26 April 2016.

5. Pan-Asian cinema refers to 'talent sharing, cross-border investment, co-productions (which may be unofficial, or backed by formal treaties), and market consolidation, through distribution and investment in foreign infrastructure'. Darrell Davis and Emilie Yueh-yu Yeh, *East Asian Screen Industries* (London: British Film Institute, 2008), 85.

6. Gary Bettinson, 'Once Upon a Time in China and America: Transnational Storytelling and the Recent Films of Peter Chan', in *Chinese Cinemas: International Perspective*, ed. Felicia Chan and Andrew Willis (Abingdon and New York: Routledge 2016), 47–8.

7. From the website of We Pictures, We Distribution: <http://www.wepictures.com/en/about-distribution.php>; last accessed 1 May 2021.

8. Yiu-Wai Chu, *Lost in Transition: Hong Kong Culture in the Age of China* (Albany: SUNY Press, 2013), 109.

9. 'Director Peter Chan: What Is a Hong Kong Movie?' China.org.cn, 12 June 2006: <http://www.china.org.cn/english/features/film/171069.htm>; last accessed 1 May 2021.

10. 'Actor Jet Li Breaks Record with $13M Paycheck', Reuters, 25 November 2007: <https://www.reuters.com/article/idINIndia-30677420071125>; last accessed 1 May 2021.

11. Huang Ying, 'Shift of Focus', *China Daily*, 12 March 2015.

12. 'Hong Kong 2012 Diary: Specials – Peter Ho-Sun Chan, Filmmaker in Focus', Asia-Europe Foundation, 19 March 2012: <https://culture360.asef.org/news-events/

hong-kong-2012-diary-specials-peter-ho-sun-chan-filmmaker-focus/>; last accessed 1 May 2021.

13. Mirana M. Szeto and Yun-chung Chen, 'To Work or Not to Work: The Dilemma of Hong Kong Film Labor in the Age of Mainlandization', *Jump Cut: A Review of Contemporary Media* 55, Fall 2013: <https://www.ejumpcut.org/archive/jc55.2013/SzetoChenHongKong/index.html>; last accessed 1 May 2021.

14. Chu, *Lost in Translation*, 109–10.

15. For further details, see Yingjin Zhang, *Screening China: Critical Interventions, Cinematic Reconfigurations, and the Transnational Imaginary in Contemporary Chinese Cinema* (Ann Arbor: University of Michigan Press: 2002), 272.

16. Thomas Shin, 'Nomadism vs. Stability', in *Peter Ho-sun Chan: My Way*, ed. Cheuk-to Li (Hong Kong: Joint Publishing Co. Ltd., 2012), 200–3.

17. Lisa Odham Stokes, *Peter Ho-Sun Chan's He's a Woman, She's a Man* (Hong Kong: Hong Kong University Press, 2009).

18. Shu Kei, 'The Age of Miracles' (in Chinese) 〈嫲嫲帆帆〉, in *Hong Kong Films 1996* 《1996香港電影回顧》, ed. Hong Kong Film Critics Society: <https://www.filmcritics.org.hk/film-review/node/2015/06/22/%E5%AB%B2%E5%AB%B2%E5%B8%86%E5%B8%86>; last accessed 1 May 2021. For example, the female protagonist is willing to make a deal with God, using ten years of her own life to save her child's life. This is utilitarianism rather than maternal love, according to Shu, because a mother would simply trade her own life for her son's.

19. Sheldon Lu, *Chinese Modernity and Global Biopolitics: Studies in Literature and Visual Culture* (Honolulu: University of Hawaii Press, 2007), 123.

20. Rey Chow, *Sentimental Fabulations, Contemporary Chinese Films: Attachment in the Age of Global Visibility* (New York: Columbia University Press, 2007), Chapter 5.

21. Norman Abjorensen, *Historical Dictionary of Popular Music* (Lanham, MD, Boulder, CO, New York and London: Rowman and Littlefield, 2017), 501.

22. Chow, *Sentimental Fabulations, Contemporary Chinese Films*, 114.

23. Sheldon Lu, 'Transnational Chinese Masculinity in Film Representation', in *The Cosmopolitan Dream: Transnational Chinese Masculinities in a Global Age*, ed. Derek Hird and Geng Song (Hong Kong: Hong Kong University Press, 2018), 63.

24. Kwai-cheung Lo, *Chinese Face/Off: The Transnational Popular Culture of Hong Kong* (Urbana and Champagne: University of Illinois Press, 2005), 120.

25. Esther M. K. Cheung, 'In Love with Music: Memory, Identity and Music in Hong Kong's Diasporic Films', in *At Home in the Chinese Diaspora: Memories, Identities and Belonging*, ed. Kuah-Pearce Khun Eng and Andrew P. Davidson (New York: Palgrave, 2008), 235. Cheung has provided a lucid and inspiring analysis of the relation of song to the issues of the rootlessness of the diaspora in the film; see 234–9.

26. Chow, *Sentimental Fabulations, Contemporary Chinese Films*, 118; in other words, 'is not this love story, too, in the end only an "almost" – not quite the simple encounter with capitalism and happiness that they once naively dreamt of . . .' (120).

27. Michael Curtin, 'Sweet Comrades: Historical Identities and Popular Culture', in *In Search of Boundaries: Communication, Nation-States, and Cultural Identities*, ed. Joseph M. Chan and Bryce T. McIntyre (Westport, CT: Ablex, 2002), 277.

28. Lo, *Chinese Face/Off*, 121.

29. Jin Long Pao, 'The Pan-Asian Co-Production Sphere: Interview with Director Peter Chan', *Harvard Asia Quarterly* 6(3): 45.

30. Prasenjit Duara, 'Hong Kong as a Global Frontier: Interface of China, Asia, and the World', in *Hong Kong in the Cold War*, ed. Priscilla Roberts and John M. Carroll (Hong Kong: Hong Kong University Press, 2016), 219–20.

31. Chow, *Sentimental Fabulations, Contemporary Chinese Films*, 117.

32. Yingchi Chu, *Hong Kong Cinema: Coloniser, Motherland and Self* (London and New York: RoutledgeCurzon, 2001), 124. In 1995, the November issue of *Ming Pao Monthly* featured a special issue entitled 'The Death of Hong Kong Cinema'.

33. Esther C. M. Yau, 'Watchful Partners, Hidden Currents: Hong Kong Cinema Moving into the Mainland of China', in *A Companion to Hong Kong Cinema*, ed. Esther M. K. Cheung, Gina Marchetti and Esther C. M. Yau (Malden, MA: Wiley-Blackwell, 2015), 35.

34. Bliss Cua Lim, 'Generic Ghosts: Remaking the New "Asian Horror Film"', in *Hong Kong Film, Hollywood and New Global Cinema: No Film Is an Island*, ed. Gina Marchetti and Tan See Kam (Abingdon and New York: Routledge, 2007), 118–19.

35. Ti Wei, 'In the Name of "Asia": Practices and Consequences of Recent International Film Co-productions in East Asia', in *East Asian Cinemas: Regional Flows and Global Transformations*, ed. Vivian P. Y. Lee (Basingstoke and New York: Palgrave Macmillan, 2011), 195. '*The Eye* was directed by the Chinese-Thai filmmakers Pang brothers (Danny Pang-fat and Oxide Pang Shun) and the cast included Malaysian Taiwanese actress Angelica Lee, Chinese-Canadian singer Lawrence Chou, and Thai actress Chutcha Rujinanon. Not only the cast and the crew are pan-Asian, the film's main action and setting straddle Hong Kong and Thailand. *The Eye* achieved considerable market success in several Asian countries and was soon followed by two sequels, *The Eye 2* (2004) and *The Eye 10* (2005). Also in 2002, Peter Chan conducted another pan-Asian co-production project, two omnibus horror films *Three* (2002) and *Three: Extremes* (2004), involving altogether six directors from Hong Kong, South Korea, Thailand, and Japan, including Chan himself.'

36. Beng Huat Chua, *Structure, Audience and Soft Power in East Asian Pop Culture* (Hong Kong: Hong Kong University Press, 2012), 141–2.

37. Chu, *Lost in Translation*, 104–5.

38. 'Director Peter Chan: What Is a Hong Kong Movie?'

39. Yiu-Wai Chu, *Found in Transition: Hong Kong Studies in the Age of China* (Albany: SUNY Press, 2018), 132–3.

40. Ai Erh 艾爾 and Lin Yü-ju 林譽如, '*Perhaps Love* Accomplished the Ideals of My Love Films: An Interview with World-class Director Peter Chan' 〈《如果．愛》實現了我對愛情片的所有想：國際級名導陳可辛專訪〉, *Funscreen* 《放映週報》 41, 4 September 2006: <http://www.funscreen.com.tw/headline.asp?H_No=54>; last accessed 1 May 2021.

41. G. Andrew Stuckey, *Metacinema in Contemporary Chinese Film* (Hong Kong: Hong Kong University Press, 2018), 18. The author offers an insightful reading of *Perhaps Love* as a global musical in this chapter; see 18–37.

42. Ibid., 18–19.

43. Stephen Teo 'Promise and Perhaps Love: Pan-Asian Production and the Hong Kong-China Interrelationship', Inter-Asia Cultural Studies 9:3 (2008): 351–2.

44. Chu, Lost in Transition, 109.

45. Szeto and Chen, 'To Work or Not to Work'.

46. Karen Chu, 'Cannes Q&A: Wu Xia's Director Peter Ho-sun Chan', The Hollywood Reporter, 12 May 2011: <https://www.hollywoodreporter.com/news/cannes-qa-wu-xia-director-187902>; last accessed 1 May 2021.

47. Ibid.

48. Vivienne Lo, 'Dead or Alive? Martial Arts and the Forensic Gaze', in Film and the Chinese Medical Humanities, ed. Vivienne Lo, Chris Berry and Guo Liping (London and New York: Routledge, 2020), 11; in this chapter, the author offers an informative and thoughtful discussion of the film with reference to Chinese anatomy and the wuxia classic The One-Armed Swordman (1967).

49. Emilie Yueh-yu Yeh and Shi-yan Chao, 'Policy and Creative Strategies: Hong Kong CEPA Films in the China Market', International Journal of Cultural Policy 26:2 (March 2020): 189.

50. Li Yizhuang 李以莊 and Xi Yue 席悅, 'Back to the Local: The New Age of Co-productions' 〈回歸本土：新合拍片年代〉, Bloomberg Businessweek (Chinese Version), 14 February 2010: <http://read.bbwc.cn/askybl.html>; last accessed 1 May 2021.

51. Elizabeth Kerr, 'American Dreams in China: Film Review', Hollywood Reporter, 17 May 2013: <https://www.hollywoodreporter.com/review/american-dreams-china-film-review-524792>; last accessed 1 May 2021.

52. For a further discussion of this, see Lu, 'Transnational Chinese Masculinity in Film Representation', 69–70.

53. Fan Yang, Faked in China: Nation Branding, Counterfeit Culture, and Globalization (Bloomington and Indianapolis: Indiana University Press, 2016), 191.

54. Lu, 'Transnational Chinese Masculinity in Film Representation', 69.

55. Yang, Faked in China, 191. The author writes: '"America" is still imagined as 'a powerful "Other"' for a story purportedly about the 'rise of China. Due to this binary construction of "America versus China," as cultural critic Wang Yan points out, the film has perhaps missed out on an opportunity to re-imagine a "different" China within a postcolonial global order.'

56. Kerr, 'American Dreams in China'.

57. Bettinson, 'Once Upon a Time in China and America', 40.

58. See, among others, the following for an elaborated account of Dearest: Kobe Chan Yan Chuen, 'The Abducted Child Movie in Chinese Cinema', in The Child in World Cinema, ed. Debbie Olson (London: Lexington Books, 2018), 355–72.

59. See the news related to the two films issued by We Pictures on their website: <http://www.wepictures.com/en/news-detail.php?id=1024> and <http://www.wepictures.com/en/news-detail.php?id=1020>; both last accessed 1 May 2021.

60. Xu Fan, 'Gong Li's New Hit "Leaps" to Top China's Box-office Charts', China Daily, 29 September 2020.

61. For a very abbreviated history of the sports film in the West, see Bruce Babington, *The Sports Film: Games People Play* (London and New York: Wallflower, 2014), 3–4.

62. Seán Crosson, *Sport and Film* (London and New York: Routledge, 2013), 1964.

63. Laikwan Pang, *Building a New China in Cinema: The Chinese Left-wing Cinema* (Lanham, MD and Oxford: Rowman and Littlefield, 2002), 49; see also 69.

64. Liu Li and Fan Hong, *The National Games and National Identity in China: A History* (London and New York: Routledge, 2017), 39.

65. Ibid., 73.

66. Zhou Xuelin, *Young Rebels in Contemporary Chinese Cinema* (Hong Kong: Hong Kong University Press, 2007), 51.

67. For cases of successful films about sports heroines, see Viridiana Lieberman, *Sports Heroines on Film: A Critical Study of Cinematic Women Athletes* (Jefferson, NC: McFarland & Company, 2015).

68. For further details, see 'Chinese Women's Volleyball Team's Solemn Declaration' (in Chinese) 〈中國女排嚴正聲明〉, 17 January 2020: <https://news.sina.cn/gn/2020-01-17/detail-iihnzahk4680961.d.html?from=wap>; last accessed 1 May 2021.

69. Alice Yan, 'Former Coach of China's Women's Volleyball Team Chen Zhonghe Outraged at "Ugly" Film Portrayal', *South China Morning Post*, 9 January 2020.

70. 'Why Do We Need Chinese Women's Volleyball?' (in Chinese) 〈為什麼需要中國女排〉, *China Youth Daily* 《中國青年報》, 14 October 2020.

71. He Yingzi, 'Leap, But Not Soaring', *The World of Chinese*, 30 September 2020: <https://www.theworldofchinese.com/2020/09/leap-but-not-soaring/>; last accessed 1 May 2021.

72. 'Peter Chan: *Leap* Was the Most Difficult among All the Movies I Made' (in Chinese) 〈陳可辛：《奪冠》是拍過那麼多電影里最難的一部〉, sina.com.hk, 27 September 2020: <https://sina.com.hk/news/article/20200927/0/4/2/陳可辛-奪冠-是拍過那麼多電影里最難的一部-12232458.html>; last accessed 1 May 2021.

73. Zhang Rui, '*Leap* Shows the Spirit of Chinese Women's Volleyball Team', China.org.cn, 22 January 2020: <http://www.china.org.cn/arts/2020-01/22/content_75639894.htm>; last accessed 1 May 2021.

74. 'Peter Chan: *Leap* Was the Most Difficult among All the Movies I Made'.

75. See 'Why Does Chinese Women's Volleyball Spirit Always Fill Our Eye with Tears" (in Chinese) 〈女排精神為什麼總讓我們含著淚水〉, Xinhua Net, 3 October 2020: <http://big5.xinhuanet.com/gate/big5/www.xinhuanet.com/comments/2020-10/03/c_1126571065.htm>; last accessed 1 May 2021.

76. 'Peter Chan: *Leap* Was the Most Difficult among All the Movies I Made'.

77. Heidi Hsia, 'Peter Chan on Casting Gong Li in Volleyball Movie', Cinema Online Exclusively for Yahoo Newsroom, 30 September 2020: <https://sg.style.yahoo.com/peter-chan-casting-gong-li-065000650.html>; last accessed 1 May 2021.

78. Kevin Latham, *Pop Culture China!: Media, Arts, and Lifestyle* (Santa Barbara, Denver and Oxford: ABC-CLIO, 2007), 173.

79. Lisa Funnell, *Warrior Women: Gender, Race, and the Transnational Chinese Action Star* (Albany: SUNY Press, 2014), 85; for an account of the 'transnational appeal' of Gong Li, see Chapter 4.

80. Liu Wei, 'Shining Gong Li Chimes Louder', *China Daily*, 2 November 2006.
81. Amy Qin, 'Q. and A.: Peter Chan on Making Movies in China', *Sinosphere: Dispatches from China*, 19 May 2015: <https://sinosphere.blogs.nytimes.com/2015/05/19/q-and-a-peter-chan-on-making-movies-in-china/>; last accessed 1 May 2021.
82. Chu, *Lost in Translation*, 109.
83. 'Director Peter Chan: What Is a Hong Kong Movie?'
84. Ibid.
85. Davis and Yeh, *East Asian Screen Industries*, 93.
86. Peter Chan made this clear in an interview: 'As a creative person one has to find a good balance. *Leap* should be the movie that has the most positive energy I have ever made, and at the same time it keeps my own personal appeal.' 'Peter Chan: *Leap* Was the Most Difficult among All the Movies I Made'.
87. James Mottram, 'Peter Chan's Film *Dearest* Is Based on a True Story of Child Abduction', *South China Morning Post*, 22 October 2014.
88. Bettinson, 'Once Upon a Time in China and America', 39; see also Bono Lee, 'The Possibility of China for Hong Kong Directors: The Transformation of Peter Chan's Identity', in *My Way*, 187–95.
89. Gary Bettinson, 'Yesterday Once More: Hong Kong-China Coproductions and the Myth of Mainlandization', *Journal of Chinese Cinemas* 14:1 (2020): 22. 'Like other Hong Kong filmmakers, Chan practices self-censorship only during preproduction (i.e. when anticipating nettlesome subjects); during filming, he grants himself creative autonomy, shooting without restrictions. Drastically reworking the script's dramaturgy could raise the censors' ire, but minor plot revisions are apt to go unnoticed: "Censors don't go back to the approved script and compare it frame-by-frame with the film you've shot," notes Nansun Shi. Thanks to the Hong Kong director's guile, censored material sometimes survives by stealth.'
90. Aynne Kokas, *Hollywood Made in China* (Oakland: University of California Press, 2017), 137.
91. Bettinson, 'Yesterday Once More', 21.
92. Ibid.

Chapter 4

Founding an Army with Soft Power: Captain Andrew Lau

'I do not fear these dark times, for I have seen worse. I can say with confidence that this is only darkness before dawn.'

— Andrew Lau, *The Founding of an Army*

Introduction

A filmmaker wearing multiple hats as cinematographer, director and producer, Andrew Lau began his film career as a cinematographer in the 1980s. Growing up as a film fan, Lau often watched 'after-work showings' (second-run films with cheaper tickets) with his uncle, and thanks to the coupons he received from his schoolmate's father, who was a cinema manager, he was able to watch many films when he was young. After graduating from secondary school, Lau wanted to find a job related to his interest in photography. He started his career taking photos for tourists but quit after two days because that was not what he desired. Before he actually found his life-changing job, he had a very brief tenure at a gold trading company, which was absolutely not his cup of tea. He finally had the opportunity to join Shaw Brothers in 1981 as a production assistant. He enjoyed the job and worked extra hard, and his effort paid off as he was soon promoted to camera assistant, having the chance to participate in *Legendary Weapons of China* (1982), directed by the kung-fu film master Kar-Leung Lau. Back then, Hong Kong's film industry was growing swiftly, and there was a great demand for new talent. Lau moved to Cinema City, the new force of the Hong Kong film industry, and then to Golden Harvest, where he made his cinematographic debut with his mentor Peter Ngor, *Mr. Vampire* (1985), directed by Ricky Lau, which was so popular that it triggered a wave of vampire films in Hong Kong in the late 1980s.[1] Lau soon became one of the most sought-after cinematographers, and his works included, among others, commercial blockbusters such as Sammo Hung's *The Millionaires' Express* (1986) and Jackie Chan's *Armour of God*

(1987), as well as stylistic crime thrillers such as Ringo Lam's *City on Fire* (1987) and Kar-Wai Wong's directorial debut, *As Tears Go By* (1988). He also worked with Christopher Doyle on Wong's all-time classics *Days of Being Wild* (1990) and *Chungking Express* (1994).

In order to cultivate more self-determined creativity, Andrew Lau became a director and released his debut, *Against All* (1990), a youth crime story produced by Danny Lee. He continued to focus on cinematography while directing films, and he was also the cinematographer for most of his own directed works. His subsequent collaboration with Jing Wong proved to be career-changing. After *Lee Rock* (1991) and its sequel *Lee Rock II* (1991), produced by Jing Wong and directed by Lawrence Lau, he worked closely with Wong, and his directed works *Ghost Lantern* (1993) and *Raped by an Angel* (1993) did better at the box office than his previous films. Lau started as a film producer with *1941 Hong Kong on Fire* (1994), directed by Man-Kei Chin and masterminded by Jing Wong. Lau continued to have opportunities to direct commercial films of different genres, such as the Qing Dynasty sexy romance *Lover of the Last Empress* (1995) and the young gangster thriller *Mean Street Story* (1995). The latter is worth noting here: Andrew Lau started working with the male lead, Ekin Cheng, who later became the leading gangster hero in the *Young and Dangerous* film series (1996–2000). In 1996, Lau co-founded the BoB and Partners production company ('BoB' meant 'Best of Best') with Jing Wong and Manfred Wong.[2] Not only was the *Young and Dangerous* series immensely popular, BoB and Partners' teenage romance *Feel 100%* (1996), produced by Andrew Lau and directed by Ringo Ma, and martial arts fantasy *The Storm Riders* (1998), directed by Andrew Lau, both adapted from comics like the *Young and Dangerous* films, were also very well received. Due to the shrinking market in the aftermath of the Asian financial crisis and the bursting of the dot-com bubble, the triumvirate of BoB – Andrew Lau, Jing Wong and Manfred Wong – disbanded after *The Duel* (2000), adapted from *wuxia* fiction and directed by Lau. For Lau it was certainly a blessing in disguise. He then founded the film production company Basic Pictures and partnered with Alan Mak to co-direct the police and gangster classic trilogy *Infernal Affairs* (2002–3). The trilogy won both critical acclaim (mainly for the first episode) and commercial success. His collaboration with Alan Mak continued to succeed, albeit to a lesser extent, with *Initial D* (2005) and *Confession of Pain* (2006).

Having won international fame with *Infernal Affairs*, which was remade by Martin Scorsese as *The Departed* (2006) and would go on to win the Best Picture and Best Director awards at the 78th Academy Awards, Andrew Lau began his overseas venture with the Korean romance *Daisy* (2006) and the American thriller *The Flock* (2007). Despite the star-studded casts, such as

Gianna Jun in the former and Richard Gere in the latter, these transnational collaborative projects did not meet expectations. It was therefore not surprising that Andrew Lau turned his attention to the swiftly developing mainland market in the 2010s. He continued to showcase his versatility with the contemporary romantic drama *A Beautiful Life* (2011) and the period martial arts flick *The Guillotines* (2012). Besides his filmic productions, he directed a five-minute short film for Vision Beijing in 2007, a project for the Beijing Foreign Cultural Exchanges Association and the Information Office of the Beijing Municipal Government. Starring Tony Chiu-Wai Leung, Shu Qi and Jay Chou, it was meant to showcase Beijing cuisine to the world before the 2008 Olympics. Notwithstanding this, it was still somewhat unexpected that he would later direct *The Founding of an Army* (2017), a main melody film commissioned by the government to commemorate the ninetieth anniversary of the founding of the People's Liberation Army. Although this strengthened Andrew Lau's authority as well as demonstrated his status in the mainland film industry, the film was not very well received among mainland audiences (I will come back to this later). After another lacklustre performance with the *wuxia* fantasy *Kung Fu Monster* (2018), Andrew Lau's light shone again in *The Captain* (2019), a main melody film whose genre was different from that of *The Founding of an Army*. With *The Founding of an Army* and *The Captain*, Lau showcased his versatility in the genres of main melody films. Before looking at these two projects in detail, I will first re-examine his signature works and the early stage of his northern venture.

Once Young and Dangerous

BoB and Partners was a watershed in Andrew Lau's film career. In the role of director, Lau was a 'Jack-of-all-trades', involved mainly in different commercial films. His signature work with personal style did not appear until the *Young and Dangerous* film series, which was adapted from a popular comic series penned by Ow Man and scripted by Manfred Wong. When Jing Wong, Manfred Wong and Andrew Lau founded BoB and Partners, they had very clearly set goals and objectives:

> The target audience was adolescents (below 25 years old), and the main cast was up-and-coming young actors (such as Ekin Cheng, Jordan Chan, Shu Qi and Eric Got). On top of themes (of the comic series) and story-telling skills (such as stylistic cinematography and the emphasis on unity and synergy), keen market sense and rapid response enabled BoB and Partners to become the most vigorous and powerful new film company at that time.[3]

This proved to be a successful formula for the *Young and Dangerous* films. The comic series (the literal translation of the original Chinese title was *Teddy Boy*) was considered the most representative work of Hong Kong gangster comics,[4] but its cinematic adaptation exceeded everyone's expectations. The first episode of *Young and Dangerous* was released in 1996, and it was so successful that the second and third episodes premiered in the same year, followed by the fourth (1997), fifth (1998) and sixth and final episode, *Born to be King* (2000). There was also the prequel *Young and Dangerous: The Prequel* (1998), directed by Lau, and numerous spinoffs by various directors. In the midst of the post-Asian financial crisis period, *Young and Dangerous*, out of the blue, became the most popular and profitable film series in Hong Kong.

While Andrew Lau had accumulated considerable experience from his previous gangster films, such as *Against All*, *Mean Street Story* and *To Live and Die in Tsimshatsui* (1994), *Young and Dangerous*, as an adaptation from comics, gave him the chance to hybridise his stylistic cinematography (showcased, for example, in his work with Kar-Wai Wong) with commercial gangster films. As a cinematic adaptation of comics, the gangster genre had acquired a creative synergy:

> In complicating the relationship between the audience and the cinematic medium by means of which it itself exists, the *Young and Dangerous* series makes it impossible to mistake the movie for reality at the same time that, as in [John] Woo's film, the excitement of the adventure is present as well.[5]

Despite its commercial success, however, the *Young and Dangerous* series did not receive due attention from the film critics. As rightly remarked by Martha Nochimson, the *Young and Dangerous* series was (mistakenly) undervalued:

> None of the books on Hong Kong cinema mentions them or their principal director, Andrew Lau. Online reviews express continual surprise at the quality of each new film, so thoroughly are these movies relegated to the province of disposable low culture.[6]

In fact, this film series centred on a group of honourable young street triads who deal with both the police and other triads with new modes of 'street smart'. The series conjured up a fantasy based on an alternative imagination of law and order, through which the changing social order in Hong Kong before and after the handover was presented in an entertaining manner.[7] From a different perspective, the series was a kind of creative *bildungsroman* envisioned by Hong Kong people in the (post)colonial context, in which they were trying hard to write their own stories. The male lead, Ho-Nam Chan (portrayed by Ekin Cheng), grows up later in the series, especially in the fifth episode. In that episode, 'deliberately loaded with the issue of identity', the production team refuses to admit the fact that 'Hong Kong has become middle-class'.[8] In other words, the protagonists and the production team, as well as Hong Kong per se, had grown up, and their youth identity was lost when the gangster groups started to collaborate with transnational corporations as Hong Kong merged with the national and the global.

Trying to duplicate the success formula of *Young and Dangerous* with a larger budget, BoB and Partners targeted the international market with *The Storm Riders*, which was based on Wing-Shing Ma's martial arts comic classic. 'Like Andrew Lau's other popular film series, *Young and Dangerous*, which is also based on local comics', as noted by Kwai-Cheung Lo, '[t]he Stormriders is often injected with animated and hand-drawn comic scenes to highlight its fantasy nature.'[9] Ironically, the most well-known catchphrase of *The Storm Riders* (the literal translation of the Chinese title was *Wind and Cloud* – Wind and Cloud are the names of the two protagonists) is arguably 'Succeed because of Wind and Cloud, and fail because of Wind and Cloud'. Success and failure in the comic series hinges on the two protagonists, but success and failure in the film industry cannot be predicted with a formula. Perhaps owing to the big budget, *The Storm Riders* was made as a high-concept blockbuster, selling Chinese fantasy adapted from martial arts comics to the world. However, as it 'mimicked Hollywood marketing strategies' and packaged 'a strong Chinese flavour',[10] it lacked the aleatory, creative and, at times, playful style of the *Young and Dangerous* series.

As mentioned above, shortly after *The Duel*, his last collaboration with Manfred Wong and Jing Wong at Bob and Partners, Andrew Lau founded Basic Pictures in 2002. Not only had the youth gang in *Young and Dangerous* grown up in the later episodes, Andrew Lau had also won enough fame to become a blockbuster director. With the support of Media Asia Films, Basic Pictures released its inaugural film, *Infernal Affairs*, co-directed by Andrew Lau and Alan Mak. In terms of investment, the outlay was much greater than for the *Young and Dangerous* film series, and the star-studded cast, including Andy Lau, Tony Chiu-wai Leung and Anthony Chau-sang Wong, almost guaranteed that this typical police and gangster film would be a box-office success. That said, it shattered expectations by doing extremely well as well as winning critical acclaim, grossing HK$55 million at the box office and becoming Hong Kong's top box-office draw of the year, bringing new hope to the local film industry, which had been in dire straits after the Asian financial crisis. It also swept up major awards, including, among others, Best Picture, Best Director, Best Actor (Tony Chiu-Wai Leung) and Best Supporting Actor (Anthony Wong), at the 40th Golden Horse Awards and the 22nd Hong Kong Film Awards. It was so successful that it was one of the two Hong Kong films picked by CNN in 2008 as the best Asian films of all time (the other was Kar-Wai Wong's *In the Mood for Love* [2000]): '*Infernal Affairs* breaks the mould of much of contemporary Hong Kong cinema by steering clear of over-the-top-action in favour of a slow-burning build up of psychological tension. Engrossing.'[11] In short, this film brought the signature genre of Hong Kong cinema to new heights. Gina Marchetti offered a comprehensive and informative account of *Infernal Affairs* in her book dedicated to this trilogy, including but not limited to its link to New Wave cinema, the use of music and its relation to time, memory and space.[12] Given the emphasis of this chapter, I will limit my focus to the notion of identities, which can be linked to the issue of identity that surfaced in the *Young and Dangerous* series.

The young idols in the *Young and Dangerous* films became superstars in the blockbuster crime drama *Infernal Affairs*. Police and gangster films have been the signature genre of Hong Kong cinema for many years, and going undercover was a common theme in these films since Alex Cheung's *Man on the Brink* (1981) – actually, Andrew Lau's *To Live and Die in Tsimshatsui* was the unofficial sequel to this Hong Kong New Wave classic. Partnered with Alan Mak, Andrew Lau successfully injected new dynamism into this genre using a double undercover narrative: an undercover cop in a triad gang and an undercover gangster in the police force. This reverberated with different meanings in the enduring identity crisis of Hong Kong people before and after the handover of Hong Kong in 1997.[13] For the sake of brevity, I will limit myself to highlighting the importance of the 'unhinged' identities of Andy Lau and Tony Leung here. 'They both long to "forget" their identities – as representatives of the state or representatives of forces opposed to the state or both,' as succinctly noted by Marchetti, and

> the meaning of their supposedly 'fixed' identities as cop and crook has become much less certain as the status of the state and the rule of law become less certain. Ironically, although narrative possibilities have been dramatically closed off by the new information, the status of the characters' identities has become even more malleable.[14]

Yiu Fai Chow and Jeroen de Kloet highlighted, on top of this, the importance of rooftop scenes in the film: 'the rooftop becomes the space where one can reclaim one's subjectivity', and the locality of Hong Kong is plainly underlined by Victoria Harbour and its spectacular skyline of Hong Kong – the backdrop to all rooftop scenes in the film.[15] The directors effectively used public housing estates as the setting in the early episodes of *Young and Dangerous*, and *Infernal Affairs* also skilfully juxtaposed Hong Kong's skyline and harbour with close-ups of facial expressions designed to highlight the anxiety of the protagonists. Unlike Lau's own signature moving camera, these shots deftly foregrounded the predicament of Hong Kong identity. By 'making much use of mirror reflections and gloomy illumination', the director and cinematographer (Andrew Lau and Yiu-Fai Lai) presented 'an illusory world of dim lights and shadows, smoke and mirrors, secrets and lies' in a world where people's lives are 'shackled to a prescribed plot within predetermined historical conditions' – in this case the fate of Hong Kong people and their identities in the context of 'their enforced affiliation with China'.[16] The sad but true fact about Hong Kong identity was despairingly reiterated in the introduction to the 2012 special issue published by the Hong Kong Film Critics Society to commemorate the tenth anniversary of *Infernal Affairs*:

> By its double undercover and dual/conflicting loyalties narrative, *Infernal Affairs* touched the raw nerve of the audience when Hong Kong was at its lowest point . . . after ten years Hong Kong people were still hopelessly hemmed in by this tragic story.[17]

The achievements of *Infernal Affairs* when Hong Kong cinema was at rock bottom were truly exceptional, which made Martin Scorsese interested in adapting it into *The Departed*. Perhaps not coincidentally, Andrew Lau had been linked to Scorsese before this: he had served as the cinematographer for Kar-Wai Wong's *As Tears Go By*, a tribute to Scorsese's *Mean Streets* (1973), and had directed a film with the English title *Mean Street Story*.[18] As comparisons of the original and the remake have been made by critics,[19] I would just like to direct attention to a remark made by Andrew Lau himself: 'Of course I think the version I made is better, but the Hollywood version is pretty good too. [Scorsese] made the Hollywood version more attuned to American culture.'[20] An inveterate fan of Hong Kong cinema, I must confess that I agree with Andrew Lau, but to me it is mainly because of the attunement to Hong Kong culture in the original version of this crime thriller: the locality, the identity crisis and the revitalisation of the undercover genre with typical Hong Kong characteristics. Anyway, whether one thinks *The Departed* is better or not, that the remake won Academy Awards for Best Picture and Best Director certainly further strengthened Andrew Lau's already outstanding résumé, paving the way for his Hollywood venture.

A Beautiful Life in China?

Not unlike his predecessors, such as Tsui Hark, Andrew Lau's Hollywood trip was brief and unconvincing. Although it was graced by the stars Richard Gere and Claire Danes, his first English-language film, *The Flock*, was not well received. The mountain that he had to climb was arguably taller than those of the Hong Kong directors in the 1990s, as Hong Kong cinema was no longer trendy in Hollywood. Worse still, it was reported that this American thriller was edited by the producers, which took away the director's vision.[21] In fact, Andrew Lau and Alan Mak's collaboration continued to catch attention in *Initial D*, also an adaptation, from a Japanese street-racing classic manga series written by Shu-ichi Shigeno. Starring Taiwanese superstar Jay Chou, Japanese actress Anne Suzuki and Hong Kong rising stars Edison Chen and Shawn Yue, this film was meant to be a pan-Asian project eyeing larger markets. The pan-Asian subject, however, failed to appear, as deconstructed by Kwai-Cheung Lo in his inspiring account of the film, and its racial impersonation merely unfolded the 'extimacy' of being (Hong Kong) Chinese in the twenty-first century: 'Hong Kong people are learning to become Chinese with an interior that is still foreign and colonial.'[22] As the once young and dangerous departed from the local, regrettably, their vigour began to wane. After *Confession of Pain*, another crime drama co-directed by Andrew Lau and Alan Mak, fell short of expectations in terms of both box-office receipts and critical response, the two parted company and Lau tried to look to new pastures. He directed the tragic love story *Deiji* (*Daisy*), produced by South Korea's Ifilm, in 2006. Shot in Amsterdam, this pan-Asian collaboration did not steal the limelight for Lau, and while his international film career was similar to Peter Chan's (though with a reverse direction from Asia to Hollywood), it was even shorter. As Peter Chan was struggling with his mainland film career after *The Warlords* (2007), Lau returned to Hong Kong, but not to work on films in which he excelled. *Look for a Star* (2009) and *Legend of the Fist: The Return of Chen Zhen* (2010) were romantic comedy and martial arts superhero films starring Andy Lau and Donnie Yen, respectively. Although these commercially viable products were not difficult to handle for a versatile director like Andrew Lau, they did not add any particular accolades to his already well-polished résumé. To break through this bottleneck in his career, it is therefore understandable that he chose to go north in the 2010s, a time during which the reconfigured mainland film industry needed more diverse voices – not just in terms of film genres but also directorial styles.

In fact, Andrew Lau was not completely new to the mainland market. In 2007, he directed a five-minute short film on Beijing cuisine for Vision Beijing. Starring his favourite cast, Tony Chiu-Wai Leung, Shu Qi and Jay Chou, this short film packaged a new Beijing for the world audience before the Olympics in 2008. That said, it was unfortunate that Lau did not have the chance to do what he did best, because films about the police and gangsters were not a main genre in mainland China, except for anti-drug and anti-corruption themes echoing the main melody. The romantic story *A Beautiful Life* (2011) was a transitional work of Andrew Lau's northern venture. Jointly produced by Media Asia, Basic Pictures, China Film Media Asia and Beijing Polybona Film, this was a trans-border love story between a Beijing cop (portrayed by Liu Ye) and a Hong Kong woman (portrayed by Shu Qi). It reminded Hong Kong audiences of Peter Chan's masterpiece *Comrades, Almost a Love Story* (1996), but it featured, as sharply noted by Helen Hok-sze Leung, 'a reverse trajectory that is the new reality: it is now a Hong Kong woman who is a migrant seeking her fortune in Beijing'.[23] The director adopted longer takes and slower cutting for his cross-border love story, but this was not the main reason Hong Kong audiences missed the typical Andrew Lau; the locality and identity issues in *Young and Dangerous* and *Infernal Affairs* turned into a backdrop, to say the least, of the director's northbound imaginary. Because 'the northbound filmmaker now views Hong Kong as both a suffocating place from which to escape, as well as a morally weak character in need of redemption . . . the film was not particularly well received in Hong Kong'.[24] The a-bad-woman-meets-a-good-man motif was seen by many Hong Kong fans as a blatant metaphor to butter up the booming Beijing and mainland market. In his review of *A Beautiful Life*, Mark Jenkins made a remark that sounded bitter to many Hong Kong fans' ears: 'the movie is among the first to suggest that the balance of power has shifted north. Economic migrants now travel from Hong Kong to Beijing to make their fortunes, and are regarded with suspicion by their new neighbors.' Jenkins's conclusion was also bitterly sarcastic: 'The fact that Lau now has a Beijing office, and is pursuing opportunities on the mainland is probably just a coincidence.'[25]

Given the trajectory of Andrew Lau's filmic career, it was not surprising that he would collaborate with Peter Chan, who shared a similar experience of moving from Hong Kong, Asia and Hollywood to mainland China. Directed by Andrew Lau and produced by Peter Chan, *The Guillotines* was actually a reboot of the Shaw Brothers Studio classic martial arts film *The Flying Guillotine* (1975), directed by Meng-hwa Ho. This fatal weapon stole the spotlight again in the Taiwanese *wuxia* film star Jimmy Wang's self-directed *Master of the Flying Guillotine* (1976). After more than a third of a century, Lau and Chan selected this as their *wuxia* blockbuster, kind of a sister production to *Dragon* (2011), with which Peter Chan wanted to bring something fresh to the *wuxia* genre. It was reported that Lau was Chan's third choice as director, replacing Teddy Chen who himself had taken over from Dante Lam, but Chan made it very clear in an interview that 'such elements as the plot, its focus on the brotherhood theme, its visual style and choice of end song all come from him'.[26] Andrew Lau was interested in this project because he grew up watching *wuxia* films and was therefore influenced by their action and visual effects, and he also wanted 'to create a brand-new version of *The Guillotines* that feels closer to our time'.[27] In this *wuxia* blockbuster, described by the director as his 'Qing Dynasty-set *Young and Dangerous*',[28] Andrew Lau tried luring the mainland audience by inserting many elements of his previous works. Moreover, in his own words, beneath the 'shell' of *Young and Dangerous*, Peter Chan's *The Warlords* was adopted as the 'nucleus' of *The Guillotines*.[29] As with *The Warlords*, the main theme of brotherhood (and betrayal) lay at the heart of *The Guillotines*, and the use of young idols to package this period *wuxia* actioner was borrowed from the success formula of *Young and Dangerous*. Stylish, handsome young men from the mainland, Taiwan and Hong Kong, including Huang Xiaoming, Ethan Juan, Shawn Yue and Jing Boran, teamed up with Andrew Lau on this film. Certain scenes in *The Guillotines*, such as the confrontation between Ethan Juan and Shawn Yue along a cliff bank, also reminded the audience of *Infernal Affairs*. Thanks to its generous budget of US$20 million (the film was a co-production by Chan's We Pictures, Media Asia Film Production, Stellar Mega Films, Dingsheng Cultural Industry Investment and Polyface Films), Lau could spend big on 3D special effects for this period *wuxia* actioner. Touted as 'the most expensive 3D film in the history of Chinese language cinema',[30] *The Guillotines* hybridised state-of-the-art 3D effects with martial arts. 'The action sequences are seriously stylized affairs, featuring speed changes, explosions, smouldering glares and a curiously high-tech take on the flying guillotine'; they were so spectacular that the film was called the Chinese version of *Transformers* (2007).[31] The director kept his promise of bringing something new to the *wuxia* genre with his scientific, hi-tech treatment of the mechanics of the flying guillotines, which was very much in line with Peter Chan's *Dragon*.

As Andrew Lau was a fan of Edward M. Zwick's *The Last Samurai* (2003), he also put due emphasis on the last days of the flying guillotine as a lethal weapon in the film. Not only the weapon but also the youngsters who used it became victims of the social, political and even technological changes of the era: 'As Emperor Qianlong [who deemed the flying guillotines outdated] said in the film: "The flying guillotines kill people within ten steps, but a gun can kill beyond a hundred steps, a canon beyond a thousand steps".'[32] Perhaps not unlike the secret squad of assassins who killed with flying guillotines, Hong Kong cinema seemed to have seen the beginning of its end, and so Andrew Lau wanted to pay tribute to Hong Kong martial arts films by alluding to Chang Cheh's *Blood Brothers* (1973), the film on which Peter Chan's *The Warlords* is based: 'To pay tribute to the classic scene of dismemberment by five horses in *Blood Brothers*, I shot a similar scene using five bulls ... but it had to be cut because of its horrific goriness.'[33] Despite their genre-redefining attempts, *The Guillotines* and *Dragon* shared a similar fate of failing to make their due impacts on the mainland market. *The Guillotines* received a failing score of 4.6 on Douban, a Chinese social networking website, and received unpromising box-office receipts of RMB 71.72 million. The major reason behind the under-achievement of *The Guillotines* was that the wave of period *wuxia* actioners was already near its end, and this genre was simply not the director's speciality.

Andrew Lau then returned to Hollywood, co-directing with Andrew Loo the American action crime drama film *Revenge of the Green Dragons* in 2014. Although Martin Scorsese was the executive producer, this Chinese-American gangster drama set in New York was not successful enough to develop Lau's Hollywood career. In short, 'this crime drama wants to be a Chinese-American *Goodfellas*, but it ends up just looking bad'.[34] Lau then co-directed *From Vegas to Macau III* (2016), the third episode of Jing Wong's reboot of *God of Gamblers*, with Jing Wong, but apparently it was not a story that Andrew Lau would have chosen to tell. After reaching a relatively low point in his career, it was not sur-prising that he tapped the mainland market again, but it was quite unexpected that his new venture would begin with a main(land) melody blockbuster.

The Founding of a New Market

As mentioned in the introduction, it was a surprise when Andrew Lau was invited to direct *The Founding of an Army*, which was commissioned by the gov-ernment to commemorate the ninetieth anniversary of the founding of the PLA, especially given that the two previous similar main melody films, *The Founding of a Republic* (2009) and *Beginning of the Great Revival* (2011), were both directed by veteran mainland filmmakers Huang Jianxin and Han Sanping. As the final piece of the 'epic' trilogy of the Communist Party, *The Founding of an Army* had a special position in Chinese main melody films. It is also worthwhile noting that the first two instalments featured a number of Hong Kong film stars, such as Jackie Chan, Leon Lai, Andy Lau and Donnie Yen in *The Founding of a Republic*, and Nick Cheung, Yun-Fat Chow, Tony Ka-Fai Leung and Simon Yam in *Begin-ning of the Great Revival*. *The Founding of a Republic* and *Beginning of the Great Revival* were attempts to sing the main melody in praise of the Party through commercialised blockbusters,[35] and that a Hong Kong director took the helm of *The Founding of an Army* showed that something new was meant to be injected into the final episode. In *The Founding of an Army*, there were no more Hong Kong superstars,[36] as the main cast was studded with young mainland idols commonly known as 'little fresh meat' (similar to 'stud-muffin') to Chinese neti-zens, such as Han Geng, Lu Han, Oho Ou and Lay Zhang. Branded as 'the war film that has the best appearance value (physical attractiveness) in history',[37] the target audience of this final episode was largely young people, and this was arguably one of the major reasons Andrew Lau was commissioned to direct. Lau took this project very seriously. In an interview, he confessed that he had never tackled the subject matter of *The Founding of an Army*, and, having accepted the challenge, he used the strength needed to make four films in making that one:

> I spent two to three years on learning the history. I also spent time on deciding how to approach the subject matter. Even though it's a 'main melody film', the fact that they asked me to do it meant I had to bring my own style and sensibility to the film. So they gave me quite a lot of freedom. They foresaw that even a main melody film could be done by a commercial director, from a commercial point of view.[38]

Lau tried adding a touch of sensibility to this war film, such as with how Zhu De – later known as one of the Ten Marshals of the PLA – bit the bullet and left his young soldiers behind to fight till their death during the Sanhe Ba Battle. Unfortunately, his thoughtful effort was glaringly overshadowed by the star-studded but controversial cast.

'At one point, online promotional materials included posters that branded the Communist military heroes as Chinese *Avengers*, and claimed that the movie was as good as the best gangster films in Hong Kong.'[39] Andrew Lau's treatment of ambiguous identities in the *Infernal Affairs* trilogy was indeed not suitable for this staunchly patriotic film about the founding of the army of the people, but his experience in handling young idols in the *Young and Dangerous* series (and even *The Guillotines*) surely made his résumé stand out from those of other directors. Although the police and gangster theme could not be sung together with the main(land) melody, Andrew Lau's experience in *Infernal Affairs* could be applied to the bloody battle scenes in the film, the key theme of which was Mao Zedong's famous saying: 'Political power grows out of the barrel of a gun'.[40] In addition, Lau's mainland experience and collaboration with young idols accumulated from *The Guillotines* also benefited his main melody project. In short, the casting of this main melody film was both daring and problematic. On the one hand, these young idols could attract more young fans to watch a propaganda film that they normally would not be interested in; on the other hand, the choice of young idols to play the roles of well-known military leaders stirred up heated controversies.

It was actually quite common for war films to have all-star casts though. There were countless film stars in Hollywood war classics, from Fred Zinnemann's *From Here to Eternity* (1953), David Lean's *The Bridge on the River Kwai* (1957), Ken Annakin, Andrew Marton and Bernhard Wicki's *The Longest Day* (1962), Michael Cimino's *The Deer Hunter* (1978), Francis Ford Coppola's

Apocalypse Now (1979), and Oliver Stone's *Platoon* (1986) to Steven Spielberg's *Saving Private Ryan* (1998) and the like. Chinese war films were no exception. The Taiwanese 'main melody' films in praise of the Kuomintang (Nationalist Party), such as *Eight Hundred Heroes* (1975), directed by Shan-Hsi Ting, and *Victory* (1976), directed by Chia-chang Liu, also featured star-studded casts of handsome actors and beautiful actresses, such as Chun-Hsiung Ko, Brigitte Lin, Sylvia Chang and Han Chin in the former, and Chun-Hsiung Ko, Sylvia Chang, Ming-Lun Ku and Terry Hu in the latter. The problem with *The Founding of an Army* was that the young Chinese male actors, emulating the success of K-Pop idols, were mostly good-looking but feminine (unlike the masculinity of Chun-Hsiung Ko). One of the harshest criticisms came from Ye Daying, a film director and the grandson of Communist Party General Ye Ting, who attacked Oho Ou, who portrayed his grandfather in the film, as 'a sissy who can't even stand straight'.[41] Ye Daying made this accusation based on the fact that war films had long been dominated by masculine stereotypes.[42] It was rather unfortunate for the director because the trend of young feminine male idols, which was unfitting in the war film genre, was simply far beyond his control. Perhaps this was why Lau said in an interview that he liked the way he handled female characters in the film, such as in the sentimental scene in which Mao Zedong's wife, Yang Kaihui, bids farewell to her husband.[43] Ironically, the catchphrase in *The Storm Riders* mentioned earlier might also be applicable to this film: 'Succeed because of Wind and Cloud, and fail because of Wind of Cloud'. Both the success and failure of this film could be attributed to the strategy of using young idols to package the main melody war theme.

Actually, Andrew Lau was not inexperienced in dealing with politically sensitive issues, albeit in a different context. After Steven Spielberg resigned as artistic adviser to the Beijing 2008 Olympic Games in protest over China's failure to distance itself from genocide and human rights abuses in Darfur, Lau, in the capacity of the director of a short film promoting China's preparation for the Olympics, was asked to express his opinion about this. He responded by saying that he was very surprised at Spielberg's decision, because '[i]t's sports, it's not political'.[44] In the light of this, it was Andrew Lau's strategy to highlight 'history', not politics, in this main melody war film. He was very firm about treating history seriously:

> I will not tamper with history . . . some said I made a lot of money by shooting a main melody film and kowtowing to the Communist Party, and I never think about this. I have been making co-productions for many years.[45]

Be that as it may, the historical narratives of the Communist Party and of others are, of course, very different. In *The Founding of a Republic* and *Beginning of the Great*

Revival, for example, 'star cameos, gentle humor, and quotidian details operate alongside substantial political revisions of twentieth-century Chinese history'.[46] It was totally understandable that in a main melody film celebrating the PLA there would be little, if any, room for the director to tell the story in his own way. Because of this, there was not much the director could do about the lacklustre storytelling, which was another reason behind the far from impressive achievement of the film. Besides *The Founding of an Army*, there were two other main melody films released during the ninetieth anniversary of the founding of the PLA: *Wolf Warrior 2* (2017), directed by Wu Jing, and *The War of Loong* (2017), directed by Gao Feng. Despite having the most fitting title and theme to echo the anniversary, *The Founding of an Army* was totally eclipsed by *Wolf Warrior 2*, which broke the all-time box-office record in China. The poor performance of *The Founding of an Army* was starkly reflected at the box office: RMB 0.4 billion compared with RMB 5.6 billion for *Wolf Warrior 2*. This drastic difference should not be interpreted as the result of different directorial abilities. Despite being a main melody film, *Wolf Warrior 2* did not have the burden of history, and its exceptional success was something that could not be imagined by an orthodox main melody film, no matter how it was commercialised:

> While *The Founding of an Army* had to tread a precariously narrow line between the need to appeal to star-chasing millennials and to honor political orthodoxy, another movie, stripped from any obligation to historical accuracy, found a potent formula to launch itself into the stratosphere of Chinese blockbusters.[47]

Borrowing what Jacques Rancière astutely argued and applying it here – 'there is a stark political choice in art: it can either reinforce a radical democracy or create a new reactionary mysticism'[48] – the problem with *The Founding of an Army* seemed to have been its failed attempt to achieve the latter, either abroad or at home.

If Tsui Hark's *The Taking of Tiger Mountain 3D* (2014) invited the audience to trace the intertextual references between the main melody film and his previous representative works, without which they would not have been able to fully appreciate the undertones, the trace of *The Founding of an Army* remained at the technical level – it was unable to carry rich overtones beyond the main melody. In terms of execution, Andrew Lau showcased in *The Founding of an Army* his ability to handle spectacular war scenes, thanks to his typical, ingenious use of the camera. His experience in highlighting the images of the protagonists also benefited the characterisation, but owing to the mismatch between the 'little fresh meat' and the heroic figures they portrayed, the director could not effectively engage audiences, not even the younger ones. The effect of using a Hong

Kong director to sing the main(land) melody was much limited, I would argue, without the intertextual trace between the main melody film and his previous works. Apart from their highly professional execution, there were not many added values for using Hong Kong directors instead of mainland directors. That said, although *The Founding of an Army* did not meet, let alone exceed, expectations, it did pave the way for Andrew Lau's northern venture. His next film, *Kung Fu Monster*, a *wuxia* fantasy, was also a co-production of Beijing Polybona Film, Media Asia and Film Unlimited Production founded by Derek Yee. Once again, it was not the type of film with which Andrew Lau could make the best use of his cinematic skills, and owing to the lack of creative handling in this over-produced genre, the result was not promising at all. However, a new opportunity for him to direct another main melody film soon presented itself, and this time he had much more space to juggle his cinematic skills – in the new main melody genre of modern Chinese heroes.

The Captain with Chinese Characteristics

If *The Founding of an Army* was an unsuccessful Chinese version of *The Avengers* (2012), Andrew Lau avenged with *The Captain*. The following remark on *The Captain* succinctly summed up his film career before this main melody project:

> That it's also Lau's best directing effort in years says more about his recent poor choices than it does about this film's qualities. After such underwhelming movies as *Revenge of the Green Dragons*, *From Vegas to Macau III*, *The Founding of an Army* and *Kung Fu Monster*, the law of averages would suggest that the director is due for a rebound.[49]

The Captain was released together with two other main melody films, *My People, My Country* (2019) and *The Climbers* (2019), during National Day to celebrate the seventieth anniversary of the People's Republic of China. Raking in RMB 2.68 billion at the box office, *The Captain* joined the list of the top ten films of all time at mainland China's box office and ranked third in box-office receipts of Hong Kong directors in the mainland market – the first was RMB 3.65 billion for Dante Lam's *Operation Red Sea* (2018) and the second RMB 3.39 billion for Stephen Chow's *The Mermaid* (2016). *The Captain* was a very close second to the star-studded seventieth anniversary film *My People, My Country* – the title itself spoke volumes for its status as an 'official' tribute to the anniversary – helmed by seven famous mainland Chinese directors: Chen Kaige, Zhang Yibai, Guan Hu, Xue Xiaolu, Xu Zheng, Ning Hao and Wen Muye. It was surprising that Andrew Lau's new project completely overshadowed another new main melody genre film, the Chinese adventure drama *The Climbers*, directed by Daniel Lee from Hong Kong, and starring Wu Jing, who became a typical Chinese national hero after *Wolf Warrior 2* (2017), and internationally acclaimed actress Zhang Ziyi. Based on real stories, both *The Captain* and *The Climbers* belonged to a new kind of main melody film that upheld patriotism through 'ordinary' Chinese heroism. Touted as the first Chinese film about the two trips made by Chinese climbers to the summit of Mount Everest, *The Climbers* combined the biopic with the adventure genre, which itself incorporated elements of patriotism, as the catchphrase goes: 'climbing for our country, refusing to yield an inch'. Similarly, *The Captain* blended the biopic with the disaster genre, paying homage to real heroes who helped prevent a tragic disaster on a Sichuan Airlines flight. The unimpressive box-office takings and critical acclaim of main melody films such as *The Founding of an Army* showed that, having watched a greater variety of films from around the world, mainland audiences had higher demands, to borrow the words of Chris Berry, 'based on quite similar values and styles of filmmaking to those used in the West'.[50]

With a history almost as long as that of cinema itself, disaster films constitute 'a sufficiently numerous, old, and conventionalized group to be considered a genre rather than a popular cycle that comes and goes'.[51] After early examples, such as the Georges Méliès' 'docudrama' *Collision and Shipwreck at Sea* (1898) and the little-seen Italian silent film *The Last Days of Pompeii* (1913) (which, adapted from Edward Bulwer-Lytton's book, may have been 'the first attempt at a narrative'), the '1930s saw the first real wave of narrative disaster films from major Hollywood studios', and later, as 'film technology progressed, sound became commonly used, and special effects improved', filmmakers 'discovered a new, untapped source for terror – commercial airlines'.[52] Disaster films were ushered into their golden era in Hollywood in the 1970s, thanks to the success of the air-disaster classic, George Seaton's *Airport* (1970). Although Ronald Neame's *The Poseidon Adventure* (1972) and John Guillermin's *The Towering Inferno* (1974) skyrocketed higher in the box office, air-disaster films were very popular, and *Airport* had three sequels: Jack Smight's *Airport 1975* (1974), Jerry Jameson's *Airport '77* (1977) and David Lowell Rich's *The Concorde . . . Airport '79* (titled *Airport '80: The Concorde* in the United Kingdom and Japan). All in all, these films basically adopted the formula set up by William A. Wellman's *The High and the Mighty* (1954): 'a plane on a doomed course is piloted by a crew dealing with personal drama while the lives of some of the passengers are shown in flashback in order to give us reasons to care about their fates'.[53] *The Captain* can be seen as a derivative of this. Meanwhile, biopics 'have [also] been around since the beginning of cinema, with subjects in the silent era ranging from Florence Nightingale to Cleopatra, Abraham Lincoln, Napoleon, Benjamin Disraeli, and Jesus Christ'; although

> [t]hey have persisted in infuriating historians and film critics, for perpetuating falsehoods, for their formulaic nature, and in elevating ordinary individuals (actors) to stardom . . . Hollywood biopics have become routes to nominations for Best Actor/Actress category in the Academy Awards.[54]

With respect to elevating ordinary individuals to stardom (heroism), *The Captain* was also formulated with a similar blueprint.

Based on a real near disaster on a flight from Chongqing to Lhasa, *The Captain* depicted the heroics of a pilot who, like the 'Miracle on the Hudson' pilot, Chesley 'Sully' Sullenberger, miraculously landed his airliner, despite the shattered cockpit windscreen at 30,000 feet, somewhere over the Tibetan Plateau in May 2018. This high-in-the-sky thriller, hence called the 'Chinese answer to *Sully*',[55] echoed the main melody in a similar manner as *The Founding of an Army*, but the narrative here was free from the burden of the official history of the latter. Even more important, the official history in this film was dramatised, as the director and screenwriter wanted to highlight Chinese heroism and/as patriotism (more on this to follow). The 'based on a true story' tag gave the film a sense of verisimilitude, which also made the main melody that paid brazen tribute to real heroes in the end credits look less unabashed. The theme of *The Captain* was not different from other air-disaster films: 'a situation of normalcy erupts into a persuasive image of death'.[56] In regard to the plot, there was not much unexpected in this Chinese rendition of the genre, but the state-of-the-art CGI special effects polished the nerve-shredding emergency with awesome visuals, embellishing the commercialised main melody with spectacular representations of the near disaster. The following review underlined the enjoyable but formulaic, soulless plot of this nail-biter on the one hand, and may have sounded sweet to the Chinese film industry on the other: 'This brazenly manipulative but undeniably effective disaster movie is as corny as an industrial-sized bag of week-old popcorn but proves that the Chinese film industry really has entered the late stages of capitalist aesthetic degeneration.'[57] Indeed, the Chinese industry was not trying to produce a genre-(re)defining film with this main melody blockbuster.

Nevertheless, that Andrew Lau made an air-disaster film on a par with its Hollywood counterparts was considered a remarkable achievement of Chinese cinema. The original English title of this fascinating air-disaster drama was *Chinese Captain*, later changed to *The Captain*, while the literal translation of the Chinese title remained *Chinese Captain*. The 'de-Sinicisation' of the English title, which sounded less jingoistic, was a clever move to make it clear that the film was not an answer to Clint Eastwood's *Sully* (2016), nor was it a derivative of *Captain America* (2011). At the same time, it also tackled, albeit unintentionally, the problem that Rey Chow warned of, an old issue related to Orientalism:

> The use of 'Chinese' as a specifier signals a new kind of care and a new kind of attentiveness to the discursive imperatives ... In the name of investigating 'cultural difference,' ethnic markers such as 'Chinese' easily become a method of differentiation that precisely blocks criticism from its critical task by reinscribing potentially radical notions such as 'the other' in the security of fastidiously documented archival detail.[58]

Andrew Lau was commissioned to pilot *The Captain* mainly because the objectives of the film were to use heroism to echo the main melody in a commercially attractive mainstream genre film. In this sense it was an air-disaster biopic. However, the production team reiterated in an interview that the film was not meant to be an answer to *Sully*, and apparently, the main melody was one of the most important factors behind this.[59] *Sully*, like most Hollywood blockbusters, developed dramatic tension with the conflicts between the individual and the institution, a plot not welcomed in Chinese cinema, let alone main melody films. One of the greatest challenges for the director was arguably how to let the charisma of the captain (portrayed by Zhang Hanyu) permeate in the face of danger on the one hand, and the professionalism of the aircrew shine through on the other. Moreover, the team spirit of a series of government institutions, such as the Southwest Regional Administration of the Civil Aviation Administration of China and the Aviation Division of the Western Theater Command of the PLA Air Force, was also highlighted in the film. It was a collective effort that prevented the disaster, so to speak. As underlined by Yu Dong, President of the production company Polybona Films:

> Over the years Polybona has continued to tell Chinese stories, convey Chinese messages, promote Chinese spirit, and showcase Chinese style. *The Captain* unfolds the unity and professionalism of Chinese aviation, the professional attitude that respects lives, rules, and responsibilities. This is the de facto Chinese spirit.[60]

In the end, Andrew Lau successfully delivered what was promised, as evidenced by the fact that the film was hailed by official media, such as *China Daily* and CCTV, as 'a disaster film with Chinese characteristics' that 'focus on the spirit and professional integrity of the crew in defiance of the danger'.[61] The director handled the obligatory main melody in an ingenious manner, saving part of the nationalistic refrain for the end in the form of an epilogue – the end credits included photos of the actual crew and statistics about Chinese aviation's exceptional safety record. There were also other required elements for the main melody biopic, and so Andrew Lau had to spend the first thirty minutes or so taking care of realistic details, such as mini-biographies, control rooms, safety inspections and weather forecasts. Thanks to his expertise in cinematography, his adroit use of the camera made these otherwise uninteresting or even unpleasant scenes acceptable. Another strategy worth mentioning is his treatment of the passengers. Given that the feelings as well as panic of the passengers cannot but be part of the formula of disaster films, clichéd subplots such as scenes about loved ones (e.g., the captain's wife waiting anxiously) are inevitable. Knowing very well that not much could be done with these themes in this main(land) melody film, Andrew Lau simply aimed to achieve minimal compliance with the rule, as the main(land) melody must be about institutions, not individuals, and he even diplomatically let passengers (such as an aged soldier visiting his deceased comrade and a reunited Tibetan family) share responsibilities to echo the main(land) melody. Having fulfilled the major requirements, Lau could turn his attention to what he is best at: going all in on action, with stunning sequences that made the audience collectively hold its breath, reminding veteran fans of typical air-disaster films such as the *Airport* series. 'Unfortunately, the criticisms of Lau being a proponent of style over substance are fully in evidence here too though,' as noted by a film reviewer:

> When coupled with a co-director who has the grit needed to rein in Andrew Lau's excesses, great things can be accomplished – the *Infernal Affairs* trilogy was a perfect example of this. *The Captain*, however, was Lau in his subtle-as-a-sledgehammer-to-the-face mode here and has no-one to pull him back to the story.[62]

This is a reasonable criticism, but, as I see it, a bit wide of the mark for a main(land) melody film. Andrew Lau was neither good at nor interested in Eastwood's slow-paced, nuanced plot development in *Sully*, as it was simply not possible to put the emphasis on the story with *The Captain*, such as with flaws in the air traffic investigation in *Sully*.

Concluding Remarks

Andrew Lau recalled that when Yu Dong approached him in September 2018, he was a bit intimidated by the very short deadline for the film's release. Perhaps the tight deadline and the firm release date (on the eve of the seventieth anniversary of the PRC on 1 October 2019) were some of the reasons behind asking a highly effective director to take the helm of this main melody film. Some aspects of this based-on-a-true-story film could not be handled fast though. For the sake of authenticity in his fictionalisation of the true story, the director asked the actors 'to talk to real-life prototypes of their roles to get deeper understanding and knowledge of their personal lives and their work'.[63] Moreover, he was determined to introduce something very Andrew Lau into this main melody project. The main setting was of course the aircraft. 'People told me to make the inside of the plane wider because it would be easier to shoot, but I insisted on the plane design being similar to that of the real aircraft,' Lau told *China Daily*, and despite this he managed to use his expertise as an experienced cinematographer to complete the shoot in the narrow space inside the plane.[64] Thanks to rattling shots, fast editing, visual effects and narrative momentum, this nail-biter moves with such a breath-taking pace that the audience does not have time to linger on any particular scenes. At times, the audience doesn't even have a chance to focus on anything except screaming, so to speak. There may be minor blunders, but 'windscreen aside, the brisk editing doesn't linger on anything long enough for the cracks to show'.[65] All in all, I think Lau can take the following remark as a compliment: '*The Captain* is another propaganda film, albeit a more or less tolerable one given that it's also a very good disaster film.'[66]

It is not without reason that Andrew Lau has been hailed as 'perhaps the most representative Hong Kong director in the post-Handover era'.[67] His *Young and Dangerous* and *Infernal Affairs* projects are among the most successful series in post-handover Hong Kong cinema. Not unlike Peter Chan, he did begin to falter a bit in his pan-Asian and Hollywood ventures. It then took him some time to translate his directorial and cinematographic talents into the mainland market. For someone who was versatile enough to be among the very few who could work closely with Kar-Wai Wong and Jing Wong, it was not difficult for him to regather momentum after his initial backfires. Interestingly, the literal translation of the Chinese title of the first film in which Andrew Lau participated, *Legendary Weapons of China*, is *Eighteen Kinds of Weapons*, meaning different kinds of martial arts/weapons. It seems that Lau is an all-rounder who is good at all kinds of film work/genres. He is prolific compared with Peter Chan and Ann Hui, and, more notably, able to handle different genres, moving 'between art films and commercial features throughout his career'.[68] With his keen commercial filmmaking instincts, he successfully packaged the main melody with a mainstream commercial genre: '*The Captain* has all of the director's trademark love of slick style; the film is as polished as any of the Hollywood blockbusters it aspires to.'[69] *The Captain* also proved Andrew Lau's ability to make a commercially attractive genre film that fulfilled main melody requirements, especially with a very tight schedule (one year). The effectiveness of Hong Kong directors is clearly one of their most important edges. It was reported that Andrew Lau immediately started to prepare the script and study the special effects after accepting the challenge; shooting started on 3 January 2019, and it just took three months to complete the whole project. 'Usually a film like this would take two years to shoot and make, including the postproduction period, which normally takes a year,' Lau said.[70] Despite the tight schedule, he managed to accomplish his task, and in reality, Captain Andrew Lau also made a safe and sound landing for his mainland career flight.

It has long been the major goal of China's film industry to produce mainstream genre films that can lure not only local but also overseas audiences. Towards this end, the case of Andrew Lau and *The Captain* can be seen as successfully killing two birds with one stone. Of course, this main melody air-disaster biopic was not the first of its kind in China. *Emergency Landing* (1999), directed by Zhang Jianya, was also an air-disaster film based on the real story of the forced landing of a China Eastern Airlines flight in 1998. It was also enhanced by CGI special effects, but back then the technology of the Chinese film industry was of course lagging far behind that of Hollywood. However, this was not the most significant difference between the two films. In 2014, there was a similar film, *Last Flight*, directed by Vincent Zhou. Adapted from a novel by Singaporean writer-cum-actress Megan Tay and starring English actor Ed Westwick, this supernatural air-disaster actioner, enhanced by 3D special effects, set its target at the international audience, but in the end, it was not well received, even by the local audience. Remarkably, *The Captain* did well at the box office in Singapore, second only to Todd Phillips's Hollywood blockbuster *Joker* (2019):

> Singaporeans have 'started to embrace the concept of a China movie block-buster' and are not just limited to watching Hollywood movies. The success of *The Captain* and other Chinese films in the box office is a testament to this trend.[71]

More recently, Andrew Lau was commissioned to direct the ground-breaking main melody medical humanities blockbuster *Chinese Doctors* (2021), a tribute to the centenary of the founding of the Party as well as to the Chinese doctors who fought selflessly and valiantly against the Covid-19 pandemic. Although there is still a long way to go before commercial Chinese films can draw crowds in the West, there are signs that overseas markets are not unreachable, and the Hong Kong director should take major credit for this. Comparing *The Founding of an Army* with *The Captain*, however, it is safe to conclude that mainstream Hong Kong directors such as Andrew Lau are better at singing the main(land) melody in commercial blockbusters without the burden of orthodox historical narratives. While they have managed to commercialise obligatory propaganda in creative ways, for something as official as *The Founding of an Army*, it was just too ideological to handle.

Notes

1. Cited from an interview with Andrew Lau: 'Self-learning and Goal-setting, Shining Bright: Andrew Lau Our Senior' (in Chinese), 〈自學立志，散發光芒：劉偉強學長〉, *Lingnan Secondary School Newsletter* 《嶺南中學校園通訊》 29, 2015.

2. The three co-founders had different versions of the founding of the company and its inaugural work: they co-founded the company in 1995, and the inaugural work was the first episode of *Young and Dangerous* (it was listed as the work of Jing's Production Limited though), or they co-founded the company in 1996 and the inaugural work was the third episode; see Wei Junzi 魏君子, *Spindrift in Light Shadow: Contextual Memories of Hong Kong Films* (in Chinese) 《光影裏的浪花：香港電影脈絡回憶》 (Hong Kong: Chunghwa, 2019), 386.

3. Wei Junzi 魏君子, 'New Navigation Marks' (in Chinese) 〈新航標〉, *Sina Entertainment*, 22 November 2012: <https://ent.sina.cn/film/chinese/2012-11-22/detail-iawzunex5998715.d.html?from=wap>; last accessed 1 May 2021.

4. Wing-Chung Fan 范永聰, *We Grew Up Reading Hong Kong Comics This Way* (in Chinese) 《我們都是這樣看港漫長大的》 (Hong Kong: Fei Fan Book, 2017), 117; see also Wendy Siuyi Wong, 'The History of Hong Kong Comics in Film Adaptations: An Accidental Legacy', in *The Oxford Handbook of Adaptation Studies*, ed. Thomas Leitch (New York: Oxford University Press, 2017), 398–9.

5. Martha P. Nochimson, *Dying to Belong: Gangster Movies in Hollywood and Hong Kong* (Malden, MA, Oxford and Victoria: Blackwell, 2007), 163.

6. Ibid., 85. 'The most extensive comments to be found on *Young and Dangerous* are at <http://www.chinesecinemas.org/young.html>. This website contains an extensive history of the films which finishes with a statement that the series may be more ambitious than was at first thought.'

7. See Chung-tai Li, 'From Lawlessness to Lawfulness: Representation of Law and Order in Andrew Lau's *Young and Dangerous* Series', MPhil thesis, the University of Hong Kong, Hong Kong, 2017.

8. Yiu-Wai Chu, *Lost in Transition: Hong Kong Culture in the Age of China* (Albany: SUNY Press, 2013), 95–6; Sek Kei, 'The Wrong Positioning of *Young and Dangerous*' (in Chinese), *Ming Pao*, 13 June 1998, C11.

9. Kwai-Cheung Lo, *Chinese Face/Off: The Transnational Popular Culture of Hong Kong* (Champaign: University of Illinois Press, 2005), 101.

10. Ibid.

11. Mairi Mackay, 'Pick the Best Asian Films of All Time', CNN, 23 September 2008: <https://edition.cnn.com/2008/SHOWBIZ/Movies/08/12/asiapacific.top10/index.html>; last accessed 1 May 2021.

12. Gina Marchetti, *Andrew Lau and Alan Mak's Infernal Affairs: The Trilogy* (Hong Kong: Hong Kong University Press, 2007).

13. See, among others, Wing-Sang Law, 'The Violence of Time and Memory Undercover: Hong Kong's Infernal Affairs', *Inter-Asia Cultural Studies* 7:3 (2006): 383–402; Allan Cameron and Sean Cubitt, 'Infernal Affairs and the Ethics of Complex Narrative', in *Puzzle Films: Complex Storytelling in Contemporary Cinema*, ed. Warren Buckland (Chichester: Wiley-Blackwell, 2009), 151–66; and Marchetti, *Andrew Lau and Alan Mak's Infernal Affairs*.

14. Marchetti, *Andrew Lau and Alan Mak's Infernal Affairs*, 12, 37.

15. Yiu Fai Chow and Jeroen de Kloet, 'Flânerie and Acrophilia in the Postmetropolis: Rooftops in Hong Kong Cinema', *Journal of Chinese Cinemas* 7:2 (2013): 140, 146–7. Actually, the directors made ingenious use of local settings in Hong Kong; for the key locations in this film, see, for instance, Kevin Ma, 'Where *Infernal Affairs* Was Filmed in Hong Kong', *Discovery: Cathay Pacific Inflight Entertainment*, 19 February 2019.

16. Janet Ng, *Paradigm City: Space, Culture, and Capitalism in Hong Kong* (Albany: SUNY Press, 2013), 26; as pointedly asked by the author: 'Is there a Hong Kong identity deeply buried beneath this nationalist narrative to be excavated or is Hong Kong merely glass and steel and what their glossy surfaces reflect?'

17. Editor, 'Ten Years of Infernal Affairs' (in Chinese) 〈《無間道》十年〉, Hong Kong Film Critics Society: <https://www.filmcritics.org.hk/taxonomy/term/7/101>; last accessed 1 May 2021.

18. Gina Marchetti, 'Departing from *The Departed*: The *Infernal Affairs* Trilogy', in *Hong Kong Culture: Word and Image*, ed. Kam Louie (Hong Kong: Hong Kong University Press, 2010), 150. The author writes: 'In fact, Lau's signature moving camera may not be so far removed from Scorsese's own sense of movement on the "mean streets" of New York City.'

19. Such as Marchetti, 'Departing from *The Departed*', 147–67; Li Jinhua, 'From *Infernal Affairs* to *The Departed*', *CineAction* 93, Spring 2014: 29–35; Martin Lüthe, 'Hellish Departure? The Departed, Infernal Affairs and Globalized Film Cultures', *Remakes and Remaking: Concepts – Media – Practices*, ed. Rüdiger Heinze and Lucia Krämer (Bielefeld: Transcript.Verlag, 2015), 81–96; Panos Kotzathanasis, '6 Reasons Why *Infernal Affairs* Is Better Than *The Departed*', *Taste of Cinema*, 5 February 2017: <http://www.tasteofcinema.com/2017/6-reasons-why-infernal-affairs-is-better-than-the-departed/>, last accessed 1 May 2021; Li Wanlin, 'A Cross-Cultural Comparison of *Infernal Affairs* and *The Departed*', *Style* 52(3), 2018: 321–44.

20. 'In Brief: My *Infernal Affairs* Is Better Than Scorsese's says Lau', *The Guardian*, 10 October 2006.

21. Lisa Odham Stokes and Rachel Braaten, *Historical Dictionary of Hong Kong Cinema* (2nd ed.) (Lanham, MD: Rowman and Littlefield, 2020), 252.

22. Kwai-Cheung Lo, *Excess and Masculinity in Asian Cultural Productions* (Albany: SUNY Press, 2010), 55–6.

23. Helen Hok-sze Leung, 'Love in the City: The Placing of Intimacy in Urban Romance Films', *A Companion to Hong Kong Cinema*, ed. Esther M. K. Cheung, Gina Marchetti and Esther C. M. Yau (Malden, MA: Wiley-Blackwell, 2015), 274.

24. Leung, 'Love in the City', 276–7. Worse still, 'many critics and audience members were offended by its treatment of Hong Kong, both as a city and as a "character" embodied by Peiyu initially'. See also the two references made by Leung: Ka-Ming Chan 陳嘉銘, 'Won't Let You Be Alone, Won't Let You Be Underserving' (in Chinese) 〈不再讓你孤單, 不再讓你高攀〉, *Hong Kong Film* 《香港電影》 42, August 2011: 78–9; Siu-Wa Tang 鄧小樺, 'The Resurrection of the Hong Kong Girl' (in Chinese) 〈港女之轉生〉, *Hong Kong Economic Journal* 《信報》, 2 June 2011.

25. Mark Jenkins, 'In Booming Beijing, A Bad Girl Meets A Good Cop', NPR, 19 May 2011: <https://www.npr.org/2011/05/20/136394173/in-booming-beijing-a-bad-girl-meets-a-good-cop>; last accessed 1 May 2021.

26. Yvonne The, 'Andrew Lau: The Master Multitasker', *South China Morning Post*, 23 December 2012.

27. Edmund Lee, 'Andrew Lau on *The Guillotines*', *Time Out Hong Kong*, 19 December 2012–1 January 2013, 79.

28. Ibid.

29. Bai Ying 白瀛, 'Director Andrew Lau Disclosing the Eye-Catching Points of *The Guillotines*' (in Chinese) 〈導演劉偉強揭秘《血滴子》看點〉, Xinhua Net, 20 December 2012: <http://politics.people.com.cn/BIG5/n/2012/1220/c70731-19962553.html>; last accessed 1 May 2021.

30. Lee, 'Andrew Lau on *The Guillotines*', 79.

31. Tim Youngs 'The Guillotines', Far East Film Festival Udine 2020: <https://www.fareastfilm.com/eng/archive/2013/the-guillotines/?IDLYT=15535>; last accessed 1 May 2021. See also 'The Guillotines as if The Transformers' (in Chinese) 〈《血滴子》宛如「變形金剛」〉, @movies, 22 December 2012: <http://app2.atmovies.com.tw/news/NF1212221600/ >; last accessed 1 May 2021.

32. Siu-Pan Ho 何兆彬, 'The Guillotines: Say Goodbye to Double Boiled Winter Melon Soup' (in Chinese) 〈血滴子：跟冬瓜盅說再見〉, *Apple Daily*, 20 December 2012.

33. Ibid.

34. Jordon Hoffmann, '*Revenge of the Green Dragons*: Movie Review', *New York Daily News*, 23 October 2014. Moreover, it was reported that Scorsese's participation was obviously minimal, and '[r]umor has it that Scorsese's involvement was merely a favor to Lau for his support in his film, *The Departed*, the American remake of Lau's blockbuster, *Infernal Affairs*'. Oneleaf, '*Revenge of the Green Dragons* (2014) Review', *City on Fire*, 21 January 2051: <https://cityonfire.com/revenge-of-the-green-dragons-2014-review/>; last accessed 1 May 2021.

35. For a detailed account of the two films, see Shenshen Cai, *State Propaganda in China's Entertainment Industry* (Abingdon and New York: Routledge, 2016), Chapter 2.

36. In that there are only minor roles played by Hong Kong actors, including William Chen, Alex Fong and Andrew Lau himself; for a full list of Hong Kong actors' and directors' participation in the three main melody blockbusters, see Sonny Shiu-Hing Lo, Steven Chung-Fun Hung and Jeff Hai-Chi Loo, *China's New United Front Work in Hong Kong: Penetrative Politics and Its Implications* (Singapore: Palgrave Macmillan, 2019), 300.

37. 'The War Film That Has the Best "Appearance Value"?' (in Chinese) 〈最高顏值戰爭片?〉, Chung T'ien Television News, 27 July 2017: <https://www.youtube.com/watch?v=-fmbXL1SBuE>; last accessed 1 May 2021.

38. Karen Chu, 'Hong Kong Director Andrew Lau on Not Being "Bored" by the Films He Makes', *The Hollywood Reporter*, 19 March 2018.

39. 'Soft Power, Hard Sell', *Chublic Opinion*, 18 September 2017 <https://u.osu.edu/mclc/2017/09/20/soft-power-hard-sell/>; last accessed 1 May 2021.

40. English translation Gucheng Li, *A Glossary of Political Terms of the People's Republic of China* (Hong Kong: The Chinese University of Hong Kong Press, 1995), 325.

41. 'Soft Power, Hard Sell'; see also 'Director Ye Daying Queries the Entertainmentization of *The Founding of an Army*' (in Chinese) 〈導演葉大鷹質疑《建軍大業》娛樂化〉, *M Time*, 25 July 2017: <http://news.mtime.com/2017/07/25/1571758.html>; last accessed 1 May 2021.

42. Ralph Donald and Karen MacDonald, *Reel Men at War: Masculinity and the American War Film* (Lanham, MD: Scarecrow Press, 2011), 41–112.

43. Hiu-Ling Tsang 曾曉玲, 'Skimming the Old Main Melody in *The Founding of an Army*' (in Chinese) 〈《建軍大業》撇去舊有主旋律〉, *Ming Pao*, 21 July 2017.

44. For more details, see Tom Scocca, *Beijing Welcomes You: Unveiling the Capital City of the Future* (New York: Riverhead Books, 2011), Chapter 14.

45. Tsang, 'Skimming the Old Main Melody in *The Founding of an Army*'.

46. Gina Marchetti, 'The Feminine Touch: Chinese Soft Power Politics and Hong Kong Women Filmmakers', in *Screening China's Soft Power*, ed. Paola Voci and Luo Hui (Abingdon and New York: Routledge, 2018), 233.

47. 'Soft Power, Hard Sell'.

48. Jacques Rancière, *The Future of the Image* (London: Verso, 2007), from the publisher.

49. Edmund Lee, '*The Captain* Film Review: Andrew Lau Returns to Form with Air-disaster Movie Based on Real-life Accident', *South China Morning Post*, 17 October 2019.

50. Sarah Zheng, 'Xi Jinping Takes Leading Role in Hit Propaganda Film Extolling "Amazing" China', *South China Morning Post*, 4 March 2018.

51. Maurice Yacowar, 'The Bug in the Rug: Notes on the Disaster Genre', in *Film Genre Reader IV*, ed. Barry Keith Grant (Austin: University of Texas Press, 2012), 313.

52. Glenn Kay and Michael Rose, *Disaster Movies* (Chicago: Chicago Review Press, 2006), 2.

53. Nik Havert, *The Golden Age of Disaster Cinema: A Guide to the Films, 1950–1979* (Jefferson, NC: McFarland, 2019), 37.

54. Deborah Cartmell, 'The Hollywood Biopic of the Twentieth Century', *A Companion to the Biopic*, ed. Deborah Cartmell and Ashley D. Polasek (Chichester: Wiley-Blackwell, 2020), 89. Moreover, 'Oscar voters love them because the "based on a true story" tag gives them a veneer of seriousness, and because it's easy to judge whether or not the central impersonation is any good.' Ellen Cheshire, *Bio-pics: A Life in Pictures* (London and New York: Wallflower, 2015), 2.

55. Richard Kuipers, 'Film Review: *The Captain*', *Variety*, 18 October 2019: <https://variety.com/2019/film/reviews/the-captain-review-1203374961/>; last accessed 1 May 2021.

56. Yacowar, 'The Bug in the Rug', 313.

57. Leslie Felperin, '*The Captain* Review: Airline Disaster Nail-biter Plays by the Rules', *The Guardian*, 4 October 2019.

58. Rey Chow, *Writing Diaspora: Tactics of Intervention in Contemporary Cultural Studies* (Bloomington and Indianapolis: Indiana University Press, 1993), 6.

59. Ching Lee 李青, 'What's Left of the Hero besides the Audiovisual Impact?' (in Chinese) 〈視聽震撼之外，英雄還剩下什麼？〉, *HK 01 Weekly*, 25 October 2019: <https://www.hk01.com/周報/388609/中國機長-影評-視聽震撼之外-英雄還剩下什麼>; last accessed 1 May 2021.

60. 'Trailer of *The Captain* Exposed' (in Chinese) 〈《中國機長》曝預告〉, *Ifeng Entertainment*, 25 September 2019: <https://ent.ifeng.com/c/7qFrCh1XBya?_zbs_baidu_bk>; last accessed 1 May 2021.

61. Liu Yang 劉陽, 'National Day Films Highly Vigorous: *My People, My Country* and *The Captain* Performing Exceedingly Well' (in Chinese) 〈國慶檔活力旺：《我和我的祖國》《中國機長》等表現突出〉, *People's Daily*, 10 October 2019.

62. Andrew Saroch, '*The Captain*', *Far East Films: Reviews*, 7 April 2020.

63. Zhang Rui, 'Andrew Lau: Making an Air Accident into a Visual Roller Coaster', China.org.cn, 16 October 2019: <http://www.china.org.cn/arts/2019-10/16/content_75306468.htm>; last accessed 1 May 2021.

64. Li Yingxue, 'More Than a Safe Landing', *China Daily*, 4 November 2019.

65. Wendy Ide, '*The Captain*: Review', *Screen Daily,* 18 November 2019: <https://www.screendaily.com/reviews/the-captain-review/5144773.article>; last accessed 1 May 2021.

66. Sean Gilman, '*The Captain* (Andrew Lau, 2019)', *Seattle Screen Scene*, 17 October 2019: <https://seattlescreenscene.com/2019/10/17/>; last accessed 1 May 2021.

67. Ibid.

68. Gina Marchetti, *Andrew Lau and Alan Mak's Infernal Affairs: The Trilogy* (Hong Kong: Hong Kong University Press, 2007), 5.

69. Saroch, '*The Captain*'.

70. Li, 'More Than a Safe Landing'.

71. 'Disaster Film *The Captain* Sees Strong Performance in Singapore', *China Daily*, 22 October 2019.

Chapter 5

Stepping to the Fore: Dante Lam's *Operation* Trilogy

'When we struggle for life to the last breath, that breath is courage itself.'
— Dante Lam, *The Rescue*

Introduction

Compared with the directors discussed in the previous chapters, Dante Lam may be less experienced, but for a thorough study of Hong Kong directors' participation in main melody films, he cannot be left unexamined. Lauded as 'the flagship works of main melody action films',[1] his *Operation Mekong* (2016) and *Operation Red Sea* (2018) reaped both commercial success and critical acclaim. Similar to Andrew Lau, Dante Lam began his film career as an apprentice from below. He once said that he was a big fan of Hong Kong films when he was young, and he watched at least two films every week.[2] In 1985, when the twenty-year-old was looking for a summer job, he was not aware that he would find a life-changing one in the film industry. During his brief tenure as a trainee at an advertising company, some friends introduced him to Cinema City, one of the leading companies in Hong Kong's thriving film industry back then, and this changed his life as well as the history of Hong Kong cinema. That summer job gave him the chance to be involved in blockbusters such as *Aces Go Places IV* (1986), directed by Ringo Lam, but his role in the production unit was so minor that he did not even have to go to the studio. In the late 1980s, he had the opportunity to become the assistant of Gordon Chan, who later became his mentor as well as *Bo Le*. Lam accumulated precious experience in filmmaking during the heyday of Hong Kong cinema in the late 1980s and early 1990s, especially in Gordon Chan's blockbusters of various genres, such as Stephen Chow's undercover cop comedy *Fight Back to School* (1991), Jackie Chan's car-racing crime thriller *Thunderbolt* (1995) and Andy Lau's sci-fi romance *Armageddon* (1997). With the support of Gordon Chan, Lam made his directorial debut, *Option Zero*, in 1997, a typical police and gangster film which he later revitalised with a series of exceptional crime actioners in the new millennium. After a satisfactory but unexceptional debut, Lam co-directed with Gordon Chan *Beast Cops* (1998), another police and gangster film that won them the Best Director title at the 18th Hong Kong Film Awards. In this genre-bending thriller, the roles of the police and the gangsters were ambiguous, but they were not undercovers such as those in the *Infernal Affairs* (2002–3) trilogy.

The award-winning *Beast Cops* was arguably the biggest achievement in the first stage of Dante Lam's film career. He noted in an interview that his film career could be broadly categorised into three stages, the first stage being from *Option Zero* to *The Twins Effect* (2003).[3] Thanks to the success of *Beast Cops*, he had more opportunities shortly before and after the turn of the millennium. Prior to *The Twins Effect*, Lam had directed a variety of genres, and this first stage was quite promising in general, given the fact that Hong Kong cinema had started to decline at that juncture. Unfortunately, according to the director himself, he had a painful experience in the second stage of his career, when he was at a loss as to what to do and how to move forward. This stage was relatively short, but the two embarrassingly symbolic works made the director feel really bad: 'these films really sucked . . . I almost wanted to quit my film career'.[4] Lam understood very well that being a director was often an art of compromise, but the case of *Heat Team* (2004), starring Aaron Kwok and Eason Chan, was simply too hard to take, as the hard-core actioner (the literal translation of the original Chinese title was 'to charge and break through enemy lines') was mandated by investors to be repackaged into a comedy only two weeks before the film began shooting. 'I had only two options: to do or not to do. Given that all preparation has been done, it would be too difficult to abort the project . . . I was the one to blame, because I compromised and accepted reality.'[5] In 2006, Lam joined forces with Gordon Chan again, co-directing *Undercover Hidden Dragon*, which was a farcical parody of police and gangster films and directors such as Johnnie To and Andrew Lau. This became a farce in itself, as this was apparently not Lam and Chan's cup of tea, and, more tragically, police and gangster films were in fact Dante Lam's favourites. Gordon Chan went north after this fiasco, and Dante Lam took a short break and returned after two years with *Beast Stalker* (2008). As his fans could tell by the title, it was a loose sequel to *Beast Cops*, at least in terms of style, and he subsequently found the creative space he needed to develop his individual style in a series of creative treatments of the police and gangster genre in *The Stool Pigeon* (2010), *Fire of Conscience* (2010), *The Viral Factor* (2012) and *That Demon Within* (2014) (plus, the 2013 film *Unbeatable*, in which a middle-aged boxer cheered himself as well as the city up). In these psycho-actioners, Lam's signature – the psychological analysis of the dark side of the human mind – was almost everywhere.

Despite the decent achievements of these crime thrillers, the major trend for established Hong Kong directors was to eye bigger markets as the local one was continuing to shrink at that time. After his pan-Asian venture *To the Fore* in 2015, which was an innovative sports film genre attempt, Lam headed squarely to the mainland market. In 2016, the main(land) melody film *Operation Mekong* changed his film career, and his subsequent *Operation Red Sea* set a new record (the second-highest grossing Chinese-language film at the China box office at that time, and the seventh-highest grossing film of 2018 globally), making him the Hong Kong director with the highest box-office record in mainland China. Lam was awarded the Daniel A. Craft Award for Excellence in Action Cinema at the 17th New York Asian Film Festival (NYAFF), perhaps mainly because of the phenomenal success of *Operation Red Sea*. Nevertheless, his achievements were duly recognised at the ceremony, which praised his first psycho-thriller, *Beast Stalker*, as 'an instant modern classic when it was released in 2008', and '[s]ince then, Lam has been at the creative forefront of the action genre'.[6] Dante Lam's film career was shorter than that of the directors discussed in the previous chapters, but in terms of main melody films, he was the one who made history.

Finding a Viral Factor

Having worked with Gordon Chan on a series of police and gangster films, Dante Lam had amassed considerable experience before he chose the signature genre of Hong Kong cinema to make his directorial debut. *Option Zero* was about the G4 VIP Protection Unit (Section G, Division 4; commonly known as G4) of the Hong Kong Police Force. As evident in the English title of the film, this debut was in the same series as *The Final Option* (1994) and *First Option* (1996), directed by Gordon Chan with Dante Lam as the assistant director, crime action-ers involving the Special Duties Unit (commonly known as the Flying Tigers) of the Hong Kong Police Force. His debut film might not have been exceptional, but it was good enough to impress veteran film critics such as Shek Kei, who saw his potential with this film, one that injected new elements into the common Special Duties Unit genre: 'notwithstanding the formulaic plot, the timely cinematic sense, technological knowledge and human touch caught attention of the audience'.[7] His typical style of noir-tinged thrillers first surfaced in the award-winning *Beast Cops*, which was considered an outstanding collaboration of Gordon Chan and Dante Lam in the sense that the film stemmed from their collaborative projects *The Final Option* and *First Option*. More importantly, the interactions of the protagonists in *Beast Cops* can be seen in the light of similar relationships in the romantic comedy *Tom, Dick and Hairy*, produced by Gordon Chan and co-directed by Chi-ngai Lee and Peter Chan, whereas the violent noir underworld theme was more fully developed in Dante Lam's later works. The hopelessly equivocal distinction between hero and villain helped explore issues more philosophical than those of other anti-hero triad films, and through outrageously disgusting violence, the directors exposed the 'beast' logic of the noir world.

Notwithstanding the success of *Beast Cops*, Lam did not enjoy the luxury of young New Wave directors in the early 1980s, who had experimented with different styles and genres as the Hong Kong cinema market quickly expanded. He faced a mountain that was very difficult to climb at the beginning of the new millennium. Despite his take on his favourite police and gangster genre in *Hit Team* (2001), and a derivative in the crime comedy *Jiang hu: The Triad Zone* (2000), which was a stylised, parodic critique of Hong Kong action cinema similar to but much more successful than the later *Undercover Hidden Dragon*, Lam had to make numerous commercial films that were, in the end, critically and even commercially maligned, including banal romantic stories such as *When I Look Upon the Stars* (1999), *Tiramisu* (2002), *Love in the Rocks* (2004) and even the sex comedy *Naked Ambition* (2003), co-directed with Hing-Kar Chan. As mentioned above, Dante Lam considered *Heat Team* an embarrassing, if not humiliating, experience, probably because it was meant to be a hard-core police and gangster actioner – his favourite genre. As also mentioned, Gordon Chan went north after the miserable *Undercover Hidden Dragon*, but Dante Lam chose to stay in Hong Kong. Besides *Sparkling Red Star* (2007), an animated remake of the 1974 Chinese children's propaganda film, and *Storm Rider Clash of the Evils* (2008), an animated feature film based on the comic series *Wind and Cloud* (aka *Storm Rider*) by Wing-shing Ma, he did not direct any films for two years before *The Sniper* (2009), during which he had a chance to stop and think about what to do next. After that brief time off, he 'began to focus on storytelling and communication with the characters in his films'.[8] The release of *The Sniper* was unexpectedly delayed by the sex photo scandal of one of the male leads, Edison Chen, and *Beast Stalker* became his 'come-back' work.

Before the two *Operation* actioners, Dante Lam had already won international fame with his psycho-suspense thrillers, such as *Beast Stalker* and *The Stool Pigeon*. Although he did not win major personal awards with *Beast Stalker*, he did win the Best Director award at the Bucheon International Fantastic Film Festival in 2009, and the film caught international attention as Nick Cheung bagged a total of seven Best Actor awards, including from the 2009 Asia-Pacific Film Festival. Cheung's performance was enhanced by the director's emphasis on incisive characterisation on top of the strong visual impacts created by camera shakes and brisk editing, which mixed jittery sentiment and continued violence with psychoanalytical perspectives. In *Beast Stalker*, *The Stool Pigeon* and even *Fire of Conscience* (to a lesser extent due to the male lead, Leon Lai, who was arguably bound by his long-time idol image), Dante Lam fully developed the elaborated characterisation of (problem) cops and gangsters, and the extreme predicaments faced by both policemen and gangsters in his noir world. The powerful restlessness of Dante Lam's actioners reminded the audience of Ringo Lam's renowned *On Fire* series (*City on Fire* [1987], *Prison on Fire* [1987] and *School on Fire* [1988], as well as the later *Full Alert* [1997] and *Victim* [1999]).[9] 'He was my idol. The final massacre scene in my previous movie, *The Stool Pigeon*, was actually my salute to his film *School on Fire*.'[10] Lam acknowledged this when he expressed sadness over the death of Ringo Lam in December 2018. Stephen Teo's remark on Ringo Lam's *Full Alert* (called 'one of the darkest of films ever made in Hong Kong' by Teo), therefore, nicely applied to Dante Lam: 'Lam has succeeded in delineating a mood that comes as close to the inner despair of the darkest allegories of good versus evil in literature – and in half the time than [Michael] Mann's overblown *Heat*.'[11]

From *Beast Cops* and *Beast Stalker* to *The Stool Pigeon*, Dante Lam's films 'proffer bleak visions, wounded bodies and fatal endings tempered with fraternal bonds', to borrow the words of Esther Yau and Tony Williams in their introduction to Hong Kong 'neo-noir'.[12] Built around the notion of blurring the boundaries between good and evil, these films exposed a noir world in which the protagonists – be they cops or gangsters – faced an impasse in their utterly failed lives and tried fighting back, albeit in vain. In this sense, Lam's psycho-actioners did not try to depict typical psychopaths in noir thrillers[13] but, rather, fated, tragic characters in real life. In an interview before the release of *Unbeatable*, Lam made it clear that his films embodied a harsh view of life: 'We're living in a very cruel world. We try, but are always cruelly hit hard. Everyone is "baptized" by cruelty, and only after that one can reach a new realm in one's life.'[14] In this context, one of the films he made in the first five years of the new millennium, *Runaway* (2001), is especially worth mentioning (although *The Twins Effect* was obviously much more commercially successful, collecting HK$28.4 million at the box office). The main theme of this comic mimicry of gangsters is clearly expressed in the Chinese title, which means the opposite of 'no way out' in Chinese. In the midst of his ludicrous predicament, the fallen teddy-boy protagonist (portrayed by Nick Cheung) runs away from his enemies and finds himself in Phuket, where he is able to find an alternative way out in his life. As perceptively noted by film critic Fatmoonba, *Runaway* and *Unbeatable* are actually two sides of the same coin. The 'runaway' was found by Dante Lam, together with Nick Cheung, in this absurd world: in both films, they are actually trying to imagine what one has to do at the lowest point of one's life (more about *Unbeatable* to follow).[15]

With the support of Emperor Motion Pictures, his long-term collaborator, Dante Lam made a stunning attempt to demonstrate his ability to handle an action blockbuster with *The Viral Factor* in 2012. Lam was indeed not inexperienced in dealing with blockbusters; he was the assistant director of the big-budget *Thunderbolt* and *Armageddon*, and the director of *The Twins Effect*. *The Viral Factor* was a big-budget, high-concept film shot mainly in Malaysia and Jordan. Starring Hong Kong, Taiwanese and mainland stars (Nicholas Tse, Jay Chou and Michelle Bai, respectively), this was an ambitious project targeted at the pan-Asian market. Some of the fierce firearm and bomb scenes were genuinely spectacular, and this was probably the major reason Lam was later invited to helm *Operation Mekong*. However, *The Viral Factor* was widely criticised as lacking a subtle use of plot and characterisation, something that Dante Lam had shown he could achieve in his previous psycho-actioners. Surely this was not the only reason, but it was an important one in choosing to reunite with Nick Cheung in *Unbeatable* and *That Demon Within*. 'Director Dante Lam and actor Nick Cheung are a match made in cinema heaven',[16] a Hong Kong film critic noted. Even though this might have sounded a bit exaggerated, it nevertheless spoke volumes about the very creative synergy between the duo.

(Not) the Unbeatable

When *Unbeatable* was released in August 2013 in Hong Kong, the city was caught in a very unsettled atmosphere, owing to the escalating tension between Hong Kongers and mainlanders and the controversies related to universal suffrage in Hong Kong. Despite being a co-production, the sports drama, directed by Dante Lam, generated positive energy for Hong Kong people. In this story about an ageing boxer who tries to regain his lost pride at the lowest point in his life, Dante Lam underlined the importance of fighting back. Although he did not say it explicitly, as Derek Kwok and Clement Cheng did in their award-winning *Gallants* (2010), what he had in mind was the often-cited words of Sylvester Stallone in *Rocky Balboa* (2006):

> You, me, or nobody is gonna hit as hard as life. But it ain't about how hard you hit. It's about how hard you can get hit and keep moving forward; how much you can take and keep moving forward.

The catchphrase of *Unbeatable* was probably inspired by Rocky: 'You're in the rings. Don't be afraid. Once you fear, you lose.' In a sense, Dante Lam and Hong

Kong cinema per se were facing a similar predicament at that juncture. The theme of ageing was central to Hong Kong cinema, if not Hong Kong culture and society at large. Dante Lam's message was echoed by the male lead, Nick Cheung, who explained in an interview why he was determined to train hard to build a body with a rippled torso and bulging biceps at the age of forty-eight:

> . . . after people saw this body, it has made some citizens realize: if Ka-Fai Cheung [Nick Cheung] can have this body because of his determination, so can I. It has become a kind of 'Ka-Fai Cheung inspiration', and this impact has made me realize that I can also make some positive contribution to society. To me, that was unexpected.[17]

It was perhaps equally unexpected that the film not only effectively cheered Hong Kong people up, but was also well received in the mainland. *Unbeatable* premiered at the Shanghai International Film Festival in June 2013, where Nick Cheung won the Golden Goblet award for Best Actor with his outstanding performance in the film. Chosen as the opening film of the Hong Kong Film Festival, co-organised by Kino Arsenal and the Hong Kong Economic and Trade Office, Berlin, in May 2014, *Unbeatable* also won international recognition for the director.

The impasse of Hong Kong films, and the city per se, was a common theme in Hong Kong cinema in that special context, and it was precisely the subject of Pou-Soi Cheang's *Motorway* (2012). Let me briefly recapitulate what I have written elsewhere on the subject of this film.[18] Unlike other car-racing classics, *Motorway* set its main car chase scenes not on motorways but in small alleys; a sharp right-angle turn in a tight alleyway was one of the most spectacular scenes in the film. The '8000 rpm, 2 km/h' skill to spin the wheels like mad while inching 2 km/h is the secret to making the almost impossible 90-degree turn. Apparently, for the Hong Kong film industry to move forward, doing so at '8000 rpm, 2 km/h' was the key. In one of the most remarkable tyre-screeching scenes in the film, Anthony Chau-Sang Wong shows his mentee Shawn Yue, who is deeply frustrated by not being able to make the 90-degree turn, how to perform it. I have also argued that Cheang made thoughtful use of the mentor–mentee relationship and the '8000 rpm, 2 km/h' ace in the hole to underscore the philosophy of motoring forward: 'Don't let other cars distract you. Take control of your car. Focus on your own lane, and give all you got when you have the chance.' This heartfelt advice was made not only to the young cop but also to the Hong Kong film industry, if not to Hong Kong culture at large. In this sense, *Motorway* attempted to hybridise different genres by celebrating driving as martial arts, presenting the skill of car racing with grace, not with an adrenalin rush. The introduction of martial arts elements in the film was not just an attempt to cross genres. More importantly, it gave the director the opportunity to highlight the importance of inheritance and transmission with high-octane energy. In short, Pou-Soi Cheang made a beautiful attempt at showing how to go one's own way. Ironically, Cheang's next project after *Motorway* was *The Monkey King* (2014), a big-budget (reportedly around US$60 million) fantasy epic starring megastars Donnie Yen, Yun-Fat Chow and Aaron Kwok, followed by episodes 2 and 3. To quote the Chinese scholar and writer Qian Zhongshu, who was famous for his erudition as well as pointed cynicism, 'It is the price of wisdom, a trick life has played on the philosophy of life.'[19]

When Pou-Soi Cheang hazarded north to produce blockbusters, Dante Lam stayed in Hong Kong for his next project, *That Demon Within*, a further development of his previous psycho-actioners, in which the boundaries between good and evil were not only blurred but actually wiped out, as reflected by the line at the end of the film: 'there is always a spot of darkness in the human mind'. This psychodrama was inspired by the real story of Po-Ko Tsui, who was called 'the devil cop' (the literal translation of the Chinese title of the film) for robbing banks and killing his colleagues. Although Nick Cheung plays an important role as a robber in this film, the de facto protagonist is Daniel Wu as a cop who coincidentally transfuses blood to save Cheung, who is severely wounded in a police ambush. Subsequently, Wu continues to be troubled by his guilt and begins hallucinating Cheung as his alter ego. Unlike with Dante Lam's previous psycho-thrillers, the camera style and the overall aura of *That Demon Within* was less jittery, but the film was even more noir as the director stamped his personal mark by digging deeper into the psychological complexity of Wu, with an eye to exploring that demon within. The film was less well received than *Beast Stalker* and *The Stool Pigeon*, mainly because it looked 'clumsy', as the director tried taking on 'too many themes', and – more important perhaps – the emphasis rested on Daniel Wu, not Nick Cheung: '*That Demon Within* is a murky thriller that is clumsy in execution. Partly it is because the reliable Cheung takes a backseat to the less compelling Daniel Wu here.'[20] There was no denying that Dante Lam and Nick Cheung were perfect partners, as evidenced by their chemistry from *Runaway* to *Unbeatable*, but it was unfair to put the blame on Wu, because Cheung was admittedly in a better position – in terms of experience and character – to play the demon within. As the director wanted to deal more with psychological and even philosophical complexity in this film, his typical brisk shooting slowed down at times and zeroed in on Wu as the protagonist, with Cheung playing only his alter ego. By saying that Lam's psychodrama had turned philosophical, I mean that he was not satisfied with letting the protagonist's psychological complexity surface; he was on the verge of conveying the message that 'to conquer a demon one must become a demon'.[21] Noir is not just a style but the substance, so to speak. In this sense, *That Demon Within* was even darker than Lam's previous works, but for fans who enjoyed the turbulent aura of his action-ers, the spirit might not have been powerfully restless enough. Moreover, it was not without irony that *That Demon Within* was released in April 2014, a little more than five months before the Occupy Central with Love and Peace campaign (also subsequently known as the Umbrella Movement), which strived for genu-ine universal suffrage in Hong Kong. During the same period, *The Midnight After* (2014) also premiered in April, and one of the main themes of that dystopian noir film adapted from an internet novel was 'Hong Kong was lost overnight'. Hong Kong people were more concerned with the dystopian future of their city than the noir nature of the human psyche. Worse still, the Umbrella Movement had exerted a big impact on the image of the Hong Kong Police Force, which made Dante Lam's signature psychoanalysis of problem cops and gangsters almost a taboo.

It was therefore not surprising that Dante Lam picked up the sports film genre again in his next project, *To the Fore*, this time moving the spotlight on to young, handsome stars in his pan-Asian cycling film featuring Taiwanese Eddie Peng, Korean Si-won Choi and Chinese Canadian Shawn Dou. *Unbeatable* and *To the Fore* were both Dante Lam's attempt to develop a film genre not quite estab-lished in Hong Kong or Chinese cinema. A fan of cycling, he said that he had been thinking of making a cycling film since 2001 but had not had the chance to do so, as sports films were rare in Hong Kong:

> As a matter of fact, *To the Fore* has a strong relation with *Unbeatable* because the film received positive responses two years ago, I eventually managed to make the film that I have been longing for . . . The theme of *Unbeatable* is about how a middle-aged man faces his middle age crisis and reclaims his glory. After *Unbeatable*, I had a strong passion to make a film about teenagers pushing up their limits and overcoming their boundaries, dedicating for the team yet upholding one's belief.[22]

While boxing was quite a common theme in sports films, cycling was not a very popular genre in commercial cinema. Many well-known cycling films were documentaries, such as Jørgen Leth's classic *A Sunday in Hell* (1976) – hailed as the 'greatest cycling film of all time'.[23] *The Flying Scotsman* (2006), directed by Douglas Mackinnon and based on Scottish amateur cyclist Graeme Obree, was also a notable example of a cycling drama biopic. Ranked number eight by the American Film Institute's 100 Most Inspiring Movies of All Time, Peter Yates's *Breaking Away* (1979) was the only film related to cycling on that list.[24]

Written by cycling enthusiast Steve Tesich, who won the Academy Award for Best Original Screenplay, *Breaking Away* might have had a cycling theme, but it was largely a coming-of-age story about a cycling-obsessed teenager. The sports drama film about cycle racing, *American Flyers* (1985), directed by John Badham and also written by Tesich, was commonly seen as less successful than *Breaking Away*.[25] It was therefore a challenging task for Dante Lam, who wanted to present a new pan-Asian imaginary with this genre. The conflicts between individual and group goals, as well between friends, created the dramatic tension in *To the Fore*. The young, handsome stars were attractive indeed, and the shooting locations in the film, which spanned Asia – including Kaohsiung, Kenting, Wuling, Shanghai, Tenggeli (Inner Mongolia), Busan and Hong Kong – and Italy, were also spectacular. The racing scenes in this film enabled Dante Lam to showcase his talents in handling actioners. However, fans of Dante Lam found the cycling races across Asia more like footage from sports and/or travel channels. In the end, the film received a total of RMB 145 million at the box office, which was not outstanding by mainland standards. In terms of critical acclaim, this new endeavour did not win any major awards and lagged significantly behind *Unbeatable*.

In a cycling race, 'breakaway' means that 'a single-rider or, more usually, a group of riders, breaks away from the main pack, taking the lead in an effort to win the race, often referred to as going off the front'.[26] In *To the Fore*, Dante Lam foregrounded the similar, but different, tactic of 'the lead-out':

> . . . the process in which a rider, most often a team's designated sprinter, is strategically 'delivered' to the finale of a race by his team-mates in optimum condition, to be able to execute his speciality: an explosive sprint for the victory.[27]

In other words, the exhausted lead-out man moves aside and lets his team-mate race in the final sprint. In a sense, Lam was trying to 'break away' from the local Hong Kong market to enter the pan-Asian market. In the end, not unlike his chosen focus on the team spirit of the lead-out, *To the Fore* really became 'the lead-out film' that strategically delivered him into a good position to sprint towards the mainland market. This film might not have been a genuine breakthrough for Dante Lam, but it did pave the way for his subsequent big-budget, high-concept main melody projects. Moreover, Lam reunited with Eddie Peng in *To the Fore*, who played a supporting role in *Unbeatable*, and since then Peng has replaced Nick Cheung as his 'match made in cinema heaven'. Their collaboration shone even more brightly in the subsequent *Operation Mekong*.

The 'Northern' Operation

Although Dante Lam had successfully broken away and entered the mainland market with his main melody project *Operation Mekong*, he said that he made films according to his own feelings, and it did not have anything to do with whom he collaborated: 'I do not have main melody in my mind. I have made two already, but still do not know exactly what main melody means.'[28] Veteran Hong Kong producer John Chong, who worked with Andrew Lau on the *Infernal Affairs* series and Dante Lam on *Option Zero* and *Beast Cops*, explained why Hong Kong's top filmmakers chose to make Chinese propaganda films, underlining the entertainment factor:

> The Hong Kong film industry has always made the entertainment factor a priority, so Hong Kong directors are able to inject entertainment value into something that the Chinese audience is overly familiar with . . . Some Hong Kong directors might have reservations about directing propaganda-type films, but many of them have no baggage.[29]

Apparently, Dante Lam was among those who had no baggage. As the only 'post-1997' director – he made his directorial debut after the handover – discussed in this book so far, he explored the dark side of the human mind with restless action in his signature psycho-thrillers. 'There are many different roads to take to realize one's dream. Having long been creative and flexible, Hong Kong people should continue to make best use of their strengths,'[30] Lam maintained. With the psychological dimension de-emphasised, if not erased, his action fit nicely with the new genre of main melody war films. He touched on this in an interview at the NYAFF in 2018, saying that he felt more comfortable directing *Operation Mekong* and *Operation Red Sea* because they 'had more of an international scope, and used more of an international language, and they're both commercial films', and he could combine his own experiences of filming and the topics of the two films.[31] As argued in the previous chapter, Andrew Lau's *The Founding of an Army*, also a main melody war film, was not successful because it was difficult for a Hong Kong director to deal with the orthodox main melody of the People's Liberation Army. Inasmuch as praise should go to Dante Lam for his genuinely professional handling of war action, one of the reasons behind the success of the *Operation* series, as pointedly noted by Candy Leung, producer and Lam's long-term collaborator, was that the incidents did not happen inside mainland China:

> If you asked Dante to shoot a movie like how to build the army during Chairman Mao, that is out of our knowledge, because we come from Hong Kong. But speaking of *Operation Mekong*, it was about chasing a drug king,

and *Operation Red Sea* was a real story talking about the 2015 retrieval of the Chinese people coming back to China. So, both of them have the space for Dante *to use those incidents as a global language,* and then to combine with his experience and his technique in action films, it comes together perfectly well.[32]

Inspired by a real story known as the Mekong River Massacre in 2011, *Operation Mekong* tells the story of the patriotic mission of Chinese officers in the waters of the Golden Triangle, where gangs demand protection money from boats and/or hijack them to transport drugs. In the film, thirteen sailors on two Chinese commercial vessels are executed, and a group of elite narcotics officers led by Captain Gao (portrayed by Zhang Hanyu) is sent there to investigate what was reportedly the deadliest attack on Chinese nationals abroad in modern times.[33] Assisted by the intelligence officer (portrayed by Eddie Peng) and others, they find that the massacre was plotted by the notorious drug lord Naw Khar. What to anticipate in such a story is usually a series of dangerous and even deadly action scenes, the signature of Dante Lam. Under the shell of drug films (anti-drug being a main melody in itself), the main melody was actually patriotism. *Operation Mekong* was a message to the world, to borrow Chinese netizens' favourite *Wolf Warrior* (2015) tagline: 'Anyone who offends China will be killed no matter how far the target is'.[34] The film was praised by *Global Times,* China's national English-language newspaper under *People's Daily,* as follows: 'Patriotic films rarely become big box-office earners in China, yet *Operation Mekong* has defied the odds to become the surprise critical hit of the Chinese mainland's week-long National Day Holiday. It's secret? Plenty of action.'[35] As *People's Daily* is the official newspaper of the Central Committee of the Communist Party of China, this was official recognition. Equally important, the film won both critical acclaim and commercial success. Named Best Picture at the 31st Golden Rooster Awards, it brought in RMB 1.17 billion at the box office, becoming the sixth highest-grossing film in mainland China in 2016. In terms of its large-scale show of firepower, this illegal-drug actioner was categorically the most spectacular work of Dante Lam up to that point, and the director displayed his expertise in stunning action scenes.

In her review of *Operation Mekong,* Jessica Kiang made a very perceptive remark regarding the two ways in which Dante Lam handled the film:

Either the gravity of the real-life subject matter would see Lam suppress his trademark exuberance, last seen slightly defanged in cycling drama *To The Fore,* or he'd take vast liberties with the truth and deliver a slam-bam manhunt thriller . . . To the evident delight of the Chinese audience, who have made *Mekong* the No. 1 film in the region for the last two weekends running, Lam takes the latter route.'[36]

Mainland Chinese audiences, especially the younger ones, were not interested in subtle characterisation. A main melody film with a similar theme, *Extraordinary Mission* (2017), also helmed by Hong Kong directors (co-directed by Alan Mak and Anthony Pun), was much less well received than Dante Lam's work. Both films 'emulate *Wolf Warrior* in terms of the setting of the Golden Triangle', upholding nationalist expansion which 'by definition does not stop at the borders: China's millennial dream looms large over parts of the world'.[37] The review by Tim Youngs, programme consultant for the Far East Film Festival, on Mak and Pun's mission was intended to be complementary, but it also underlined the reason for its reduced popularity in mainland China:

> While *Extraordinary Mission* may lack the sheer sensationalism of last year's big actioner *Operation Mekong*, which also focused on mainland authorities tackling a Golden Triangle drug lord, the filmmakers instead follow a more character-driven thriller approach to draw on their strengths while trying something different.[38]

The sheer sensationalism of *Operation Mekong* was exactly the key to success for this main melody crime thriller. Mak and Pun and the screenwriter Felix Chong, who also penned the stories in the *Infernal Affairs* series, wanted to integrate the subtly ambiguous characterisation of *Infernal Affairs* into this main(land) melody project, but clearly they did not have the discursive space to do what they were good at. On the contrary, in *Operation Mekong* Dante Lam foregrounded sensationalism with his signature action, which merged well with the main melody, even though it was simply jingoistic patriotism. The plot was formulaic but meticulously calculated, climaxing in the jungle clash towards the finale. Spectacular action scenes, including everything from car chases to shopping mall combat, were perfectly timed to pin the audience to their seats. Meanwhile, although Lam also tried making the characters less flat by describing Zhang Hanyu's family affection and Eddie Peng's personal trauma, the subtleness of characterisation was by no means near that of his previous psycho-actioners. According to a mainland film critic, there was nevertheless a major breakthrough in this main(land) melody film: there was interrogation under torture (not allowed by mainland standards), and the heroes killed someone who did not deserve to be killed. Owing to this, Dante Lam said *Operation Mekong* should be considered an ordinary commercial film rather than a main melody film.[39] Whichever way, the plot and characterisation did not matter much, as it was designed to be a Hollywood-style action thriller, one which, in terms of production standards, was virtually on a par with its counterparts in the West. The audience, amazed by the spectacular action scenes, felt like they were watching a Michael Bay film, and 'if Benicio Del Toro were the male lead, the setting moved to Columbia, and China Airlines changed to American Airlines, this would easily become an American production' promoting Americanism.[40]

Mainland film critics, and even *Global Times*, agreed that *Operation Mekong* 'is much more effective than other patriotic films because it wraps its message in the veneer of the action genre' and, as movie critic Yuan Dengyu told the Party's newspaper, 'telling a story in a way that everyone enjoys is much better than simply beating people over the head with how they should love their country and party'.[41] Action-pack(ag)ed patriotism was welcomed by the mainland audience, but actually, 'if it makes for a breathlessly assaultive, vastly entertaining couple of hours, it can be discomfiting whenever there's a brief pause in the pelting gunfire and we glimpse the contours of the actual, flesh-and-blood tragedy'.[42] The film did not draw crowds beyond mainland China because those who did not buy into the patriotic, if not jingoistic, theme would certainly prefer a Michael Bay production, not its Chinese version. One just has to take a look at the box-office record to be convinced: *Operation Mekong* grossed a worldwide total of US$173,839,072, 99.22 per cent (US$172,477,764) of which was from mainland China.[43] Critics also compared *Operation Mekong* with Tsui Hark's *The Taking of Tiger Mountain 3D* (2014). Even though Dante Lam had adopted a strategy that was similar to Tsui Hark's version of a model drama, successfully turning 'a patriotic mission of Chinese armed security officers into one of the most accomplished action films of recent years', Lam's version required no prior knowledge 'to navigate this sprawling tale of a violent manhunt',[44] nor did it have the intertextual trace on Tiger Mountain (see Chapter 1) to produce subtle undertones: the only relatable role was the intelligence officer portrayed by Eddie Peng, who is 'saddled with a personal trauma and a major slice of coincidence – both Lam's signatures, you may say'.[45] However, Eddie Peng was not Nick Cheung, who had so many years of Hong Kong cinema experience under his belt, and Peng's reference was limited to *Unbeatable*. Perhaps the value added by Dante Lam's new favourite partner was mainly in his being young and handsome. In addition, interestingly, Peng gave Dante Lam the title 'the devil director',[46] which effectively accentuated the demanding verisimilitude of action in his films.

From Red Sea to Blue Ocean?

Both *Operation Mekong* and *Operation Red Sea* 'celebrate the military actions of the Chinese People's Liberation Army (PLA) in the overseas, and foster strong patriotic sentiments'.[47] Owing to the unexpected success of *Operation Mekong*, the same success formula was reproduced in *Operation Red Sea*, but with a massive escalation in terms of budget, action, sensationalism and the wolf warrior mentality. To borrow the words of the director, '*Operation Red Sea* is not just a film, but actually a national project. We were not making an ordinary film, but a film supported by the Chinese [People's Liberation Army] Navy!'[48] A 'gift' to commemorate the founding of the PLA, this Chinese military film was meant to 'show off confidence of nation and individuals', promoting patriotism by showcasing the strengths of China's naval force. 'China's naval force long lagged behind. But entering the second decade of the 21st century, China's overall maritime force has surpassed countries like Japan, the UK and France, and is even better than the US in some areas,' the Beijing-based naval expert Li Jie told *Global Times*, and therefore the Chinese government 'pays more attention to people's recognition of their homeland and how to generate pride in the nation'.[49]

Grossing a total of US$579.33 million – $575.85 million of which was in mainland China[50] – *Operation Red Sea* was just second to *Wolf Warrior II* in the all-time Chinese box-office record at that time (fifth as of May 2020). It was apparent that the main melody film was immensely popular in, but not beyond, mainland China (not in Hong Kong either, with a miserable box-office record of only US$1 million). However, as *Operation Red Sea* was jointly produced by Polybona and Hong Kong's Emperor Motion Pictures, the film was selected to be submitted by Hong Kong to the Academy Award for Best Foreign Language Film category for review, although the film said nothing about or for the Special Administrative Region. Notwithstanding this, to simply slam the choice as 'a transparent attempt to curry favour somewhere in Beijing'[51] may be missing the most important point. To submit a film having to do more with the mainland than Hong Kong was not unprecedented. *Raise the Red Lantern* (1991), directed by Zhang Yimou, was submitted by Hong Kong and nominated to compete at the 64th Academy Awards back in 1991, not to mention that Mandarin films were often selected to represent Hong Kong before the rise of local Cantonese films in the 1970s. The selection of *Operation Red Sea* was, of course, linked to the expansion of China's role in the global order, related to not just its military power but also its soft power to make films. If I may borrow Chris Berry's point when he asked, 'If China Can Say No, Can China Make Movies?'[52], *Operation Red Sea* arguably proved that China has begun to learn how to increase its soft power by making movies. Admittedly, the film was part of a series of Chinese main melody films that had shown that 'the Chinese military begins to play an important role in overseas rescues and UN peacekeeping operations'.[53] At the same time, however, *Operation Red Sea* proved that, with the expertise of a Hong Kong director who had masterminded breathless spectacles (in terms of production quality, I consider *Operation Red Sea* higher than that of *Wolf Warrior II*), China made main melody films on top of films that helped to make China. Called 'China's *Black Hawk Down*',[54] *Operation Red Sea* aimed to tell the world that China could make movies, and more importantly, not just Michael Bay spectacles of action in the style of his breathless filmic worlds constructed by extraordinary production budgets,[55] but also Hollywood-style commercial war films that could churn box-office returns by promoting patriotism. Therefore, *China Daily* stressed that *Operation Red Sea* was called by the NYAFF website 'a major breakthrough in action cinema' and 'a nonstop barrage of shootouts, deadly hand-to-hand combat, high-powered chases and nail-biting suspense'.[56] In addition, Dante Lam also successfully convinced his audience that, unless they found Americanism less propagandist than Chinese nationalism, a Chinese main melody war film could be entertaining. In this sense, although *Operation Red Sea* had attracted local but not global audiences, it reminded them that Hollywood blockbusters were entertaining simply because one did not pay attention to what America was trying to say.

Adapted from a real story, *Operation Red Sea* let the Chinese Navy flex its muscles through an operation during the 2015 Yemeni Civil War. After the Dragon Commando, the Special Forces of the PLA's Navy Marine Corps, completed their mission of rescuing hostages kidnapped by pirates in Somali, they were sent to Yemen for their dangerous mission. On top of the evacuation of nearly 600 Chinese nationals and 225 foreigners from Aden, the southern port of Yemen ('Yewaire' in the film), the Commando also had to prevent terrorists from seizing nuclear weapons. Different from *Operation Mekong*, Dante Lam's new operation held 'not a single Chinese will be left behind' as its mission. According to Major General Ji Mingkui, former Director of Education at the PLA's National Defence University:

> As China gains a greater voice in international affairs, China's approach to economic globalization is also eliciting an enthusiastic response. Changing times are giving the Chinese military brand new missions – it must protect China's overseas interests, support economic cooperation among nations, safeguard the security of China's overseas enterprises and the rights of overseas Chinese, and carry out evacuation when they find themselves in danger. At the same time, the Chinese army must shoulder a series of international duties, including peacekeeping, combating pirates, sea rescue, and maintaining maritime order.[57]

This nicely summed up the mission of *Operation Red Sea* as a main melody military film. Strictly bound by this theme, Dante Lam had even less room to showcase his cinematic skills. In the eyes of mainland critics, however, *Operation Red Sea* ingeniously 'discards the propaganda-laden historicism we are so used to seeing in traditional Chinese war movies': 'instead of stirring battle scenes, we witness death and suffering in its naked, terrifying reality. Instead of infallible generals and invincible heroes, we follow a cohesive unit of soldiers taught to treat war with a studied coldness.'[58] In other words, from the mainland perspective, death and suffering in its naked, terrifying reality were the factors that made Dante Lam stand out. Thanks to the astronomical budget and the support of the Chinese Navy, the director, whose hands were tied by the plot, managed to further enhance the verisimilitude of actions in his film by devising 'the bloodiest and most propulsive battle scenes ever allowed on mainland screens (in Hong Kong the film was classified for over-18 audiences)'.[59] 'The devil director' wanted to make everything real, not just real-looking:

> I'm interested in reality, in real things, for my movies, I want everything to be as real as possible . . . in a regular action movie, when you throw a hand grenade, what happens on screen is not what happens in real life – there's no huge explosion, bodies don't go flying through the air. I try to show what really happens.[60]

With the support of the Chinese Navy as well as the Moroccan Royal Guard (from arms and ammunition to tanks), the military scenes were excruciatingly nerve-racking, designed by the director as a backdrop against which heroic acts in tragic situations were portrayed. Despite military support, there were certainly many difficulties in shooting big scenes with huge setups in Morocco, a place with which the director and his crew were not familiar. It was the flexibility of the Hong Kong director that counted: 'Candy and I had to both be very flexible in our problem-solving.'[61] On the face of it, this was not a Hong Kong film because the film featured a mainland cast (except for a minor role played by Simon Yam), but in fact, in addition to the director and his long-term collaborator and producer Candy Leung, the production team included many Hong Kongers, such as co-screenwriter Ming-Kit Lam and film scorers Elliot Leung and Edmond Fung. Not unlike *Operation Mekong*, *Operation Red Sea* put the emphasis on the production of the action scenes, not characterisation, and perhaps because this film highlighted the Chinese Navy, no psychological ambiguity of individual characters was allowed. Therefore, it is fair to say:

> The physically capable cast, boasting illustrious backgrounds in military, martial arts or dance, all look indistinguishably rugged, but feeble attempts to give them touching moments, such as a soldier feeding candy to a jawless comrade, instead can play like an unintentional gag.[62]

And this was perhaps also the reason Dante Lam did not need any Hong Kong film stars, not even Eddie Peng, in this epic main melody war film. All in all, as rightly noted by Laikwan Pang, 'It is probably a commercial decision more so than a political decision to trust a Hong Kong director with this important "main melody" project,'[63] and the commercial decision proved to be well made, at least in terms of box-office returns.

Operation Red Sea has made Lam the highest-grossing Hong Kong director in Chinese-language cinema to date. His remarkable success proved that a Hong Kong director was capable of shooting a main(land) melody war blockbuster with overt political messages similar to those in *Wolf Warrior*. In this sense, the red sea did become a blue ocean in terms of market development, creating new demand by opening up a new space for Hong Kong directors and Chinese main melody films. However, despite being the highest-grossing film of a Hong Kong director, *Operation Red Sea* was still unable to go beyond the domestic market, as 99.4 per cent of the box-office returns were generated by mainland China, with an almost negligible 0.3 per cent from the US and, even worse, 0.18 per cent from Hong Kong.[64] Nevertheless, with the remarkable success of *Operation Red Sea* gracing his résumé, Dante Lam moved on to the third operation with a reported budget of RMB 700 million, totally unimaginable for a Hong Kong director. Well known for his unwillingness to use CGI, Dante Lam opted to shoot scenes on expensive real-life sets for *The Rescue* to help the actors become immersed in their characters.[65] Without an exceptionally big budget – even in terms of a Chinese main melody blockbuster – this would not have been possible. Originally scheduled to premier during Chinese New Year in 2020, the release of *The Rescue*, like Peter Chan's *Leap*, was delayed due to the coronavirus outbreak. When the pandemic situation became less serious in China, cinemas reopened in July after a six-month closure. *The Rescue* finally hit cinemas in December 2020, raising the curtain on a brand-new movie season in 2021. As this book focuses primarily on main melody films in the 2010s, I will not dwell at length on it here. Nevertheless, by way of conclusion, a brief look at the third operation of Dante Lam's main(land) melody venture will shed further light on the foregoing discussion in this chapter.

Concluding Remarks

Touted as a film that 'brings Chinese bravery to big screens' by *Global Times*,[66] *The Rescue* was meant to be a love letter written by the director to China Rescue & Salvage (CRS), a paramilitary force that had yet to receive due attention in Chinese cinema. Lam told *China Daily* that he had decided to make a main(land) melody film about this organisation in the Ministry of

Transport, which is responsible for the security of navigation, shipping and seamen in Chinese waters, because he was 'instantly hooked' after he saw a six-minute clip of a documentary about marine rescue and salvage in 2014: 'It was extremely dangerous and I really admired the courage of the rescuers. It felt so thrilling to see the destructive power of nature, which I realized I could easily paint as the ultimate "villain" in a movie.'[67] With nature as the 'villain' of the film, *The Rescue* was more ambitious than the two previous operations, as the director was no longer content with sheer sensationalism. As Laikwan Pang plainly underlined, 'These Hong Kong-trained male directors are given projects of such high dosages of adrenaline, which are then be [*sic*] properly contained by the patriotic ideology.'[68] Dante Lam seemed to be trying to inject something other than adrenaline into this episode of his main(land) melody operations. Generally seen as another Michael Bay-esque big-budget action drama packed with explosions and screaming ('mostly along the lines of "Live, dammit, live!" and "Don't give up on me, man, don't give up"'), *The Rescue* showed that Dante Lam wanted to induce genuine differentiation on top of specialisation in this 'explosive popcorn disaster movie'.[69]

Even though the film proved the director's ability to handle Bay's typical high-octane action, Dante Lam had no intention of emulating Bay's cinematography, which 'has heavily relied on camera perspectives that are so shaky in nature that even viewers who are able to halt the flow of images find it difficult to say what they see in the first place'.[70] As evidenced by the choices of Peter Pau as a cinematographer (*Crouching Tiger Hidden Dragon* [2000]) and Martin Laing as a production designer (Art Director of *Titanic* [1997] and *Pearl Harbor* [2001]), although Dante Lam's cameras swirled in and around the action, he wanted to let the audience see the spectacles clearly. Fans who did not like CGI would certainly have enjoyed the four jaw-dropping scenes in the film: a flaming offshore oil rig, a landslide near a raging river, a plane's emergency landing as it crashes into the water and a sinking tanker about to explode. These disasters were carefully set to manifest CRS's amazing commitment to maritime rescues and salvaging, as well as the director's capability in mastering high-octane action scenes with giant sets. The four major scenes were certainly the high points of this main melody disaster blockbuster, which promoted, if not propagandised, the bravery of CRS as well as Chinese officials. Because of the nature of the duties of CRS, the 'action' in the film centred around the rescue function rather than law enforcement: 'In that sense, *The Rescue* lacks the gun battles that pumped Lam's prior works full of adrenaline, but still contains daring rescues and demonstrations of bravery.'[71] Fans of *Operation Red Sea*, however, were disappointed, as reflected by the unpersuasive 6.3/10 score on Douban (compared with 9/10 for *Operation Red Sea*), and the box-office returns of RMB 0.44 billion were unacceptable (compared with RMB 3.65 billion for *Operation Red Sea*), falling far behind Han Yan's *A Little Red Flower* (2020), a romantic drama starring young idol actor Jackson Yee, and Herman Yau's *Shockwave 2*, a crime thriller that premiered during the same period (box-office returns for both films were over RMB 1 billion). As noted in a film review written by a Chinese audience member, this could have been attributed to the lack of Dante Lam's trademark in *The Rescue*: 'insanely over-the-top action'.[72] This may be a fair comment, but it has to be stated that the 'trademark' referred only to Lam's two previous operations in mainland China.

As mentioned above, from *Beast Cops*, *The Stool Pigeon* and *That Demon Within* to *Unbeatable*, Dante Lam built his own signature style with actioners about the psychological analysis of the dark side of the mind. It was indeed impossible to deal with the darkness of the human mind in a main melody blockbuster about Chinese bravery, but, without a 'villain' except nature, the director chose to create dramatic tension with his characters. While *Operation Red Sea* – because its main theme was the Chinese Navy – did not allow the director to probe into the psychological ambiguity of individual characters, there was more flexibility for him in *The Rescue*. Therefore, different from the immaculately professional crew in *The Captain* (2019), the team in *The Rescue*, especially the male lead Eddie Peng, looked more like 'ordinary' people open to various feelings and emotions. As apparent from the Douban reviews, fans did not buy the non-action scenes. For example, as a film blogger said, 'Director Dante Lam wanted to prove that people who did not appreciate his non-action scenes were wrong, but in the end he did the opposite. His non-action scenes are lousy.'[73] This was indeed an unfair comment that had not taken into consideration Lam's track record. It should not have been surprising that characterisation in a main melody film could not take on internal psychological conflict such as seen in *The Demon Within*; nor was it possible to have a thorough and extensive account of a fallen character such as in *Unbeatable*. Although the characterisation of Eddie Peng as a single dad coping with loss may have been cookie-cutter,[74] and the struggle between looking after his son after surgery and performing a rescue mission may have looked a bit cheaply sensational, these aspects of character were meant to depict the rescue team members as human beings when they were back on land. The emphasis on the female pilot (portrayed by Xin Zhilei) could also be considered an innovative move in the trilogy, as the two previous operations focused exclusively on brave men. Sadly, though, the audience, especially those in mainland China, simply expected more lavish action and sensationalism out of Dante Lam, such as in *Operation Red Sea*. The 'human' plots in the film were undeniably thin (probably because it was politically incorrect to put too much emphasis on the ambivalence of human characters in a main melody film that promoted bravery), but that was arguably all Dante Lam could do. In the end, they were believed to be out of place, looking particularly awkward when juxtaposed with his breath-taking action scenes. One of the major related reasons was the clichédly predictable plot. Without a well-designed plot it was difficult, if not impossible, to build the characters. It was an open secret, however, that there was a formula with which every main melody film had to stick.

In terms of box-office returns and even review scores, *The Rescue* was indeed far from successful compared with the two previous operations. Its unconvincing performance may have been partly attributed to the fact that it was not very timely for the film to premier when China and the world was heavily hit by the coronavirus pandemic – a similar natural disaster. However, besides fulfilling the minimum requirement of beating Patty Jenkins's *Wonder Woman 1984* (2020), which premiered on the same day, at the box office in mainland China, it also received some positive reviews, which are especially worth mentioning in the sense that the film was compared with those of Michael Bay: 'This Michael Bay-esque love letter to China Rescue & Salvage may be propaganda, but its enjoyably bonkers melodrama and grippingly engaging action are a lot less obnoxious than any film Bay has made.'[75] Contrary to the comment that *The Rescue* had sunk into worn-out domestic clichés, proving that Dante Lam was simply not good at non-action scenes, the film evinced the experiment of the Hong Kong director to make Chinese main melody blockbusters go global. Although 'the aesthetic cut that separates consequences from intentions and prevents their [*sic*] from being any direct passage to an "other side" of words and images' could not be avoided, Dante Lam had, in a sense, been able to, borrowing Jacques Rancière's words about film's power, 'rework the frame of our perceptions and the dynamism of our affects' and 'open up new passages for political subjectivation'.[76] Unfortunately, there was no simultaneous release in cinemas in other parts of the world because of the pandemic. It remains to be seen whether Chinese main melody blockbusters will be able to go global, but it would be reasonable to conclude that Dante Lam's third operation, together with Andrew Lau's *The Captain*, have brought a new trend of disaster films to Chinese main melody films.

Notes

1. Shen Jiequn 沈杰群, 'Dante Lam the Director of *The Rescue*' (in Chinese) 〈《緊急救援》導演林超賢〉, *The China Youth Daily* 《中國青年報》, 21 January 2020: <http://media.people.com.cn/BIG5/n1/2020/0121/c40606-31557663.html>; last accessed 1 May 2021.
2. Freddie Wong 黃國兆 (ed.), *A Compendium of Hong Kong Film Directors, 1979–2013* (in Chinese) 《香港電影導演大全 1979–2013》: <http://www.hkfilmdirectors.com/zh-hk/director/lam-dante>; last accessed 1 May 2021.

3. An Dong 安東, 'Dante Lam: I Don't Have Main Melody in My Mind' (in Chinese) 〈林超賢：我心中沒有主旋律〉, Sina Entertainment 《新浪娛樂》, 2 October 2018: <http://ent.sina.com.cn/m/c/2018-10-02/doc-ihkvrhpr9627771.shtml>; last accessed 1 May 2021.

4. Ibid.

5. 'Main Melody, Positive Energy, Dante Lam' (in Chinese) 〈主旋律、正能量、林超賢〉, *Next Magazine* 《壹周刊》 1324, 24 July 2015.

6. 'Hong Kong Films Debut at New York Asian Film Festival', The Government of the Hong Kong Special Administrative Region Press Releases, 14 June 2018 <https://www.info.gov.hk/gia/general/201806/14/P2018061400464.htm>; last accessed 1 May 2021.

7. Shek Kei, '*Option Zero*: Dante Lam Worthy of Attention' (in Chinese) 〈G4特工：林超賢值得注意〉, *Reminiscences of Hong Kong Films in 1997* (in Chinese) 《1997香港電影回顧》: <https://www.filmcritics.org.hk/film-review/node/2015/06/22/g4-特工：林超賢值得注意>; last accessed 1 May 2021.

8. Wei Junzi 魏君子, *Sprays in Electric Shadows: Contextual Memories of Hong Kong Cinema* (in Chinese) 《光影裏的浪花：香港電影脈絡回憶》 (Hong Kong: Chunghwa, 2019), 624.

9. Law Kar, 'Hero on Fire: A Comparative Study of John Woo's "Hero" Series and Ringo Lam's "On Fire" Series', in *Fifty Years of Electric Shadows: Hong Kong Cinema Retrospectives*, trans. Stephen Teo (Hong Kong: HKIFF/Urban Council; 21st Hong Kong International Film Festival, 1997), 67–73.

10. 'Dante Lam Misses Chance to Work with Ringo Lam', *Cinema Online*, 2 January 2019: <https://www.cinema.com.my/articles/news_details.aspx?search=2019.n_dantemisschance_44810&title=Dante-Lam-misses-chance-to-work-with-Ringo-Lam>; last accessed 1 May 2021.

11. Stephen Teo, 'Sinking into Creative Depths: Hong Kong Cinema in 1997', in *Hong Kong Panorama 97–98* (Hong Kong: Provisional Urban Council; Hong Kong International Film Festival Society, 1998), 11–13.

12. Esther C. M. Yau and Tony Williams, 'Introduction: Hong Kong Neo-Noir', in *Hong Kong Neo-Noir*, ed. Esther C. M. Yau and Tony Williams (Edinburgh: Edinburgh University Press, 2017), 4. For an elaborated account of the different meanings of Hong Kong noir, see Kim-Mui E. Elaine Chan, *Hong Kong Dark Cinema: Film Noir, Re-conceptions, and Reflexivity* (Cham: Palgrave Macmillan, 2019).

13. For an informative account of psychopaths in noir thrillers, see Lee Horsley, *The Noir Thriller* (Basingstoke and New York: Palgrave Macmillan, 2001), 119–24.

14. 'Interview: Director Dante Lam' (in Chinese) 〈專訪導演林超賢〉, *Mtime*, 19 August 2013: <http://news.mtime.com/2013/08/07/1515973-6.html>; last accessed 1 May 2021.

15. 月巴氏 Fatmoonba, *Romantic Fatmoonba Watching Old Movies* (in Chinese) 《浪漫月巴睇舊戲》, 23 August 2013: <http://fatmoonba.blogspot.com/2013/08/blog-post_23.html>; last accessed 1 May 2021.

16. Edmund Lee, 'Nick Cheung and Dante Lam Are Near the Peak of Their Creative Power', *South China Morning Post*, 16 April 2014.

17. Edmund Lee, 'Body of Work: Nick Cheung on His Physical and Professional Trans-formation', *South China Morning Post*, 15 August 2013; see also Yiu-Wai Chu, *Found in Transition: Hong Kong Studies in the Age of China* (Albany: SUNY Press, 2018), 158.

18. Chu, *Found in Transition*, 124–5.

19. Qian Zhongshu, 'On Happiness', trans. Zhu Liya, *Genre: Forms of Discourse and Culture* 43:3–4 (September 2010): 282.

20. Boon Chan, '*That Demon Within*: Clumsy HK Thriller Takes on One Too Many Themes', *Strait Times*, 16 April 2014.

21. Mandyrun, '*The Demon Within*: To Conquer a Demon One Must Become a Demon' (in Chinese) 〈《魔警》一抓魔，必先成魔〉, pixnet.net, 9 April 2014: <https://mandyrun.pixnet.net/blog/post/361781636>; last accessed 1 May 2021.

22. 'Q&A World Focus: *To the Fore* by Dir. Dante Lam', Tokyo International Film Festival 2015, 23 October 2020: <http://2015.tiff-jp.net/news/en/?p=9877>; last accessed 1 May 2021.

23. William Fotheringham, *Sunday in Hell: Behind the Lens of the Greatest Cycling Film of All Time* (London: Yellow Jersey Press, 2018).

24. *Breaking Away* is also the only cycling film included in Bruce Babington's study of sports films, *The Sports Film: Games People Play* (London and New York: Wallflower, 2014).

25. K. Edgington, Thomas Erskine and James M. Welsh, *Encyclopedia of Sports Films* (Lanham, MD, Toronto and Plymouth, UK: The Scarecrow Press, 2011), 15.

26. Ibid., 73

27. Joseph Caron Dawe, 'How a Leadout Works in Pro Cycling – And How You Could Benefit from It', Red Bull Content Pool, 16 August 2019: <https://www.redbull.com/gb-en/cycling-leadout-guide-how-it-works>; last accessed 1 May 2021.

28. Dong, 'Dante Lam: I Don't Have Main Melody in My Mind'.

29. Karen Chu and Patrick Brzesk, 'Why Hong Kong's Top Filmmakers Are Making China Propaganda Films', *The Hollywood Reporter*, 17 May 2017: <https://www.hollywoodreporter.com/news/why-hong-kongs-top-filmmakers-are-making-china-propaganda-films-1004572>; last accessed 1 May 2021.

30. 'Main Melody, Positive Energy, Dante Lam'.

31. Diva Vélez, 'New York Asian 2018 Interview: Hong Kong Action Legend Dante Lam and Producer Candy Leung Talk *Operation Red Sea*', *Screen Anarchy*, 18 July 2018: <https://screenanarchy.com/2018/07/new-york-asian-2018-interview-hong-kong-action-legend-dante-lam-and-producer-candy-leung-talk-operati.html>; last accessed 1 May 2021.

32. Ibid.; my emphasis.

33. Sally Huang and Michael Martina, 'Laos Extradites Suspect to China in Mekong Massacre Case', *Chicago Tribune*, 10 May 2012: <https://www.chicagotribune.com/lifestyles/ct-xpm-2012-05-10-sns-rt-china-mekongmurder-tvl4e8ga36l-20120510-story.html>; last accessed 1 May 2021.

34. '*Operation Mekong* Told the World: Anyone Who Offends China Will be Killed No Matter How Far the Target Is' (in Chinese) 〈《湄公河行動》告訴世界犯中華者雖遠必誅〉, *The China Youth Daily Online* 《中青在線》, 11 October 2016: <http://mil.news.sina.com.cn/china/2016-10-11/doc-ifxwrhpn9660250.shtml>;

last accessed 1 May 2021. English translation of the tagline Beijing Bureau, '*Wolf Warrior 2*: The Nationalist Action Film Storming China', *BBC News*, 4 August 2017: <https://www.bbc.com/news/blogs-china-blog-40811952>; last accessed 1 May 2021.

35. 'Patriotic Action Flick *Operation Mekong* Becomes Critical Darling during National Day Holiday', *Global Times*, 8 October 2016.

36. Jessica Kiang, 'Film Review: *Operation Mekong*', *Variety*, 22 October 2016: <https://variety.com/2016/film/reviews/operation-mekong-review-1201897197/>; last accessed 1 May 2021.

37. Sheng-mei Ma, *Off-White: Yellowface and Chinglish by Anglo-American Culture* (New York, London, Oxford, New Delhi and Sydney: Bloomsbury Academic 2019), 188.

38. Tim Youngs, '*Extraordinary Mission*', Far East Film Festival 22 Udine, 26 June–4 July 2020: <https://www.fareastfilm.com/eng/archive/2017/extraordinary-mission/?IDLYT=15535>; last accessed 1 May 2021.

39. '*Operation Mekong*: This Is a Major Breakthrough for Main Melody Films!' (in Chinese) 〈《湄公河行動》：這是一次「主旋律」電影的大突破！〉, *KK News*, 11 October 2016: <https://kknews.cc/entertainment/yajnm9g.html>; last accessed 1 May 2021.

40. 'Reflections on an American-style Made-in-China Drug Film' (in Chinese) 〈《湄公河行動》觀後感：「美」味國產緝毒片〉, Kazuohk Blogspot, 1 November 2016: <http://kazuohk.blogspot.com/2016/11/operation-mekong.html>; last accessed 1 May 2021.

41. 'Patriotic Action Flick *Operation Mekong* Becomes Critical Darling during National Day Holiday'.

42. Kiang, 'Film Review: *Operation Mekong*'.

43. Box Office Mojo: <https://www.boxofficemojo.com/title/tt6044910/?ref_=bo_rl_ti>; last accessed 1 May 2021.

44. Edmund Lee, '*Operation Mekong*: Dante Lam's Action-film Master Class', *South China Morning Post*, 5 October 2016.

45. Ibid.

46. Eddie Peng called Dante Lam 'Devil Lam' on Weibo after Lam won the 32nd Golden Rooster Best Director award with *Operation Red Sea*; '"The Devil Director" Dante Lam Famed at the Golden Rooster Awards' (in Chinese) 〈「魔鬼導演」林超賢揚威金雞獎〉, *Sky Post* 《晴報》, 25 November 2019.

47. Jieyu Liu and Junko Yamashita (eds), *Routledge Handbook of East Asian Gender Studies* (Abingdon and New York: Routledge, 2020), 324.

48. Chu Xiaohui 初曉慧, 'Dante Lam: *Operation Red Sea* Is Not Just a Film, But Actually a National Project!' (in Chinese) 〈林超賢：《紅海行動》不止是電影, 更是國家行為！〉, *Sina News*, 5 March 2018: <http://news.sina.com.cn/c/nd/2018-03-05/doc-ifyrztfz8024736.shtml>; last accessed 1 May 2021.

49. Wei Xi, 'Chinese Military Movie *Operation Red Sea* Shows off Confidence of Nation, Individuals', *Global Times*, 6 February 2018.

50. Box Office Mojo: <https://www.boxofficemojo.com/releasegroup/gr2180010501/?ref_=bo_rl_su>; last accessed 1 May 2021.

51. Elizabeth Kerr, '*Operation Red Sea*: Film Review', *The Hollywood Reporter*, 10 May 2018: <https://www.hollywoodreporter.com/review/operation-red-sea-honghai-xingdong-film-review-1149626>; last accessed 1 May 2021.

52. Chris Berry, 'If China Can Say No, Can China Make Movies? Or, Do Movies Make China? Rethinking National Cinema and National Agency', in *Modern Chinese Literary and Cultural Studies in the Age of Theory*, ed. Rey Chow (Durham, NC, and London: Duke University Press, 2000), 160.

53. Xi, 'Chinese Military Movie *Operation Red Sea* Shows off Confidence of Nation, Individuals'.

54. Stanley Rosen mentioned this in a seminar; Gerlinde Goschi, '*Operation Red Sea*', USC US-China Institute, 19 May 2019: <https://china.usc.edu/k12/forums/film-festival/operation-red-sea-0>; last accessed 1 May 2021.

55. See, for instance, Lutz Koepnick, 'World Cinema in the Age of Populism', in *Michael Bay: World Cinema in the Age of Populism* (Urbana, Chicago and Springfield: University of Illinois Press, 2018), 1–146.

56. Hong Xiao, 'Action Film Director Takes Top Honors', *China Daily USA*, 20 July 2018.

57. Ji Mingkui, '*Operation Red Sea* Reflects the Real Battle', *China Focus*, 1 March 2018: <http://www.cnfocus.com/operation-red-sea-reflects-the-real-battle/>; last accessed 1 May 2021.

58. Li Yang, 'Why *Operation Red Sea* Isn't Like Other Chinese War Movies', *Sixth Tone: Fresh Voices from Today's China*, 11 March 2018: <https://www.sixthtone.com/news/1001880/why-operation-red-sea-isnt-like-other-chinese-war-movies>; last accessed 1 May 2021.

59. Maggie Lee, 'Film Review: *Operation Red Sea*', *Variety*, 2 March 2018: <https://variety.com/2018/film/asia/operation-red-sea-review-1202710157/>; last accessed 1 May 2021.

60. Hong Xiao, 'Action Film Director Takes Top Honors'.

61. Vélez, 'New York Asian 2018 Interview'.

62. Lee, 'Film Review: *Operation Red Sea*'.

63. Laikwan Pang, 'Sexualizing Cinematic Border: Gender, Spectatorship and Citizenship in Hong Kong-Mainland Cinema', in *Routledge Handbook of East Asian Gender Studies*, 324–5.

64. Box Office Mojo: <https://www.boxofficemojo.com/releasegroup/gr2180010501/?ref_=bo_rl_su>; last accessed 1 May 2021.

65. Xu Fan, 'Hook, Line and Sinker', *China Daily Global*, 16 January 2020.

66. '"The Rescue" brings Chinese Bravery to Big Screens in China', *Global Times*, 22 December 2020.

67. Ibid.

68. Pang, 'Sexualizing Cinematic Border', 325.

69. MaryAnn Johanson, '*The Rescue* Movie Review: China's Coast Guard at Action-thriller Work', *Flickfilosopher*, 24 January 2020: <https://www.flickfilosopher.com/2020/01/the-rescue-movie-review-chinas-coast-guard-at-action-thriller-work.html>; see also 'Review: *The Rescue* Is an Explosive Popcorn Disaster Movie', *Yahoo Lifestyle*, 22 December 2020: <https://sg.style.yahoo.com/review-the-

rescue-explosive-popcorn-disaster-movie-200533311.html; both last accessed 1 May 2021.

70. Koepnick, *Michael Bay*, 25.

71. Richard Yu, 'Review: Dante Lam's *The Rescue* Glorifies China's Ascendant Coast Guard', *Cinema Escapist*, 29 December 2020: <https://www.cinemaescapist.com/2020/12/review-the-rescue-chinese-movie/>; last accessed 1 May 2021.

72. Daniel Eagan, 'Dante Lam's Action Spectacle *The Rescue*: Review', *Film Legacy*, 17 December 2020: <https://www.filmlegacy.net/blog/2020/12/17/dante-lams-action-spectacle-the-rescue-review/>; last accessed 1 May 2021. According to the reviewer, 'One shot that travels from a helicopter cockpit through the fuselage of a passenger jet sinking in the ocean and from there up and out over the rescue team spread out below gives an indication of how jaw-dropping Lam's vision can be.'

73. '*The Rescue*'s Box-office Tumble' (in Chinese) 〈《緊急救援》票房慘敗〉 published in *The Paper*《澎湃》, 24 December 2020; last accessed 1 May 2021.

74. As per Koepnick's analysis, the characterisation of Bay's heroes is similar: 'Bay's heroes, often against their own initial will or better knowledge, consistently find themselves in situations that ask them to ignore self-interest; forget about personal goals and allegiances; functionalize their adamant narcissism, self-centeredness, and stubborn egotism for ongoing acts of sacrifice; and in so doing rescue many lives unknown to them, at times even the future of the entire planet Earth. They always reside firmly in the present and have few outspoken commitments to pressing pasts and futures.' Koepnick, *Michael Bay*, 31.

75. Johanson, '*The Rescue* Movie Review'.

76. Jacques Rancière, *Dissensus: On Politics and Aesthetics* (London and New York: Bloomsbury Academic, 2015), 159.

Chapter 6

Underneath the Shock Waves:
The (Un)told Stories of Herman Yau

'Refusing to give up is what success is all about.'
— Stephen Chow and Herman Yau, *New King of Comedy*

Introduction

To shed further light on the development of the Hong Kong model (of film-making), it is necessary to have a flexible consideration of the idea of 'main melody' itself. Notwithstanding its diversification, the genre of main melody films must promote national rejuvenation and enhance the images of the nation, the Party and the Army. From a volleyball team to a pilot, the main melody has been played to win glory for the country. Owing to the continued commercialisation of Chinese cinema, however, some mainstream films with less overt political messages have also been produced to sing 'quasi-main melodies'.[1] Anti-crime topics, in general, are central in Chinese cinema; good and evil is a clear-cut dichotomy, and justice must be done in the mainland market. More specifically, anti-terrorist, anti-drug and anti-corruption have become key themes echoing the national rejuvenation project. It will be argued in this chapter that, besides propaganda works that paid tribute to the nation, the Party and the Army, those loosely defined 'quasi-main melody' films were also very important.

The flow of this chapter is a bit different from that of the previous five. In the previous chapters, I first sketched the trajectories of the directors' film careers in Hong Kong, based on which their main(land) melody projects were further discussed. In this chapter, I will begin with a main(land) melody film directed by Herman Yau in 2011, and then move on to his earlier projects before going back to his 'quasi-main melody' blockbusters towards the end of the 2010s. As mentioned in the Introduction, the main melody films that paid tribute to the 100th anniversary of the Xinhai Revolution in 2011 kick-started a new decade of main melody blockbusters. Besides Teddy Chan's *Bodyguards and Assassins* (2009) and Jackie Chan's *1911* (2011), Herman Yau's *The Woman Knight of Mirror Lake* (2011) was also an example of early pioneering main melody projects helmed by a Hong Kong director. Hong Kong film fans who knew Herman Yau well must have had ambivalent feelings about his participation in this co-produced film in commemoration of the centenary of the Xinhai Revolution: surprised because he was most well known for his cult horror films and B-list 'quickies', but not unexpected at the same time as he was arguably the most versatile Hong Kong director and could handle many film genres of different budgets with extreme efficiency. However, perhaps owing to the poor results of the film (probably due to copyright controversies; see below) and/or the fact that the blockbusterisation of main melody films had not yet become the main melody at the beginning of the 2010s, Herman Yau did not have the chance to direct main melody blockbusters after *The Woman Knight of Mirror Lake*.

Herman Yau is actually one of the most prolific directors in Hong Kong, with more than 100 works (as director, producer and/or cinematographer) spanning more than three decades since his directorial debut, *No Regret*, in 1987. Hong Kong managed to produce around 400 films a year in the early 1990s, so it was not so unusual to be so highly productive, but after the number dropped to less than 60 in the 2010s (including the loosely defined 'Hong Kong' films), it was an exceptional achievement to continue to be as productive as Yau, who remained very much central to the dwindling film industry in Hong Kong. He has long been considered a B-movie expert who has directed some cult horror classics, but more recently, his high-concept films have involved enormous production costs and amassed huge box-office totals. He is also well known in the industry as a stalwart technician, or 'the fireman', to borrow the term of renowned Hong Kong film titan Tsui Hark, 'for his ability to rescue troubled productions'.[2] Herman Yau was the de facto bomb disposal expert (the literal Chinese translation of his 2017 crime thriller *Shock Wave*) in the Hong Kong film industry, so to speak. Perhaps this was exactly why Stephen Chow invited him to be the associate director of *New King of Comedy* (2019), as he was not only exceptionally able and professional but also self-effacing. The shooting of *New King of Comedy* took just a month or so from start to finish, but to Herman Yau it was a very generous schedule – he managed to complete his award-winning *True Women for Sale* (2008) in nine days. As one of the most productive directors in Hong Kong during the past three decades, Herman Yau's contributions to Hong Kong cinema throughout the years, especially his 'daring to challenge authority and tackle sensitive subjects' with his 'bold choice of themes and extraordinary cinematography'[3], were duly acknowledged by his alma mater, Hong Kong Baptist University, which conferred on him an Honorary University Fellowship in 2019 in recognition of his outstanding support and contributions to society.

Herman Yau's works throughout the years are too numerous to discuss individually in this chapter. For the sake of brevity, let me use the period from 2016 to 2020 as an example, during which he mastered big-budget blockbusters, such as *Shock Wave* and *The Leakers* (2018), the gangster thriller *The Mobfathers* (2016), the psychological film noir *Nessun Dorma* (2016), the Category III extreme horror film *The Sleep Curse* (2017), the small-budget ghost story *Always Be with You* (2017), the romantic comedy *77 Heartbreaks* (2017) and the black comedy *Home with a View* (2019). It is simply amazing that he had three films – *Shock Wave*, *The Sleep Curse* and *77 Heartbreaks* – screened in the same period in 2017. He was also the executive producer of the cult thriller *G Affairs* (2018), the directorial debut of young talent Cheuk-Pan Lee. Shortly before the release of the blockbuster sequels *The White Storm 2: Drug Lords* (2019) and *Shock Wave 2* (2020), Yau juggled his packed schedule to take part in Stephen Chow's *New King of Comedy*, which had an extremely tight deadline as mentioned above. Apparently, he was not just versatile but also highly efficient. As Herman Yau has made a great variety of films in different genres as well as (quasi-)main melody films, his works can be used to shed light on reflections on the Hong Kong model of filmmaking raised at the beginning of this book.

The Woman Knight of Mirror Lake

A quick glance at Herman Yau's filmography would explain why *The Woman Knight of Mirror Lake* was a surprise for his fans. Well known for his cult horror films, social critiques and commercial 'quickies', main melody projects did not quite fall within his expertise. A co-production by National Arts Films Production Limited (Hong Kong), Mei Ah Culture Communication (Xian) and Roc Pictures (Zhejiang), this film was closely related to the Xinhai Revolution and can therefore be considered a main melody film. The film was about Qiu Jin, a feminist-cum-poet also known as the 'Woman Knight of Mirror Lake'. Arguably more importantly in terms of a main melody film, she was a revolutionist who fought and died for the Revolution that later overthrew the feudal monarchy. Given the subject matter of this Chinese period film, shooting in mainland China was necessary, and thus in the end this project became a co-produced film. A biopic about the feminist revolutionary had long been in Herman Yau's plan, but it was not until the 100th anniversary of the Xinhai Revolution that he had the chance to secure investors, as 'there was a variety of celebrations and activities in China and other overseas Chinese communities of the world'[4] and the topic fit nicely with the revolutionary theme of the main melody. *The Woman Knight of Mirror Lake* was not a genuine biopic, and similar to *Bodyguards and Assassins*, it was slanted towards martial arts action, probably because of the major trend of commercial considerations of mainland–Hong Kong co-productions back then. The director 'intentionally made the film with more action and packaged it as an action or martial arts film'; on the other hand, '[t]he screenwriter and I self-censored ourselves; we avoided in the screenplay all the "sensitive" materials, perspectives and issues that might have been unwelcome to the Chinese Government.'[5] From the perspective of commercialisation, it was indeed a reasonable strategy not to stick too much to historical events. Some fans liked the so-called '70% real and 30% fabricated' plot, seeing it as a flexible way to handle commercial main melody films.[6] However, some others, especially Qiu Jingwu – the grand-nephew of Qiu Jin (the grandson of Qiu Jin's elder brother) – thought differently. He vehemently condemned the film, which did not get his personal endorsement, as 'vulgar, tasteless and kitsch' because the fabricated plot turned Qiu Jin into a martial arts exponent.[7] This controversy almost derailed Herman Yau's project.

In fact, there were a number of films about Qiu Jin before Herman Yau's, and they had also tried to adopt creative ways to present the historical figure. Back in the Republican period, there was *Qiu Jin and Xu Xilin* (1948), directed by Mei Qian. While this could also be seen as a typical main melody film during Republican China, in which Qiu Jin frequently preaches revolutionary ideals, it also underlined the intimate relationship between Qiu Jin and her cousin Xu Xilin – as apparent from the English title of the film. Working closely in the Restoration Army, Qiu and Xu strived to overthrow the Qing Dynasty. This early version also placed significant emphasis on action. As 'Qiu Jin's story was not given particular prominence in the PRC until after Mao Zedong's death with the winding back of radical, revolutionary politics from 1978 under Deng Xiaoping',[8] it was not until 1983 that another film about Qiu Jin was released, helmed by renowned mainland director Xie Jin: *Qiu Jin: A Revolutionary*. Between the two there was actually another film about Qiu Jin entitled *The Fury of King Boxer* (1972) made by Taiwanese director Shan-Hsi Ting and produced by Hong Kong First Film Organization Limited. As one can tell from the English title, the film was actually an actioner rather than a biopic, although it did provide quite a comprehensive account of Qiu Jin's life. Qiu Jin was depicted as a martial arts heroine more than a revolutionary. Following the then major trend of the kung-fu genre, the film attended to the chivalrous more than the nationalist spirit.[9] Unlike the previous directors, Xie Jin, widely considered an auteur in Chinese cinema, wanted his film to be more poetic, and thus he chose to de-emphasise action in this biopic.[10] Xie Jin chose to pay special attention to historical 'facts' in that context, which was seen as a response to the Cultural Revolution during the early stage after the open-door policy, but in the end it was Xie Jin's film aesthetics rather than historical reality that attracted film critics' attention.[11]

Although Qiu Jin was a staunch feminist who had published many articles about gender equality and established the journal *China Women's News* in 1907, feminism was muted and patriotism amplified in *Qiu Jin: A Revolutionary* as much as in *The Woman Knight of Mirror Lake*.[12] In terms of the ecology of Chinese cinema, things had changed drastically by 2011. Given the structural changes in the film industry in mainland China, Herman Yau's 2011 version had many more commercial considerations. Louise Edwards made a perspicacious comparison between the two versions:

> Audiences of Xie Jin's 1983 film witness the intense training – ideological and physical – that went into crafting Qiu Jin as a soldier. These old communist values of striving hard to continuously improve one's skills are central to her success as a martyr in 1983. In Yau's 2011 film, audiences are told that she was a child prodigy – skilled in martial arts from an early age, naturally rebellious and filled with patriotic fervour.[13]

Similar to the mode of *The Founding of a Republic* (2009), Herman Yau's main melody version of Qiu Jin was also commercialised, with greater emphasis on martial arts action. Even though Yau was not famous for action films, action was the signature of Hong Kong cinema, and, arguably, the director's rock and roll spirit (he was a big fan of rock and roll) and cult style also gave a rebellious touch to the heroine in particular and the film in general.[14] Despite its slant towards action, the film was an ambitious attempt, as noted by Ma Lunpeng, to present the whole life of Qiu Jin with a non-linear, multi-perspectival narrative.[15] In this sense, it was actually a pioneering attempt to commercialise a main melody film at the beginning of the 2010s. Unfortunately, however, in the eyes of mainland audiences back then, 'this was unequivocally a dedication film, but Herman Yau has no good sense of the main melody genre; as a matter of fact, it was an entertainment film with stunning action'.[16] Apparently, the main melody was still understood in a strict sense at that time, and this did not radically change until 2014 with the remarkable achievement of Tsui Hark's *The Taking of Tiger Mountain 3D*.

Owing to various issues, including censorship and the influential power of Qiu Jingwu, *The Woman Knight of Mirror Lake*, despite being the number two film on the SARFT's list of recommendations for celebrating the 100th anniversary of the Xinhai Revolution, 'ended up with disastrous box-office takings although it was generally well received by critics and praised by the audiences who had watched it' – in Herman Yau's own words.[17] My sense is that whether Qiu Jin was really good at martial arts or not was not a key issue; nor is it important to argue whether historical facts were presented accurately in this commercial film. I do not intend to go into detail about the (self-)censorship Yau faced – he has offered a thorough, detailed analysis of this in his doctoral thesis. What I would like to highlight here is that Yau had to consider all the various commercial and censorship factors in the production of the film. In fact, Herman Yau was possibly one of the most qualified persons to talk about film censorship. He completed a doctoral thesis entitled 'The Progression of Political Censorship: Hong Kong Cinema from Colonial Rule to Chinese-style Socialist Hegemony' in 2015, providing a penetrating account of film censorship from the perspective of a critic-cum-director. Astutely theoretical, the thesis is one of the most thorough and insightful studies of film censorship in the context of Hong Kong. In the thesis, Yau explicitly used *The Woman Knight of Mirror Lake* as an example of a mainland–Hong Kong co-produced film, through which he 'encountered almost all of the problems embedded in mainland-HK co-productions'.[18] Although Herman Yau had carefully calculated how to sing the main melody of a revolutionary narrative in a commercial co-production, and a biopic about Qiu Jin would have had fewer restrictions than those about political leaders of the Party, he did not expect to have to deal with another kind of 'main melody' – Confucianism. 'In the context of the tradition laid by *xiao* [filial piety], Qiu Jingwu's interference in *The Woman Knight* was regarded as an act of *xiao* by the government officials.'[19] The film company therefore had to put a lot of effort into dealing with the copyright issues raised by Qiu Jingwu in the name of *xiao*, which is considered a Confucian virtue as important as the revolutionary narrative.

This unconvincing main(land) melody project did not have too much of an adverse impact on Herman Yau though. 'Significantly, it illustrated, empirically, what filmmaking is under Chinese-style socialism and what the Chinese mainland censorship means for Hong Kong filmmakers', and he concluded the experience of his doctoral research in a reflexive manner:

> . . . the Hong Kong filmmakers, in the main, just went with the flow in politics as they sought opportunities to make profitable films and continue their film business. Such business-orientation motive still persists today and has developed into an internal culture and a get-rich-quick mentality of the mainstream Hong Kong cinema, which, in addition to the economic and geo-political reality, make CEPA a successful institution that embodies the PRC's film censorship.[20]

Yau clearly and painstakingly understood the changing rules of the game, and this was the reason for his ability to adapt to them effectively and continue to gather momentum over the years. Having accumulated precious experience in shooting a main melody film, he returned to Hong Kong cinema (including mainland–Hong Kong co-produced films) and continued to be a prolific director after this. Later, he produced some blockbusters – such as *Shock Wave* and *The White Storm 2: Drug Lords*, echoing anti-terrorism and anti-drug themes, respectively – that could be considered 'quasi-main melody' blockbusters (this will be further discussed in Chapter 7). Let me go back to his earlier films to trace how he gained momentum before revisiting these two quasi-main melody crime thrillers.

Tracing the Momentum: All Too Extravagant, but Professionally Controlled

Not only was Herman Yau extremely productive in the 2010s, he also gradually gained recognition from mainstream audiences as well as film critics. Although Yau won fame – some would say infamy – with his signature cult classics *The Untold Story* (1993) and *Ebola Syndrome* (1996), he has long been considered a B-movie expert swinging between small cult films and commercial ventures. The true-crime horror film *The Untold Story* successfully captured the audience's attention, but it was leading actor Anthony Chau-sang Wong who stole the spotlight, winning the Best Actor award at the 13th Hong Kong Film Awards in 1993. Furthermore, Yau was the mainstay of many of the twenty episodes of the *Troublesome Night* series (1997–2017), which evidently were the most popular and influential Hong Kong ghost films over the past couple of decades. He was nominated for Best Director for *From the Queen to the Chief Executive* (2001) and *Give Them a Chance* (2003) at the 7th and 9th Golden Bauhinia Awards organised by the Hong Kong Film Critics Association, respectively. His films *Walk In* (1997), *Troublesome Night 3* (1998), *From the Queen to the Chief Executive*, *Shark Busters* (2002), *On the Edge* (2006), *Whispers and Moans* (2007), *Love Lifting* (2012), *Ip Man: The Final Fight* (2013), *Sara* (2014), *Always Be With You* and *New King of Comedy* were 'recommended films' awarded by the Hong Kong Film Critics Society, and he was among the most frequently bestowed directors at this award ceremony. *From the Queen to the Chief Executive*, which tackled serious social issues with innovative tabloid filmmaking, was an official selection at the 51st Berlin International Film Festival and the opening film of the Panorama. Yau did not simply go with the flow in politics. His crime-thriller blockbuster *The White Storm 2*, which ranked at the top after taking RMB 1.295 billion at the mainland box office, was selected to be the representative film of Hong Kong in the Best International Feature Film category at the 2020 Oscars. Despite all this, Herman Yau has been nominated only once for Best Director at the Hong Kong Film Academy Awards, for *Shock Wave*. These achievements speak volumes on the distinctiveness of this self-effacing director.

Very Hong Kong, Yau was also familiar with mainland productions – at least Hong Kong films funded by mainland capital. His debut, *No Regret*, was produced by the left-wing Sil-Metropole Organisation Ltd., which was closely affiliated with mainland China. *Fascination Amour* (1999) and *An Inspector Calls* (co-director) (2015), among others, were mainly produced for the Lunar New Year market in mainland China. *Always Be With You*, the twentieth episode in celebration of the twentieth anniversary of the *Troublesome Night* series, was mainland–Hong Kong co-produced. Given the 'no-ghost protocol' of the mainland censorship system, it was made clear towards the end of the film that everything was simply the illusion of the schizophrenic female protagonist. This was a common disclaimer in Hong Kong ghost films in order to pass censorship in the mainland market. The following comment nicely summed up the fluid style of Yau as

> one of Hong Kong film's strangest fruits . . . Granted, he can hardly be called an auteur, and often seems unapologetic about his status as a gun-for-hire, yet his B-movie portfolio is – while highly uneven – still miles above the bottom of the barrel that is, say, Jing Wong.[21]

It is perhaps not wrong to say that some of Herman Yau's films, owing to the consistently high number of productions, are lousy. For example, *An Inspector Calls*, which he co-directed with Raymond Wong, was ranked by the Golden Plum Awards – Hong Kong's version of the Golden Raspberry Awards – as the second worst director/movie of the year. Yau knew very well that he had to juggle different budgets and multiple schedules, but the important point was that he was willing to do this and was able to do it extremely well. He described 'this in-between role as an art of making-do, borrowing from Michel de Certeau'.[22] Having written a critical essay on the theorist,[23] he had a thorough grasp of the theory of 'making do', and, more importantly, he had put it into practice throughout his film career. 'Making do' was of the utmost importance for Hong Kong cinema in the age of China and its cinema. Yau also knew very well what (not) to do: 'You see what I produced, but you do not know what I have turned down; actually, one can control one's will to do or not to do something,' he said, emphasising that he had his own bottom line.[24] If 'all too extravagant, too gratuitously wild'[25] – David Bordwell's often-cited summary of Hong Kong cinema – can be applied to *The Untold Story*, *Ebola Syndrome* and even the more recent *The Sleep Curse*, Yau could also be 'all too calculated, too professionally controlled' at the same time.

Given the limited scope of this chapter, let me focus on two films among Yau's enormous output that span different genres – *Sara* and *Ip Man: The Final Fight* – in order to further elaborate on his outstanding ability to deal with different themes.[26] Alongside a whole raft of horror and triad flicks that kept him highly productive despite Hong Kong's shrinking film market, I have chosen these two films, in one way or another related to Hong Kong, to underscore the fluidity and adaptability of Herman Yau, which may be used to point towards a Hong Kong model of filmmaking.

Besides his growing commercial ventures, Yau also showed a continued commitment to social commentary in the context of Hong Kong. *Sara* would have been just another melodrama had he not wanted to inject his keen social awareness into the film. Often known as the third episode of Yau's sex workers trilogy, the film caught the limelight by winning the female lead, Charlene Choi, her first nomination for Best Actress at the 34th Hong Kong Film Awards held in 2015. A journalist who vows to rescue a child prostitute in Thailand from exploitation, Choi's character is sexually abused as a child by her stepfather in the film. Prostitution was one of the recurring themes of Yau's work. *No Regret* and the later *Whispers and Moans* were also about teenage prostitution. *Whispers and Moans* – the literal Chinese translation was 'Ten Days of Discussions with Sex Workers' – was a social commentary, which was one of Yau's preferred genres throughout his film career, albeit less well known than his B-movie portfolio. This film and its sequel, *True Women for Sale*, were based on Elsa Yee-shan Yang's (aka Elsa Chan) investigative study on sex workers.[27] Yau regularly worked with Yang to produce social films in a more documentary vein, including the well-received *From the Queen to the Chief Executive*. Also drawing on Yang's eponymous documentary literature, this was a fictitious account based on a real story of juvenile delinquents before and after Hong Kong's handover. In *Sara*, the female protagonist leaves home after being sexually abused by her stepfather with her mother's knowledge. She later meets a man (played by Simon Yam) thirty years older than her, and in exchange for school fees she provides sex services to him for the next eight years. The film seemed not to go deep into the characters' emotions, and the director's attempt to include too many things made everything look superficial. This may have been the case, but it was ultimately irrelevant if the film was approached from another angle. Herman Yau did not aim to delve into the female protagonist's sentiments; rather, he wanted to paint a social backdrop against which issues such as child prostitution and sex tourism could be explored. Sebastian Veg's comment on *Whispers and Moans* is applicable here: '[B]y constructing his film as a series of questions without answers, Yau meets the challenge of showing the fascination held by the shady world of clubs and prostitutes in Kowloon without romanticising it.'[28]

Yau explained in an interview that if the three films about sex workers formed a trilogy, the definition of prostitution had broadened significantly.[29] *Whispers and Moans* was about night clubs, a one-woman brothel, and a gigolo, which were all affiliated with sex workers. In the second film, Prudence Liew is a hooker and Race Wong marries an old man and gives birth to a baby in order to get a Hong Kong identity card, which could be seen as a different kind of prostitution. That Sara sells her body to a man thirty years older than she is in exchange for school fees was another kind of prostitution. In a sense, the protagonist, her mother, and Dok-my – the underage Thai prostitute she wants to save – were all selling their bodies for survival. In this light, *Sara* was less about sex workers than prostitution in a broader sense. The director may have been exaggerating, but perhaps only a little, when he asked: 'Aren't we actually prostitutes when being asked by our investor and boss to write something for the sake of money?'[30] In other words, as pointedly underscored by Yau, directors and screenwriters could also be seen as providing a similar service. From a macroscopic point of view, people are also selling their free will and dignity when doing something they are reluctant to do. Chapman To, the producer of *Sara*, would not disagree with this. He once starred in the comedy *Vulgaria* (2012), in which he played the role of a film producer who has to beg a triad head in Guangxi Province for an investment. In a disgustingly vulgar scene, Chapman To is forced to eat a dish of cow's reproductive tract and is later told that there will be no deal unless he has sex with a mule. In this sense, *Sara*, which had no mainland market because of its controversial contents, was also an endeavour not to compromise the director's commitment to Hong Kong productions. In a seminar hosted by Hong Kong Shue Yan University, the director clearly stated that the mainland market should not be the only hope for the future of Hong Kong cinema.[31] Without mainland market considerations, *Sara* could be deemed the Hong Kong director's commitment to the local market. As apparent in this example, Herman Yau had a strong commitment to Hong Kong and its cinema.

When asked what he would like future movie buffs to say about his legacy, Yau answered: 'That I was an honest filmmaker that loved Hong Kong.'[32] *Ip Man: The Final Fight* is an excellent example of this. Not unlike *Sara*, this episode of the *Ip Man* series placed an emphasis on the political and social backdrop of the era as much as, if not more than, the protagonist. Unlike other episodes, *Ip Man: The Final Fight* shed light on the era of transition, if not unrest, and took on social issues in Hong Kong in the 1950s and 1960s, including, but not limited to, police corruption, social unrest and new immigrants. Wilson Yip's *Ip Man* series (2008–19) packaged Donnie Yen's Ip Man as a kung-fu legend who upholds Chinese nationalism,[33] and Kar-Wai Wong used a historical backdrop to foreground the martial arts world and the importance of inheritance and transmission. Herman Yau's prelude *The Legend Is Born: Ip Man* (2010) stressed Ip Man as a rising Wing Chun master, but apparently Yau's and Kar-Wai Wong's older Ip Man was not an omnipotent grandmaster, as he hopelessly failed to save his own wife trapped on the other side of the border. It is well known that Yau and Anthony Chau-sang Wong's partnership had roots in the Category III creepy, disturbing horror films *The Untold Story* and *Ebola Syndrome*. Besides Elsa Yang, Anthony Wong was another long-term partner of Yau's. Their first joint effort in *The Untold Story* changed not just the career of Anthony Wong, but also the impression of Hong Kong audiences regarding cult horror films. They won further acclaim for their subsequent collaborations on *Taxi Driver* (1993) and *Ebola Syndrome*, but after the latter, they did not have any signature joint ventures for many years.

Herman Yau and Anthony Wong worked together later in films such as *Fascination Amour*, *On the Edge*, *True Women for Sale*, *Turning Point* (2009) and *The Woman Knight of Mirror Lake*, but they lacked the chemistry of their previous signature works. It would be reasonable to assume that their genuine reunion came with the Category III horror film *The Sleep Curse*, which was perhaps even more grotesque and paranormal than *The Untold Story* and *Ebola Syndrome*. Despite this, I have chosen to discuss *Ip Man: The Final Fight* here, as I think the duo generated another kind of chemistry in this side story riding on the wave generated by Donnie Yen's *Ip Man* series. Produced by Emperor Entertainment Group, this episode of Ip Man could easily be seen as following suit after the success of Yen's *Ip Man*. Be that as it may, I think that Herman Yau and Anthony Wong managed to tell a story that was something more than Ip Man. Perhaps the city of Hong Kong was the real protagonist of Yau's Ip Man film, which was about the final years of the grandmaster, but there were also many shots of daily life in old Hong Kong. Compared with most of Herman Yau's works, this film had a generous budget, allowing the director to build a huge set of old Hong Kong in Foshan, the hometown of Ip Man. Philip Yung, the director of the award-winning *Port of Call* (2015), made a discerning comment when he said, 'I believe the duo would agree with me if I chose *Ip Man: The Final Fight* to be their signature collaboration.'[34] As described by Yung, the film was about the vanishing of Hong Kong, such as the fading of the martial arts spirit, ethical relationships and cultural hybridisations. More importantly, the secret to the success of the duo's chemistry rested in their long-term collaboration:

> Yau and Wong's perfect harmony can be seen in the characterisation of the protagonist . . . and the film, albeit opposite to *The Untold Story* in terms of style, is a sequel to the latter and an extension of their heartfelt writing of Hong Kong.[35]

If *The Grandmaster* (2013) was the best Ip Man film, and one which introduced Wing Chun as well as Hong Kong cinema to the world, I consider *Ip Man: The Final Fight* the best film to touch the hearts of veteran local fans of Hong Kong cinema. Kar-Wai Wong's *The Grandmaster* also adopted an alternative, ingenious strategy of singing the main(land) melody. While *The Grandmaster* was generally seen as a story of Ip Man, a 'Hong Kong' grandmaster of the martial arts Wing Chun, Kar-Wai Wong's take on the early, mainland China life of this legendary figure could be seen as tracing the roots of Hong Kong in the Chinese tradition. When he was preparing for the film, Wong collected extensive materials and interviewed various masters, paying due respect to the tradition of Chinese kung fu. In this sense, Wong evinced the possibility of producing a main(land) melody film that could capture the attention and respect of a global audience. That said, neither Wong's nor Yau's film was really a typical martial arts film. Yau accentuated inheritance and transmission as much as Kar-Wai Wong did, although in a different manner. As a catchphrase in the film goes, '[i]t is difficult for a disciple to find a good *sifu* [teacher], but it is even more difficult for a *sifu* to have a good disciple'. Kar-Wai Wong said in an interview that he decided to make *The Grandmaster* because he was deeply touched by a video in which Ip Man asked his son to tape his Wing Chun skills so they could be passed on to the next generations. This scene was included in *Ip Man: The Final Fight*, but, different from Kar-Wai Wong's, Herman Yau's presentation seemed a bit sceptical about inheritance and transmission. As clearly depicted in the interaction between Ip Man and his disciple Bruce Lee, towards the end of the film, the master was rather indifferent to the achievements of the global kung-fu star. All in all, *Ip Man: The Final Fight* was about the changing community relationships in old Hong Kong, and the philosophy behind Wing Chun was much more important than its actual practice. In Yau's episode, Ip Man summarised his philosophy of life as follows:

> Living in this secular world, take as your model Fine Trees;
> With strong and deep roots, let the branches and leaves sway with the breeze.
> The shape of an Old Coin, one's attitude in life should follow –
> The outside edge should be round, and the inside, square and hollow.[36]

This could well be applied to Yau's film career in Hong Kong, a city he called home, and beyond.

A Shock Wave of (Anti-)Crime Thrillers

Herman Yau may have been a filmmaker who embodied the spirit of Hong Kong cinema, but, arguably, he did not have the opportunity to make a typical

Hong Kong crime blockbuster until *Shock Wave*. Yau was such a prolific film-maker that he was, of course, no stranger to the police and gangster genre. *Best of the Best* (1992), the third film he directed, was about a mission of the Special Duties Unit of the Hong Kong Police Force. *City Cop 2* (1995), *On the Edge*, *Turning Point*, *Turning Point 2* (2011) and *The Mobfathers*, to name just a few, were all typical Hong Kong-style police and gangster films (although *The Mobfathers* had a marked political undertone of using triad politics as a metaphor for the electoral system of Hong Kong). A highly efficient director, Yau was invited to take the helm of some blockbusters made for the Chinese Lunar New Year market, such as *All's Well, Ends Well Too 2010* (2010) and *An Inspector Calls*. Nevertheless, it was not until *Shock Wave* that Herman Yau truly had the chance to master a typical Hong Kong-style high-concept, big-budget crime film. His collaboration with Andy Lau can be traced back to *Don't Fool Me!* (1991), the second film he directed. Interestingly, the highly productive director and megastar actor did not have an opportunity to work together again until *Shock Wave*, after more than a quarter of a century. Experienced and prolific, Herman Yau had made films with different budgets, from non-mainstream social critiques to comedies tailor-made for the Chinese New Year, before *Shock Wave*. He also had a track record of police and gangster films. *Shock Wave* was a big-budget, high-concept co-production, with the mainland as the key target market. Herman Yau's original intention was not about making a grand invested film, but about wanting to make this particular film.[37] The plot and the main setting, Hung Hom Cross Harbour Tunnel, which had a role in the film as important as the leading actor-cum-producer Andy Lau, required enormous resources and investment. As the main plot of the tunnel hostage in the film was played out over an hour, and most of the important scenes in the film happened inside or near the tunnel, it was necessary to have a 'real' setting. However, it was simply impossible to shoot the film on location owing to the tunnel's daily traffic capacity of 110,000 vehicles. The director therefore felt it was essential to build a 1:1 set of the tunnel. Without the handsome budget of a co-production, it would not have been possible for the RMB 100 million replica concept to become reality. In the end, the replica tunnel and more than 200 cars were blown up, but the budget was not. Notwithstanding the high production costs, Yau said that he did not actually overshoot his budget: 'I am always a moderate spender with self-restraint, and perhaps owing to this, the investors are willing to let me spend whatever I have to spend for production.'[38] Yau's excellent track record of budget control – he had long masterminded small-budget films – enabled him to manage the huge complexity of this blockbuster. Moreover, it was almost mission impossible to complete a film of this scale in less than four months.

Despite being a co-production, *Shock Wave* was a signature Hong Kong crime film. 'I tried to make *Shock Wave* a very exciting film, a very Hong Kong style'[39] film, said the director. Veteran fans of Hong Kong cinema felt a sense of déjà vu – a typical Hong Kong police and gangster classic reminiscent of those of the 1980s and 1990s. The film had a sad ending as the male lead sacrificed himself, but its real-world ending was a happy one, as it did well at the box office in both the mainland and Hong Kong, ranking second among all Chinese films in 2017 in Hong Kong with HK\$25.5 million and a decent RMB 400 million in the mainland. Furthermore, if Yau's commercialisation of the main melody in *The Woman Knight of Mirror Lake* fell below expectations owing to the various reasons discussed above, the timing of *Shock Wave* was so much better than his main(land) melody project released at the beginning of the decade. Although it might not have been conceived as a genuine main melody blockbuster, *Shock Wave* nicely fit into the main melody blockbuster trend well developed by Hong Kong directors, in the sense that the theme of terrorist threats and attacks acted as a sort of echo of the main melody of anti-crime. The success of *Shock Wave* showcased the extraordinary execution ability of Herman Yau, who managed to handle a high-concept blockbuster within budget and on schedule, and his mastery of action and explosive scenes earned him the nomination for Best Director at the Hong Kong Film Academy Awards. The unimpressive Douban score of 6.3, however, showed that the crime thriller with a strong Hong Kong flavour – not just the action and the setting but also the plotline of the bomb disposal hero's tragic end – did not gain wide recognition among mainland audiences. Nevertheless, producer Andy Lau must have been very happy with *Shock Wave*, as he worked with Yau again in *The White Storm 2* and *Shock Wave 2*, both of which were high-concept blockbusters with budgets even bigger than that of *Shock Wave*. Actually, both projects were thematic sequels in title only, and in a sense, they were also 'main melody' films as crime – narcotics in the former in particular – was a state-approved theme. It is therefore safe to argue that Yau began a new chapter in his career with *Shock Wave*.

As I have argued elsewhere, Johnnie To's *Drug War* (2012) could be seen as a trail-blazing northern venture of Hong Kong directors and their signature gangster films.[40] I do appreciate Johnnie To's 'mixing' of business and pleasure and 'zigzagging' his way to creative achievement in this mainland production that he was commissioned to produce. However, as the whole project was filmed in the mainland, unlike *The White Storm 2*, there was an important piece missing in the puzzle of Hong Kong crime thrillers – the setting. In fact, in 2017, Jing Wong also released an anti-narcotic blockbuster, *Chasing the Dragon* (aka *King of Drug Dealers*). Jing Wong has long been (in)famous for his strong market sense, if not opportunism. *Chasing the Dragon* was a reboot of Jing Wong's own crime classics *To Be Number One* (1991) and *Lee Rock* (1991). Given the casting of megastars Andy Lau and Donnie Yen, the mainland box-office return of RMB 584 million was not particularly impressive. While the anti-narcotic theme was highlighted in the film, it was set in British Hong Kong back in the 1960s and 1970s, as the director's strategy was to echo the anti-colonial melody. Named after *The White Storm* (2013), directed by Benny Chan, a story about three middle-aged undercover cops' operation against a Thai drug lord that sought to draw upon the collective memory of several generations of Hong Kong people,[41] *The White Storm 2* was an in-name-only sequel. Andy Lau took on the producer role once again in this thriller co-produced by his Focus Films, Hong Kong's Universe Entertainment and Chinese partners, including Guangdong Sublime Media. Given the fact that main melody blockbusters had not been developed in the mainland at that juncture, although the box-office record of RMB 235 million for Benny Chan's film was reasonably good, it did not generate too much critical attention. When *The White Storm 2* premiered in the summer of 2019, it was another story as the Chinese film industry, especially the development of main melody blockbusters, had changed extensively.

Having established an excellent working relationship with Andy Lau in *Shock Wave*, Herman Yau had an even bigger budget to produce this crime thriller with an unabashedly explicit anti-drug plot. Andy Lau portrays a gangster-turned-philanthropist and staunch supporter of actions against drugs, as his son, whom he did not know, has died young from a drug overdose. In the film, Andy Lau and Louis Koo are gang brothers, and at the beginning of the film, the latter is punished by the leader because he is suspiciously involved in drug dealing, which is strictly forbidden by the gang. Ordered to do so by the gang leader, Andy Lau chops off three of Koo's fingers, who is then expelled from the gang and later turns into the biggest drug lord in the territory. The state-approved theme of narcotics prevention was the main conflict between 'heaven' and 'earth', also represented by the Chinese names of the two male leads, Andy Lau and Louis Koo, in the film, respectively. (The literal translation of the Chinese subtitle was 'The showdown between heaven and earth'.) To increase the dramatic tension of the plot, a narcotics squad officer (portrayed by Michael Miu), whose policewoman wife died fifteen years earlier in a drug war on the same night that Louis Koo's fingers were chopped off by Andy Lau, stands between Lau and Koo. In the film, the key message that drugs are bad is repeated so heavy-handedly that it almost sounds like preaching. The director did not mind singing the main(land) melody explicitly with an eye to the mainland market, because he could then turn his attention to effectively enthralling the audience with the dramatic showdown between 'heaven' and 'earth' in the film. Compared with the lacklustre anti-narcotic propaganda *Dealer Healer* (2017), directed by

Lawrence Lau and starring Sean Lau and Nick Cheung, who were leading actors in *The White Storm*, Herman Yau's film excelled in its restless, if not relentless, action, including vigilantism. The billionaire anti-drug vigilante, Andy Lau, was the Dark Knight in this anti-drug film. Not only does he form a heavily armed team to tackle drug gangs, he also publicly offers a bounty of HK$100 million to the one who kills the biggest drug lord in Hong Kong – the 'earth', Louis Koo. This was indeed controversial, but at least it was not impossible in Hong Kong. It would have been totally unimaginable in the mainland. The film's setting in contemporary Hong Kong was ingeniously used by the director and his long-time scriptwriter Erica Lee to generate dramatic tension and pulsating action scenes to detract from the too overtly presented theme.

In *The White Storm 2*, there is a wow factor similar to that in *Shock Wave*: a climactic set-piece right inside the Central Mass Transit Railway (MTR) station, a 1:1 replica built for this scene. The fast and furious car chase scene extends from the crowded streets in the Central Business District of Hong Kong down to the subway station, followed by a duel between Lau and Koo in the MTR tunnel, who are soon joined by Michael Miu, recalling the big showdowns in classic Hollywood Westerns. Both Lau and Koo are then shot to death, with a totally devastated Miu standing till the end. The ending was evidently more politically correct than that of *Shock Wave*, as justice was finally done and was seen to be done, as both the drug lord and the vigilante are dead, with the anti-crime theme shining through the dark tunnel. In other words, this Truth will prevail in the mainland: the power of Evil will never triumph over the power of Good. Although the director was criticised by Hong Kong film critics of placing too much emphasis on the anti-crime theme and therefore undermining the social background and rhythm of the film, the production quality and pop entertainment of this typical Hong Kong crime thriller were duly recognised.[42] It was selected by the Federation of Motion Film Producers of Hong Kong as their submission to the International Feature Film category at the 2020 Oscars. At the box office, the film was also a success, ranking second among Chinese films in Hong Kong with HK$24.8 million,[43] which was especially remarkable in a summer in which the city was deeply unsettled by a series of anti-ELAB (Anti-Extradition Law Amendment Bill) protests almost everywhere in the territory. Its performance was even more amazing in the mainland, as it raked in more than RMB 1.311 billion and ranked twelfth in the annual box office.[44] With its outstanding box-office record, the film successfully prompted critics to see the future of Hong Kong cinema: 'Having been sidelined by mainland blockbusters for years, Hong Kong films are back with a vengeance.'[45] It was indeed a main melody – at least quasi-main melody – blockbuster, but at the same time, it was also an 'old-fashioned' Hong Kong crime thriller with mainland and modern flourishes.

Thanks to Herman Yau's exceptional execution abilities and thorough under-standing of the rules of the game, this (anti-)crime blockbuster hit new heights before the end of the decade. Its success in the mainland could also be attributed to the director's self-effacing style. Without the auteur's signature, such as in Johnnie To's *Drug War*, it was more flexible for the film to make ends meet, which was espe-cially important for a blockbuster with the mainland as the primary market. From *Shock Wave* and *The White Storm 2* to *Shock Wave 2*, fans of Hong Kong cinema had the feeling that the films were more Andy Lau than Herman Yau. Built upon the suc-cess of *The White Storm 2*, *Shock Wave 2* further proved that Yau, who produced *The Woman Knight of Mirror Lake* at the beginning of the 2010s, had acquired the secret skill to sing the main(land) melody beautifully in the signature Hong Kong police and gangster genre. The in-name-only sequel *Shock Wave 2* was originally scheduled to premiere in the mainland and in Hong Kong in the summer of 2020, but was postponed owing to the COVID-19 pandemic. It finally hit mainland multiplexes in December 2020, but was delayed in Hong Kong once again owing to another wave of Covid-19. It was so well received in the mainland during this extraordinary time that *Global Times* reported that the goals of the 2020 box office could be met in the mainland 'thanks to highly qualified releases in late December', and the major responsibility fell on the shoulders of *Shock Wave 2*.[46] More importantly for Hong Kong cinema, according to *Global Times* (under the auspices of *People's Daily*, the Chinese Communist Party's newspaper), the reputation of Hong Kong cinema had been declining in recent years, but the innovative film techniques, including the plot twists, the major explosion scenes at the Hong Kong International Airport and Tsing Ma Bridge and the 'real and down-to-earth image of a bomb disposal officer' turned this trend around.[47] Despite the plot twist involving the amnesia of Andy Lau that prevented him from knowing whether he was good or bad, the film was not about ambiguous identities, unlike *Infernal Affairs* (2002). Herman Yau creatively added a much-welcome dimension, underneath the main melody, of memory and amnesia, to Hong Kong's signature police and gangster genre.[48] As *Shock Wave 2* does not fall within the central scope of this book, I will not dwell upon a further discussion, except to note that Herman Yau successfully upgraded a Chinese main melody film to the standard of a blockbuster without sacrificing too much of the signature style of Hong Kong police and gangster thrillers, and this would not have been possible, I would argue, without the self-effacing style – or what I call 'the absent presence' – of the director.

The Absent Presence

It would not be sufficient to focus only on Herman Yau's extraordinary execu-tion ability discussed above. I will use the example of Stephen Chow's *New King*

of Comedy (2019) to further unpack my ideas about Yau's self-effacing character, or 'absent presence'. Arguably one of the most representative of Hong Kong
icons, Stephen Chow was generally seen as leaving the city for the mainland
market after *CJ 7* (2008), if not earlier. When the Hong Kong audience learned
that he was going to make a sequel to one of his all-time classics, *King of Comedy* (1999), they were sceptical about the loss of Hong Kong characteristics in
the new version, with a new cast consisting almost entirely of mainland actors.
Given the cast, the film was shot in Putonghua, and the Hong Kong version,
just like Chow's previous films such as *The Mermaid* (2016), was dubbed into
Cantonese. Although Cecilia Cheung, one of the female leads in the 1999 version, and the local popular hip-hop duo Fama were invited to be the voice actress
and actors in the Cantonese version, this was still seen by the Hong Kong audience as a critical flaw. One of the talking points among the Hong Kong audience was the inclusion of Cantopop classics: Danny Chan's 'Flurry' (or 'Gusty
Wind') (1982) and George Lam's 'Need You Every Single Minute' (1980). More
importantly, even though the original Cantonese songs could be heard in the
mainland version of the movie, 'Gusty Wind' had a new Mandarin version with
new lyrics penned by Zhai Jian and sung by the group Flurry Girls (or Gusty
Wind Girls). The seven young girls were handpicked by Stephen Chow from *Produce 101*, a Chinese reality television show on Tencent Video that premiered in
2017. In the end, the show selected eleven winners to form the group Rocket
Girls 101. As noted by Chow in an interview about the formation of this group,
'I heard that they had failed, but that doesn't matter, for who hasn't failed?' –
'Gusty Wind' was the song Chow used to encourage himself when he was an
extra.[49] The Putonghua version, with its new lyrics carrying meanings similar to
those in the original version, was sung by the group at the press conference to
release the new film, but the original Danny Chan Cantonese version was used
in the Hong Kong version of the film. In the end, the opinions of the Hong Kong
audience were rather diverse: some appreciated that Hong Kong could still be
felt in the mainland version of a Hong Kong classic, whereas others slammed
Stephen Chow for merely selling Hong Kong's surplus value. Like it or not, this
was a mainlandised Hong Kong classic that embodied the complex, entangled
politics of domination and resistance. There is no denying that 'Gusty Wind'
perfectly echoed the main theme of the two episodes, which was spoken loudly
by Wang Baoqiang in the sequel: 'refusing to concede is success in itself', and
this was applicable in Hong Kong as well as across the border. Not only did the
theme resonate with the catchphrases of many Hong Kong films, such as *The
Unbeatable* (2013), *The Way We Dance* (2013), *Weeds of Fire* (2016) and the like, it
also creatively connected Hong Kong cinema to Cantopop and television – when
Stephen Chow was still an extra. That said, this sequel may have been seen as a

display of tactics, but the display itself also had to be considered. Towards this end, I must add that the associate director, Herman Yau, should also be seen as a very 'Hong Kong' component in the film.

It was reported that Stephen Chow originally planned to make *The Mermaid 2* for the 2019 Lunar New Year, but owing to production and other reasons, it could not be made in time for the traditional golden period for film releases in China. He decided to use *New King of Comedy*, which could be completed in time, as a substitute. Owing to the tight schedule, Herman Yau was invited to be the associate director of this typical Stephen Chow comedy. As mentioned above, Yau was not just versatile but also highly efficient. Perhaps this was exactly why Chow decided to invite him to be his associate director, as he was exceptionally able and professional but self-effacing. It was reported that when the film started shooting, Stephen Chow was the producer and Herman Yau the director, but in the end it was branded as a Stephen Chow work, with Yau as just an associate director; in other words, he was 'made to disappear'.[50] In short, *New King of Comedy* was a de facto Stephen Chow signature work, but without the 'absent presence' of Herman Yau, it would probably not have been possible to complete it on schedule.

As discussed previously, Yau had a well-earned reputation as a sure and quick marksman who was willing as well as able to produce different film genres with different subject matters and budgets. He was also shrewdly pragmatic, as he knew the rules of the game very well: 'My films, perhaps not high-quality, usually earn good profits for the investors.'[51] He was good at making do, putting into practice the typical Hong Kong way of doing things. Anyhow, his making-do spirit was only part of the Hong Kong model of filmmaking. Tai-lok Lui was right in saying that the components of the 'Hong Kong model' (the success formula of Hong Kong) were interrelated, and when some of them changed, the other components did not work anymore.[52] The major reason for this, I would also argue, was the waning of not only the major factors behind the success of the Hong Kong model, but also, more importantly, diversity. Diversity is the magic word for Herman Yau's body of work as well as Hong Kong culture. When asked about the fading away of the typical 'Hong Kong flavour' in Hong Kong films, Yau said that he did not agree, and if that was the case, it was 'mainly reflected in the reducing of quantity of films'.[53] It is thus not surprising that Yau was a big fan of Rainer Werner Fassbinder and his legendary productivity: 'He truly loves films. Forty some films in his short life! With or without money he continued making films . . . Kar-wai Wong also loves films, but that is another kind of love. I love *making* films.'[54] In other words, if Ann Hui, as discussed in Chapter 2, used her films to show how to live an ordinary life calmly in uncertainty, Herman Yau showed how to continue to make films in these extraordinary times.

Herman Yau beautifully demonstrated how to uphold diversity in a shrinking market. In a time of accelerating cultural and social political changes, his films addressed profound issues about how to live in the film industry, as well as about what it means to live in a swiftly changing world. He gained his reputation (and arguably some degree of notoriety) from his cult, true-crime horror films, but he was not satisfied with this. He produced all kinds of commercial films while staying committed to his social commentaries. In fact, he did not even discriminate the two types of work:

> As a movie director, it is always my ultimate dream that, as long as I can manage and be able to secure an investor, I am able to make good movies of different topics and categories that would please myself and be shared with the others.[55]

He welcomed mainland–Hong Kong co-productions, but at the same time he wished to be remembered as an honest filmmaker who loved Hong Kong. Yau explained his view on co-productions in this manner:

> I will produce film [sic] whenever it is appropriate. I do not have the concept of developing business in the mainland China. Prior to exploring other parts of the world, I certainly hope that Hong Kong is the base of my career development.[56]

Having completed an excellent doctoral thesis on film censorship, he is one of the most intellectual filmmakers in Hong Kong, but admits that he is an 'opportunist', and his films are not made for intellectual audiences:

> To confirm my location, in 2006. I went back to school to examine the value system that was in my heart a long time ago, and define film as mass communication. I know I care for the ordinary people more and I have no objection that some people target the intellectual people, but I choose the mass audience and popular films over art films.[57]

In sum, he was at once keenly self-aware and aware of how things really are in the film industry:

> I've made over 80 films – a lot of them are crap. Ask people on the street and they'll tell you the same. But I enjoyed the process, even when a movie was doomed. Even the worst football player can still enjoy the game.[58]

In this sense, Herman Yau *is* Hong Kong filmmaking.

Concluding Remarks

Equally if not more important to Hong Kong cinema is that Herman Yau's 'absent presence' was also felt by the next generation of Hong Kong directors: when he continued his film business, his strategic planning encompassed succession planning. Similar to Johnnie To, who worked to develop the mainland market and to promote inheritance and transmission locally at the same time,[59] Herman Yau has been active in nurturing young directors by, among other things, being a producer of their films. *From Where We've Fallen* (2017), with which Nanjingese rookie director Wang Feifei made his directorial debut, was invited to premier in the New Directors Section at the San Sebastián Film Festival. Adapted from two short stories written by the director, the artistic film weaved together threads of romance, revenge and mystery. In the story, situated in a modern society characterised by anxiety and despair about human relationships, the male protagonist suffers from an identity crisis after finding out about his wife's extramarital affairs. Even though Yau was such a prolific filmmaker, the genre and style of this film was unfamiliar to his fans. According to Wang, Yau offered him precious suggestions on 'editing and related issues'.[60] Given the modest budget, one of the most important issues was the executive production of the film, in which Yau excelled.

The *Rashomon*-esque thriller *G Affairs* was at once similar to and different from *From Where We've Fallen* – similar in the sense that Cheuk-Pan Lee was nominated for Best New Director at the 38th Hong Kong Film Awards for his debut, and different in the sense that this bleakly stylish suspense film looked more familiar to Yau's fans. Thanks to the Hong Kong Government's First Film Initiative funding support of HK$5.5 million, *G Affairs* had a decent cast compared with similar films. Alongside new actors were the Chinese indie queen Huang Lu and the controversial Hong Kong actor-producer Chapman To. Notwithstanding commercial considerations, the director decided to adopt the experimental techniques of independent cinema in this story about a bad cop, underage sex and social discontent, which were obviously unwelcome by mainland China's censors. The film's focus was on Hong Kong, in addition to a dystopian take on its future (as implied by "GG" – Good Game – at the end of the film). Cheuk-Pan Lee's cranky debut greatly benefited from executive producer Yau's experience in the industry as well as in cult films. The styles of films in which Yau was the executive producer were almost as diverse as those he directed himself. Unlike the previous two, *Give Me One Day* (2021), with which veteran lyricist and novelist Erica Lee – who was also the scriptwriter of many of Yau's recent films, including *Shock Wave*, *The White Storm 2*, *Ip Man: The Final Fight* and *Sara* – made her directorial debut, is a romance film adapted from her own novel. The director connected this local love story to the collective memories of the city, a theme rarely touched by Yau over the years.

While it is right for experts to call on Hong Kong filmmakers to set their sights on lower-budget films, my sense is that the future development of Hong Kong cinema will not rely completely on the outcomes of such movies. As a sure and quick marksman, Yau has contributed consistently to all parts of the Hong Kong film industry with his body of work, from cult horror films, ghost story series and social commentaries to, more recently, high-concept blockbusters. As argued in this chapter, Yau's exceptional ability to execute and self-effacing style were brilliantly showcased in the examples discussed above. He also demonstrated his commitment to social commentaries and Hong Kong in films such as *Sara* and *Ip Man: The Final Fight*. At the same time, he used signature Hong Kong police and gangster films to effectively generate the genre of 'quasi-main melody' blockbusters, attracting audiences in different regions. He also embraced co-productions and local productions indiscriminately. 'I don't object to the co-productions, but for a healthy film market all kinds of films need to find a way to co-exist,'[61] he said clearly. He understood the operational logic of the film industry well enough to make different kinds of commercially profitable films – some of which he considered 'crap'. Filmmaking, however, was not just 'prostitution' to him. He continues to assist new and rising directors in the industry to develop their careers in the city they call home. He also embodies diversity as much as conformity, and, more importantly, as a value. His contributions to Hong Kong cinema in a dwindling time, as well as to Chinese cinema in its commercialisation and blockbusterisation, have not been duly recognised. Should there be a Hong Kong mode of filmmaking, Herman Yau would be an exemplary case.

Notes

1. The term 'quasi-main melody' is borrowed from Hongmei Yu, 'Visual Spectacular, Revolutionary Epic, and Personal Voice: The Narration of History in Chinese Main Melody Films', *Modern Chinese Literature and Culture* 25:2 (Fall 2013): 191.

2. Elizabeth Kerr, 'Popcorn Flicks with a Message: Herman Yau's Hong Kong Movies', Zolima CityMag, 24 March 2016: <https://zolimacitymag.com/popcorn-flicks-with-a-message-herman-yaus-hong-kong-movies/>; last accessed 1 May 2021.

3. 'Dr. Herman Yau Lai-to: Honorary University Fellow', Hong Kong Baptist University, 2019: <https://www.hkbu.edu.hk/eng/about/honlist/2019_HUF_YauLaito.jsp>; last accessed 1 May 2021.

4. Herman Lai-to Yau, 'The Progression of Political Censorship: Hong Kong Cinema from Colonial Rule to Chinese-style Socialist Hegemony' (Hong Kong: Lingnan University Doctoral Thesis, 2015), 285–7. As explained by Yau: 'The Qiu Jin film had to be filmed in the Chinese mainland for, at least, two reasons. Firstly, it is a period

film with certain inevitable, predetermined, big scenes, which pushed up the budget to a sum that would make the Chinese mainland market the only conceivable place where it could make a profit; secondly, the Chinese mainland provides filmmakers with various locations and scenery essential to Chinese period film' (285).

5. Ibid., 311, 320.
6. Ke Erte 柯爾特, 'The Woman Knight of Mirror Lake: Swift, Powerful and Not Baffling' (in Chinese) 〈《競雄女俠秋瑾》：迅猛但不讓人暈血的風格〉, Sina Entertainment 新浪娛樂, 14 October 2011: <http://ent.sina.com.cn/r/c/2011-10-14/19313450356.shtml>; last accessed 1 May 2021.
7. 'Qiu Jin's Descendant Questioning the Three Vulgarities of the Film: An Appeal to Premier Wen Jiabao' (in Chinese) 〈秋瑾後人質疑秋瑾影片三俗：致信溫總理反映〉, chinanews.com, 1 September 2011: <http://www.chinanews.com/yl/2011/09-01/3301088.shtml>; last accessed 1 May 2021.
8. Louise Edwards, *Women Warriors and Wartime Spies of China* (Cambridge: Cambridge University Press, 2016), 64.
9. Ma Lunpeng, 'Don't Say Women Can't Be Heroic: A Study of Qiu Jin's Biopics and Their Theoretical Issues' (in Chinese) 〈漫云女子不英雄：秋瑾傳記片研究及其理論問題〉, *Journal of Modern Life Writing Studies* 《現代傳記研究》 9, Fall 2017: <https://www.163.com/dy/article/FQT71B730536QGL3.html>; last accessed 1 May 2021.
10. Xie Jin, *Selected Essays on Xie Jin's Films: History* (in Chinese) 《謝晉電影選集：歷史卷》 (Shanghai: Shanghai University Press, 2007), 24; see also Xia Xiaohong 夏曉虹, 'Styles of the Times: Qiu Jin's Images in Literature' (in Chinese) 〈秋瑾文學形象的時代風貌〉, *Modern Chinese Literature Studies* 《中國現代文學研究叢刊》 4 (2009): 49–65.
11. Ma, 'Don't Say Women Can't Be Heroic'. There was also a documentary about Qiu Jin entitled *Autumn Gem* made by Rae Chang and Adam Tow.
12. Edwards, *Women Warriors and Wartime Spies of China*, 64.
13. Ibid., 65.
14. Yun Feiyang 雲飛揚, 'The Woman Knight of Mirror Lake: Using Cult Style to Tell a Story about Revolution' (in Chinese) 〈《競雄女俠·秋瑾》用CULT片說革命往事〉, *Southern Metropolis Weekly* 《南都娛樂週刊》, 17 October 2011: <https://web.archive.org/web/20150924103001/<http://www.smweekly.com/appraise/201110/27746.aspx>; last accessed 1 May 2021.
15. Ma, 'Don't Say Women Can't Be Heroic'.
16. Ibid.
17. Yau, 'The Progression of Political Censorship', 318.
18. Ibid., 284.
19. Ibid., 325.
20. Ibid., 284, 347.
21. Timo, 'The B-Movie Splendor of Herman Yau', *Screen Anarchy*, 14 May 2008: <https://screenanarchy.com/2008/05/twitch-o-meter-the-b-movie-splendor-of-herman-yau.html>; last accessed 1 May 2021.

22. Esther M. K. Cheung, Gina Marchetti and Tan See Kam, 'Hong Kong Screenscapes: An Introduction', in *Hong Kong Screenscapes: From the New Wave to the Digital Frontier*, ed. Esther M. K. Cheung, Gina Marchetti and Tan See Kam (Hong Kong: Hong Kong University Press, 2011), 7.

23. Herman Yau, 'Michel de Certeau's "Making Do": Uses and Tactics', hermanyau.com, April 2008: <http://www.hermanyau.com/cArticleDeCerteau.htm>; last accessed 1 May 2021.

24. 'Interview Herman Yau: Director of *The White Storm 2*' (in Chinese) 〈專訪《掃毒2》導演邱禮濤〉, *KK News*, 24 July 2019: <https://kknews.cc/zh-hk/entertainment/ml39ooz.html>; last accessed 1 May 2021.

25. David Bordwell, *Planet Hong Kong: Popular Cinema and the Art of Entertainment* (Cambridge, MA: Harvard University Press, 2000), 1.

26. There have been studies on Yau's cult horror films; see, among others, Tony Williams, 'Hong Kong Social Horror: Tragedy and Farce in Category 3', in *Horror International*, ed. Steven Jay Schneider and Tony Williams (Detroit: Wayne State University Press, 2005), 203–19; for an informative and thorough account of Hong Kong horror cinema in the context of Hong Kong–China co-productions, see Vivian P. Y. Lee, 'Ghostly Returns: The Politics of Horror in Hong Kong Cinema', in *Hong Kong Horror Cinema*, ed. Gary Bettinson and Daniel Martin (Edinburgh: Edinburgh University Press, 2018), 204–22.

27. Elsa Yee-shan Yang 楊漪珊, *Old Business New Profession* (in Chinese) 《古老生意新專業》 (Hong Kong: Cosmos Books, 2001).

28. Sebastian Veg, 'Hong Kong by Night: Prostitution and Cinema in Herman Yau's *Whispers and Moans*', *China Perspectives* 2 (2007): 87–8.

29. Siu-pan Ho 何兆彬, 'Herman Yau's *Sara*: Aren't We All Prostitutes?' (in Chinese) 〈邱禮濤《雛妓》: 我們何嘗不是妓〉, *Hong Kong Economic Journal* 《信報》, 23 March 2015.

30. Ibid.

31. Wai-yan Lee 李蔚茵, 'Herman Yau: *Sara* Is a Hong Kong Story' (in Chinese) 〈邱禮濤:《雛妓》屬於香港故事〉, Hong Kong Shue Yan University, 10 February 2015: <http://hknews.hksyu.edu/index.php/邱禮濤:《雛妓》屬於香港故事>; last accessed 1 May 2021.

32. Kerr, 'Popcorn Flicks with a Message'.

33. For an inspiring account on this, see Siu-Keung Cheung and Wing-Sang Law, 'The Colony Writes Back: Nationalism and Collaborative Coloniality in the *Ip Man* Series', *Social Transformations in Chinese Societies* 13:2 (2017): 159–72.

34. Philip Yung, 'The "Selfless" Realm of Herman Yau and Anthony Wong' (in Chinese) 〈邱禮濤與黃秋生的「無我」境界〉, *HK01*, 29 May 2017: <https://www.hk01.com/ 01博評-藝. 文化/94365/邱禮濤與黃秋生的-無我-境界>; last accessed 1 May 2021.

35. Ibid.

36. English translation Frank C. Yue, *Chinese Poetry in English Verse*: <http://chinese-poetryinenglishverse.blogspot.com/2013/08/blog-post.html>; last accessed 1 May 2021.

37. 'Audiences Are Mysterious Crowds, Keep Own Style: An Interview with Herman Yau', *The Chinese Film Market*, 17 April 2017: <http://mag.chinesefilmmarket.com/en/article/audiences-are-mysterious-crowds-keep-own-style/>; last accessed 1 May 2021.

38. May Or 柯美, '*Shock Wave* Director Herman Yau Praises Producer Andy Lau for Being Willing to Settle Things through Discussion' (in Chinese) 〈《拆彈專家》導演邱禮濤讚監製劉德華凡事有商量〉, *Ming Pao* 《明報》, 30 April 2017.

39. Martin Sandison, 'Exclusive: Interview with Hong Kong Filmmaker Herman Yau', *City on Fire*, 2 January 2018: <https://cityonfire.com/exclusive-interview-with-hong-kong-filmmaker-herman-yau/>; last accessed 1 May 2021.

40. Yiu-Wai Chu, *Found in Transition: Hong Kong Studies in the Age of China* (Albany: SUNY Press, 2018), 132.

41. The three cops grew up together in a public housing estate in Hong Kong, sharing the same childhood memories, which were represented by the song they sang together: 'Pledged to Go into Knife Mountain'. Chu, *Found in Transition*, 160–1.

42. Chi-kang Fu 傅紀鋼, '*The White Storm 2*: The Exclusive Focus on Drugs Undermined the Social Background and Filmic Rhythm' (in Chinese) 〈《掃毒2天地對決》：全片聚焦毒品，卻破壞了整個社會背景與電影節奏〉, *The News Lens*, 20 July 2019: <https://www.thenewslens.com/article/122389>; last accessed 1 May 2021.

43. 'The Overall Situation of the Hong Kong Film Market in 2019' (in Chinese) 〈2019年香港電影市道整體情況〉, Hong Kong Box Office Ltd, 2 January 2020: <http://www.mpia.org.hk/upload/file/00276/2019%E5%B9%B4%E5%BA%A6%E5%8D%81%E5%A4%A7%E7%A5%A8%E6%88%BF.pdf>; last accessed 1 May 2021.

44. Endata: <https://www.endata.com.cn/BoxOffice/BO/Year/index.html>; last accessed 1 May 2021.

45. Clarence Tsui, 'Hong Kong Cinema Is Not Dead, As Recent Chinese Box Office Successes Show', *South China Morning Post*, 29 August 2019.

46. Gong Qian, '2020 Box Office Goal Can Be Met in Chinese Mainland Thanks to Highly Qualified Releases in Late December', *Global Times*, 27 December 2020.

47. Ibid.

48. See Herman Yau, 'Memory/Amnesia: A Cultural Translation of Hong Kong' (in Chinese) 〈記不了/忘不掉：誰的香港〉, *Cultural Studies@Lingnan* 12, 2009: <http://commons.ln.edu.hk/mcsln/vol12/iss1/3/>; last accessed 1 May 2021. The epigraph of the essay is Milan Kundera: 'The struggle of man against power is the struggle of memory against forgetting.' Milan Kundera, *The Book of Laughter and Forgetting*, trans. Michael Henry Heim (London: Penguin, 1983), 3.

49. Zhang Rui, 'Stephen Chow Seeks to Inspire Losers with New Film', China.org.cn, 13 January 2019: <http://www.china.org.cn/arts/2019-01/13/content_74368080_2.htm>; last accessed 1 May 2021.

50. See 'Herman Yau Made to Disappear' (in Chinese), *Apple Daily*, 16 January 2019.

51. Ho, 'Herman Yau's *Sara*: Aren't We All Prostitutes?'

52. Tai-lok Lui, *Hong Kong Model: From Present Tense to Past Tense* (in Chinese) 《香港模式：從現在式到過去式》 (Hong Kong: Chunghwa, 2015).

53. 'Audiences Are Mysterious Crowds, Keep Own Style'.

54. Chin-Wai Chan 陳芊憓, 'To Do Whatever One Pleases Notwithstanding Restraints: An Interview with Herman Yau' (in Chinese) 〈在限制中率性而為：專訪邱禮濤〉, *Cinezen*, 13 June 2014: <https://www.cinezen.hk/?p=1387>; last accessed 1 May 2021.

55. Herman Lai-to Yau, 'Three Months After the Production of *From the Queen to the Chief Executive*', trans. Vicky Yau: <http://www.hermanyau.com/efromQtoCE.htm>; last accessed 1 May 2021.

56. 'HKBU Alumnus Mr. Herman Yau', *The Buddy Post*, June 2010: <http://thebuddypost. hkbu.edu.hk/web/jun12/eng/people.html>; last accessed 1 May 2021.

57. Robert Hamilton, 'Hong Kong Film Director Herman Yau Talks to *Northern Soul*', *Northern Soul*, 31 October 2017: <https://www.northernsoul.me.uk/herman-yau-hong-kong-cinema-home-manchester/>; last accessed 1 May 2021.

58. Kerr, 'Popcorn Flicks with a Message'.

59. Chu, *Found in Transition*, 132–42.

60. Zhang Lan 張楠, 'Post-80s Nanjing Director's Debut *From Where We've Fallen*' (in Chinese) 〈南京80後導演處女作《何日君再來》〉, *Yangtse Evening Post*, 13 September 2017.

61. Kerr, 'Popcorn Flicks with a Message'.

Chapter 7

Jumping on the Bandwagon: The Ensemble of Hong Kong Film Directors

'How do we know there's no hope if we don't try?'
— John Woo, *The Crossing*

Introduction

As mentioned in the Introduction, the commercialisation of main melody films can be traced back to Feng Xiaogang's war blockbuster *Assembly* (2007), and Hong Kong film directors' participation in this genre began with the 'privately run' main melody film *Bodyguards and the Assassins* (2009), a film that paid homage to the Xinhai Revolution in 1911. Jackie Chan's *1911* (2011) was also made in commemoration of the 100th anniversary of this revolution, which overthrew China's last imperial dynasty. On a different but related topic, Herman Yau's *The Woman Knight of Mirror Lake* (2011) was a mainland–Hong Kong co-produced biopic about Chinese revolutionary heroine Qiu Jin. The 2010s then ushered in a decade of commercial main melody blockbusters, in which the genre was diversified in order to attract more young local, and hopefully overseas, audiences. Main melody blockbusters were no longer restricted to the nation, the Party and the Army. Thanks to the commercialisation and diversification of main melody blockbusters, more and more Hong Kong film directors had an opportunity to helm these kinds of big-budget, high-concept films, as it was no longer possible to make such films in Hong Kong because of market considerations. In a sense, the situation was similar to the quickly expanding film market in Hong Kong in the late 1970s and 1980s, when Hong Kong film directors had more scope to try different genres. Of course this time, mostly, if not only, well-established Hong Kong film directors had the opportunity to go north. Previous chapters have discussed the participation of different generations of Hong Kong film directors in main(land) melody blockbusters, and their contributions to the genre as well as, possibly, to Hong Kong cinema. Besides the main(land) melody films that had a great impact, there were also other less successful examples by other Hong Kong directors. In this chapter, I will move on to discuss some of these examples, through which other perspectives on how Hong Kong directors sang the main(land) melody will be exposed.

As Hao Jian, Professor at the Beijing Film Academy, has noted, the major difference between the Hollywood and Chinese film industries is that the former does not have a main melody, or, if it does have one, it is the theme of criticising the government.[1] For obvious reasons, it is not possible for Chinese main melody films to utilise such a refrain. Notwithstanding, Chinese main melody films have, at least on top of the main melody, emulated the diversity of Hollywood blockbusters in terms of genres. Towards this end, Chinese main melody blockbusters have become more commercial as well as diversified. Besides the sports film genre taken on by Peter Chan and Dante Lam and the disaster film genre by Andrew Lau discussed in previous chapters, some main melodies were sung differently by Hong Kong directors in this decade. In this chapter, I will first examine John Woo's disaster and war epic, and then move on to Alan Mak's undercover cop thriller. Together with other Hong Kong directors, such as the Pang brothers' and their firefighter actioner *Out of Inferno*, Woo and Mak have added new themes to the main melody genre in the past decade. Oxide Pang, the elder twin of the Pang brothers, who is well known for his ghost horrors, was invited to direct two war films, albeit not very successful ones, which introduced new elements to this genre. Besides the main melodies, there have also been themes, especially anti-corruption and anti-drug, that have resonated with the government's major policies. The participation of Hong Kong's film directors – such as Jing Wong and David Lam – in these secondary or 'quasi-main' melodies has also contributed important dimensions to the diversification of the main melody film genre.

Trapped in the Crossing

Needless to say, John Woo is world-famous for his action films. Having worked as the protégé of kung-fu film master Chang Cheh (for example, as his assistant in *The Boxer from Shantung* [1972] and *Blood Brothers* [1973]), he further developed 'the intense emphasis on male bonding in many of Chang Cheh's films' in his 'gun-fu' films,[2] from *A Better Tomorrow* (1986) and *A Better Tomorrow II* (1987) to *The Killer* (1989), *Bullet in the Head* (1990) and *Hard Boiled* (1992). After making his directorial debut with the kung-fu film *The Young Dragons* in 1975 (excluding his experimental films[3]), John Woo chose not to follow the path of his mentor and focus only on the kung-fu genre. He did make some lacklustre kung-fu films, but also directed films of various genres, from the Cantonese opera film *Princess Chang Ping* (1976) and the comedy *Money Crazy* (1977) to the midnight-sex-talk-show-inspired *Hello, Late Homecomers* (1978). As *Money Crazy* and the loose sequel *From Riches to Rags* (1980) were quite popular and profitable, Woo had the opportunity to direct Cinema City's debut comedy *Laughing Time* (1980). Despite these different endeavours, the 'John' of all trades was of course best at action inspired by male bonding. He shot the warfare actioner *Heroes Shed No Tears* in 1983, which did not premier until 1986 owing to contractual issues between John Woo and the producer, Golden Harvest. In the same year, he released the gangster-hero thriller *A Better Tomorrow*, which was so successful that it changed not only his career but also the history of Hong Kong cinema. His subsequent signature 'gun-fu' films won him international fame,[4] and after *Hard Boiled* he left Hong Kong, releasing his Hollywood debut, *Hard Target*, in 1993.

As noted in Chapter 1, John Woo, Tsui Hark and Ringo Lam were all initially given the chance to work with Jean-Claude Van Damme, the Muscles from Brussels, and in the end only John Woo passed this initial stage successfully, moving on to *Broken Arrow* (1996) and *Face/Off* (1997). Having won the Saturn Award for Best Director with the latter, he further developed his Hollywood career with the blockbuster *Mission: Impossible 2* (2000). Woo's signature gunshot scenes turned Tom Cruise into Yun-Fat Chow, and with Ethan Hawke's mission impossible, John Woo reached the height of his career in Hollywood.[5] However, the new millennium witnessed the recession of the second American reception of Hong Kong action cinema triggered by 'the cult discovery of John Woo and Tsui Hark',[6] and perhaps owing to this, John Woo tried something new in Hollywood with the war epic *Windtalkers* (2002). Thanks to his fame in Hollywood, it was a big-budget, high-concept war film, but unfortunately, although Woo was not totally inexperienced (*Heroes Shed No Tears* was actually a warfare actioner, but the budget in no way compared to that of a Hollywood blockbuster), his expertise obviously did lie with this genre. Based on Navajo 'code talkers' during the Second World War, *Windtalkers* was a US$115 million flop (it took in only US$40 million in the US),[7] and John Woo knew very clearly why his Hollywood career had begun to falter:

> The main themes of *Windtalkers* are friendship and understanding. Unfortunately, the studio wanted a John Wayne movie, just a typical American hero film with explosions every few minutes. I had to make them understand that this wasn't a story about heroes. It's a story about a man and his own demons, trying to redeem himself from war. I made the movie that way, but some people in the studio didn't appreciate it and, in the end, I guess neither did the audience.[8]

Friendship and understanding were definitely not what the American audience wanted from John Woo. His subsequent film, *Paycheck* (2003), a bit underrated in my opinion, did not do well at the box office either. The performance of this sci-fi thriller, about an engineer (portrayed by Ben Affleck) who voluntarily has his memory erased, was adversely affected, at least in part, by the decline of post-*Gigli* Affleck.

Back in 1993, John Woo's *Hard Boiled*, the last film he made in Hong Kong before relocating to Hollywood, was screened at the University of Miami Film School. The film held the audience in awe, as it was believed to distil 'the essence of the action genre and overwhelmed the viewer with two hours of destruction elevated to art form like no other film had ever done', and one of the questions asked by the audience was very inspiring: 'Why would you want to come and work in Hollywood when in Hong Kong you can make films like this?'[9] If the reason was to reach a larger audience, I think Woo was successful. But if it was about bringing his distinctive film aesthetics to the West, I would say that it was a mission incomplete. Elyssa Szeto was right in noting that Woo was 'facing off East and West', proving that 'he can make films transnationally without sacrificing the themes and styles that have won him acclaim in his latest Chinese-language films, such as *Red Cliff* and its sequel (2008–2009)'.[10] From a different perspective, Kwai-cheung Lo made a very inspiring remark about Woo's style:

> In what way does the audience conceive of how Woo's films – whether they are made in Hong Kong or produced by Hollywood – work for them? . . . There is, for example, the posture of having both guns outstretched; characters leaping through the air while shooting; guns tossing through the air in slow-motion to be caught by the protagonist; a superhero withstanding the impact of hundreds of bullets; aestheticized violence; well-choreographed action sequences; all kinds of glorifying slow-motion, tracking shots, dramatic dolly-in, freeze-frames, and dissolves; themes of friendship, loyalty, chivalry, and code of honor; and so on . . . Are these stylistic particulars just appearances that cannot represent Woo's 'real thing'?[11]

While Lo provided a meticulous Lacanian reading of this, I would just like to highlight here, as a big fan of John Woo when he was still in Hong Kong, that most, if not all, of his Hollywood projects can be said to have the form but without the spirit. So, when the audience got used to the forms – his signature scenes Kwai-cheung Lo mentioned and, of course, white doves – they no longer appreciated what the director wanted to convey in his films. For example, in *Windtalkers*, he failed to impress his target audience because they did not have many opportunities to see how Woo showcased his signature styles. John Woo wanted to deliver something more than stylistic particulars.

After the flops of *Windtalkers* and *Paycheck*, John Woo took a short rest and then turned to the quickly emerging mainland market with the co-produced period drama *Red Cliff*, which represented a typical genre of co-productions back then. This was a project that Woo had dreamed of making. As Stephen Teo has examined in detail, the film, based on the novel *Romance of the Three Kingdoms*, gave Woo a chance to pay tribute to Akira Kurosawa, whose *Kagemusha* (1980) and *Ran* (1985) were also inspired by this Chinese literary classic. Perhaps more importantly,

> a film such as *Red Cliff* typifies the convergence of nationalism and transnationalism in the Chinese thrust towards global soft power – a kind of convergence that resonates with the objectives of other Asian cinemas to compete with Hollywood and with each other.[12]

Shortly after *Red Cliff* won both critical acclaim and, to a certain extent, box-office success, John Woo was awarded the Golden Lion for Lifetime Achievement at the 67th Venice International Film Festival in 2010. Expectations were therefore high when he started shooting *The Crossing* (2014), even though *Reign of Assassins* (2010), a *wuxia* film that he produced and co-directed with Taiwanese director Chao-pin Su, was 'a bit run-of-the-mill'.[13] At a press conference at the 4th Beijing International Film Festival on 16 April 2014, John Woo said that he had long wanted to make this *Doctor Zhivago*-style epic,[14] although the film was billed by mainland media as the 'China's *Titanic*', and he explained why as follows: 'This film is an epic love story. The humanity and history will touch people's hearts.'[15] This sounded similar to what he had said about *Windtalkers*, and unfortunately, the result was not very different from his previous failed project. Although Woo might not have had to convince the producer that this was a film about humanity, not heroes, it was clear that the audience expected a typical war film with heroism and action. Loosely based on the true story of the *Taiping*, an overloaded steamer sailing from Shanghai to Taiwan that sank in 1949, this main melody film in two parts was about the Kuomintang's defeat at the Huaihai Campaign in 1948, which marked the beginning of the end of its rule over China. In 2008, Woo first heard about this story, in which more than 1,500 passengers were killed, from the Taiwanese screenwriter Hui-Ling Wang, who had worked with Ang Lee in *Eat Drink Man Woman* (1994), *Crouching Tiger, Hidden Dragon* (2000) and *Lust, Caution* (2007). As the re-examination of the Republican period was also one of the main melodies emphasised by Beijing, John Woo had the chance to sing the main(land) melody with this epic romance after *Red Cliff*. *The Crossing* seemed closer to his idea of fusing the love theme with the grand framework of a historical epic like *Gone with the Wind* (1939).

Understandably, however, those who had expected to watch 'China's *Titanic*' were hugely disappointed, as the first instalment, which was focused more on love stories against the backdrop of the battle that the Kuomintang lost, ended exactly where the fateful voyage on the *Taiping* began. It was seen by the audience as overly long-winded, and this could have been attributed to its design in two parts (*The Crossing II* was released eight months after the first episode), which was meant to boost box-office revenues to cover its huge blockbuster budget. There was also speculation that the director's poor health – he was diagnosed with Stage 3 lymphoid cancer in 2011 – was an important reason why Woo had fumbled. In the end, the first part grossed only RMB 195 million in mainland China and a total of US$32.38 million worldwide, ranking a miserable forty-fifth at the Chinese box office for 2014.[16] John Woo did not think the two-part design was a flaw, and he even said that *The Crossing* was the best work of his life before the film premiered in 2014, to which I suppose his fans would beg to differ.[17] John Woo attributed the lacklustre reception to insufficient promotions, wrong timing and, above all, incorrect marketing strategy – the film was erroneously branded as the 'Chinese *Titanic*': 'It is completely different. *The Crossing* focuses on war and its impact on the love stories. Their fate will change as they board the ship,' he said.[18] Owing, perhaps, to the audience's frustration, *The Crossing II* (2015) was even more poorly received by critics and audiences than the first instalment. Widely reviewed as 'a sinker and a stinker', the sequel was a disaster in itself:

> Like passengers who overpaid for tickets to escape war-ravaged Shanghai on the Taiwan-bound liner *Taiping* in 1949, only to end up on a sinking ship, audiences get a pretty lousy deal with John Woo's *The Crossing II*, an inert follow-up that doesn't deliver enough visual or emotional payoff in its overdue yet short-lived shipwreck climax.[19]

For a big-budget blockbuster epic, the box office of US$8.07 million worldwide was simply abysmal. It reportedly topped the list of the biggest-loss films in the history of Chinese cinema.[20]

Besides the two-part design and/or the poor health of the director, an equally important reason behind the flop was arguably that John Woo was best at male bonding stories, not love stories. I do not doubt that John Woo had long wished to make an epic romance, but it was clear he would botch it if he did so solely for the following reason: 'People tend to think I can only do male films, but I want to prove that I can do a female film from a female perspective.'[21] As mentioned above, some of his stylistic particulars, such as white doves, did appear in the film, but obviously it was not the John Woo that his fans wanted to see. The film included most, if not all, of his signature ticks, from slow-motion action, male bonding and Mexican standoffs to, of course, white doves. The CG-assisted scenes, such as in the Shanghai Bund where the steamer was moored, were actually made beautifully, but this was not what his old fans or the young mainland audiences expected. The abashed appearance of flapping doves, for example, alongside the *Taiping* rendered the director's signature symbol more awkward than ever. In sum, *The Crossing* was a great disappointment to John Woo's fans, both old and new, and this was succinctly summed up by the following comment:

> When the Taiping eventually sinks, it brings a tear to the eye – not for the thousands lost at sea, but rather the resigned acceptance that Hong Kong cinema has lost one of its truly great directors. Woo built his career as a pioneering visual stylist, whose signature flourishes inspired a generation of filmmakers both local and abroad. To see him churn out such generic bilge provokes a mournful sinking feeling.[22]

Ironically, John Woo's steamer launched at the same time as Tsui Hark's *The Taking of Tiger Mountain 3D* (2014) premiered. The former was totally eclipsed by the latter in terms of both commercial success and critical acclaim. It was reported that Tsui Hark helped with a new cut of the second part of *The Crossing*, but this just made the failure of the second part more stark. Tsui Hark's model worked well when he sang the main(land) melody, but John Woo's did not, because the aesthetics of violence and male bonding in his films were organically woven into his works. In my view, grand narrative was not John Woo's expertise. *Bullet in the Head* had a larger epochal backdrop, but it was precisely because of this that it was less well received than *A Better Tomorrow*, *The Killer* and *Hard Boiled*. Perhaps he knew this as well, as he said that the love stories in the film involved humanity, not politics: 'There was a political backdrop of civil war. There were winners and losers, but it was the love in the midst of upheavals that counted.'[23] He also told *The Beijing News* that the original title, *1949*, was changed to *The Crossing* because he (and/or the film company) did not want to be misunderstood. As this was not supposed to be a political film, it was not unreasonable for the film company to brand the film as China's *Titanic*.[24] In any case it was simply mission impossible for a main melody film to avoid politics. That Tsui Hark squarely tackled politics in *The Taking of Tiger Mountain 3D* was the major reason for its success. 'The transition from *Hard Target* to *Face/Off* through *Broken Arrow* may explain how Woo could become himself only by renouncing being himself', and '[i]n general discussions of John Woo's movies there is conspicuous consensus as to the concrete existence of a "Woo film-style." This style is presumed to be stable and not vary across time and place.'[25] The style of John Woo was just not a film style that could be easily translated across the border. It was a pity that Woo was seen by the Hollywood industry as just another action film director, as pointedly summarised by Tony Williams:

> He is not recognized for being the serious artist that he is and this affects the funding of projects that would really reflect the complex nature of his talent. He is just another transnational artist brought into an industry that now shows little respect and understanding for creativity.[26]

As such, post-Hollywood John Woo had become just another action film director. Similarly, the corporate Chinese establishment saw him as an established action film director who could internationalise main melody films. Even without the benefit of hindsight, it was possible to see that this was a mismatched mission. I had hoped naively that John Woo would reunite with Yun-Fat Chow and Hong Kong to revitalise his work, but at the same time I fully understood that his international career was a no-return one. Perhaps he also knew he had to revitalise himself, but he chose to remake Junya Satō's *Manhunt* (1976) his subsequent project. The major reason behind this was that Ken Takakura, the male lead of this Japanese crime classic who passed away in 2014, was his favourite actor. However, once again, the transnational – pan-Asian – framework iced with John Woo's signature ticks looked embarrassingly old-fashioned.

Extraordinary but Mismatched Mission

Besides those from internationally renowned veteran director John Woo, other Hong Kong directors also made main(land) melody projects that were mismatched missions. Gordon Chan, for example, was another well-established Hong Kong director who took up an incompatible main(land) melody project. As mentioned in the chapter on Dante Lam, Gordon Chan was Lam's mentor and collaborator for many years. With *Beast Cops* (1998), they were jointly named Best Director at the 18th Hong Kong Film Awards. While Hong Kong cinema was rapidly declining in the new millennium, they reunited to make the farcical parody *Undercover Hidden Dragon* (2006), which was a total failure. Gordon Chan went north to develop his mainland career after this, and his mainland debut, *Painted Skin* (2008), a supernatural period fantasy adapted from Qing Dynasty writer Pu Songling's *Strange Tales from a Chinese Studio*, made about RMB 200 million at the box office, making it the annual highest grossing domestic film in China.[27] His subsequent works were mainly period dramas, including *Mural* (2011) and the martial arts actioner trilogy *The Four* (2012, 2013, 2014; the first episode was co-directed with Janet Chun). As period martial arts films became less popular in the 2010s, Gordon Chan's fame gradually faded, and when he picked up the period main(land) melody project *God of War* (2017), it was argu- ably not good timing.

Gordon Chan started his film career at Shaw Brothers, first as a special effects technician and later as a scriptwriter (he co-scripted *Behind the Yellow Line* [1984], starring Leslie Cheung, Maggie Cheung and Anita Mui and dis- tributed by Shaw Brothers). He once said that his main job was scriptwriter, and director was just a part-time role.[28] However, after he made his successful directorial debut, *Yuppie Fantasia* (1989) (actually, he was the executive direc- tor of another 1988 romantic comedy, *Hearts to Hearts*), Chan became one of the most sought-after directors in Hong Kong. He had many opportunities to work on different genres with various superstars, including Stephen Chow's classic 'non-sensical' comedy series *Fight Back to School* (1991) and its sequel *Fight Back to School II* (1992) and Jackie Chan's car-racing crime thriller *Thun- derbolt* (1995).[29] Although these were box-office winners, his career-defining films were police and gangster actioners, including *The Final Option* (1994), *First Option* (1996) and *Beast Cops*, the film that won him and Dante Lam the Best Director award. Similar to many other Hong Kong directors, Gordon Chan was versatile and able to handle different themes and genres. *Painted Skin* was released during the heyday of period dramas in the mainland market, and thanks to Gordon Chan's excellent executive ability, it did very well there. When period dramas started declining later, however, it became obvious that period dramas were not Gordon Chan's strong suit. In this sense, it was not surprising that *God of War* was seen as failing to meet expectations. It was a main melody film in the sense that this historical action film was about Ming Dynasty Commander Qi Jiguang beating a force of pirates led by Japanese sam- urai, which chimed nicely with the anti-Japanese theme of main melody films. Actually the film was quite well made in all aspects, and the male lead, Vincent Zhao, was excellently cast as the stiff military strategist general. That said, this was a fair comment on the film: 'Competent on all fronts but never dazzling, it should please genre devotees but won't cross over to a broader audience.'[30] Because of the declining popularity of period martial arts dramas in the 2010s, this main melody film attracted only genre devotees, not young local fans, let alone overseas audiences. If it had been shot a decade earlier, I guess the results would have been better. In 2017, the mainland audience had different choices, even of main melody films, owing to the commercialisation and diversification of this genre.

Two younger, but also already established, Hong Kong directors similarly took charge of main(land) melody films, one not unexpected but the other quite a surprise. Firstly, it was totally expected that Alan Mak, the long-time collaborator of Andrew Lau, would be commissioned to direct main melody films. One of the most successful Hong Kong directors in the new millennium, Mak had worked closely with Andrew Lau on the *Infernal Affairs* trilogy (2002–3), *Initial D* (2005) and *Confession of Pain* (2006), and then with Felix Chong, his long-time scriptwriter partner, on the *Overheard* trilogy (2009–14). That Alan Mak first headed north with *The Lost Bladesman* (2011), co-directed with Felix Chong, was a bit surprising though. This mainland–Hong Kong co-produced film was a historical war biopic inspired by the story of Guan Yu, also known as the God of War, of the Three Kingdoms Period. Mak had never directed a period martial arts or war film before this northbound project. Obviously, the reason for taking it on was that period martial arts dramas were the major trend of mainland–Hong Kong co-productions at that time. However, as repeatedly mentioned in previous chapters, Chinese cinema started striving for the diversification of genres in the 2010s, and this was a rather untimely mainland debut for Mak and Chong, especially because this genre was not their speciality at all.

Their second mainland project was *The Silent War* (2012), which can virtually be considered a main melody film. As one can tell from the title, this film was similar to their *Overheard* series, although the subject matter was completely different. Starring Hong Kong, mainland and Taiwanese stars Tony Chiu-wai Leung, Zhou Xun and Mavis Fan, respectively, *The Silent War* was a spy thriller romance set in 1949, shortly after the founding of the People's Republic of China. It was adapted from the first tale in the award-winning spy novel *In the Dark* penned by mainland writer Mai Jia (hailed as the Chinese equivalent to John Le Carré). Patriotic symbols like flags and saluting were arguably a standard tribute paid to the Party and the Army, but at least the directors did not demonise the enemy when singing the main melody in this film about the battles between agents from the Communist Party of China and the Kuomintang. On the face of it, this was similar to the mainland spy blockbuster *The Message* (2009), but the directors placed more emphasis on romance in this story about the government's Unit 701, which was responsible for stopping an invisible enemy. This seemed to be an ingenious design because the directors could not slam surveillance or, most importantly, the complicities between the government and big business/real estate developers – something they did beautifully with the *Overheard* series. Yet exactly because of this design, Mak and Chong could not do what they did best. Although the *Overheard* series was co-produced by mainland's Bona Entertainment and Hong Kong's left-wing production company Sil-Metropole Organization, the directors were free to direct their critiques as the setting was Hong Kong. Both Mak and Chong were excellent writers, but without Andrew Lau, the execution seemed less spectacular than in *Infernal Affairs*. Lacking the meticulous plot of the *Overheard* series,[31] *The Silent War* ended up being a mediocre spy film. Understandably, the film was not well received in Hong Kong due to its blatant glorification of the Party, but it grossed a promising total of RMB 0.24 billion at the mainland box office. Perhaps owing to this, mainland investors seemed happy about the outcome, and Alan Mak continued to helm a main(land) melody blockbuster in his next mainland project. This time, he co-directed *Extraordinary Mission* (2017) with Anthony Pun, a veteran cinematographer making his directorial debut with this main(land) melody war film.

Alan Mak's new mission was similar to the operations taken up by Dante Lam. *Extraordinary Mission* was a typical commercial main melody blockbuster that paid homage to the police force for their valiant, patriotic deeds against crime. At the premiere of the film at the Communication University of China in March 2017, the directors said directly and overtly: 'Police officers are ordinary people, but they have to take up extraordinary mission. *Extraordinary Mission* aims to pay homage to them for their righteousness, sense of responsibility and patriotism.'[32] The theme of the story was staunchly main melody: an undercover cop (portrayed by Huang Xuan) risks his life and infiltrates a drug gang in the Golden Triangle after finding out that another undercover (portrayed by Xing Jiadong) has been captured. In the end, as expected, he collaborates with his superior in charge of his undercover mission (portrayed by Zu Feng), who sacrifices his life in this extraordinary mission, destroying the gang and saving his colleague. With a plot blatantly similar to Dante Lam's *Operation Mekong* (2016), this film was designed to be a combination of *Infernal Affairs* and *Operation Mekong*. Unfortunately, in spite of Alan Mak's proven track record of handling an undercover's ambiguous identity and its unsettling transformation, there was simply not much, if any, room for him to depict the ambiguity and complexity of the undercover in a main melody film. After the first half or two-thirds, which was a new version of *Infernal Affairs* (for example, Huang Xuan reminded the audience of the undercover played by Tony Chiu-wai Leung in *Infernal Affairs*) with more action, the film turned into a shorter, lighter version of *Operation Mekong*. Most mainland audiences were either not attracted by or not familiar with *Infernal Affairs* (the mainland version they saw was different, at least the ending where, unlike the Hong Kong version, poetic justice was done), and, as evidenced by the outstanding result of *Operation Mekong*, they were attracted by breathless, nearly ceaseless action. Obviously, Mak and Pun, with screenwriter Felix Chong, were no Dante Lam. Perhaps not coincidentally, the following review of *The Lost Bladesman* seemed largely applicable to *Extraordinary Mission*:

> Mak and Chong, whose expertise lies in setting taut psychological dramas in urban, westernized Hong Kong, are out of their depth when projecting a historical vision steeped in ancient folklore. A move to modernize the protagonists by besetting them with philosophical doubts about their raison d'etre and values of their time is not developed in line with their course of action, which remains orthodox.[33]

Although their extraordinary mission was set in modern times, they were equally out of their depth when translating psychological dramas in urban, westernised Hong Kong to a main melody crime thriller somewhere in the Golden Triangle. To be fair, the undercover theme did let the directors make a film different from typical main melody crime thrillers like *Operation Mekong*, and this was arguably why it was quite positively reviewed by international film critics, such as in this one by Tim Youngs:

> . . . the filmmakers instead follow a more character-driven thriller approach to draw on their strengths while trying something different. Now with Pun joining them as co-director, Mak and Chong are showing no lack of ambition in extending their brand of filmmaking into new territory.[34]

Unfortunately, this was not welcomed by mainland audiences, who expected sheer sensationalism, nor was it welcomed by Hong Kong audiences, who thought it was, at best, an incomplete version of *Infernal Affairs*. The co-director Anthony Pun once explained in an interview what he understood as main melody: 'I do not know how to define main melody. Actually top Hollywood box-office earners are often main melody films about the country and patriotism. This film of ours is about responsibility, justice and sacrifice.'[35] Clearly, he did not fully understand the difference between Hollywood and Chinese main melodies, as noted by Hao Jian mentioned at the beginning of this chapter. Even in films about the country and/or patriotism, Hollywood did not have a main melody, or, if it did, it was the theme of criticising the government. While Tsui Hark squarely dealt and effectively coped with this in *The Taking of Tiger Mountain 3D*, Mak and Pun simply tried evading the issue in their extraordinary mission.

As mentioned above, it was a bit surprising to see Oxide Pang in the director's seat in the main(land) melody war film *My War* (2016), as the director had won his fame with ghost horrors. Oxide Pang and his twin brother Danny Pang caught critics' attention with their horror series *The Eye* (2002–5) and a Hollywood version in 2007. Back in 1997, Oxide Pang made his own directorial debut, the experimental project *Who Is Running?* (1997) in Thailand. The twin's joint directorial debut crime film, *Bangkok Dangerous* (1999), enjoyed international acclaim – winning the International Federation of Film Critics FIPRESCI Award at the Toronto International Film Festival in 2000. Co-produced by the Singapore-based MediaCorp Raintree Pictures and its Hong Kong counterpart, Applause Pictures, masterminded by Peter Chan, the Pang brothers 'pulled in a multinational cast and crew for *The Eye*', and after this pan-Asian success, they continued 'with almost similar formulas, transnational casts and narratives taking place on Hong Kong and Thailand' in the next instalments, and the side-track *Ab-Normal Beauty* (2004) was ground-breaking in the sense that it 'offers a psychologically complex variation on this theme and pushes its implications for queer female subject formation further than most of its predecessors'.[36] Oxide Pang started his career at Thailand's well-known Kantana Film Lab, where he began to make commercials, and later became well known as one of the best colour correction technicians in all of Asia in the early 1990s. He later joined forces with his Hong Kong-based twin brother, who was an established film editor, and together became 'Directors of Ghostly Talent'.[37] As mentioned in the chapter on Peter Chan, the pan-Asian project turned a bit sour later, and so Oxide Pang put more emphasis on the Hong Kong market. In terms of solo efforts, Oxide Pang's stylistic series *The Detective* (2007), *The Detective 2* (2011) and *Conspirators* (aka *The Detective 3*) (2013), which made ingenious, expert use of colour tones, was hailed as 'a new generation of Hong Kong noirish crime thrillers with a Thai flavor'.[38] Their fans were quite surprised when the Pang brothers co-directed *Out of Inferno* (2013), a mainland–Hong Kong co-production, touted as Hong Kong's 'first 3D disaster film', displaying the professionalism of the Chinese firefighters who serve the southern Chinese city of Guangzhou. Oxide Pang's next solo northbound project was the suspense romantic comedy *Detective Gui* (2015), which was almost unnoticed by the local audience in Hong Kong.

Perhaps owing to these new items on his résumé, Oxide Pang was commissioned to take charge of China Film Group's big film of the year, *My War*. This main melody historical war film about the Korean War was based on the novel *Reunion* penned by the literary master Ba Jin in 1961. A tribute to commemorate the sixty-fifth anniversary of the Korean War, in which China fought on the side of North Korea against American forces, *My War* was a typical main melody war film glorifying the PLA. Despite this, Oxide Pang said that he was not trying to make a main melody film:

> When I first went to China Film Group to attend a meeting, I was thinking why they thought of me. There are so many outstanding directors in the mainland. If they asked me to make a main melody film, and to praise the main melody, I would have run away from this project.[39]

China Film Group chose him because they wanted to have something different from typical main melody war films, and according to Oxide Pang himself, 'China Film Group set an objective for me, which was to make a commercial film with my style and from my perspective.'[40] In a sense, this was arguably the main reason that led to the flop of this film. From my perspective, it was a beautiful misunderstanding if Pang really thought that was what he had been tasked to do. It was a main melody film, and the main melody had to be sung in a standard way, without changing the melody, although one might sing the melody in his/her own style. In other words, the most important point was the commercialisation of main melody films, not inserting a main melody theme into a commercial film. In the end, it was embarrassing that Oxide Pang's hands were, to a significant extent, tied. Although he did bring into the production crew a Thai special effects team and some Korean filmmakers, he was not able to fully exhibit his alternative style as in *The Detective*. It was reported that he had to put the emphasis on war scenes involving the Chinese side after discussing with the screenwriter Liu Heng, who had penned the scripts of many mainland blockbusters, including *Assembly* and *The Flowers of War* (2011) directed by Zhang Yimou, and he decided to abort his plan to shape the character of the male lead (portrayed by Liu Ye) differently, sticking with the typical heroism of a main melody war film.[41] In the end, even if he wanted to bring something new to the main melody, they were only stylistic ticks like a hand-held camera and slow motion, and the war scenes were condemned by mainland critics as routine, making heroism 'pale and weak'.[42] The lesson told by Tsui Hark was that if one wanted to take Tiger Mountain, one had to go into the mountain, not try to find a detour. To be fair, *My War* was decently made, but it did not exactly meet the expectations of mainland audiences for a main melody war film. Worse still, the promotional trailer of the film stirred up heated controversies before its release:

> It starred a literal busload of famous old Chinese actors playing the grandparents of the film's stars on a sightseeing trip to Seoul. When the enthusiastic young South Korean tour guide starts telling them about her city, the old people interrupt. 'Miss,' says one with a grin, 'we've been here before.' She is surprised, saying that according to their passports, they'd never been to Korea. 'We didn't use passports back then,' one responds cheerfully. The tour guide is confused. Another explains: 'We came carrying the Red Flag'. She still doesn't get it, so the old people tell her to check out the film *My War* – she'll understand then, they assure her.[43]

The trailer went viral on the internet, and many Chinese netizens were highly critical of it because it unashamedly created hard feelings among the South

Koreans. Subsequently, '[s]ome called for a boycott of the film even though Oxide Pang protested that he had had nothing to do with the trailer'.[44]

Oxide Pang's next main(land) melody take was *Towards the River Glorious* (2019), another propaganda war film to commemorate the end of the Chinese Civil War in 1949. This film focused on the Yangtze River Crossing Campaign, during which – as per the PLA's slogan 'Fight across the Yangtze River and liberate all of China' – the PLA crossed the Yangtze River and occupied Nanjing, the then capital of the Kuomintang. Pang must have known very well that it was a main melody project. The following review succinctly summed up the lacklustre performance of the director; although he had adopted more hard-core war scenes with countless bombs and gunfire: to this film 'he brings little else than his trademark showiness: heavy filters (one battle scene is so damn orange it would give even the late, great Tony Scott a seizure), extreme slow-motion, a few first-person-shooter angles, and that's about it.'[45] My sense is that main melody war films were a mismatched mission for Oxide Pang. Not unlike John Woo, what he had brought to main melody war blockbusters was at most his style without its essence. The producers might have wanted him to introduce something new to main melody war films, but bound by the genre itself, they could not but, to borrow a traditional Chinese proverb, 'buy a wooden box and return the pearls inside'.

Quasi-Main Melodies

As mentioned in the previous chapter, the continued commercialisation of Chinese cinema has led to more quasi-main melodies being made. Renowned for its police and gangster films, Hong Kong cinema found more and more opportunities with anti-crime topics in the 2010s. The top-grossing local film in Hong Kong in 2012, the signature Hong Kong police and gangster film *Cold War* (2012), co-directed by Longman Leung and Sunny Luk, received HK$42.8 million at the local box office, but raked in RMB 252.18 million at the mainland box office,[46] showing that Hong Kong-style crime thrillers, as long as they could pass the censorship system, had an enormous market in the mainland. Mainland–Hong Kong co-produced (anti-)crime films were very popular in the 2010s, including, among others, *Cold War*, *Firestorm* (2013), directed by Alan Yuen, *Overheard 3* (2014), directed by Felix Chong and Alan Mak, *Helios* (2015) and *Cold War 2* (2016), directed by Longman Leung and Sunny Luk, *Line Walker* (2016) and *Line Walker 2* (2019), directed by Wai-Hung Man, *Shock Wave* (2017), directed by Herman Yau, and *Project Gutenberg* (2018), directed by Felix Chong. The achievements of Hong Kong crime films were recognised by China's national English language newspaper. According to an essay published in *Global Times* in 2019, crime suspense thriller was one of the major characteristics of Hong Kong-related films:

> In recent years, crime and suspense thrillers such as *Project Gutenberg*, *Chasing the Dragon* [2017] and the *Storm* series [2014–2019] did very well at the box office in the mainland, which was a confidence booster for Hong Kong filmmakers. It showed that Hong Kong films have not been abandoned by the mainland market, as long as their stories can touch the hearts of the audience.[47]

Given the limited scope of this chapter, I will briefly discuss just two key crime themes especially welcomed by the mainland market: drugs and corruption.

First of all, drug use is a severe social problem that has hindered national rejuvenation. Some of the main(land) melody films discussed above and in previous chapters (such as *My War* and *Operation Mekong*) glorified the PLA and the police by their fighting against drug lords. In a sense, the anti-drug theme can be seen as a secondary or 'quasi-main' melody. Indeed, anti-drug has been a national policy for many years, but a new anti-drug law that abolished the modality of re-education through labour, which was considered a milestone, was rolled out in 2008:

> It called for a boost in community treatment, encouraged drug users to seek treatment voluntarily, and set compulsory isolated rehabilitation as the only government-ordered treatment modality. China has also rapidly expanded methadone maintenance treatment programmes. These policies are good attempts to shift the penalty-oriented management of drug users to one that is health-oriented.[48]

Anti-corruption is another national policy repeatedly stressed by senior government officials. After the Eighteenth National Congress of the Communist Party of China in 2012, an unprecedentedly large-scale campaign was launched to fight corruption on all fronts, involving the party, government, military and state-owned company officials. This 'has opened a new chapter of anti-corruption campaign in China'.[49] Be it an anti-drug or an anti-corruption campaign, popular cultures, such as television dramas and films, were effective means to supplement the policies. Having won fame for their police and gangster crime films for many decades, Hong Kong directors found these anti-crime topics perfectly suited to them. In the past decade or so, there have thus been many mainland–Hong Kong co-produced, albeit not fully main melody, films that sang these quasi-main melodies.

As I have argued elsewhere, Johnnie To's *Drug War* (2012) represented 'a reverse border crossing', where the presence of Hong Kong was in mainland cinema. Opposite to the border crossing of mainland gangsters committing crimes in Hong Kong films in the 1980s, this film featured Hong Kong drug dealers crossing the border into the mainland. Johnnie To understood the rules of the game of the mainland market very well: 'We are the production team. *Drug War* is not a co-production; it is a mainland production.'[50] Besides the standard requirements, such as a perfectly righteous *gongan* (portrayed by Sun Honglei) and poetic justice done at the end of the film (the Hong Kong drug cartel boss, portrayed by Louis Koo, is sentenced to death), Johnnie To managed to keep some of his Hong Kong characteristics in his northern venture.[51] The anti-drug theme was also picked up by Benny Chan in his *The White Storm* (2013), which was about three middle-aged undercover cops' operation against a Thai drug lord. The use of the Cantopop classic 'Pledged to Go into Knife Mountain' as the theme song, I have argued, can be interpreted as a metaphor of the northbound ventures of Hong Kong directors: the mainland market was similar to 'knife mountain'.[52] These directors successfully broke into the knife mountain, and as the anti-drug theme fit nicely with the main melody, more and more (anti-)drug films were made, such as Jing Wong's *Chasing the Dragon* (2017) and *Chasing the Dragon II: Wild Wild Bunch* (2019), Herman Yau's *The White Storm 2: Drug Lords* (2019) and Lawrence Lau's *Dealer Healer* (2019).

Based on the story of a repentant gangster who later won the Ten Outstanding Young Persons award for his contributions to gospel addiction treatment, *Dealer Healer* was nothing more than uninspiring propaganda against drugs, despite the star-studded cast (Louis Koo, Sean Lau and Gordon Lam). Actually, this story had already been adapted into a film version by Billy Tang as *Those Were the Days . . .* in 1995. Without the generous support of Sil-Metropole and the mainland market, this new version would not have been possible. A sequel in name only, *The White Storm 2: Drug Lords* enjoyed huge success at the mainland box office, taking RMB 1,312 million compared with RMB 37 million for *Dealer Healer*. In addition to the two leading stars, Andy Lau and Louis Koo, Herman Yau's directorial skills were a key factor behind the film's popularity (more on this in Chapter 6). Most importantly, *The White Storm 2: Drug Lords* proved that the commercialisation of the anti-drug theme in an action thriller was overwhelmingly welcomed by mainland audiences.

Meanwhile, *Chasing the Dragon* was a reboot of Jing Wong's own crime classic *To Be Number One* (1991), inspired by the true story of the Hong Kong drug lord 'Crippled Ho' (the Chinese title of the film). Wong also worked another crime classic of his, *Lee Rock* (1991), into *Chasing the Dragon*. *Lee Rock* was about a police officer notorious for corruption in the 1960s and 1970s. Donnie Yen and Andy

Lau portrayed the roles of Cripple Ho and Lee Rock, respectively, and Wong effectively recycled the surplus value of Hong Kong cinema into an upgraded package for the mainland market, grossing a promising RMB 584 million at the mainland box office. An in-name-only sequel, *Chasing the Dragon II* was in fact inspired by the story of the notorious gangster who kidnapped a Hong Kong billionaire (also one of the three felons in *Trivisa* [2016]). This was arguably not so attractive to the mainland audience. Owing to the formulaic treatment by Wong, this sequel received only around RMB 300 million in mainland China. Notwithstanding the different degrees of popularity in the mainland, the two instalments of *Chasing the Dragon* evinced Jing Wong's shrewd and highly pragmatic treatment of crime themes. The films were intentionally set in colonial Hong Kong, with special emphases on criminals before the handover. On the one hand, this was a strategy to avoid censorship because the crimes did not have anything to do with the present-day Hong Kong Special Administrative Region; on the other hand, these corrupt stories could also be seen as debunking the myth of the 'good old colonial days' hailed by some Hong Kong people.

Before Xi Jinping's far-reaching anti-corruption campaign in 2012, corruption had long been seen as one of the biggest enemies of the PRC. *Fatal Decision* (2000), a film based on Zhang Ping's best-selling novel *Decision* and directed by Yu Benzheng, was 'so well received that a former Central Disciplinary Committee member gave an order: "Leading cadres should take their families to watch this film."'[53] Back then, it was 'the single most popular film in the relative new genre of "anticorruption cinema",' and as noted by Michael Berry, despite its being 'a work of thinly veiled entertainment propaganda, *Fatal Decision*'s realism and boldness struck a genuine chord'.[54] *In the Name of the People* (2017), the anti-corruption television drama masterminded by The Supreme People's Procuratorate, was another example of government policy. This was perhaps the reason why the *Storm* series directed by David Lam was so well received in the mainland market. Less propagandist, this commercial series pinpointed the major issue of corruption with different typical crime-thriller plots. Well known for his anti-corruption television dramas and films, David Lam, albeit not as popular as his contemporaries Tsui Hark and Ann Hui, was an excellent person to helm this series. He started his career with TVB and joined Hong Kong's ICAC in 1980, masterminding two television-film series, *Anti-Corruption Pioneers* (1981) and *Anti-Corruption Pioneers II* (1985). After leaving ICAC, he went on to direct, among others, the corruption-related crime films *Powerful Four* (1992) and *First Shot* (1993). The alphabets of the *Storm* series, including *Z Storm* (2014), *S Storm* (2016), *L Storm* (2018) and *P Storm* (2019), referred to different kinds of corruption activities: 'Z' for the criminal 'Z Fund' in the film; 'S' for soccer-betting-related corruption; 'L' for laundering and ICAC's 'L' group, responsible for investigating breaches of staff discipline; and 'P' for prison as the film was about corruption related to the Correctional Services Department. This series was not particularly well received in Hong Kong because David Lam did not make any innovative attempts, but it did introduce something new to the genre of 'anti-corruption cinema' in the mainland, showing that overtly didactic messages could be covered – in both senses of this word – by crime thrillers. Jing Wong also knew this very well. Back in 2009, he released the (anti-)corruption film *I Corrupt All Cops* (2009), as implied by the first letters of the four words (ICAC) of the cryptic English title. Similar to *Chasing the Dragon*, the film, set in colonial Hong Kong before the setting up of the ICAC, can be seen as anti-corruption as well as uncovering deep-seated social problems in Hong Kong under British rule.

Concluding Remarks

While the commercialisation of main melody films remained a key task of the mainland film industry, quasi-main melodies also continued to be sung in the mainland market. On the one hand, new Hong Kong directors had more opportunities in diversified main melody films. *The Bravest* (2019), for example, was produced by Andrew Lau and directed by Tony Chan, a young director who had only (co-)helmed a few romantic comedies – such as *Fall in Love Like a Star* (2015) – before this tribute to firefighters adapted from Mongolian writer Balguy Yuanye's non-fiction work *The Deepest Water Is Tears*. Billy Chung's *Eternal Wave* (2017), a loose remake of the early revolutionary-themed spy film *The Eternal Wave* (1958), was another example. On the other hand, besides Hong Kong directors being commissioned to make main(land) melody films, Hong Kong genre films with a less overt main melody were equally if not more important for the development of Hong Kong directors in mainland China. Two anti-corruption blockbusters, originally scheduled for release in early 2020, were deferred because of the coronavirus pandemic: Philip Yung's *Theory of Ambitions* and Jing Wong's loose sequel to *I Corrupt All Cops* (the former would have premiered earlier had it not been for censorship issues). In a previous section, I noted that Alan Mak took up some main(land) melody projects that were not his area of expertise. When he sang the quasi-main melody, however, he seemed to be more comfortable. In *Integrity* (2019), which was loosely based on a case of smuggling illicit cigarettes in 1993, he regained some of his momentum as, with fewer restrictions, he could rely more on 'intricate plotting rather than action scenes to grip audiences'.[55] This was a good example of how some Hong Kong directors could sing quasi-main melodies more proficiently.

Tsui Hark, Ann Hui, Peter Chan, Dante Lam and Andrew Lau were among those whose styles were more effectively translated into main melody films.

When mainland Chinese media talked about the *Storm* series, for example, it was stressed that its popularity in the mainland could be attributed to its suspense and action, the success formula of Hong Kong police and gangster films:

> We have watched a lot of main melody films, but few had left deep impressions on us. The major reason was that there was only main melody but no film. Main melody films, of course, should be an organic fusion of main melody and films.[56]

Therefore, the repackaging of main melody films as genre films would arguably be an important direction to take.[57] However, it is still necessary to see the main melody as equally if not more important than the commercial value of a genre blockbuster – the main(land) melody – in the mainland market. Daniel Lee's *The Climbers* (2019) ranked third, with a promising RMB 1 billion box-office gross, but third to *My People, My Country* and *The Captain*, despite the leading role of Wu Jing, who had set amazing box-office records with *Wolf Warriors 2* (2017) and *The Wandering Earth* (2019). In terms of critical acclaim, it also fell short of expectations. It was reported by the mainland media as a lost battle.[58] As argued by a mainland film critic, the background music and emotional scenes reminded the audience of the director's *Dragon Blade* (2015) and *Time Raiders* (2016), but perhaps owing to a lack of thorough understanding of revolutionary beliefs, Lee had to find secular rationales for the characters, which could not but dilute the impact of the main melody: 'these motivations do not fit nicely with the mission of our time, turning cardinal national principles into trivial romances'.[59] The blockbusterisation of main melody films, in other words, should not be seen as genuine Hollywoodisation.

Having said this, entertainmentisation and blockbusterisation were nonetheless crucial to the development of Chinese main melody films in the 2010s. It was argued by mainland critics that the rise of main melody war films in China was a result of the rise of national consciousness, and some even used Slavoj Žižek's 'post-ideological society' – albeit not in an unproblematic manner – to account for the rise of a market of healthy national consciousness in the mainland.[60] Be that as it may, this was what Žižek said when he talked about the 'post-ideological':

> One of the commonplaces of the contemporary 'post-ideological' attitude is that today, we have more or less outgrown divisive political fictions (of class struggle, etc.) and reached political maturity, which enables us to focus on real problems (ecology, economic growth . . .) One could thus claim that what the 'post-ideological' attitude of the sober, pragmatic approach

to reality excludes as 'old ideological fictions' of class antagonisms, as the domain of 'political passions' which no longer have any place in today's rational social administration, is the historical Real itself.[61]

In the light of this, it was the entertainmentisation/blockbusterisation of main melody films that masked 'old ideological fictions'. Hong Kong directors' participation in main melody films, at least to some extent, has contributed to that sober, pragmatic approach to reality.

Notes

1. Hao Jian 郝建, 'How Are the Hollywood and Chinese Main Melodies Different?' (in Chinese) 〈好萊塢與中國的主旋律有什麼不同？〉, *BBC News*, 4 March 2018: <https://www.bbc.com/zhongwen/trad/world-43280703>; last accessed 1 May 2021.
2. Man-Fung Yip, *Martial Arts Cinema and Hong Kong Modernity: Aesthetics, Representation, Circulation* (Hong Kong: Hong Kong University Press, 2017), 191.
3. *The Evil One* (1968), *Secret Killer* 《秘密殺手》 (1968), *Learning by Doing* 《學而時習之》 (1969), *Accidentally* 《偶然》 (1969) and *Dead Knot* 《死結》 (1969); for details see Robert K. Elder (ed.), *John Woo: Interviews* (Jackson: University of Mississippi Press, 2005), xix–xx.
4. Yip, *Martial Arts Cinema and Hong Kong Modernity*, 187–91.
5. Anne T. Ciecko, 'Transnational Action: John Woo, Hong Kong Hollywood', in *Transnational Chinese Cinemas: Identity, Nationhood, Gender*, ed. Sheldon Lu (Honolulu: University of Hawaii Press, 1997), 237.
6. Poshek Fu and David Desser, 'Introduction', *The Cinema of Hong Kong: History, Arts, Identity* (Cambridge: Cambridge University Press, 2000), 4; for a detailed discussion of the first American reception see David Desser, 'The Kung Fu Craze: Hong Kong Cinema's First American Reception', in *The Cinema of Hong Kong*, 19–43.
7. Rob Mackie, 'Windtalkers', *The Guardian*, 28 February 2003.
8. Keith Staskiewicz, 'John Woo on John Woo: My Hits and Misses', *Entertainment Weekly*, 17 November 2009: <https://ew.com/gallery/john-woo-john-woo-my-hits-and-misses/>; last accessed 1 May 2021.
9. Barna William Donovan, *The Asian Influence on Hollywood Action Films* (Jefferson, NC, and London: McFarland & Company, 2008), 4.
10. Kin-Yan Szeto, *The Martial Arts Cinema of the Chinese Diaspora: Ang Lee, John Woo, and Jackie Chan in Hollywood* (Carbondale and Edwardsville: South Illinois University Press, 2011), 9.
11. Kwai-Cheung Lo, *Chinese Face/Off: The Transnational Popular Culture of Hong Kong* (Urbana and Chicago: University of Illinois Press, 2005), 164.
12. Stephen Teo, *The Asian Cinema Experience: Styles, Spaces, Theory* (Abingdon and New York: Routledge, 2013), 68–71. See also Stephen Teo, *Chinese Martial Arts Cinema* (2nd ed.), (Edinburgh: Edinburgh University Press, 2016), 195–203.

13. Peter Bradshaw, *Reign of Assassins*: Review', *The Guardian*, 14 February 2013.

14. 'John Woo: *The Crossing* Is the Most Self-satisfied Work in My Life' (in Chinese) 〈吳宇森：《太平輪》是一生最滿意之作〉, *The Beijing News* 《新京報》, 20 October 2014. He also made this very clear in an interview: 'I was very interested in doing a film that concerned love. I wanted to make an epic like *Doctor Zhivago*. When the KMT [Kuomintang political party] was being defeated [by the CCP], there were many people who wanted to flee to Taiwan. Many people were on the Taiping when it sank and even though this was a tragedy, it's also a story of hope, kindness, survival and faith.' 'Interview: John Woo', *Time Out Hong Kong*, 16 December 2014: <https://www.timeout.com/hong-kong/film/interview-john-woo>; last accessed 1 May 2021.

15. Zhang Rui, 'John Woo's *The Crossing* as Epic as *Gone with the Wind*', China.org.cn, 18 April 2014: <http://www.china.org.cn/arts/2014-04/18/content_32135893.htm>; last accessed 1 May 2021.

16. 'Chinese Box Office for 2014', Box Office Mojo: <https://www.boxofficemojo.com/year/2014/?area=CN>; last accessed 1 May 2021.

17. 'John Woo: *The Crossing* Is the Best Work of My Life', *People's Daily*, 14 October 2014.

18. Heidi Hsia, 'John Woo Defends *The Crossing*', Cinema Online Exclusively for Yahoo Newsroom, 16 December 2014: <https://sg.news.yahoo.com/john-woo-defends-crossing-060900945.html>; last accessed 1 May 2021.

19. Maggie Lee, 'Film Review: *The Crossing II*', *Variety*, 1 August 2015: <https://variety.com/2015/film/reviews/the-crossing-ii-review-john-woo-1201554194/>; last accessed 1 May 2021.

20. Shi Fan 釋凡, 'The Biggest Loss in the History of Chinese Cinema: John Woo Fallen into a Second-rate Businessman?' (in Chinese) 〈史上賠錢最慘《太平輪》讓吳宇森墮落二流生意人？〉, *Shi Fan Film and Television*, 23 July 2017: <https://www.sohu.com/a/159392331_120022>; last accessed 1 May 2021.

21. Rui, 'John Woo's *The Crossing* as Epic as *Gone with the Wind*'.

22. James March, 'Film Review: Start the Bilge Pump – John Woo's Leaky Vehicle *The Crossing II* Is a Sinker and a Stinker', *South China Morning Post*, 19 October 2015.

23. 'John Woo: *The Crossing* Is the Best Work of My Life'.

24. Ibid.

25. Lo, *Chinese Face/Off*, 164.

26. Tony Williams, *John Woo's Bullet in the Head* (Hong Kong: Hong Kong University Press, 2009), 107.

27. 'Stars return to *Painted Skin 2*', chinadaily.com, 22 March 2011: <https://www.chinadaily.com.cn/life/2011-03/22/content_12210503.htm>; last accessed 1 May 2021.

28. 'Gordon Chan', in *A Compendium of Hong Kong Film Directors, 1979–2013*, ed. Freddie Wong 黃國兆 (in Chinese) 《香港電影導演大全 1979-2013》: <http://www.hkfilmdirectors.com/zh-hk/director/chan-gordon>; last accessed 1 May 2021.

29. 'The director credit for *Thunderbolt* reads "Gordon Chan," but the movie obviously features recognizable styles. Jackie explained why to journalist Paul Sherman. "We had four units – he [Gordon] had one unit, I had one unit, Sammo Hung had one

unit. He [Gordon] was the main director.'" Renée Witterstaetter, *Dying for Action: The Life and Films of Jackie Chan* (New York: Warner Books, 1997), 156.

30. John DeFore, '*God of War*: Film Review', *The Hollywood Reporter*, 2 June 2017: <https://www.hollywoodreporter.com/review/god-of-war-1009979>; last accessed 1 May 2021.

31. Critics said that *Overheard* evinced 'technological nationalism', not 'cultural nationalism'; see J. Macgregor Wise, *Surveillance and Film* (New York and London: Bloomsbury Academic, 2016), 113.

32. An Yue 安岳, 'Main Melody + Commercial Blockbusters: The Extraordinary Mission of *Extraordinary Mission*' (in Chinese) 〈主旋律+商業大片：《非凡任務》的非凡任務〉, *Journal of China Federation of Literary and Art Circles* 《中國藝術報》, 30 March 2017.

33. Maggie Lee, '*The Lost Bladesman*: Film Review', *The Hollywood Reporter*, 1 June 2011:   <https://www.hollywoodreporter.com/review/lost-bladesman-film-review-193899>; last accessed 1 May 2021.

34. Tim Youngs, 'Extraordinary Mission', Far East Film Festival 2017: <https://www.fareastfilm.com/eng/archive/2017/extraordinary-mission/?IDLYT=15535>; last accessed 1 May 2021.

35. Yue, 'Main Melody + Commercial Blockbusters'.

36. Liew Kai Khiun, *Amnesia, Nostalgia and Heritage: Transnational Memory and Popular Culture in East and Southeast Asia* (London and Lanham, MD: Rowman and Littlefield, 2016),15; Helen Hok-Sze Leung, *Undercurrents: Queer Culture and Postcolonial Hong Kong* (Vancouver and Toronto: UBC Press, 2008), 44. For a detailed discussion on *The Eye*, see Liew, 11–24.

37. 'Oxide Pang', in Wong, *A Compendium of Hong Kong Film Directors, 1979–2013*: <http://www.hkfilmdirectors.com/en/director/pang-oxide>; last accessed 1 May 2021.

38. Ruby Cheung, *New Hong Kong Cinema: Transitions to Becoming Chinese in 21st-Century East Asia* (New York and Oxford: Berghahn Books, 2016), 97; for a further discussion of the series, see 97–9.

39. 'Interview with Oxide Pang on *My War*: If This Were a Main Melody Film, I Would Have Run Away' (in Chinese) 〈彭順受訪談《我的戰爭》：如果這是主旋律電影，我一定會跑掉〉, sohu.com, 31 August 2016: <https://m.sohu.com/n/467044917/?wscrid=95360_5>; last accessed 1 May 2021.

40. Ibid.

41. 'The RMB 150 Million-Budget *My War* Has So Far Grossed Less Than 30 Million' (in Chinese) 〈1.5億《我的戰爭》至今票房不足3千萬〉, Flying Fish Original 飛魚原創, 20 September 2016: <https://kknews.cc/entertainment/lm8grg.html>; last accessed 1 May 2021.

42. Ibid.

43. Linda Jaivin, 'Culture: In and Out of Control', in *China Story Yearbook 2016: Control*, ed. Jane Golley, Linda Jaivin and Luigi Tomba, (Canberra: ANU Press, 2017), 154.

44. Ibid., 155.

45. '*Towards the River Glorious* (2019) Short Review', *Asian Film Strike*, 19 April 2020: <https://asianfilmstrike.com/2020/04/19/towards-the-river-glorious-2019-short-review/>; last accessed 1 May 2021.

46. Hong Kong Motion Picture Industry Association 香港影業協會, *Compilation of Data of Hong Kong Films 2012* (in Chinese) 《香港電影資料彙編2012》 (Hong Kong: CreateHK, 2013), 11, 49.

47. Luo Xiaoding 羅曉汀 and Dong Ming 董銘, 'From Anti-Triad to Anti-Terrorist/ Corruption/ Drug' (in Chinese) 〈從反黑到反恐反貪反毒〉, *Global Times*, 9 April 2019.

48. Mei Yang, Liang Zhou, Wei Hao and Shui-Yuan Xiao, 'Drug policy in China: Progress and Challenges', *The Lancet* 383:9916 (February 2014): 509.

49. Yuwa Wei, *Issues Decisive for China's Rise or Fall: An International Law Perspective* (Singapore: Springer, 2019), 169; for further details, see 169–71.

50. Zhao Yan 趙妍, 'Johnnie To's New Mainland Production: *Drug War* Considered Expanding the Dimensions of Mainland Movies' (in Chinese) 〈杜琪峰國產新片《毒戰》打開內地電影尺度〉, *Time Weekly* 《時代週報》 228, 11 April 2013.

51. Yiu-Wai Chu, *Found in Transition: Hong Kong Studies in the Age of China* (Albany: SUNY Press, 2018), 120–42.

52. Ibid., 160–2.

53. Laifong Leung, *Contemporary Chinese Fiction Writers: Biography, Bibliography, and Critical Assessment* (New York and London: Routledge, 2017), 305.

54. Michael Berry, *A History of Pain: Trauma in Modern Chinese Literature and Film* (New York: Columbia University Press, 2008), 350.

55. Edmund Lee, '*Integrity* Film Review', *South China Morning Post*, 8 February 2019.

56. Lao Yue 勞月, 'Entertainmentization and the Main Melody: Starting with the *Storm* Series' (in Chinese) 〈娛樂化與主旋律：從《反貪風暴》系列電影說起〉, *The Paper* 《澎湃》, 24 April 2019: <https://www.thepaper.cn/newsDetail_forward_3336536>; last accessed 1 May 2021.

57. 'Becoming Genre Films: The New Direction of Main Melody Films' (in Chinese) 〈類型片化，主旋律影片走出新路〉, *Xinhua Daily* 《新華日報》, 19 April 2018, 14.

58. For example, 'Wu Jing Lost! Why *The Climber* Fell during the National Day Holiday' (in Chinese) 〈吳京輸了！《攀登者》為何國慶檔掉隊〉, <https://kknews.cc/entertainment/bzo5ppm.html>; last accessed 1 May 2021.

59. 'Beijing Style vs. Hong Kong Style: Who Is Going to Lead the Future Development of Main Melody Blockbusters?' (in Chinese) 〈京派 vs 港派：誰能引導主旋律大片的未來？〉: <https://www.360kuai.com/pc/966088583a89db459?cota=3&kuai_so=1&sign=360_e39369d1>; last accessed 1 May 2021.

60. Chen Yucheng 陳俞成 and Ma Ningyu 馬寧宇, 'An Investigation into the National Consciousness of Main Melody War Films' (in Chinese) 〈主旋律戰爭類型電影的民族意識探究〉, *Media Today* 《今傳媒》, 16 August 2018: <http://media.people.com.cn/BIG5/n1/2018/0816/c420925-30232612.html>; last accessed 1 May 2021.

61. Slavoj Žižek, *The Plague of Fantasies* (London and New York: Verso, 1997), 163.

Epilogue

Since the beginning of the 2010s, there has been a radical transformation of the scale and the nature of the Chinese film industry. In just ten years, the number of movie screens in China increased more than ten-fold, from 6,256 to 69,787, and the number of cinemas from 1,646 to 12,000.[1] As noted in a special account published by Mtime – a mainland Internet movie and TV database – on the development of the Chinese film industry, the 2010s will probably enter the annals of Chinese film history as the decade of change, and the major changes included, among others, the declining influence of Hollywood and Chinese period blockbusters and the rise of Chinese main melody and genre films.[2] The ecology of the Chinese film industry also changed a great deal in the 2010s. As noted in a report published by Deloitte China in 2017, there were new transformations of the business model in the mainland market after China's culture and entertainment industry entered into an unprecedented 'golden age', such as the emergence of 'new giants' (e.g., Wanda Group) driven by policy, the Internet and capital, which 'used resource advantages to gradually penetrate the entertainment industry and build an ecosystem'.[3] Moreover, 'the current singular profitability model will require a diversified strategy', and the '[r]evenue structure will be rebalanced, shifting from "Long Tail" to "Thick Tail"':

> For example, with Disney as its model, Huayi Brothers has launched a 'de-cinematic' strategy that integrates the traditional film business, Internet entertainment, and location-based entertainment, and expands into upstream and downstream industry chains to alleviate dependence on the film industry.[4]

It is also true that the emphasis of the industry has shifted from 'Made in China' to 'Made for the World', but given the special nature of a film industry with Chinese characteristics, the changes have been sticking with the main melody, although this genre was 'blockbusterised' in the 2010s. There was a need to diversify the genre of main melody films, for example, moving from a focus on political figures to 'ordinary' heroes – pilots, firefighters, coast guard members, climbers, sportspeople and the like – in order to attract more local as well as global audiences. What is clear in the rise of these Chinese genre films, from crime, sci-fi and disaster to sports films, is that they were all in one way or another, albeit to different extents, singing the main melody.

Hollywood Made in China?

The blockbusterisation of Chinese main melody films should be seen as similar to but different from Hollywoodisation.[5] Hollywood has long been the film production centre of the world, assuming such a key role that 'world cinema' is widely used to refer to national cinemas that are 'not Hollywood' (a marketing label covering the film productions of non-English-speaking countries at the edges of the market, 'world cinema' still, ironically, exists in the age of globalisation).[6] *The Oxford History of World Cinema*, for instance, outlined the evolution of national cinemas round the world and the development of these varied and distinctive film traditions alongside Hollywood.[7] Similarly, the Film Foundation's World Cinema Project established by Martin Scorsese aims to preserve and restore 'neglected films from around the world'; 'We created the World Cinema Project to ensure that the most vulnerable titles don't disappear forever,' Scorsese explained when The Film Foundation joined forces with the Pan African Federation of Filmmakers and UNESCO in 2017 to launch a long-term project 'to help locate, restore and preserve films made on the African continent'.[8] Although this model of world cinema has been problematised by film scholars over the past several decades,[9] Hollywood is still the centre of film production that the rest of the world is trying to emulate.

Bollywood, as evident in the name itself, is an excellent example of seeing in Hollywood a model to emulate, and the result is 'an Indian film industry which is clearly "mediated" by Hollywood, and a case of a "strategic making-do, not of being overwhelmed" by Hollywood'.[10] Simply put, 'Bollywood Emulating Hollywood meant, at some level, producing action spectacles with high budgets and mainstream international audiences'.[11] This was one of the goals identified by Chinese main melody films. As Chris Berry has noted, China's contact with blockbusters began with the box-office-split deals in 1995, and some Chinese big-budget, high-concept films were 'spurred by a desire to emulate Hollywood blockbusters following their Chinese success'.[12] However, as these big-budget films (*dapian*) had to sing the main melody, which was the distinctive characteristic of post-socialist Chinese films, they were not very popular among the general audience. As noted in the Introduction, 80 per cent of the Chinese films produced between 1995 and 2000 (80 to 100 each year) could be considered main melody films – they 'consumed huge resources yet accounted for few market profits'.[13]

Obviously, echoing the Chinese dream upheld by President Xi Jinping, the Chinese film industry has not aimed to be a place for national cinema in world cinema, but to be on a par with Hollywood. In her *Hollywood Made in China*, Aynne Kokas made an insightful link between Xi Jinping's 'Chinese dream' and Hollywood's 'dream factory', as the former is 'a branding strategy that has a lot in common with the mythology of Southern California': 'When trying to build a global vision of the Chinese Dream, what could be better than turning to the *original* dream factory?'[14] Therefore, there have been new Sino-US media 'brandscapes': 'capital-driven, real estate-intensive projects that accelerate the growth of marketing infrastructure in China' and that have created 'a space for Chinese financiers to invest their capital, a site to absorb the wealth of Chinese consumers, and a location for Hollywood content providers to expand the presence of their media brands within an important global market'.[15] In this context, Marvel superhero films, among others, have successfully entered the market of mainland China and have become enormously popular. Yet the rise of China in the age of global capitalism has been complex, and its integration into the global economy has also involved an attempt to change the rules of the game. In the film sector, the 'widespread, crushing influence that Hollywood hits had on the Chinese film industry' can be seen as 'a double-edged sword':

> On the one hand, it led to a cinematic space loaded with tensions and anxieties, yet, on the other, it simultaneously provoked the rise of Chinese blockbusters and opened up the domestic industry to both the perils and benefits of Hollywood and global capitalism.[16]

As mentioned in the previous chapters, Chinese main melody blockbusters are often touted as China's answer to a Hollywood production, such as *The Captain* (2019) to *Sully* (2016), *Operation Mekong* (2016) to *Black Hawk Down* (2001), *The Crossing* (2014) to *Titanic* (1997) and *Wolf Warrior* (2015) to *Rambo* (2008). Critics may argue that, using *Wolf Warrior 2* (2017) as an example, 'its success is largely due to its translation of some of the worst elements of Hollywood formulas into a Chinese context', but it is also important to note that it 'does show signs of being shaped by Chinese concerns and conditions as much as by Hollywood'.[17]

Indeed, these Hollywood-made-in-China versions were not designed to attract overseas audiences. They aimed, at least at that stage of the development of Chinese cinema, to attract local audiences, especially younger ones, that would be willing to sing the main melody more than to watch Marvel heroes. In this sense, the 2010s was a decade of significance. The last year of that decade saw Chinese box-office takings hit a new high, a total of RMB 64.3 billion (~US$9.2 billion) in box-office revenue. More importantly, according to the China Film Administration, 'domestic films grossed RMB 41.2 billion in 2019, which is 64.07% of the annual total gross revenue of both domestic and foreign films in the market, and a significant 8.65% increase from last year'.[18] In addition, Chinese cinema was led for the first time by two domestic blockbusters. Two of the three main melody tributes to the seventieth anniversary of the founding of the PRC and another main melody disaster film were also on the list, whereas only two Hollywood productions made the top-ten highest-grossing films of 2019 in China:

1. *Ne Zha* – RMB 5.035 billion
2. *The Wandering Earth* – RMB 4.686 billion
3. *Avengers: Endgame* – RMB 4.25 billion
4. *My People, My Country* – RMB 3.17 billion
5. *The Captain* – RMB 2.912 billion
6. *Crazy Alien* – RMB 2.213 billion
7. *Pegasus* – RMB 1.728 billion
8. *The Bravest* – RMB 1.707 billion
9. *Better Days* – RMB 1.558 billion
10. *Fast & Furious Presents: Hobbs & Shaw* – RMB 1.435 billion

It was reported by *The Washington Post* that the film sector has, or at least will, become 'another US export China is learning to do without': 'China is exhibiting signs of becoming India or Nigeria, two large movie-going markets whose film ecosystem thrives independently of Hollywood.'[19] The two highest-grossing films of the year, the ground-breaking Chinese sci-fi *The Wandering Earth* and the 3D computer animation fantasy *Ne Zha*, were helmed by the young Chinese directors Frant Gwo and Yang Yu (commonly known as *Jiaozi*, meaning 'dumpling' in Chinese), respectively. Both directors, who were in their thirties at the time, said that they were influenced by Hollywood films; Frant Gwo cited James Cameron's *Terminator 2: Judgment Day* (1991).[20] Kokas commented on this paradigm shift as follows: 'They [the Chinese audience] don't want a nationalist agenda but they want a movie to feel Chinese. If they can get that in big-budget blockbusters, they're going to see them.'[21] The overwhelming success of Chinese films in 2019 can be interpreted as a result, at least in part, of the productive synergy between main melody and genre films.

Blockbusterisation of Main Melody Films

In 2016, China replaced Japan as the second largest global film market. Although the growth rate began to slow down after that, the number of new screens doubled between 2015 and 2019. It was widely believed that 'this market growth (of screens, audience numbers and box-office revenues) was due to a number of factors: a new wave of film-makers, a diversification of genres, and changes in government regulations', and in the midst of these changes, main melody films experienced a 'renaissance'.[22] In the 2010s, main melody films had grown into the main genre in Chinese cinema, and its blockbusterisation was arguably the most phenomenal development of the mainland film industry during this time. If any stronger proof were needed of this, the three main melody blockbusters that commemorated the seventieth anniversary of the founding of the People's Republic of China in October 2019 were excellent cases that epitomised the development of the mainland film industry during this decade. Just take the box office on National Day, 1 October 2019, as an example. The three main melody blockbusters – *My People, My Country*, *The Captain* and *The Climber* – brought in RMB 3.170 billion, RMB 2.912 billion and RMB 1.103 billion, respectively, accounting for more than ninety per cent of the total revenue during the National Day holidays, which was a new record in the history of Chinese cinema. Equally important was that the three films scored 8.2, 7.4 and 7.0, respectively on Douban, China's biggest portal of book and film reviews, showing that they were well received by both general audiences and critics.[23] As already noted in the Introduction to this book, two of these films were directed by Hong Kong filmmakers (Andrew Lau for *The Captain* and Daniel Lee for *The Climbers*), which was strong proof of Hong Kong directors' impact on main(land) melody commercial blockbusters.

At its peak, Hong Kong cinema was first in the world in terms of per capita productions, as well as the second largest exporter of films, behind only the United States. More importantly, Hong Kong filmmakers from the small city once dubbed the 'Hollywood of the East' developed their careers with the Hollywood operation logic,[24] and they had accumulated enough experience to produce commercial blockbusters according to that standard. Although the winner of the National Day box office was *My People, My Country*, this epic of seven stories about seven significant moments after the founding of the country was co-directed by seven famous mainland directors (Chen Kaige, Zhang Yibai, Guan Hu, Xue Xiaolu, Xu Zheng, Ning Hao and Wen Muye). It is also worth noting that in the 2019 top-ten list cited above, three films were helmed by Hong Kong directors: *The Captain*, *The Bravest* and *Better Days* (another three were in the top twenty: *The White Storm 2: Drug Lords*, *The Climbers* and

P Storm). This was testament to the importance of Hong Kong directors in this distinctive genre of Chinese cinema.

In the forum 'Chinese Cinema Investment and Development in the New Era' held during the 28th Golden Rooster and Hundred Flowers Film Festival in November 2019, Huang Qunfei, Deputy General Manager of the Huaxia Film Company (the producer of *My People, My Country*), categorised main melody films into three types: (1) traditional main melody films on great people and/ or major incidents; (2) commercial main melody films presented by Polybona productions; and (3) films embodying mainstream values.[25] Hong Kong directors made significant contributions to all three types. As a matter of fact, even mainland critics agreed that Hong Kong filmmakers took an active part in every important juncture of the commercialisation of main melody films: the privately run *Bodyguards and Assassins* (2009) as a paradigm shift of a main melody blockbuster, the successful blockbusterisation of the typical main melody with *The Taking of Tiger Mountain 3D* (2014) and the diversification of main melody film genres in, among others, *The Captain* and *Leap* (2020). In sum, 'Hong Kong directors' experience in making commercial films resulted in various genres, such as police and gangster, action, *wuxia* and disaster films, revitalizing the otherwise stereotypic, clichéd main melody genre.'[26]

As shown in the previous chapters, Hong Kong directors made different kinds of contributions to the blockbusterisation as well as entertainmentisation of the main melody film genre, and its repackaging as genre films was a key direction for Chinese cinema as the industry continued to develop. In regard to this, Bona Film Group, led by Yu Dong, was a very successful market leader. This Beijing-based production company specialised in mainland–Hong Kong co-productions, from the very locally Hong Kong story *A Simple Life* (2011) to the genuinely global masterpiece *The Grandmaster* (2013). Owing to its well-established network in co-productions, the company also knew very well how to commission Hong Kong directors to make main(land) melody films. Hong Kong directors plus mainland producers plus main melody themes became its success formula. According to Yu Dong, a star-studded cast, shooting style and production crew were the three key factors in the successful production of main melody films.[27] Tsui Hark's *The Taking of Tiger Mountain 3D*, Ann Hui's *Our Time Will Come* (2017) and Dante Lam's 'operations' were all excellent examples, although Andrew Lau's *The Founding of an Army* (2017) may have been less fruitful. Even Wu Jing of *Wolf Warrior 2* was closely affiliated with Hong Kong cinema during his early film career. 'The Hong Kong film industry has always made the entertainment factor a priority, so Hong Kong directors are able to inject entertainment value into something that the Chinese audience is overly familiar with', as pointedly noted by veteran Hong Kong producer John Chong.[28] In short, Hong

Kong directors made significant contributions to the blockbusterisation and entertainmentisation of the main melody film genre, as well as its diversification with various kinds of genre films.

In regard to the integration of the Hong Kong film industry into the mainland, new relaxation measures were rolled out by the State Film Administration to facilitate the further development of the Hong Kong and Macao film industries in April 2019.[29] Apparently, this sounded attractive enough to many ears, but the measures were basically commercially oriented, designed to enhance the integration of Hong Kong and Macao into the mainland. No wonder Edward Yau, Hong Kong Secretary for Commerce and Economic Development, was among the first to respond: 'I hope that the film industry will tap the new measures, while continue [sic]to leverage existing advantages, to expand mainland and overseas markets and further promote the brand of "Hong Kong films."'[30] The Greater Bay Area has enormous potential to 'supercharge an economic dynamo', as argued by Peter Wong, Deputy Chairman and Chief Executive of The Hongkong and Shanghai Banking Corporation Limited.[31] Be that as it may, an economic dynamo is not a guarantee of the brand 'Hong Kong films'; if Hong Kong directors cannot bring their characteristics across the border, they will forfeit the 'Hong Kong' brand.

After Hong Kong directors were commissioned to make main melody blockbusters, were their individual styles erased by the main melody, or were they able to retain their styles and convey their messages in those blockbusters? Andrew Lau, for one, was confident that he had been able to keep his Hong Kong style in *The Founding of an Army*.[32] While Ann Hui's *Our Time Will Come* was believed to have hidden messages related to Hong Kong, some other Hong Kong directors claimed that they were able to preserve their Hong Kong characteristics under the cliché of nationalism in main melody films.[33] In any case, Hong Kong directors were seen as being able to sing the main melody in a sophisticated way, turning propaganda into commercially acceptable blockbusters. Thanks to the advent of new, diversified productions of 'main melody films and genre films', recent main melody films began to incorporate the typical elements of Hong Kong action films and police and gangster films, arguably to such an extent that critics called them 'Chinese commercial films with a consciousness of main melody' (before 2010) and even more recently 'main melody movies in name only': 'many commercially successful main melody movies in recent years have become no different in character from entertainment films in general'.[34]

Northbound Imaginary: A Different Version

During the late-transitional period before its reversion to China in 1997, Hong Kong witnessed a rise of Hong Kong Cultural Studies in academia based on Hong

Kong's reversion and the unprecedented 'one country, two systems' framework. The 'northbound imaginary' was one of the most theoretically important issues related to the trend back then. *Hong Kong Cultural Studies Bulletin* published a research project on Hong Kong Cultural Studies masterminded by Stephen Ching-kiu Chan, a special topic on the northbound imaginary in 1995 which was later turned into a book in Chinese. Through this topic, some Hong Kong critics pointed their critiques at Hong Kong megalomania, which also referred to mainstream Hong Kong's claim that its cosmopolitanism would justify its economic and cultural expansion across the border in China.[35] It might have been wishful thinking,[36] but the northbound imaginary as such once showed the potential impact of Hong Kong on the mainland. Some even argued that Hong Kong would bring its core values, such as freedom, to the mainland in the long run. Few if any could have imagined, however, a different version of the northbound imaginary that would surface shortly after Hong Kong's reversion to China, and the problematic Hong Kong megalomania later turned into a profit-driven mindset. I have argued elsewhere that the northern ventures of Hong Kong filmmakers marked a paradigmatic shift: the northbound imaginary in the 1990s, which was supposed to change China by theorising the politics of Hong Kong's cultural penetration into the mainland, had to transform itself into a new version by tapping into the northern market for economic opportunities. 'History has since proved that it was not Hong Kong culture influencing China but, rather, the other way round.'[37]

Teddy Chan's *Bodyguards and Assassins*, an early example of Hong Kong filmmakers' participation in 'privately run' main melody films in mainland China, was arguably irony at its finest in regard to the (dis)appearance of Hong Kong cinema.[38] Interestingly, it can be interpreted as a metaphor for the predicament faced by Hong Kong (the literal translation of the Chinese title was *A Besieged City in October*). The film was about protecting Dr Sun Yat-sen, the Father of the Nation, from assassination while he was in Hong Kong meeting with allies to formulate a plan to overthrow the Qing court. Hong Kong's contribution to the revolution and its place in modern Chinese history were duly recognised in the film, which would not have been achievable without mainland resources. The handsome budget not only turned this film into a blockbuster with many superstars, it also allowed the director to build a 1:1 set of the Central District in the early twentieth century in a studio near Shanghai. The total budget of the film was reportedly HK$180 million (including the replica, which cost HK$50 million), which was simply unimaginable for local Hong Kong productions back then. In short, without the co-production and the mainland market, *Bodyguards and Assassins* would not have been possible. However, it was ironic that, as noted by Kwai-cheung Lo, the film was an effort 'to take sides and show its dedication to the "politically correct" nationalist revolution'.[39] Moreover, the film was also seen by Hong Kong critics as a poignant summary of the impasse faced by Hong Kong cinema in/as a besieged city (echoing the Chinese title) after the 1997 handover.[40]

As mentioned in the Introduction, Yu Dong made it clear that after 2009, Hong Kong filmmakers were simply commissioned to produce films with mainland themes and stories. After *Bodyguards and Assassins*, more and more Hong Kong directors started singing the main – as well as mainland – melody. As the lyricist Siu Hak declared in Eason Chan's Cantopop song 'Main Melody' (2013), a political allegory packaged as a love ballad: 'You want me to give in, and I want you to give in . . . When shall we find the new system of love?' 'Main melody' was an issue of paramount importance in finding 'the new system of love' for Hong Kong. The study of Hong Kong cinema had been marginalised, owing to what Poshek Fu termed 'the Central Plains syndrome',[41] until the late 1990s or so. Given the rise of China in the new millennium, there was a new 'Central Plains syndrome' after Beijing put increased emphasis on its soft power – this time it was not just scholarly attention on China's art cinema and political cinema but also its commercial market. It is sad but true that refusing the mainland melody seemed to be impractical. For those who cared about the distinguishing characteristics of Hong Kong culture, perhaps Derek Kwok's catchphrase in his big-budget co-production *As the Light Goes Out* (2013) served as a kind of reminder after Hong Kong media entered the enormous mainland market: 'The only way to survive is to live with the thick smoke . . . don't ever believe what you see in the thick smoke; your mind will be distorted by hallucinations.'[42] To live with the thick smoke, Rey Chow's famously inspiring reading of the gaze and the image might be helpful, and I would like to look at this briefly.

Rey Chow's interpretation of the works of 'the Fifth Generation' directors is especially worth mentioning in this context. There have been critiques on the works of Zhang Yimou and Chen Kaige, calling them 'autoethnographies' that aimed to fulfil the desirous appetite of Western audiences. According to Rey Chow, however, it is 'imprecise, though not erroneous, to say that directors such as Zhang are producing a new kind of Orientalism', and the 'self-subalternizing, self-exoticizing visual gestures of the Orientals' Orientalism is first and foremost a demonstration – a display of a tactic'.[43] The 'self-Orientalism' that turns the ambivalently victimized image of 'China' into an asset – it is both the image and the gaze at the same time – can be read as a marketing tactic that packages and sells Chineseness to the world, as I have argued elsewhere.[44] I would like to twist my original reading of the normal, if not banal, reading of the Orientalist representation of China a bit here. Not unlike the Oriental's Orientalism, the fusion of the representation of Hong Kong and the main melody can also be interpreted as displaying a tactic. Rey Chow's argument was further developed in her *Sentimental Fabulations, Contemporary Chinese Films: Attachment in the Age of Global Visibility*:

> From a comparative cultural perspective, what continues to concern me is that a certain predictable attitude tends to dominate the agenda these days whenever works inhabiting the East-West divide come under scholarly scrutiny. Instead of enabling the critical potential embedded in such works to come to light, this attitude often ends up blocking and annulling that potential in the name of political rectitude.[45]

This kind of political rectitude has appeared in another form in the mainland–Hong Kong divide, and a similar predictable attitude – entering the mainland market for the sake of money, Hong Kong has lost its distinguishing characteristics – has blocked and annulled the critical potential embedded in those works. The above-mentioned examples can be seen as self-effacing – similar to self-subalternising or self-exoticising – tactics. While Chow warned us against 'the pursuit of certain non-Western native traditions and their ideological demands on representation' with which the critique of Orientalism has become smoothly allied,[46] I have underscored the need to trace the (im)possibility of cultural translations across borders in this book.

The Hong Kong Model (of Filmmaking)

It was argued in *Lost in Transition* that Peter Chan moved north to shoot *Perhaps Love* (2005) for the mainland market, and his subsequent *The Warlords* (2007) signalled a paradigm shift from Hong Kong cinema to mainland–Hong Kong co-productions.[47] In other words, Peter Chan's filmmaking model was closely intertwined with the waning of the local characteristics of Hong Kong cinema. That said, one question was left unanswered, whether Peter Chan's business venture – from Hong Kong to Hollywood and Asia, and then to the mainland – marked the success of the Hong Kong model of filmmaking or not. The 'Hong Kong model' was actually the central issue of Hong Kong sociologist Tai-lok Lui's book bearing the same title in Chinese. As per Lui's analysis, the major factors behind the success of the 'Hong Kong model' included the features of a flexible small to medium enterprise, laissez-faire policy, professional civil service, consultative politics and hard-working, professional, and pragmatic people. He argued that owing to various social and political changes in recent years, the Hong Kong model on which Hong Kong's success was based in the past is now outdated.[48] Lui also made a related remark when he talked about the Hong Kong style throughout the unimaginable (what he called 'hyperreal') events during the Anti-ELAB protests that began in Hong Kong in June 2019: 'It is essential for us to think about what Hong Kong style(s) actually is/are. Why have both sides [pro- and anti-establishment] abandoned Hong Kong style at once?'[49] One of the most inspiring arguments made by Lui about this issue, which is closely related to his notion of the Hong Kong model, is that Hong Kong people staunchly value choices. Simply put, as the government did not provide them with desirable choices, the people took to the streets to protest for their own.

In light of this, the achievements of Peter Chan and other northbound filmmakers in co-productions can only be considered a success in parts of the Hong Kong model. These filmmakers may be equally hard-working, professional and, needless to say, pragmatic, but they can no longer provide enough choices for Hong Kong audiences. The rise of co-productions began after the signing of the CEPA in 2003, and since then, Hong Kong's film industry has been M-shaped, with big-budget co-productions on one end, small-budget and even local productions on the other and mid-budget productions, a very important component of the film industry, occupying the middle.[50] While I agree with Gary Bettinson that 'Hong Kong's film industry has not so much broken with its past traditions as channeled them into distinct modes of production',[51] the problem of shrinking diversity in low- to mid-budget films has posed a significant threat to its sustainable development. Regarding this, Peter Chan and other northbound filmmakers, no matter how successful they have been in the mainland market, are only part of the Hong Kong model of filmmaking. It is undeniably true that many Hong Kong filmmakers including, but not limited to, Tsui Hark, Andrew Lau and Dante Lam, have fared well nationally with their co-productions and main melody films. As convincingly argued by Emilie Yeh and Shi-yan Chao,

> the CEPA scheme has allowed key filmmakers to revive and extend signature creative strategies of Hong Kong cinema, in spite of the tension between Hong Kong's fears of 'mainlandization' and the allure of now the world's second largest film market.[52]

However, the so-called 'China opportunity' has been shrinking (in a quantitative sense) and 'has become rather exclusive in terms of the kinds of jobs available to Hong Kong people'.[53] This also applies to the film industry. At the other end of the spectrum, promising young local directors continued to emerge in the 2010s, such as Philip Yung of *Port of Call* (2015), Frank Hui, Jevons Au and Vicky Wong of *Trivisa* (2016), Steve Chi-fat Chan of *Weeds on Fire* (2016), Chun Wong of *Mad World* (2017), Tai-Lee Chan of *Tomorrow Is Another Day* (2017), Kearen Pang of *29+1* 《29+1》 (2017), Jun Lee of *Tracey* (2018), Oliver Siu-Kuen Chan of *Still Human* (2018) and Cheuk-Pan Lee of *G Affairs* (2018). These works effectively 'probe Hong Kong's everyday experience from the angle of the quotidian and the ordinary', as perceptively noted by Sebastian Veg.[54] Young Hong Kong director Heiward Mak has also pointed out that mid- and small-budget productions will become the mainstay of Hong Kong cinema.[55] In a nutshell, inheritance and transmission, as well as diversity, will be the most important factors in the future development of Hong Kong cinema. It is against such a critical backdrop that Herman Yau was used as an example in Chapter 6 to shed light on a preliminary answer to the question related to the Hong Kong model of filmmaking.

In the light of the rise of mainland–Hong Kong co-productions after the signing of the Closer Economic Partnership Agreement in 2003, the 'northern ventures' of Hong Kong directors can be understood in relation to the 'absent presence' of Hong Kong cinema in the age of Chinese cinema. When I was a graduate student, I was heavily influenced by postcolonial theories. This is one of my favourite quotes from Gayatri Spivak: 'When we come to the concomitant question of the consciousness of the subaltern, the notion of what the work cannot say becomes important.'[56] For example, 'You're the Best in the World', the theme song of a TVB martial arts drama, was used in Stephen Chow's *The Mermaid* (2016). This can be read as highlighting the plurality of Hong Kong culture, trying to say something that the work cannot say. Jacky Cheung's Cantonese popular song 'How Can I Let You Go?' can be interpreted as a stereotypic representation of Cantopop as cheesy romantic ballads, but in *Trivisa* it can also be interpreted as a 1997 metaphor lamenting the end of an era. I have argued in great detail about why Hong Kong Studies must imagine how to keep its erasure – which seems almost inevitable in the age of China – visible and legible, and it is pertinent to write about the plurality of Hong Kong under strategic erasure.[57] Thanks to 'selective appropriations of Hong Kong film classics in China's independent films', according to Esther Yau, 'mainland critics and cinephiles are as capable as their Hong Kong counterparts in identifying any worthy "hidden currents" in films, and many have learned to become equally watchful over the comparative achievements of other cinemas.'[58] 'Hidden currents' are similar to what I have called 'trace' in this book. In the light of this, the 'absent presence' discussed in the previous chapter is also an important point to consider.

The Trace of Hong Kong Cinema

Let me use *The Vanished Murderer* (2015), directed by Chi-leung Lo, a loose sequel to his *The Bullet Vanishes* (2012), to further illustrate the 'trace' of Hong Kong cinema. This mainland–Hong Kong co-produced suspense crime thriller featured large-scale student protests against finance magnates, and some of the scenes even gave the Hong Kong audience a sense of déjà vu. While the setting of 'Xiang Cheng' (Hong City; literal translation, 'fragrant city') may have been allusive, Hong Kong (literal translation, 'fragrant harbour') is totally absent in the vaguely set 1930s period presented in the film. As suggested by the title, the plot is about the disappearance of a murderer/prisoner, and, as pointed out by film critics, it reminded audiences of Frank Darabont's *Shawshank Redemption* (1994) and Seung-wan Ryoo's *The Berlin File* (2013). These 'rip-offs' were not as pertinent to the vanished subject of Hong Kong as the lecture given by Professor Huo (portrayed by Gordon Lam) in the film, which was based on Michael Sandel's famous lecture on the ethical problem of justice, 'The Moral Side of Murder':

> If you had to choose between (1) killing one person to save the lives of five others and (2) doing nothing, even though you knew that five people would die right before your eyes if you did nothing – what would you do? What would be the right thing to do?[59]

The plot of *The Vanished Murderer* points towards the issue of justice, which was a telling footnote to social movements in Hong Kong. The story was about (the vanished) Hong Kong. Critics may have been disappointed with the plot of this suspense thriller – it 'has no logic whatsoever'[60] – but if interpreted from another angle, this was less a genuine suspense thriller than a political allegory with 'snake feet'. The film, for understandable reasons, had to 'draw a snake and add feet to it' by ending with the revelation that Professor Huo was actually a villain who was looking out for his interests in the name of justice – in other words, justice was merely a grand narrative to mask one's own greed.

If the setting of *The Vanished Murderer* was considered deliberately metaphorical, the one in *Call of Heroes* (2016), directed by Benny Chan, was simply straightforward. When the director summoned Akira Kurosawa's samurai dramas, Sergio Leone's spaghetti Western films and even Hong Kong classics like King Hu's *Come Drink with Me* (1966) and Ka-fai Wai's *Peace Hotel* (1995) in this martial arts blockbuster, there was a deep and lingering tone in the Chinese title of the film, whose literal translation was 'an endangered city', which sounds similar to 'besieged city' in Cantonese and especially in Putonghua. Set in China circa 1910, the film is about the village of Pucheng ('Ordinary City' in Chinese), which is a refugee haven led by the honourable Sheriff Yang (portrayed by Sean Lau). Confronted by the son of a warlord (portrayed by Louis Koo) who randomly kills people, Yang arrests him and refuses to let him go, even after the village is besieged by the army of the father of the murderer. Branded as an old-school martial arts blockbuster, the film featured a star-studded cast, but, unexpectedly, there were no martial arts actors except Wu Jing and a special appearance by Sammo Hung. In addition to the obvious echoes of martial arts, samurais and Westerns, there was also a discernible reference to the 'absent presence' of the endangered city: 'For audiences from Chan's home city, the struggle between pursuing justice and maintaining everyone's livelihood may also strike a particularly resonant chord in these post-Occupy times.'[61] The director's own call for heroes, in other words, was a necessarily ventriloquistic feat of speaking to two different groups of audiences at once.

The 'absent presence' mentioned in Chapter 6 can be traced to Martin Heidegger's and Jacques Derrida's *sous-rature* ('under erasure'): 'to write a word, cross it out, and then print both word and deletion'.[62] Absence is therefore presenced through *sous-rature*, and as per Derrida, the absencing has created a new presence.[63] Since a text is to be understood by the trace of that other which is forever absent, I have also purposefully chosen the term 'trace' to foreground the importance of tracing the momentum of Hong Kong culture:

> . . . [To borrow the words of Judith Butler,] we expect that where there is a trace, there is something prior to it that has left it – the trace of a life, a book, a thought. But if the trace is the means through which what is prior is marked, then it is at once lost and found in the course of that marking. In this sense, the trace is the origin of the origin. [In her translator's preface of Jacques Derrida's *Of Grammatology*, Gayatri Spivak makes it clear that she chose the term 'trace'] because it 'looks the same' as Derrida's word, [but she also reminds readers of] at least the track, even the spoor, contained within the French word.[64]

As the absent part of a sign's presence, a trace can be sketched to display the irreducibly complex structure of presence and absence. As stated by Derrida, 'survival carries within itself the trace of an ineffaceable incision',[65] and the trace has become effaced in presenting itself: 'effacement constitutes itself as a trace – effacement establishes the trace in a change of place and makes it disappear in its appearing, makes it issue forth from itself in its very position'.[66] Although the trace itself is not present, the displacement unequivocally indicates its presence as absence. Trace, albeit invisible, presents itself, but arguably more importantly, the hidden texts, meanings and histories remain legible/visible.[67] To sum up, I fully agree with Esther Yau on her point about 'partnership imaginary and cultural memory':

> A cultural memory of narrative strategies, creative film crafting, and transregional negotiation of the Hong Kong's colonial era restrictions and industry

limitations does not vanish. Instead, this cultural memory is entangled with a retroactive identity of this cinema which infuses the co-produced films of Hong Kong and China in a particular manifestation of cultural globalization that is not entirely that of Hong Kong or of China. Partnership imaginary that engages different spatial dynamics and cultural Memory can reinforce the chances of breaking out from previous successes and present misses, and that is yet to be realized.[68]

The trace of Hong Kong reference can be creatively appropriated (for example, by 'catachresis' in the sense of Gayatri Spivak[69]) to generate insights into Hong Kong (in China) Studies.

There was a telling anecdote related to 'Hong Kong films': shortly before the unveiling of the new relaxation measures for co-productions in 2019, young Hong Kong film industry stakeholders issued an open letter to Derek Yee, chairman of the Hong Kong Film Directors' Guild and Hong Kong Film Awards Association, complaining about the lack of opportunities for local Hong Kong film industry workers because of imported labour from the mainland, as many Hong Kong films no longer employ local workers, except for production managers and set coordinators. If this is not rectified, there will be no Hong Kong filmmakers in 'Hong Kong films' before long.[70] It has thus become all the more important for Hong Kong cinema, echoing my argument in *Found in Transition* that it is not death but a new beginning for Hong Kong culture,[71] to reflect on its future development.

Coda: Hong Kong Cinema in the Future Continuous Tense?[72]

Hong Kong cinema is bound to imagine itself in the parenthetical of Hong Kong (in China) Studies at this particular juncture. Research on the paradigm shift of mainland–Hong Kong cross-border cooperation in the cultural realm will lead to a larger project on the transmission and transformation of Hong Kong culture in the mainland. Theoretical innovations lie in its turning away from the mainland–Hong Kong dichotomy, shifting the emphasis on the study of Hong Kong culture to cultural translations across the border. According to the official website of the Greater Bay Area administered by the Constitutional and Mainland Affairs Bureau:

On the one hand, Hong Kong will facilitate and support the economic development of the region, with a view to enhancing the role and functions of the Greater Bay Area in the country's two-way opening up; on the other hand, we will facilitate the development of industries in which Hong Kong's strengths lie in the Greater Bay Area, capitalizing on Hong Kong's strengths to serve the country's needs.[73]

Given that the emphasis on the development of industries, finance, trade and STEM education is now held in esteem, a Cultural Studies response to the Greater Bay Area must be in order. As Arif Dirlik has perceptively remarked in 'The Rise of China and the End of the World as We Know It', 'the PRC is a rising power in search of a paradigm that may provide an identity of its own that may also be appealing to others'.[74] Its paradigm appeals to others by following international standards, but in some respects only. As Hong Kong is the place where the impact of the rise of China will be most acutely felt, Hong Kong Studies can and will continue to shed illuminating light on politically engaged analyses of the changes and social challenges that confront the world today, with far-reaching theoretical implications for related areas, such as Inter-Asia Cultural Studies and Postcolonial Studies.

Hong Kong Studies will also contribute a vital dimension to related fields such as Asian Studies, especially against the backdrop of the recent revival of Cold War Studies in academia. As astutely noted by Poshek Fu, although peripheral to global geopolitics, Hong Kong was nevertheless 'a central battlefield of Asia's cultural Cold War', and 'Hong Kong cinema was on the front line of the cultural Cold War'.[75] The experience of Hong Kong's cultural interaction with Chinese politics back then could be inspiring in regard to the present situation, in which I am interested, although this is not exactly the same kind of cold war in a new era of 'one world two systems' global order. Hong Kong, an inseparable part of China and its window to the world, has been hopelessly bound by the unprecedented confluence of neoliberal capitalism and state capitalism, and the conflicts as well as collusion between the two capitalisms have generated a persistent storm in the Special Administrative Region. Inspired by Lawrence Grossberg's *Cultural Studies in the Future Tense*, which 'offers a modest proposal for future formations of cultural studies',[76] I will make a provisional conclusion – or prolegomenon, to be exact – by exploring Hong Kong (in China) Studies as an interdisciplinary model for future work. Grossberg made a very bold statement in the introduction of his book: 'We all want to change the world.'[77] The northbound imaginary of Hong Kong back in the 1990s might have been overbearing, but it also aimed to change China. Now that China has changed (but not for Hong Kong), if not become, the world, Hong Kong must rethink its future in this special context. Grossberg wanted to take the economy back from economists and put it back in the social world. For the future of Cultural Studies, more critically, he highlighted the importance of going beyond the established Eurocentric border. Hong Kong Studies, understood in this special context, must be inscribed between Eurocentric and Sinocentric borders, as well as between two capitalisms.

As Jackie Chan is (in)famous for making controversial statements about Hong Kong, it was not surprising to hear him say, at the Chinese People's

Political Consultative Conference's Arts Group held in March 2018, 'Now, we don't say whether a film is a Hong Kong film or a Chinese film – Hong Kong films are Chinese films as well.'[78] Although his remark may have seemed controversial, it was actually not as unreasonable as it sounded. To paraphrase Chan, it would arguably be Hong Kong Studies is China Studies and/or Greater Bay Area Studies if there is no proactive consideration of the role of Hong Kong Studies within emerging formations of global modernity with Chinese characteristics. Grossberg believed that culture can be an effective mediator, universal and specific at once, and that the new generation of scholars must foster an 'open-minded and progressive vanguard of intellectual and political movements to come'.[79] In the Hong Kong context, progressive vanguards cannot but take a step further to consider the (im)possibility of Hong Kong Studies in relation to Hong Kong (in China) Studies. I would argue that it is in this sense that the future continuity of Hong Kong cinema and even the city itself should be understood. I have repeatedly stated that after Hong Kong's reversion to China in 1997 both China and the West wanted to retain Hong Kong's status quo as a 'capital of free-wheeling capital',[80] and thus was spawned a myth of status quo that 'froze' Hong Kong as a commercial city. However, what made Hong Kong unique in the world was not its role in global capitalism, which was, in a sense, not genuinely different from that of other global cities, but its distinctive humanities-related aspects, such as its culture. As such, the study of Hong Kong culture in mainland China carries long-term significance for Hong Kong Studies as an academic discipline.

No one has a crystal ball to see what the future development of Chinese cinema will be, especially after the world was struck by an unprecedented pandemic at the beginning of the 2020s. If this book has offered a sensible account of the transformation of Chinese main melody films in regard to the impacts made by Hong Kong directors in the 2010s, it has already fulfilled its due function.

Notes

1. Lai Lin Thomala, 'Number of Cinema Screens in China from 2009 to 2019', *Statista*, 3 June 2020: <https://www.statista.com/statistics/279111/number-of-cinema-screens-in-china/>; last accessed 1 May 2021.

2. Mtime reporters and editors, '2010–2019: Ten Years of Radical Changes in the Mainland Chinese Market' (in Chinese) 〈2010–2019中國內地市場十年巨變史〉, Mtime, 3 January 2020: <https://news.mtime.com/2020/01/02/1600280-all.html>; last accessed 1 May 2021.

3. Deloitte, 'China's Film Industry: A New Era', Deloitte Culture & Entertainment report series, 2017, 1.

4. Ibid.

5. Regarding blockbusterisation, see, for instance, Keith B. Wagner, Kiki Tianqi Yu and Luke Vulpiani, 'Introduction: China's iGeneration Cinema', in *China's iGeneration: Cinema and Moving Image Culture for the Twenty-First Century*, ed. Matthew D. Johnson, Keith B. Wagner, Kiki Tianqi Yu and Luke Vulpiani (New York and London; Bloomsbury Academic, 2014), 9. 'Many main-melody films produced or co-produced by the state-owned film groups employ classic Hollywood narrative and characterization methods, and feature regional superstars to achieve the effect of "blockbusterization" of propaganda drama.'

6. Shohini Chaudhuri, *Contemporary World Cinema: Europe, the Middle East, East Asia and South Asia* (Edinburgh: Edinburgh University Press, 2005) is one of the examples.

7. Geoffrey Nowell-Smith (ed.), *The Oxford History of World Cinema* (Oxford: Oxford University Press, 1996).

8. 'Partnership with the Film Foundation's World Cinema Project and the Pan African Federation of Filmmakers to Restore African Cinema', Media Services, UNSECO, 28 February 2017: <http://www.unesco.org/new/en/media-services/single-view/news/partnership_with_the_film_foundations_world_cinema_projec/>; last accessed 1 May 2021.

9. Ella Shohat and Robert Stam, *Unthinking Eurocentrism: Multiculturalism and the Media* (London and New York: Routledge, 1994), among others, was a pioneering attempt to correct Eurocentric criticism by examining Hollywood films with a multicultural approach. Works have also theorised 'World Cinema' using a polycentric method from a plurality of critical perspectives. As tersely summed up by Stephanie Dennison and Song Hwee Lim, 'the establishment of World Cinema as a discipline promotes a truly global perspective upon a seemingly universal one (film studies) and a decidedly regional one (area studies)'. Stephanie Dennison and Song Hwee Lim, 'Introduction: Situating World Cinema as a Theoretical Problem', in *Remapping World Cinema: Identity, Culture and Politics in Film* (London and New York: Wallflower Press, 2006), 8.

10. Stephen Teo, 'Film and Globalization: From Hollywood to Bollywood', in *The Routledge International Handbook of Globalization Studies*, ed. Bryan S. Turner (London and New York: Routledge, 2010), 419.

11. Jigna Desai, *Beyond Bollywood: The Cultural Politics of South Asian Diasporic Film* (New York and London: Routledge, 2004), 65.

12. Chris Berry and Mary Farquhar, *China on Screen: Cinema and Nation* (New York: Columbia University Press, 2006), 209–10.

13. Wendy Su, *China's Encounter with Global Hollywood: Cultural Policy and the Film Industry 1994–2013* (Lexington: University Press of Kentucky, 2016), 20.

14. Aynne Kokas, *Hollywood Made in China* (Oakland: University of California Press, 2017), 4.

15. Ibid., 41.

16. Ying Xiao, *China in the Mix: Cinema, Sound, and Popular Culture in the Age of Globalization* (Jackson: University of Mississippi Press, 2017), 155–6.

17. Chris Berry, 'Wolf Warrior 2: Imagining the Chinese Century', Film Quarterly 72:2 (2018): 39–40; according to Berry, 'the film marks a new stage in Chinese cinema in the context of the global revival of nationalism' (43).

18. Zhang Rui, 'China's 2019 Box Office Gross Hits a Whopping $9.2B', China.org.cn, 2 January 2020: <http://www.china.org.cn/arts/2020-01/02/content_75572170.htm>; last accessed 1 May 2021.

19. Steven Zeitchik, 'The Chinese Film Business Is Doing the Unthinkable: Thriving without Hollywood', The Washington Post, 30 December 2019; published as 'Another US Export China Is Learning to Do Without', South China Morning Post, 1 January 2020.

20. Ibid.

21. Ibid.

22. Yongli Li, 'Rising Creativity and the Enduring Main Melody: Trends in China's 2019 Film Market', The Asia Dialogue, 16 December 2019: <https://theasiadialogue.com/2019/12/16/rising-creativity-and-the-enduring-main-melody-trends-in-chinas-2019-film-market/>; last accessed 1 May 2021.

23. 'Three Main Melody Films Broke Records during National Day Holidays' (in Chinese) 〈國慶檔三部主旋律電影合力破紀錄〉, Xinxi ShiBao 《信息時報》, 3 October 2019: <http://media.people.com.cn/BIG5/n1/2019/1003/c40606-31383920.html>; last accessed 1 May 2021.

24. See, for instance, Stephan Hammond, Hollywood East: Hong Kong Movies and the People Who Made Them (Lincolnwood: Contemporary Books, 2000).

25. Bi Yuanyuan 畢媛媛, 'The Success of My People, My Country Is Non-replicable' (in Chinese) 〈《我和我的祖國》成功不能複製〉, Daily Economic News 《每日經濟新聞》, 25 November 2019.

26. Xu Si 徐思, 'Beijing School or Hong Kong School? Who Will Lead the Future of Main Melody Blockbusters?' (in Chinese) 〈京派vs港派：誰能引導主旋律大片的未來？〉, Sina.com, 10 October 2019: <https://k.sina.com.cn/article_5594739451_1 4d78f2fb00100jziu.html>; last accessed 1 May 2021.

27. Ding Zhouyang 丁舟洋, '9 Years 81 Films! On the Secret of How Main Melody Films Changed from Political Capital to the Major Site of Capital Struggle' (in Chinese) 〈9年81部！揭秘主旋律電影如何從政治任務成為資本爭奪的主戰場〉, Daily Economic News 《每日經濟新聞》, 1 August 2017.

28. Karen Chu and Patrick Brzeski, 'Why Hong Kong's Top Filmmakers Are Making China Propaganda Films', The Hollywood Reporter, 17 May 2017: <https://www.hollywoodreporter.com/news/why-hong-kongs-top-filmmakers-are-making-china-propaganda-films-1004572>; last accessed 1 May 2021.

29. The five relaxation measures are: '1. To remove the restriction on the number of Hong Kong people participating in Mainland film productions; 2. To remove the restriction on percentage of artistes and requirement of Mainland-related plots in motion pictures jointly produced by the Mainland and Hong Kong (Mainland-Hong Kong co-productions); 3. To waive the fees for establishing Mainland-Hong Kong co-production projects; 4. To allow Hong Kong films and film practitioners to apply

for nomination for awards in Mainland film festivals; and 5. To allow Hong Kong film companies to apply for incentives for distributing and promoting outstanding Mainland motion pictures and Mainland-Hong Kong co-productions in Hong Kong, Macao and overseas.' 'HKSAR Government Welcomes Measures by Relevant Central Authorities to Further Facilitate Entry of Hong Kong Film Industry into Mainland Market', The Government of Hong Kong Special Administrative Region Press Releases, 16 April 2019: <https://www.info.gov.hk/gia/general/201904/16/P2019041600262.htm>; last accessed 1 May 2021.

30. Xinhua/chinadailyasia.com, 'New Measures to Facilitate HK-mainland Film Co-production', *China Daily*, 16 April 2019.

31. Peter Wong, 'How the Greater Bay Area Can Supercharge an Economic Dynamo', *South China Morning Post*, 6 March 2019.

32. Andrew Lau, 'Andrew Lau Confident that Main Melody Films Can Have Hong Kong "Flavor"', *Hong Kong Economic Journal*, 31 July 2017.

33. Siu-keung Cheung 張少強 and Wing-sang Law 羅永生, 'On Chinese Nationalism in *Ip Man*' (in Chinese) 〈論電影《葉問》中的華人民族主義〉, in *Hong Kong, Discourse, Media*, ed. Siu-keung Cheung et al. (Hong Kong: Oxford University Press, 2013), 117–40.

34. For the former, see Yu-liang Chang 張裕亮, 'From China's Main Melody Movies to Chinese Commercial Films with a Consciousness of Main Melody Characteristics' (in Chinese) 〈從中國主旋律電影到有主旋律意識的中國商業電影〉, *The Hong Kong Journal of Social Sciences* 39 (September 2010): 1–37; for the latter, Shuk-ting Kinnia Yau, 'From March of the Volunteers to Amazing Grace: the Death of China's Main Melody Movie in the 21st Century', *Jump Cut: A Review of Contemporary Media* 59 (Fall 2019): <https://www.ejumpcut.org/currentissue/KinnieYauMainMelody/index.html>; last accessed 1 May 2021.

35. See the 'Northbound Imaginary' Group 北進想像小組, 'Northbound Imagination: Re-positing Hong Kong Postcolonial Discourse' (in Chinese) 〈北進想像：香港後殖民論述再定位〉, in *Cultural Imaginary and Ideology: Critical Essays on Contemporary Hong Kong Cultural Politics* 《文化想像與意識形態: 當代香港文化政治論評》 (in Chinese), ed. Stephen Ching-kiu Chan 陳清僑 (Hong Kong: Oxford University Press, 1997), 3–10.

36. Shu-mei Shih 史書美, 'Problems of "Northbound Imaginary": Hong Kong Cultural Identity Politics' (in Chinese) 〈「北進想像」的問題：香港文化認同政治〉, in *Cultural Imaginary and Ideology*, 158.

37. Yiu-Wai Chu, *Found in Transition: Hong Kong Studies in the Age of China* (Albany: SUNY Press, 2018), 133.

38. Ibid., 111–12.

39. Kwai-cheung Lo, 'Hong Kong Cinema as Ethnic Borderland', in *A Companion to Hong Kong Cinema*, ed. Esther M. K. Cheung, Gina Marchetti and Esther C. M. Yau (Malden, MA: Wiley-Blackwell, 2015), 71.

40. 'Movies in a Besieged City' (in Chinese) 〈圍城電影〉 was the cover story of the May 2010 issue of *HKinema*, the quarterly published by the Hong Kong Film

Critics Association: <https://www.filmcritics.org.hk/hkinema/hkinema09.pdf>; last accessed 1 May 2021.

41. Poshek Fu and David Desser, 'Introduction', in *The Cinema of Hong Kong: History, Arts, Identity* (Cambridge: Cambridge University Press, 2000), 2.

42. Chu, *Found in Transition*, 131.

43. Rey Chow, *Primitive Passions: Visuality, Sexuality, Ethnography, and Contemporary Chinese Cinema* (New York: Columbia University, 1995), 171.

44. Chu, *Lost in Transition*, 28.

45. Rey Chow, *Sentimental Fabulations, Contemporary Chinese Films: Attachment in the Age of Global Visibility* (New York: Columbia University Press, 2007), 147.

46. Ibid.

47. Chu, *Lost in Transition*, 109–10.

48. Tai-lok Lui, *Hong Kong Model: From Present Tense to Past Tense* (in Chinese) 《香港模式：從現在式到過去式》 (Hong Kong: Chunghwa, 2015).

49. Tai-lok Lui, 'Choices Available' (in Chinese) 〈有得揀〉, *Ming Pao* 《明報》, 20 December 2019.

50. Chu, *Lost in Transition*, 112–15.

51. Gary Bettinson, 'Yesterday Once More: Hong Kong-China Coproductions and the Myth of Mainlandization', *Journal of Chinese Cinemas* 14:1 (2018): 28.

52. Emilie Yeh and Shi-yan Chao, 'Policy and Creative Strategies: Hong Kong CEPA Films in the China Market', *International Journal of Cultural Policy* 26:2 (2020): 199.

53. Tai-lok Lui, 'Fading Opportunities: Hong Kong in the Context of Regional Integration', in *Hong Kong 20 Years After the Handover: Emerging Social and Institutional Fractures after 1997*, ed. Brian C. H. Fong and Tai-lok Lui (Basingstoke: Palgrave Macmillan, 2018), 334.

54. Sebastian Veg, 'Anatomy of the Ordinary: New Perspectives in Hong Kong Independent Cinema', *Journal of Chinese Cinemas* 8 (2014): 73–92.

55. 'Young Directors and Actors' (in Chinese) 〈青年導演演員〉, Hong Kong Shue Yan University, 24 October 2019: <http://hknews.hksyu.edu/index.php/青年導演演員：香港電影進入中小型製作年代_小品電影反而更能留下印象>; last accessed 1 May 2021.

56. Gayatri Spivak, 'Can the Subaltern Speak?', in *Marxism and the Interpretation of Culture*, ed. Cary Nelson and Lawrence Grossberg (Urbana: University of Illinois Press, 1988), 287.

57. Chu, *Found in Transition*, 178. I used *Trivisa* here as an indication of the bigger picture of Hong Kong, and I am not sure if it is fortunate or unfortunate, but Hong Kong cinema's future may be a lot brighter than that of the city itself. In the face of the crisis of the city's decline, if not demise, Hong Kong filmmakers have beautifully set an example of straddling both sides: crossing the border but with succession planning at home at the same time.

58. Esther C.M. Yau, 'Watchful Partners, Hidden Currents: Hong Kong Cinema Moving into the Mainland of China', in *A Companion to Hong Kong Cinema*, ed.

Esther M. K. Cheung, Gina Marchetti and Esther C. M. Yau (Malden, MA: Wiley-Blackwell, 2015), 19.

59. Michael Sandel, 'The Moral Side of Murder', Harvard University's Justice with Michael Sandel: <http://justiceharvard.org/themoralsideofmurder/>; last accessed 1 May 2021.

60. Harris Dang, 'Movie Review: *The Vanished Murderer*', *Film-momatic Reviews*, 26 April 2016: <https://filmmomaticreviews.wordpress.com/2016/04/26/movie-review-the-vanished-murderer/>; last accessed 1 May 2021.

61. Edmund Lee, 'Film Review: *Call of Heroes*—Eddie Peng, Lau Ching-wan in Exhilarating *Wuxia* Epic', *South China Morning Post*, 18 August 2016.

62. Gayatri Spivak, 'Translator's Preface', in Jacques Derrida, *Of Grammatology*, Gayatri Spivak (trans.), introduction by Judith Butler, Fortieth Anniversary Edition (Baltimore: Johns Hopkins University Press, 2016), xxxii; Chu, *Found in Transition*, 146.

63. Winnie L. M. Yee, 'Decoding *The Trading Floor*: Charting a Postcolonial Hong Kong Identity through the TV Screen'. *SERIES: International Journal of TV Serial Narratives* 5:2 (Winter 2019): 83–94. According to the author, 'Hong Kong is also absent in the miniseries *The Trading Floor* [a 2018 TV drama produced by Andy Lau's Focus TV for Fox Networks Group], but a new space has been created by the process of erasure' (91).

64. Chu, *Found in Transition*, 116. See also Spivak, 'Translator's Preface', *Of Grammatology*, xxxv-vi and Butler, 'Introduction', *Of Grammatology*, x.

65. Jacques Derrida, *Sovereignties in Question: The Poetics of Paul Celan*, ed. Thomas Dutoit and Outi Pasanen (New York: Fordham University Press, 2005), 139.

66. Jacques Derrida, *Speech and Phenomena: And Other Essays on Husserl's Theory of Signs*, trans. David Allison (Evanston, IL: Northwestern University Press, 1973), 156.

67. For example, *Chung Wai Literary Quarterly* published a special issue (December 2016) on 'Derrida and Our Time' (in Chinese) 「德希達與我們的時代」, exploring how to use Derrida's theory to intervene in contemporary events/traces.

68. Yau, 'Watchful Partners, Hidden Currents', 43.

69. With its root in Greek denoting "misuse" or "misapplication," this term was appropriated by Gayatri Spivak as a tactic of the colonized: "a practice of resistance through an act of creative appropriation, a retooling of the rhetorical or institutional instruments of imperial oppression that turns those instruments back against their official owners." Stephen D. Moore, *Untold Tales from the Book of Revelation: Sex and Gender, Empire and Ecology* (Atlanta: SBL Press, 2014), 22; in other words, it is "a process whereby the victims of colonialism and imperialism strategically recycle and redeploy facets of colonial or imperial culture or propaganda."

70. 'An Open Letter to Derek Yee, Chairman Hong Kong Film Awards Association' (in Chinese)致香港電影金像獎主席爾冬陞先生的公開信〉, *Standnews*, 13 April 2019: <https://thestandnews.com/society/致-香港電影金像獎主席-爾冬陞先生-的公開信/>; last accessed 1 May 2021.

71. Chu, *Found in Transition*, 24–6.

72. This is paraphrased from Yiu-Wai Chu's 'Hong Kong Studies in the Future Continuous Tense', *International Institute for Asian Studies: Newsletter* Autumn 2019: 10; part of this section is a revised version of this essay.

73. Constitutional and Mainland Affairs Bureau, 'Overview', Greater Bay Area: <https:// www.bayarea.gov.hk/en/about/overview.html>; last accessed 1 May 2021. To be fair, the Constitutional and Mainland Affairs Bureau does have something to say about culture, but the statement on 'Arts & Culture, Creative Industries and Intellectual Property' focuses mainly on industries, not culture.

74. Arif Dirlik, 'The Rise of China and the End of the World as We Know It', Vancouver Institute Lectures, University of British Columbia, 27 February 2016: <https://open. library.ubc.ca/cIRcle/collections/12708/items/1.0348919>; last accessed 1 May 2021; a shorter version in *American Quarterly* 69:3 (September 2017): 533–40.

75. Poshek Fu, 'More than Just Entertaining: Cinematic Containment and Asia's Cold War in Hong Kong, 1949–1959', *Modern Chinese Literature and Culture* 30:2 (Fall 2018): 3.

76. Lawrence Grossberg, *Cultural Studies in the Future Tense* (Durham, NC: Duke University Press, 2010), 2.

77. 'This book is an expression of my own continuing belief that intellectual work matters, that it is a vital component of the struggle to change the world and to make the world more humane, and that cultural studies, as a particular project, a particular sort of intellectual practice, has something valuable to contribute.' Ibid., 6.

78. Kris Cheng, 'No Distinction between Chinese and Hong Kong Films Anymore, Says Actor Jackie Chan', *Hong Kong Free Press*, 8 March 2018: <https://www.hongkongfp. com/2018/03/08/no-distinction-chinese-hong-kong-films-anymore-says-actor- jackie-chan/>; last accessed 1 May 2021.

79. Grossberg, *Cultural Studies in the Future Tense*, 181.

80. Chu, *Lost in Transition*, 5.

Select Bibliography

14th Hong Kong International Film Festival (ed.). *The China Factor in Hong Kong Cinema*. Hong Kong: Urban Council of Hong Kong, 1990.

15th Hong Kong International Film Festival (ed.). *Hong Kong Cinema in the Eighties: A Comparative Study with Western Cinema*. Hong Kong: Urban Council of Hong Kong, 1991.

21st Hong Kong International Film Festival (ed.). *Fifty Years of Electric Shadows*. Hong Kong: HKIFF/ Urban Council, 1997.

23rd Hong Kong International Film Festival (ed.). *Hong Kong New Wave: Twenty Years After*. Hong Kong: Provisional Urban Council of Hong Kong, 1999.

Abbas, Ackbar, *Hong Kong: Culture and the Politics of Disappearance*. Hong Kong: Hong Kong University Press, 1997.

Abjorensen, Norman. *Historical Dictionary of Popular Music*. Lanham, MD, Boulder, CO, New York, London: Rowman and Littlefield, 2017.

Ahmad, Aijaz. 'Jameson's Rhetoric of Otherness and the "National Allegory"'. *Social Text* 17 (Fall 1987), 3–25.

Atkinson, Michael (ed.). *Exile Cinema: Filmmakers at Work beyond Hollywood*. Albany, NY: SUNY Press, 2008.

Babington, Bruce. *The Sports Film: Games People Play*. London and New York: Wallflower, 2014.

Badiou, Alain. *Cinema*. Cambridge: Polity, 2013.

Baker, Peter and Deborah Shaller (eds). D*etecting Detection: International Perspectives on the Uses of a Plot*. New York and London: Continuum International Publishing Group, 2012.

Bell, Daniel A. *The China Model: Political Meritocracy and the Limits of Democracy*. Princeton: Princeton University Press, 2015.

Berry, Chris. *Postsocialist Cinema in Post-Mao China: The Cultural Revolution after the Cultural Revolution*. New York and London: Routledge, 2004.

Berry, Chris (ed.). *Chinese Films in Focus II*. London: British Film Institute, 2008.

Berry, Chris. '*Wolf Warrior 2*: Imagining the Chinese Century', *Film Quarterly* 72:2 (2018), 38–44.

Berry, Chris and Mary Farquhar. *China on Screen: Cinema and Nation*. New York: Columbia University Press, 2006.

Berry, Michael (ed.). *Speaking in Images: Interviews with Contemporary Chinese Filmmakers*. New York: Columbia University Press, 2005.

Berry, Michael. *A History of Pain: Trauma in Modern Chinese Literature and Film*. New York: Columbia University Press, 2008.

Bettinson, Gary. 'Yesterday Once More: Hong Kong-China Coproductions and the Myth of Mainlandization', *Journal of Chinese Cinemas* 14:1 (2020): 26–31.

Bettinson, Gary and Daniel Martin (eds). *Hong Kong Horror Cinema*. Edinburgh: Edinburgh University Press, 2019.

Bettinson, Gary and James Udden (eds). *The Poetics of Chinese Cinema*. New York: Palgrave MacMillan.

Bliss, Michael. *Between the Bullets: The Spiritual Cinema of John Woo*. Lanham, MD: Scarecrow Press, 2002.

Bordwell, David. *Planet Hong Kong: Popular Cinema and the Art of Entertainment*. Cambridge, MA: Harvard University Press, 2000.

Buckland, Warren (ed.). *Puzzle Films: Complex Storytelling in Contemporary Cinema*. Chichester: Wiley-Blackwell, 2009.

Cai, Shenshen. *State Propaganda in China's Entertainment Industry*. Abingdon and New York: Routledge, 2016.

Callahan, William A. 'Identity and Security in China: The Negative Soft Power of the China Dream', *Politics* 35:3 (April 2015), 216–29.

Cartmell, Deborah and Ashley D. Polasek (eds). *A Companion to the Biopic*. Chichester: Wiley-Blackwell, 2020.

Chan, Felicia and Andrew Willis (eds). *Chinese Cinemas: International Perspective*. Abingdon and New York: Routledge 2016.

Chan, Joseph M. and Bryce T. McIntyre (eds). *In Search of Boundaries: Communication, Nation-States, and Cultural Identities*. Westport, CT: Ablex, 2002.

Chan, Kim-Mui Elaine. *Hong Kong Dark Cinema: Film Noir, Re-conceptions, and Reflexivity*. Cham: Palgrave Macmillan, 2019.

Chan, Stephen Ching-kiu 陳清僑 (ed.). *Cultural Imaginary and Ideology: Critical Essays on Contemporary Hong Kong Cultural Politics* (in Chinese) 《文化想像與意識形態: 當代香港文化政治論評》. Hong Kong: Oxford University Press, 1997.

Chan, Sui-jeung. *East River Column Hong Kong Guerrillas in the Second World War and After*. Hong Kong: Hong Kong University Press, 2009.

Chang, Jing Jing. 'Ann Hui's Tin Shui Wai Diptych: The Flashback and Feminist Perception in Post-Handover Hong Kong', *Quarterly Review of Film and Video* 33:8 (2016), 722–42.

Chaudhuri, Shohini. *Contemporary World Cinema: Europe, the Middle East, East Asia and South Asia*. Edinburgh: Edinburgh University Press, 2005.

Chen, Xiaomei. *Staging Chinese Revolution: Theater, Film, and the Afterlives of Propaganda*. New York: Columbia University Press, 2017.

Chen Xuguang 陳旭光 and Tien Yizhou 田亦洲. 'New Era of Chinese Cinema: New Configurations, New Norms and New Aesthetic Constructions' (in Chinese) 〈中國電影新時代: 新格局、新規範與新美學建構〉, *Commentaries on Literature And Art* 1 (2018), 74–84.

Cheshire, Ellen. *Bio-pics: A Life in Pictures*. London and New York: Wallflower, 2015.

Cheuk, Pak Tong Cheuk. *Hong Kong New Wave Cinema*. Bristol and Chicago: Intellect, 2008.

Cheung, Esther M. K., Gina Marchetti and Esther C. M. Yau (eds). *A Companion to Hong Kong Cinema*. Malden, MA: Wiley-Blackwell, 2015.

Cheung, Esther M. K., Gina Marchetti and Tan See Kam (eds). *Hong Kong Screenscapes: From the New Wave to the Digital Frontier*. Hong Kong: Hong Kong University Press, 2011.

Cheung, Ruby. *New Hong Kong Cinema: Transitions to Becoming Chinese in 21st-Century East Asia*. New York and Oxford: Berghahn Books, 2016.

Cheung, Siu-Keung and Wing-Sang Law. 'The Colony Writes Back: Nationalism and Collaborative Coloniality in the *Ip Man* Series', *Social Transformations in Chinese Societies* 13:2 (2017), 159–72.

Chow, Rey. *Writing Diaspora: Tactics of Intervention in Contemporary Cultural Studies*. Bloomington and Indianapolis: Indiana University Press, 1993.

Chow, Rey. *Primitive Passions: Visuality, Sexuality, Ethnography, and Contemporary Chinese Cinema*. New York: Columbia University, 1995.

Chow Rey (ed.). *Modern Chinese Literary and Cultural Studies in the Age of Theory*. Durham, NC and London: Duke University Press, 2000.

Chow, Rey. *Sentimental Fabulations, Contemporary Chinese Films: Attachment in the Age of Global Visibility*. New York: Columbia University Press, 2007.

Chow, Yiu Fai and Jeroen de Kloet. 'Flânerie and Acrophilia in the Postmetropolis: Rooftops in Hong Kong Cinema', *Journal of Chinese Cinemas* 7:2 (2013), 139–55.

Chu, Yingchi. *Hong Kong Cinema: Coloniser, Motherland and Self*. London and New York: RoutledgeCurzon, 2001.

Chu, Yiu-Wai. *Lost in Transition: Hong Kong Culture in the Age of China*. Albany, NY: SUNY Press, 2013.

Chu, Yiu-Wai. *Found in Transition: Hong Kong Studies in the Age of China*. Albany, NY: SUNY Press, 2018.

Chu, Yiu-Wai朱耀偉. *The (Post)Youth Age of Hong Kong Popular Culture* (in Chinese) 《香港流行文化的(後)青春歲月》. Hong Kong: Chung Hwa, 2019.

Chua, Beng Huat. *Structure, Audience and Soft Power in East Asian Pop Culture*. Hong Kong: Hong Kong University Press, 2012.

Clark, Paul. *Chinese Cinema: Culture and Politics since 1949*. Cambridge: Cambridge University Press, 1987.

Clark, Paul. *The Chinese Cultural Revolution: A History*. New York: Cambridge University Press, 2008.

Cornelius, Sheila (with Ian Haydn Smith). *New Chinese Cinema: Challenging Representations*. London: Wallflower Press, 2002.

Crosson, Seán. *Sport and Film*. London and New York: Routledge, 2013.

Davis, Darrell William. 'Marketization, Hollywood, Global China', *Modern Chinese Literature and Culture* 26: 1 (Spring 2014), 193–241.

Davis, Darrell William and Emilie Yueh-yu Yeh. *East Asian Screen Industries*. London: British Film Institute, 2008.

De Certeau, Michel. *The Practice of Everyday Life*. Berkeley and Los Angeles: University of California Press, 1984.

Deleuze, Gilles. *Cinema 1: The Movement Image*. Minneapolis: University of Minnesota Press, 1989.

Deleuze, Gilles. *Cinema 2: The Time-Image*. Minneapolis: University of Minnesota Press, 1989.

Dennison, Stephanie and Song Hwee Lim (eds). *Remapping World Cinema: Identity, Culture and Politics in Film*. London and New York: Wallflower Press, 2006.

Derrida, Jacques. *Speech and Phenomena: And Other Essays on Husserl's Theory of Signs*. Evanston, IL: Northwestern University Press, 1973.

Derrida, Jacques. *Sovereignties in Question: The Poetics of Paul Celan*. New York: Fordham University Press, 2005.

Derrida, Jacques. *Of Grammatology*, Fortieth Anniversary Edition. Baltimore: Johns Hopkins University Press, 2016.

Desai, Jigna. *Beyond Bollywood: The Cultural Politics of South Asian Diasporic Film*. New York and London: Routledge, 2004.

Dirlik, Arif. 'The Rise of China and the End of the World as We Know It', Vancouver Institute Lectures, University of British Columbia, 27 February 2016: <https://open.library.ubc.ca/cIRcle/collections/12708/items/1.0348919>; last accessed 1 May 2021; shorter version in *American Quarterly* 69:3 (September 2017): 533–40.

Donald, Ralph and Karen MacDonald. *Reel Men at War: Masculinity and the American War Film*. Lanham, MD: Scarecrow Press, 2011.

Donovan, Barna William. *The Asian Influence on Hollywood Action Films*. Jefferson, NC and London: McFarland & Company, 2008.

Edgington, K., Thomas Erskine and James M. Welsh, *Encyclopedia of Sports Films*. Lanham, MD, Toronto, Plymouth, UK: The Scarecrow Press, 2011.

Edney, Kingsley, Ying Zhu and Stanley Rosen (eds). *Soft Power with Chinese Characteristics: China's Campaign for Hearts and Minds*. Oxford and New York: Routledge, 2020.

Edwards, Louise. *Women Warriors and Wartime Spies of China*. Cambridge: Cambridge University Press, 2016.

Egan, Ronald C. *Word, Image, and Deed in the Life of Su Shi*. Cambridge, MA and London: Harvard University Press, 1994.

Elder, Robert K. (ed.). *John Woo: Interviews*. Jackson: University of Mississippi Press, 2005.

Eng, Kuah-Pearce Khun and Andrew P. Davidson (eds). *At Home in the Chinese Diaspora: Memories, Identities and Belonging*. New York: Palgrave, 2008.

Fan, Xing. *Staging Revolution: Artistry and Aesthetics in Model Beijing Opera during the Cultural Revolution*. Hong Kong: Hong Kong University Press, 2018.

Fang, Karen. *John Woo's A Better Tomorrow*. Hong Kong: Hong Kong University Press, 2004.

Fong, Brian and Tai-lok Lui (eds). *Hong Kong 20 Years After the Handover: Emerging Social and Institutional Fractures after 1997*. Basingstoke: Palgrave Macmillan, 2018.

Fotheringham, William. *Sunday in Hell: Behind the Lens of the Greatest Cycling Film of All Time*. London: Yellow Jersey Press, 2018.

Fu, Poshek. 'More than Just Entertaining: Cinematic Containment and Asia's Cold War in Hong Kong, 1949–1959', *Modern Chinese Literature and Culture* 30:2 (Fall 2018): 1–55.

Fu, Poshek and David Desser (eds). *The Cinema of Hong Kong: History, Arts, Identity*. Cambridge: Cambridge University Press, 2000.

Funnell, Lisa. *Warrior Women: Gender, Race, and the Transnational Chinese Action Star*. Albany, NY: SUNY Press, 2014.

Golley, Jane, Linda Jaivin and Luigi Tomba (eds). *China Story Yearbook 2016: Control*. Canberra: ANU Press, 2017.

Grant, Barry Keith (ed.). *Film Genre Reader IV*. Austin: University of Texas Press, 2012.

Grossberg, Lawrence. *Cultural Studies in the Future Tense*. Durham, NC: Duke University Press, 2010.

Hall, Kenneth E. *John Woo: The Films*. Jefferson, NC: McFarland, 1999.

Hall, Kenneth E. *John Woo's The Killer*. Hong Kong: Hong Kong University Press, 2009.

Hammond, Stephan. *Hollywood East: Hong Kong Movies and the People Who Made Them*. Lincolnwood, IL: Contemporary Books, 2000.

Havert, Nik. *The Golden Age of Disaster Cinema: A Guide to the Films, 1950–1979*. Jefferson, NC: McFarland, 2019.

Hird, Derek and Geng Song (eds). *The Cosmopolitan Dream: Transnational Chinese Masculinities in a Global Age*. Hong Kong: Hong Kong University Press, 2018.

Ho, Sam and Wai-leng Ho (eds). *The Swordsman and His Jiang Hu: Tsui Hark and Hong Kong Film*. Hong Kong: Hong Kong Film Archive, 2002.

Hong Kong International Film Festival Society. *Hong Kong Panorama 97–98*. Hong Kong: Provisional Urban Council, 1998.

Hong Kong Motion Picture Industry Association香港影業協會 (ed.). *Compilation of Data of Hong Kong Films 2012* (in Chinese)《香港電影資料彙編2012》. Hong Kong: CreateHK, 2013.

Horsley, Lee. *The Noir Thriller*. Basingstoke and New York: Palgrave Macmillan, 2001.

Irr, Caren and Ian Buchanan (eds). *On Jameson: From Postmodernism to Globalization*. Albany, NY: SUNY Press, 2006.

Jameson, Fredric. 'Third-World Literature in the Era of Multinational Capitalism', *Social Text* 15 (Autumn 1986), 65–88.

Johnson, Matthew D., Keith B. Wagner, Kiki Tianqi Yu and Luke Vulpiani (eds). *China's iGeneration: Cinema and Moving Image Culture for the Twenty-First Century*. New York and London; Bloomsbury Academic, 2014.

Kay, Glenn and Michael Rose. *Disaster Movies*. Chicago: Chicago Review Press, 2006.

Kendrick, James (ed.). *A Companion to the Action Film*. Chichester: Wiley-Blackwell, 2019.

Koepnick, Lutz. *Michael Bay: World Cinema in the Age of Populism*. Urbana: University of Illinois Press, 2018.

Kokas, Aynne. *Hollywood Made in China*. Oakland: University of California Press, 2017.

Kundera, Milan. *The Book of Laughter and Forgetting*. London: Penguin, 1983.

Kwong, Po-Wai鄺保威. *Ann Hui Talking about Ann Hui* (in Chinese)《許鞍華說許鞍華》. Hong Kong: Po-Wai Kwong, 1998.

Latham, Kevin. *Pop Culture China!: Media, Arts, and Lifestyle*. Santa Barbara, Denver, Oxford: ABC-CLIO, 2007.

Lau, Joseph劉紹銘, Ping-kwan Leung 梁秉鈞 and Zidong Xu 許子東. *Rereading Eileen Chang* (in Chinese)《再讀張愛玲》. Hong Kong: Oxford University Press, 2002.

Law, Kar, Frank Bren, and Sam Ho (eds). *Hong Kong Cinema: A Cross-cultural View*. Lanham, MD, Toronto, and Oxford: The Scarecrow Press, 2004.

Law, Wing-Sang. 'The Violence of Time and Memory Undercover: Hong Kong's *Infernal Affairs*', *Inter-Asia Cultural Studies* 7:3 (2006), 383–402.

Lee, Cheng-Liang李政亮. *China: The Age of Chinese Blockbusters* (in Chinese)《拆哪，中國的大片時代》. Taipei: Azure Books, 2017.

Lee, Leo Ou-fan李歐梵. *Fin de siècle Murmur* (in Chinese)《世紀末囈語》. Hong Kong: Oxford University Press, 2001.

Lee, Leo Ou-Fan. *Shanghai Modern: The Flowering of a New Urban Culture in China, 1930–1945*. Cambridge, MA: Harvard University Press, 1999.

Lee, Vivian P. Y. *Hong Kong Cinema Since 1997: The Post-Nostalgic Imagination*. Basingstoke: Palgrave Macmillan, 2009.

Lee, Vivian P. Y. (ed.). *East Asian Cinemas: Regional Flows and Global Transformations*. Basingstoke and New York: Palgrave Macmillan, 2011.

Leitch, Thomas (ed.). *The Oxford Handbook of Adaptation Studies*. New York: Oxford University Press, 2017.

Leung, Helen Hok-Sze. *Undercurrents: Queer Culture and Postcolonial Hong Kong*. Vancouver and Toronto: UBC Press, 2008.

Leung, Laifong. *Contemporary Chinese Fiction Writers: Biography, Bibliography, and Critical Assessment*. New York and London: Routledge, 2017.

Leung, Wing-fai. *Multimedia Stardom in Hong Kong: Image, Performance and Identity*. Abingdon and New York: Routledge, 2015.

Li, Cheuk-to (ed.). *A Study of Hong Kong Cinema in the Seventies*. Hong Kong: Hong Kong International Film Festival, 1984.

Li, Cheuk-to (ed.). *Peter Ho-Sun Chan: My Way*. Hong Kong: Joint Publishing, 2012.

Li, Gucheng. *A Glossary of Political Terms of the People's Republic of China*. Hong Kong: The Chinese University of Hong Kong Press, 1995.

Li, Liu and Fan Hong. *The National Games and National Identity in China: A History*. London and New York: Routledge, 2017.

Lieberman, Viridiana. *Sports Heroines on Film: A Critical Study of Cinematic Women Athletes*. Jefferson, NC: McFarland & Company, 2015.

Liew, Kai Khiun. *Amnesia, Nostalgia and Heritage: Transnational Memory and Popular Culture in East and Southeast Asia*. London and Lanham, MD: Rowman and Littlefield, 2016.

Lim, Song Hwee and Julian Ward (eds). *The Chinese Cinema Book*, 2nd edition. London: Bloomsbury, 2020.

Ling, Alex. *Badiou and Cinema*. Edinburgh: Edinburgh University Press, 2011.

Liu, Jieyu and Junko Yamashita (eds). *Routledge Handbook of East Asian Gender Studies*. Abingdon and New York: Routledge, 2020.

Lo, Kwai-cheung. *Chinese Face/Off: The Transnational Popular Culture of Hong Kong*. Urbana and Champaign: University of Illinois Press, 2005.

Lo, Kwai-cheung. 'Knocking Off Nationalism in Hong Kong Cinema: Woman and the Chinese "Thing" in Tsui Hark's Films', *Camera Obscura* 2:3 (December 2006), 37–61.

Lo, Kwai-Cheung. *Excess and Masculinity in Asian Cultural Productions*. Albany, NY: SUNY Press, 2010.

Lo, Kwai-Cheung 羅貴祥 and Eva Man 文潔華(eds). *Age of Hybridity: Cultural Identity, Gender, Everyday Life Practice, and Hong Kong Cinema of the 1970s* (in Chinese) 《雜嘜時代：文化身份、性別、日常生活實踐與香港電影1970s》. Hong Kong: Oxford University Press, 2005.

Lo, Sonny Shiu-Hing, Steven Chung-Fun Hung and Jeff Hai-Chi Loo. *China's New United Front Work in Hong Kong: Penetrative Politics and Its Implications*. Singapore: Palgrave Macmillan, 2019.

Lo, Vivienne, Chris Berry and Guo Liping (eds). *Film and the Chinese Medical Humanities*. London and New York: Routledge, 2020.

Louie, Kam (ed.). *Hong Kong Culture: Word and Image*. Hong Kong: Hong Kong University Press, 2010.

Lu, Sheldon (ed.). *Transnational Chinese Cinemas: Identity, Nationhood, Gender*. Honolulu: University of Hawaii Press, 1997.

Lu, Sheldon. *Chinese Modernity and Global Biopolitics: Studies in Literature and Visual Culture*. Honolulu: University of Hawaii Press, 2007.

Lui, Tai-lok Lui 呂大樂. *Hong Kong Model: From Present Tense to Past Tense* (in Chinese) 《香港模式：從現在式到過去式》. Hong Kong: Chunghwa, 2015.

Ma, Sen馬森. *Film China Dream* (in Chinese) 《電影中國夢》. Taipei: Showwe Information Co. Ltd., 2016.

Ma, Sheng-mei. *Off-White: Yellowface and Chinglish by Anglo-American Culture*. New York, London, Oxford, New Delhi, Sydney: Bloomsbury Academic 2019.

Marchetti, Gina. *Andrew Lau and Alan Mak's Infernal Affairs: The Trilogy*. Hong Kong: Hong Kong University Press, 2007.

Marchetti, Gina. 'Gender Politics and Neoliberalism in China: Ann Hui's *The Postmodern Life of My Aunt*', *Visual Anthropology* 22: 2–3 (2009), 123–40.

Marchetti, Gina *Citing China: Politics, Postmodernism, and World Cinema*. Honolulu: University of Hawaii Press, 2018.

Marchetti, Gina and Tan See Kam (eds). *Hong Kong Film, Hollywood and New Global Cinema: No Film is an Island*. Abingdon and New York: Routledge, 2007.

Mathews, Gordon, Eric Ma, and Tai-lok Lui. *Hong Kong, China: Learning to Belong to a Nation*. London and New York: Routledge, 2008.

Meyer-Clement, Elena. *Party Hegemony and Entrepreneurial Power in China: Institutional Change in the Film and Music Industries*. London and New York: Routledge, 2015.

Moore, Stephen D. *Untold Tales from the Book of Revelation: Sex and Gender, Empire and Ecology*. Atlanta: SBL Press, 2014.

Morris, Meaghan, Siu Leung Li, and Stephen Ching-kiu Chan (eds). *Hong Kong Connections: Transnational Imagination in Action Cinema*. Durham, NC and London: Duke University Press, 2005.

Morton, Lisa. *The Cinema of Tsui Hark*. Jefferson, NC: McFarland, 2001.

Nelson, Cary and Lawrence Grossberg (eds). *Marxism and the Interpretation of Culture*. Urbana: University of Illinois Press, 1988.

Neupert, Richard. *The End: Narration and Closure in the Cinema*. Detroit: Wayne State University Press, 1995.

Ng, Janet, *Paradigm City: Space, Culture, and Capitalism in Hong Kong*. Albany, NY: SUNY Press, 2013.

Nochimson, Martha P. *Dying to Belong: Gangster Movies in Hollywood and Hong Kong*. Malden, MA, Oxford and Victoria: Blackwell, 2007.

Nowell-Smith Geoffrey (ed.). *The Oxford History of World Cinema*. Oxford: Oxford University Press, 1996.

O'Brien, Daniel. *Spooky Encounters: A Gwailo's Guide to Hong Kong Horror*. Manchester: Headpress, 2003.

Olson, Debbie (ed.). *The Child in World Cinema*. London: Lexington Books, 2018.

Pang, Laikwan. *Building a New China in Cinema: The Chinese Left-wing Cinema*. Lanham, MD and Oxford: Rowman and Littlefield, 2002.

Pierson, Michele. *Special Effects: Still in Search of Wonder*. New York: Columbia University Press, 2002.

Polley, Jason, Vinton Poon and Lian-Hee Wee (eds). *Cultural Conflict in Hong Kong: Angles on a Coherent Imaginary*. Singapore: Palgrave Macmillan, 2018.

Rajala, Anne, Daniel Lindblom and Matteo Stocchetti (eds). *The Political Economy of Local Cinema: A Critical Introduction*. Berlin: Peter Lang, 2020.

Ramo, Joshua Cooper. *The Beijing Consensus*. London: The Foreign Policy Centre, 2004.

Rancière, Jacques. *The Future of the Image*. London and New York: Verso, 2007.

Rancière, Jacques. *Aesthetics and Its Discontents*. Cambridge and Malden, MA: Polity, 2009.

Rancière, Jacques. *Dissensus: On Politics and Aesthetics*. London and New York: Bloomsbury Academic, 2015.

Roberts, Priscilla and John M. Carroll (eds). *Hong Kong in the Cold War*. Hong Kong: Hong Kong University Press, 2016.

Rossi, Ino (ed.). *Challenges of Globalization and Prospects for an Inter-civilizational World Order*. Cham: Springer, 2020.

Schneider, Steven Jay and Tony Williams (eds). *Horror International*. Detroit: Wayne State University Press, 2005.

Schroeder, Andrew. *Tsui Hark's Zu: Warriors from the Magic Mountain*. Hong Kong: Hong Kong University Press, 2004.

Scocca, Tom. *Beijing Welcomes You: Unveiling the Capital City of the Future*. New York: Riverhead Books, 2011.

Shek, Kei石琪. *Hong Kong Cinema: New Wave* (in Chinese) 《香港電影新浪潮》. Shanghai: Fudan University Press, 2006.

Shohat, Ella and Robert Stam. *Unthinking Eurocentrism: Multiculturalism and the Media*. London and New York: Routledge, 1994.

Sison, Antonio D. *The Sacred Foodways of Film: Theological Servings in 11 Food Films*. Eugene, OR: Pickwick, 2016.

Song, Weijie. 'Cinematic Geography, Martial Arts Fantasy, and Tsui Hark's Wong Fei-hung Series', *Asian Cinema* 19:1 (Spring/Summer 2008), 123–42.

Spiridon, Monica. 'The (Meta)narrative Paratext: Coda as a Cunning Fictional Device', *Neohelicon* 37:1 (June 2010): 60.

Stokes, Lisa Odham. *Peter Ho-Sun Chans He's a Woman, She's a Man*. Hong Kong: Hong Kong University Press, 2009.

Stokes, Lisa Odham and Rachel Braaten. *Historical Dictionary of Hong Kong Cinema*. Lanham, MD: Rowman and Littlefield, 2020.

Stuckey, G. Andrew. *Metacinema in Contemporary Chinese Film*. Hong Kong: Hong Kong University Press, 2018.

Su, Wendy. *China's Encounter with Global Hollywood: Cultural Policy and the Film Industry 1994–2013*. Lexington: University Press of Kentucky, 2016.

Szeto, Kin-Yan. *The Martial Arts Cinema of the Chinese Diaspora: Ang Lee, John Woo, and Jackie Chan in Hollywood*. Carbondale and Edwardsville: South Illinois University Press, 2011.

Szeto, Mirana M. and Yun-chung Chen. 'To Work or Not to Work: The Dilemma of Hong Kong Film Labor in the Age of Mainlandization', *Jump Cut* 55 (Fall 2013): <https://www.ejumpcut.org/archive/jc55.2013/SzetoChenHongKong/index.html>; last accessed 1 May 2021.

Tan, See Kam. *Tsui Hark's Peking Opera Blues*. Hong Kong: Hong Kong University Press, 2016.

Tang, Xiaobing. *Visual Culture in Contemporary China*. Cambridge: Cambridge University Press, 2015.

Teo, Stephen. *Hong Kong Cinema: The Extra Dimension*. London: British Film Institute, 1997.

Teo, Stephen. '*Promise* and *Perhaps Love*: Pan-Asian Production and the Hong Kong-China Interrelationship', *Inter-Asia Cultural Studies* 9:3 (2008), 341–58.

Teo, Stephen. *The Asian Cinema Experience: Styles, Spaces, Theory*. Abingdon and New York: Routledge, 2013.

Teo, Stephen. *Chinese Martial Arts Cinema* 2nd edition. Edinburgh: Edinburgh University Press, 2016.

To, Nathan. 'A Revolution for Memory: Reproductions of a Communist Utopia through Tsui Hark's *The Taking of Tiger Mountain* and Posters from the Cultural Revolution', *Frames Cinema Journal* 7 (June 2015): <http://framescinemajournal.com/article/a-revolution-for-memory-reproductions-of-a-communist-utopia-through-tsui-harks-the-taking-of-tiger-mountain-and-posters-from-the-cultural-revolution/>; last accessed 1 May 2021.

Tung, Constantine and Colin Mackerras (eds). *Drama in the People's Republic of China*. Albany, NY: SUNY Press, 1987.

Turner, Bryan S. (ed.). *The Routledge International Handbook of Globalization Studies*. London and New York: Routledge, 2010.

Veg, Sebastian. 'Hong Kong by Night: Prostitution and Cinema in Herman Yau's *Whispers and Moans*', *China Perspectives* 2 (2007): 87–8.

Veg, Sebastian. 'Anatomy of the Ordinary: New Perspectives in Hong Kong Independent Cinema', *Journal of Chinese Cinemas* 8: (2014): 73–92.

Voci, Paola and Luo Hui (eds). *Screening China's Soft Power*. Abingdon and New York: Routledge, 2018.

Wei Junzi 魏君子. *Spindrift in Light Shadow: Contextual Memories of Hong Kong Films* (in Chinese)《光影裏的浪花：香港電影脈絡回憶》. Hong Kong: Chunghwa, 2019.

Wei, Yuwa. *Issues Decisive for China's Rise or Fall: An International Law Perspective*. Singapore: Springer, 2019.

Williams, Tony. *John Woo's Bullet in the Head*. Hong Kong: Hong Kong University Press, 2009.

Wise, J. Macgregor. *Surveillance and Film*. New York and London: Bloomsbury Academic, 2016.

Witterstaetter, Renée. *Dying for Action: The Life and Films of Jackie Chan*. New York: Warner Books, 1997.

Wong, Cecilia 卓男 and Stephanie Ng 吳月華 (eds). *Ann Hui: Forty* (in Chinese)《許鞍華：電影四十》. Hong Kong: Joint Publishing Co., 2018.

Xia, Xiaohong 夏曉虹. 'Styles of the Times: Qiu Jin's Images in Literature' (in Chinese) 〈秋瑾文學形象的時代風貌〉, *Modern Chinese Literature Studies* 《中國現代文學研究叢刊》 4 (2009), 49–65.

Xiao, Hui Faye. *Youth Economy, Crisis, and Reinvention in Twenty-First-Century China: Morning Sun in the Tiny Times*. Abingdon and New York: Routledge, 2019.

Xiao, Ying Xiao. *China in the Mix: Cinema, Sound, and Popular Culture in the Age of Globalization*. Jackson, MS: University of Mississippi Press, 2017.

Xie Jin 謝晉. *Selected Essays on Xie Jin's Films: History* (in Chinese)《謝晉電影選集：歷史卷》. Shanghai: Shanghai University Press, 2007.

Xie, Min 謝冕 and Zhang Yiwu 張頤武. *Major Transformation: Cultural Studies of the Post-New Period* (in Chinese)《大轉型：後新時期文化研究》. Heilongjiang Education Press, 1995.

Xin, Jinsong 辛金順. *Silent Voices: Essays on Sinophone Literature* (in Chinese)《秘響交音: 華語語系文學論集》. Taipei: Independent & Unique, 2012.

Yang, Elsa Yee-shan 楊漪珊. *Old Business New Profession* (in Chinese)《古老生意新專業》. Hong Kong: Cosmos Books, 2001.

Yang, Fan. *Faked in China: Nation Branding, Counterfeit Culture, and Globalization*. Bloomington and Indianapolis: Indiana University Press, 2016.

Yang, Yanling. 'Film Policy, the Chinese Government and Soft Power', *New Cinemas: Journal of Contemporary Film*, 14:1 (April 2017), 71–91.

Yau, Esther C. M. (ed.). *At Full Speed: Hong Kong Cinema in a Borderless World*. Minneapolis and London: University of Minnesota Press, 2000.

Yau, Esther C. M. and Tony Williams (eds). *Hong Kong Neo-Noir*. Edinburgh: Edinburgh University Press, 2017.

Yau, Herman Lai-to 邱禮濤. 'Memor /Amnesia: A Cultural Translation of Hong Kong' (in Chinese) 〈記不了/忘不掉：誰的香港〉, *Cultural Studies@Lingnan* 12 (2009): <http://commons.ln.edu.hk/mcsln/vol12/iss1/3/>; last accessed 1 May 2021.

Yau, Herman Lai-to. 'The Progression of Political Censorship: Hong Kong Cinema from Colonial Rule to Chinese-style Socialist Hegemony.' Hong Kong: Lingnan University Doctoral Thesis, 2015.

Yau, Ka-Fai. 'Looking Back at Ann Hui's Cinema of the Political', *Modern Chinese Literature and Culture* 18–19 (2006), 117–50.

Yau, Shuk-ting Kinnia. 'From *March of the Volunteers* to *Amazing Grace*: the Death of China's Main Melody Movie in the 21st Century', *Jump Cut: A Review of Contemporary Media* 59 (Fall 2019): <https://www.ejumpcut.org/currentissue/Kinnie YauMainMelody/index.html>; last accessed 1 May 2021.

Yeh, Emilie and Shi-yan Chao. 'Policy and Creative Strategies: Hong Kong CEPA Films in the China Market', *International Journal of Cultural Policy* 26:2 (2020), 184–201.

Yin Hong尹鴻and He Mei何美. 'Chinese Films after the Period of Co-production: The Historical Development of Mainland-HK Co-production in the Chinese Film Industry' (in Chinese) 〈走向後合拍時代的華語電影:中國內地與香港電影的合作/合拍歷程〉, *Communication and Society* 7 (January 2009): 31–60.

Yip, Man-Fung. *Martial Arts Cinema and Hong Kong Modernity: Aesthetics, Representation, Circulation*. Hong Kong: Hong Kong University Press, 2017.

Yu, Hongmei. 'Visual Spectacular, Revolutionary Epic, and Personal Voice: The Narration of History in Chinese Main Melody Films', *Modern Chinese Literature and Culture* 25:2 (Fall 2013), 168–218.

Yue, Audrey. *Ann Hui's Song of the Exile*. Hong Kong: Hong Kong University Press, 2010.

Yue, Audrey and Olivia Khoo (eds). *Sinophone Cinemas*. Basingstoke: Palgrave Macmillan, 2014.

Zhang, Rui. *The Cinema of Feng Xiaogang: Commercialization and Censorship in Chinese Cinema after 1980*. Hong Kong: Hong Kong University Press, 2008.

Zhang, Xudong. *Chinese Modernism in the Era of Reforms: Cultural Fever, Avant-garde Fiction*. Durham, NC and London: Duke University Press, 1997.

Zhang, Xudong (ed.). *Whither China?: Intellectual Politics in Contemporary China*. Durham, NC and London: Duke University Press, 2001.

Zhang, Xudong. *Postsocialism and Cultural Politics: China in the Last Decade of the Twentieth Century*. Durham, NC and London: Duke University Press, 2008.

Zhang Ying張瑩. *A Study of Main Melody Films since the New Period* (in Chinese)《新時期以來主旋律電影研究》. Shanghai: Sanlian, 2017.

Zhang, Yingjin. *Screening China: Critical Interventions, Cinematic Reconfigurations, and the Transnational Imaginary in Contemporary Chinese Cinema*. Ann Arbor: University of Michigan Press: 2002.

Zhang, Yingjin (ed.). *A Companion to Chinese Cinema*. Chichester: Wiley-Blackwell, 2012.

Zhongshu, Qian. 'On Happiness', trans. Zhu Liya, *Genre: Forms of Discourse and Culture* 43:3–4 (September 2010): 282.

Zhou, Xuelin. *Young Rebels in Contemporary Chinese Cinema*. Hong Kong: Hong Kong University Press, 2007.

Zhu, Ying. *Chinese Cinema during the Era of Reform: The Ingenuity of the System*. Westport, CT and London: Praegar, 2003.

Zhu, Ying and Stanley Rosen (eds). *Art, Politics, and Commerce in Chinese Cinema*. Hong Kong: Hong Kong University Press, 2010.

Žižek, Slavoj. *The Plague of Fantasies*. London and New York: Verso, 1997.

Filmography

1911 《辛亥革命》, Jackie Chan 成龍, 2011

1941 Hong Kong on Fire 《香港淪陷》, Man-Kei Chin 錢文錡, 1994

2046 《2046》, Kar-Wai Wong 王家衞, 2004

29+1 《29+1》, Kearen Pang 彭秀慧, 2017

77 Heartbreaks 《原諒他77次》, Herman Yau 邱禮濤, 2017

Ab-Normal Beauty 《死亡寫真》, Oxide Pang 彭順, 2004

Aces Go Places III 《最佳拍檔之女皇密令》, Tsui Hark 徐克, 1984

Aces Go Places IV 《最佳拍檔之千里救差婆》, Ringo Lam 林嶺東, 1986

Against All 《朋黨》, Andrew Lau 劉偉強, 1990

The Age of Miracles 《嫲嫲帆帆》, Peter Chan 陳可辛, 1996

Alan and Eric: Between Hello and Goodbye 《雙城故事》, Peter Chan 陳可辛, 1991

All About Women 《女人不壞》, Tsui Hark 徐克, 2008

All's Well, Ends Well Too 2010 《花田囍事2010》, Herman Yau 邱禮濤, 2010

All the Wrong Clues 《鬼馬智多星》, Tsui Hark 徐克, 1981

Always Be with You 《常在你左右》, Herman Yau 邱禮濤, 2017

American Dreams in China 《中國合夥人》, Peter Chan 陳可辛, 2013

Armageddon 《天地雄心》, Gordon Chan 陳嘉上, 1997

Armour of God 《龍兄虎弟》, Jackie Chan 成龍 and Eric Tsang 曾志偉, 1987

As Tears Go By 《旺角卡門》, Kar-Wai Wong 王家衞, 1988

As the Light Goes Out 《救火英雄》, Derek Kwok 郭子健, 2014

As Time Goes By 《去日苦多》, Ann Hui 許鞍華, 1997

Assembly 《集結號》, Feng Xiaogang 馮小剛, 2007

Azalea Mountain 《杜鵑山》, Xie Tieli 謝鐵驪, 1974

Baise Uprising 《百色起義》, Chen Jialin 陳家林, 1989

Bangkok Dangerous 《無聲殺手》, Danny Pang 彭發 and Oxide Pang 彭順, 1999

Battle of Triangle Hill 《上甘嶺》, Sha Meng 沙蒙 and Lin Shan 林杉, 1956

Beast Cops 《野獸刑警》, Gordon Chan 陳嘉上 and Dante Lam 林超賢, 1996

Beast Stalker 《証人》, Dante Lam 林超賢, 2008

A Beautiful Life 《不再讓你孤單》, Andrew Lau 劉偉強, 2011

Beginning of the Great Revival 《建黨偉業》, Han Sanping 韓三平 and Huang Jianxin 黃建新, 2011

Behind the Yellow Line 《緣分》, Taylor Wong 黃泰來, 1984

Best of the Best 《飛虎精英之人間有情》, Herman Yau 邱禮濤, 1992

Better Days 《少年的你》, Derek Tsang 曾國祥, 2019

A Better Tomorrow 《英雄本色》, John Woo 吳宇森, 1986

A Better Tomorrow II 《英雄本色II》, John Woo 吳宇森, 1987

The Birth of New China 《開國大典》, Li Qiankuan 李前寬 and Xiao Guiyun 蕭桂雲,1989

Black Mask 2: City of Masks 《黑俠II》, Tsui Hark 徐克, 2002

Black Sun: The Nanking Massacre 《黑太陽：南京大屠殺》, Tun-fei Mou 牟敦芾, 1995

The Blade 《刀》, Tsui Hark 徐克, 1995

Blood Brothers 《刺馬》, Cheh Chang 張徹, 1973

Boat People 《投奔怒海》, Ann Hui 許鞍華, 1983

Bodyguards and Assassins 《十月圍城》, Teddy Chan 陳德森, 2009

Born to be King 《勝者為王》, Andrew Lau 劉偉強, 2000

The Boxer from Shantung 《馬永貞》, Cheh Chang 張徹, 1972

The Bravest 《烈火英雄》), Tony Chan 陳國輝, 2019

The Bugle from Gutian 《古田軍號》, Chen Li 陳力, 2019

Bullet in the Head 《喋血街頭》, John Woo 吳宇森, 1990

The Bullet Vanishes 《消失的子彈》, Chi-leung Lo 羅志良, 2012

The Butterfly Murders 《蝶變》, Tsui Hark 徐克, 1979

Call of Heroes 《危城》, Benny Chan 陳木勝, 2016

Chairman Mao 1949 《決勝時刻》, Ning Haiqiang 寧海強 and Huang Jianxin 黃建新, 2019

The Captain 《中國機長》, Andrew Lau 劉偉強, 2019

Chasing the Dragon 《追龍》, Jing Wong 王晶 and Jason Kwan 關智耀, 2017

Chasing the Dragon II: Wild Wild Bunch 《追龍II：賊王》, Jason Kwan 關智耀 and Jing Wong 王晶, 2019

Chinese Doctors 《中國醫生》, Andrew Lau 劉偉強, 2021

A Chinese Ghost Story 《倩女幽魂》, Tony Ching 程小東, 1987

A Chinese Ghost Story II 《倩女幽魂II：人間道》, Tony Ching 程小東, 1990

A Chinese Ghost Story III 《倩女幽魂III：道道道》, Tony Ching 程小東, 1991

Chungking Express 《重慶森林》, Kar-wai Wong 王家衛, 1994

City Cop 2 《公僕II》, Herman Yau 邱禮濤, 1995

City on Fire 《龍虎風雲》, Ringo Lam 林嶺東, 1987

CJ 7 《長江7號》, Stephen Chow 周星馳, 2008

The Climbers 《攀登者》, Daniel Lee 李仁港, 2019

Cold War 《寒戰》, Longman Leung 梁樂民 and Sunny Luk 陸劍青, 2012

Cold War2 《寒戰II》, Longman Leung 梁樂民 and Sunny Luk 陸劍青, 2016

Come Drink with Me 《大醉俠》, King Hu 胡金銓, 1966

Comrades, Almost a Love Story 《甜蜜蜜》, Peter Chan 陳可辛, 1996

Confession of Pain 《傷城》, Alan Mak 麥兆輝 and Andrew Lau 劉偉強, 2006

Confucius 《孔子：決戰春秋》, Hu Mei 胡玫, 2010

Conspirators 《同謀》, Oxide Pang 彭順, 2013

Cops and Robbers 《點指兵兵》, Alex Cheung 章國明, 1979

Crazy Alien 《瘋狂的外星人》, Ning Hao 寧浩, 2019

The Creation of a World《開天闢地》, Li Xiepu 李歇浦, 1991

The Crossing《太平輪》, John Woo 吳宇森, 2014

The Crossing II《太平輪：驚濤摯愛》, John Woo 吳宇森, 2015

Crouching Tiger, Hidden Dragon《臥虎藏龍》, Ang Lee 李安, 2000

Curse of the Golden Flower《滿城盡帶黃金甲》, Zhang Yimou 張藝謀, 2006

Daisy《雛菊》, Andrew Lau 劉偉強, 2006

Dangerous Encounters of the First Kind《第一類型危險》, Tsui Hark 徐克, 1980

Days of Being Wild《阿飛正傳》, Kar-wai Wong 王家衛, 1990

Dealer Healer《毒誡》, Lawrence Lau 劉國昌, 2017

Dearest《親愛的》, Peter Chan 陳可辛, 2014

The Decisive Engagement: The Beiping Tianjin Campaign《大決戰三：平津戰役》, Li Jun 李俊 and Wei Lian 韋廉, 1992

The Decisive Engagement: The Liaoxi Shenyang Campaign《大決戰之遼沈戰役》, Li Jun 李俊, Yang Guangyuan 楊光遠, Wei Lian 韋廉, Jing Mukui 景慕逵 and Zhai Junjie 翟俊傑, 1991

The Decisive Engagement: Wei-hai Campaign《大決戰二：淮海戰役》, Li Jun 李俊 and Cai Jiwei 蔡繼渭, 1991

The Detective《C+偵探》, Oxide Pang 彭順, 2007

The Detective 2《B+偵探》, Oxide Pang 彭順, 2011

Detective Dee and the Mystery of the Phantom Flame《狄仁傑之通天帝國》, Tsui Hark 徐克, 2010

Detective Gui《宅女偵探桂香》, Oxide Pang 彭順, 2015

Don't Cry, Nanking《南京1937》, Wu Ziniu 吳子牛, 1995

Don't Fool Me!《中環英雄》, Herman Yau 邱禮濤, 1991

Dragon《武俠》, Peter Chan 陳可辛, 2011

Dragon Blade《天將雄師》, Daniel Lee 李仁港, 2015

Dragon Gate Inn《龍門客棧》, King Hu 胡金銓, 1967

The Drive to Win《沙鷗》, Zhang Nuanxin 張暖忻, 1981

Drug War《毒戰》, Johnnie To 杜琪峯, 2012

The Duel《決戰紫荊之巔》, Andrew Lau 劉偉強, 2000

Eat Drink Man Woman《飲食男女》, Ang Lee 李安, 1994

Ebola Syndrome《伊波拉病毒》, Herman Yau 邱禮濤, 1996

Eight Hundred Heroes《八百壯士》, Shan-Hsi Ting 丁善璽, 1975

Eighteen Springs《半生緣》, Ann Hui 許鞍華, 1997

Election《黑社會》, Johnnie To 杜琪峯, 2005

Emergency Landing《緊急迫降》, Zhang Jianya 張建亞, 1999

The Emperor and the Assassin《荊柯刺秦王》, Chen Kaige 陳凱歌, 1998

Eternal Wave《密戰》, Billy Chung 鍾少雄, 2017

The Eternal Wave《永不消逝的電波》, Wang Ping 王蘋, 1958

The Extra《茄喱啡》, Ho Yim 嚴浩, 1978

Extraordinary Mission《非凡任務》, Alan Mak 麥兆輝 and Anthony Pun 潘耀明, 2017

The Eye《見鬼》, Oxide Pang 彭順 and Danny Pang 彭發, 2002

Fall in Love Like a Star《怦然星動》, Tony Chan 陳國輝, 2015

Farewell My Concubine《霸王別姬》, Chen Kaige 陳凱歌, 1993

Fascination Amour《愛情夢幻號》, Herman Yau 邱禮濤, 1999

Fatal Decision《生死抉擇》), Yu Benzheng 于本正, 2000

Feel 100%《百分百感覺》, Ringo Ma 馬偉豪, 1996

The Fiery Years《火紅的年代》, Fu Chaowu 傅超武, Sun Yongping 孫永平 and Yu Zhongying 俞仲英, 1974

Fight Back to School《逃學威龍》, Gordon Chan 陳嘉上, 1991

Fight Back to School II《逃學威龍2》, Gordon Chan 陳嘉上, 1992

Fight Hard: The Champion's Story of Chinese Women's Volleyball Team《拼搏：中國女排奪魁記》, Zhang Yitong 張貽彤, Shen Jie 沈傑 and Li Hanjun 李漢軍, 1982

The Final Option《飛虎雄心》, Gordon Chan 陳嘉上, 1994

Fire of Conscience《火龍》, Dante Lam 林超賢, 2010

Firestorm《風暴》, Alan Yuen 袁錦麟, 2013

The First Incense Burner《第一爐香》, Ann Hui 許鞍華, 2021

First Option《飛虎》, Gordon Chan 陳嘉上, 1996

First Shot《廉政第一擊》, David Lam 林德祿, 1993

Flag of the Republic《共和國之旗》, Wang Jixing 王冀邢 and Lei Xianhe 雷獻禾, 1999

Flirting Scholar《唐伯虎點秋香》, Lik-Chi Lee 李力持, 1993

The Flowers of War《金陵十三釵》, Zhang Yimou 張藝謀, 2011

The Flying Guillotine《血滴子》, Meng-hwa Ho 何夢華, 1975

Flying Swords of Dragon Gate《龍門飛甲》, Tsui Hark 徐克, 2011

The Founding of a Republic《建國大業》, Han Sanping 韓三平 and Huang Jianxin 黃建新, 2009

The Founding of an Army《建軍大業》, Andrew Lau 劉偉強, 2017

The Four《四大名捕》, Gordon Chan 陳嘉上 and Janet Chun 秦小珍, 2012

The Four 2《四大名捕II》, Gordon Chan 陳嘉上 and Janet Chun 秦小珍, 2013

The Four 3《四大名捕大結局》, Gordon Chan 陳嘉上, 2014

From the Queen to the Chief Executive《等候董建華發落》, Herman Yau 邱禮濤, 2001

From Riches to Rags《錢作怪》, John Woo 吳宇森, 1980

From Vegas to Macau《賭城風雲》, Jing Wong 王晶 and Billy Chung 鍾少雄, 2014

From Vegas to Macau II《賭城風雲II》, Jing Wong 王晶 and Aman Chang 張敏, 2015

From Vegas to Macau III《賭城風雲III》, Jing Wong 王晶 and Andrew Lau 劉偉強, 2016

From Where We've Fallen《何日君再來》, Wang Feifei 王飛飛, 2017

Full Alert《高度戒備》, Ringo Lam 林嶺東, 1997

The Fury of King Boxer《驚天動地》, Shan-Hsi Ting 丁善璽, 1972

G Affairs《G殺》, Cheuk-Pan Lee 李卓斌, 2018

Gallants《打擂台》, Derek Kwok 郭子健 and Clement Cheng 鄭思傑, 2010

Ghost Lantern《人皮燈籠》, Andrew Lau 劉偉強, 1993

Give Me One Day《給我一天》, Erica Lee 李敏, 2021

Give Them a Chance《給他們一個機會》, Herman Yau 邱禮濤, 2003

God of Gamblers《賭神》, Jing Wong 王晶, 1989

God of Gamblers II: Back to Shanghai《賭俠2之上海灘賭聖》, Jing Wong 王晶, 1991

God of War《蕩寇風雲》, Gordon Chan 陳嘉上, 2017

Golden Chicken《金雞》, Samson Chiu 趙良駿, 2002

The Golden Era《黃金時代》, Ann Hui 許鞍華, 2014

The Grandmaster《一代宗師》, Kar-wai Wong 王家衛, 2013

Guerrillas on the Plain《平原游擊隊》, Su Li 蘇里 and Wu Zhaodi 武兆堤, 1955

The Guillotines《血滴子》, Andrew Lau 劉偉強, 2012

Hard Boiled《辣手神探》, John Woo 吳宇森, 1992

He Ain't Heavy, He's My Father《新難兄難弟》, Peter Chan 陳可辛, 1993

He's a Woman, She's a Man《金枝玉葉》, Peter Chan陳可辛, 1994

Hearts to Hearts《三人世界》, Stephen Shin 冼杞然, 1988

Heat Team《重案驏孖 Gun》, Dante Lam 林超賢, 2004

Heaven Can Help《上天救命》, David Chiang 姜大衛, 1984

Helios《赤道》, Sunny Luk 陸劍青 and Longman Leung 梁樂民, 2015

Hello Late Homecomers《Hello! 夜歸人》, John Woo 吳宇森, 1978

Hero《英雄》, Zhang Yimou 張藝謀, 2002

Heroes Shed No Tears《英雄無淚》, John Woo吳宇森, 1986

Heroic Sons and Daughters《英雄兒女》, Wu Zhaodi 武兆堤, 1964

Hit Team《重裝警察》, Dante Lam 林超賢, 2001

Home with a View《家和萬事驚》, Herman Yau邱禮濤, 2019

I Corrupt All Cops《金錢帝國2：四大探長》, Jing Wong 王晶, 2009

In the Mood for Love《花樣年華》, Kar-Wai Wong 王家衛, 2000

Infernal Affairs《無間道》, Andrew Lau 劉偉強 and Alan Mak 麥兆輝, 2002

Infernal Affairs II《無間道II》, Andrew Lau 劉偉強 and Alan Mak 麥兆輝, 2003

Infernal Affairs III《無間道III：終極無間》, Andrew Lau劉偉強and Alan Mak 麥兆輝, 2003

Initial D《頭文字D》, Andrew Lau 劉偉強 and Alan Mak 麥兆輝, 2005

An Inspector Calls《浮華宴》, Herman Yau 邱禮濤 and Raymond Wong 黃百鳴, 2015

Integrity《廉政風雲：煙幕》, Alan Mak 麥兆輝, 2019

Ip Man《葉問》, Wilson Yip 葉偉信, 2008

Ip Man 2《葉問2:宗師傳奇》, Wilson Yip 葉偉信, 2010

Ip Man 3《葉問3》, Wilson Yip 葉偉信, 2015

Ip Man 4: The Finale《葉問4：完結篇》, Wilson Yip 葉偉信, 2019

Ip Man: The Final Fight《葉問：終極一戰》, Herman Yau 邱禮濤, 2013

Jade Goddess of Mercy《玉觀音》, Ann Hui許鞍華, 2003

Jiang hu: The Triad Zone《江湖告急》, Dante Lam 林超賢, 2000

Jiang Ziya《姜子牙》, Li Wei 李煒 and Cheng Teng 程騰, 2020

Ju Dou《菊豆》, Zhang Yimou 張藝謀, 1990

The July Seventh Incident《七七事變》, Li Qiankuan李前寬and Xiao Guiyun 蕭桂雲, 1995

Keep Rolling《好好拍電影》, Lim-Chung Man文念中, 2021

The Killer《喋血雙雄》, John Woo 吳宇森, 1989

King of Comedy《喜劇之王》, Stephen Chow 周星馳, 1999

Kung Fu Monster《武林怪獸》, Andrew Lau 劉偉強, 2018

The Kunlun Column《巍巍昆侖》, Hao Guang 郝光 and Jing Mukui 景慕逵, 1988

L Storm 《L風暴》, David Lam 林德祿, 2018

Last Flight 《絕命航班》, Vincent Zhou 周文武貝, 2014

Laughing Time 《滑稽時代》, John Woo 吳宇森, 1980

The Leakers 《洩密者們》, Herman Yau 邱禮濤, 2018

Leap 《奪冠》, Peter Chan陳可辛, 2020

Lee Rock 《五億探長雷洛傳：雷老虎》, Lawrence Lau 劉國昌, 1991

Lee Rock II 《五億探長雷洛傳II之父子情仇》, Lawrence Lau 劉國昌, 1991

The Legend Is Born: Ip Man 《葉問前傳》, Herman Yau 邱禮濤, 2010

Legend of the Fist: The Return of Chen Zhen 《陳真：精武風雲》, Andrew Lau 劉偉強, 2010

The Legend of Zu 《蜀山傳》, Tsui Hark徐克, 2001

Legendary Weapons of China 《十八般武藝》, Kar-Leung Lau 劉家良, 1982

Li Na 《獨自·上場》, Peter Chan 陳可辛, 2021

Line Walker 《使徒行者》, Wai-Hung Man 文偉鴻, 2016

Line Walker 2 《使徒行者2：諜影行動》, Wai-Hung Man 文偉鴻, 2019

A Little Red Flower 《送你一朵小紅花》, Han Yan 韓延, 2020

Liu Hulan 《劉胡蘭》, Feng Bailu 馮白魯, 1950

Long Live Youth 《青春萬歲》, Xu Xiaobing 徐肖冰 and Lei Zhenlin 雷震霖, 1959

Look for a Star 《游龍戲鳳》, Andrew Lau 劉偉強, 2009

The Lost Bladesman 《關雲長》, Felix Chong 莊文強 and Alan Mak 麥兆輝, 2011

Love in a Fallen City 《傾城之戀》, Ann Hui許鞍華, 1984

Love in the Rocks 《戀情告急》, Dante Lam 林超賢, 2004

Love Lifting 《高舉·愛》, Herman Yau 邱禮濤, 2012

Lover of the Last Empress 《慈禧秘密生活》, Andrew Lau 劉偉強, 1995

Lover's Grief over the Yellow River 《黃河絕戀》, Feng Xiaoning 馮小寧, 1999

Lust, Caution 《色，戒》, Ang Lee 李安, 2007

Mad World 《一念無明》, Chun Wong 黃進, 2017

Man on the Brink 《邊緣人》, Alex Cheung 章國明, 1981

Mao Zedong and His Son 《毛澤東和他的兒子》, Zhang Jinbiao 張今標, 1991

Master of the Flying Guillotine 《獨臂拳王大破血滴子》, Jimmy Wang 王羽, 1976

Master Q 2001 《老夫子2001》, Tsui Hark 徐克, 2001

Mean Street Story 《廟街故事》, Andrew Lau 劉偉強, 1995

The Mermaid 《美人魚》, Stephen Chow 周星馳, 2016

The Message 《風聲》, Chen Guofu 陳國富 and Gao Qunshu 高群書, 2009

The Midnight After 《那夜凌晨，我坐上了旺角開往大埔的紅 VAN》, Fruit Chan 陳果, 2014

The Millionaires' Express 《富貴列車》, Sammo Hung 洪金寶, 1986

Missing 《深海尋人》, Tsui Hark 徐克, 2008

The Mobfathers (《選老頂》), Herman Yau 邱禮濤, 2016

Money Crazy 《發錢寒》, John Woo 吳宇森, 1977

The Monkey King 《西遊記之大鬧天宮》, Pou-Soi Cheang 鄭保瑞, 2014

Motorway 《車手》, Pou-Soi Cheang 鄭保瑞, 2012

Mr. Vampire 《殭屍先生》, Ricky Lau 劉觀偉, 1985

Mural《畫壁》, Gordon Chan 陳嘉上, 2011

My American Grandson《上海假期》, Ann Hui 許鞍華, 1991

My Intimate Partners《難兄難弟》, Kim Chun 秦劍, 1960

My People, My Country《我和我的祖國》, Ning Hao 寧浩, Chen Kaige 陳凱歌, Guan Hu 管虎, Xu Zheng 徐崢, Zhang Yibai 張一白, Wen Muye 文牧野 and Xue Xiaolu 薛曉璐, 2019

My People, My Homeland《我和我的家鄉》, Deng Chao 鄧超, Xu Zheng 徐崢, Ning Hao 寧浩, Yan Fei 閆非, Peng Damo 彭大魔, Yu Baimei 俞白眉 and Chen Sicheng 陳思誠, 2020

My War《我的戰爭》, Oxide Pang 彭順, 2016

Mysterious Buddha《神秘的大佛》, Zhang Huaxun 張華勳, 1981

Naked Ambition《豪情》, Dante Lam 林超賢 and Hing-kar Chan 陳慶嘉, 2003

The Naval Battle of 1894《甲午風雲》, Lin Nong 林農, 1962

Ne Zha《哪吒之魔童降世》, Jiaozi 餃子, 2020

Nessun Dorma《兇手還未睡》, Herman Yau 邱禮濤, 2016

New King of Comedy《新喜劇之王》, Stephen Chow 周星馳 and Herman Yau 邱禮濤, 2019

News Attack《神行太保》, Samson Chiu 趙良駿, 1989

Night and Fog《天水圍的夜與霧》, Ann Hui 許鞍華, 2009

No Regret《靚妹正傳》, Herman Yau 邱禮濤, 1987

On the Edge《黑白道》, Herman Yau 邱禮濤, 2006

Once Upon a Time in China《黃飛鴻》, Tsui Hark 徐克, 1991

Once Upon a Time in China II《黃飛鴻之二：男兒當自強》, Tsui Hark 徐克, 1992

Once Upon a Time in China III《黃飛鴻之三：獅王爭霸》, Tsui Hark 徐克, 1993

Once Upon a Time in China IV《黃飛鴻之四：王者之風》, Tsui Hark 徐克, 1993

Once Upon a Time in China V《黃飛鴻之五：龍城殲霸》, Tsui Hark 徐克, 1994

Once Upon a Time in China and America《黃飛鴻之西域雄獅》, Sammo Hung 洪金寶, 1997

The One-Armed Swordman《獨臂刀》, Cheh Chang 張徹, 1967

The One Man Olympics《一個人的奧林匹克》, Hou Yong 侯詠, 2008

Operation Mekong《湄公河行動》, Dante Lam 林超賢, 2016

Operation Red Sea《紅海行動》, Dante Lam 林超賢, 2018

The Opium War《鴉片戰爭》, Xie Jin 謝晉, 1997

Option Zero《G4特工》, Dante Lam 林超賢, 1997

Ordinary Heroes《千言萬語》, Ann Hui 許鞍華, 1999

Our Time Will Come《明月幾時有》, Ann Hui 許鞍華, 2017

Out of Inferno《逃出生天》, Oxide Pang 彭順 and Danny Pang 彭發, 2013

Overheard《竊聽風雲》, Felix Chong 莊文強 and Alan Mak 麥兆輝, 2009

Overheard 2《竊聽風雲2》, Felix Chong 莊文強 and Alan Mak 麥兆輝, 2011

Overheard 3《竊聽風雲3》, Felix Chong 莊文強and Alan Mak 麥兆輝, 2014

P Storm《P風暴》, David Lam 林德祿, 2019

Painted Skin《畫皮》, Gordon Chan 陳嘉上, 2008

Peace Hotel《和平飯店》, Ka-fai Wai 韋家輝, 1995

Pegasus 《飛馳人生》, Han Han 韓寒, 2019

Peking Opera Blues 《刀馬旦》, Tsui Hark 徐克, 1986

Perhaps Love 《如果·愛》, Peter Chan 陳可辛, 2005

Port of Call 《踏血尋梅》, Philip Yung 翁子光, 2015

The Postmodern Life of My Aunt 《姨媽的後現代生活》, Ann Hui 許鞍華, 2006

Powerful Four 《四大探長》, David Lam 林德祿, 1992

Princess Chang Ping 《帝女花》, John Woo 吳宇森, 1976

Prison on Fire 《監獄風雲》, Ringo Lam 林嶺東, 1987

Project A 《A計劃》, Jackie Chan 成龍, 1983

Project Gutenberg 《無雙》, Felix Chong 莊文強, 2018

The Protector 《威龍猛探》, James Glickenhaus, 1985

Qiu Jin and Xu Xilin 《碧血千秋》, Mei Qian 梅阡, 1948

Qiu Jin: A Revolutionary 《秋瑾》, Xie Jin 謝晉, 1983

Queen of Sports 《體育皇后》, Sun Yu 孫瑜, 1934

The Raid 《財叔之橫掃千軍》, Tsui Hark 徐克, 1991

Raise the Red Lantern 《大紅燈籠高高掛》, Zhang Yimou 張藝謀, 1991

Raped by an Angel 《香港奇案之強姦》, Andrew Lau 劉偉強, 1993

Red Cliff 《赤壁》, John Woo 吳宇森, 2008

Red Cliff II 《赤壁: 決戰天下》, John Woo 吳宇森, 2009

The Red Detachment of Women 《紅色娘子軍》, Xie Jin 謝晉, 1961

The Red Detachment of Women 《紅色娘子軍》, Pan Wenzhan 潘文展 and Fu Jie 傅杰, 1971

Reign of Assassins 《劍雨》, John Woo 吳宇森 and Chao-pin Su 蘇照彬, 2010

The Rescue 《緊急救援》, Dante Lam 林超賢, 2020

Roaring Across the Horizon 《橫空出世》, Chen Guoxing 陳國星, 1999

The Romance of Book and Sword 《書劍恩仇錄》, Ann Hui 許鞍華, 1986

Runaway 《走投有路》, Dante Lam 林超賢, 2001

S Storm 《S風暴》, David Lam 林德祿, 2016

Sara 《雛妓》, Herman Yau 邱禮濤, 2014

School on Fire 《學校風雲》, Ringo Lam 林嶺東, 1988

The Secret 《瘋劫》, Ann Hui 許鞍華, 1979

The Secret of China 《紅星照耀中國》, Wang Jixing 王冀邢, 2019

Seven Swords 《七劍》, Tsui Hark 徐克, 2005

Shanghai Blues 《上海之夜》, Tsui Hark 徐克, 1984

Shanghai Triad 《搖啊搖，搖到外婆橋》, Zhang Yimou 張藝謀, 1995

The Shaolin Temple 《少林寺》, Zhang Xinyan 張鑫炎, 1982

Shark Busters 《反收數特遣隊》, Herman Yau 邱禮濤, 2002

Shock Wave 《拆彈專家》, Herman Yau 邱禮濤, 2017

Shock Wave 2 《拆彈專家2》, Herman Yau 邱禮濤, 2020

The Silent War 《聽風者》, Felix Chong 莊文強 and Alan Mak 麥兆輝, 2012

A Simple Life 《桃姐》, Ann Hui 許鞍華, 2011

The Sleep Curse 《失眠》, Herman Yau 邱禮濤, 2017

The Sniper 《神槍手》, Dante Lam 林超賢, 2009

Song of the Exile《客途秋恨》, Ann Hui 許鞍華, 1990

The Soong Sisters《宋家皇朝》, Mabel Cheung 張婉婷, 1997

Sparkling Red Star《閃閃的紅星之孩子的天空》, Dante Lam 林超賢, 2007

The Spooky Bunch《撞到正》, Ann Hui 許鞍華, 1980

Starry Is the Night《今夜星光燦爛》, Ann Hui 許鞍華, 1988

Still Human《淪落人》, Oliver Siu-Kuen Chan 陳小娟, 2018

The Stool Pigeon《線人》, Dante Lam 林超賢, 2010

The Storm Riders《風雲：雄霸天下》, Andrew Lau 劉偉強, 1998

Storm Rider: Clash of the Evils《風雲決》, Dante Lam 林超賢, 2008

The Story of Qiu Ju《秋菊打官司》, Zhang Yimou 張藝謀, 1992

The Story of Woo Viet《胡越的故事》, Ann Hui 許鞍華, 1981

Summer Snow《女人四十》, Ann Hui 許鞍華, 1996

Swordsman《笑傲江湖》, King Hu 胡金銓, Tony Ching 程小東, Tsui Hark 徐克, Ann Hui 許鞍華, Andrew Kam 金揚樺 and Raymond Lee 李惠民, 1990

Swordsman 2《笑傲江湖II東方不敗》, Tony Ching 程小東, 1992

Swordsman 3: The East Is Red《東方不敗：風雲再起》, Tony Ching 程小東 and Raymond Lee 李惠民, 1993

The Taking of Tiger Mountain 3D《智取威虎山》, Tsui Hark 徐克, 2014

Taxi Driver《的士判官》, Herman Yau 邱禮濤, 1993

Temptress Moon《風月》, Chen Kaige 陳凱歌, 1996

Ten Years《十年》, Zune Kwok 郭臻, Fei-pang Wong 黃飛鵬, Jevons Au 歐文傑, Kwun-wai Chow 周冠威 and Ka-leung Ng 伍嘉良, 2015

A Terra-Cotta Warrior《秦俑》, Tony Ching 程小東, 1990

That Demon Within (《魔警》, Dante Lam 林超賢, 2014

Theory of Ambitions《風再起時》, Philip Yung 翁子光, 2021

Those Were the Days . . .《慈雲山十三太保》, Billy Tang 鄧衍成, 1995

Three《三更》, Jee-woon Kim 金知雲, Nonzee Nimibutr and Peter Chan 陳可辛, 2002

Three《三人行》, Johnnie To 杜琪峯, 2016

Thunderbolt《霹靂火》, Gordon Chan 陳嘉上, 1995

Tie Ren《鐵人》, Yin Li 尹力, 2009

Time Raiders《盜墓筆記》, Daniel Lee 李仁港, 2016

A Time to Remember《紅色戀人》, Ye Daying 葉大鷹, 1998

Tiramisu《戀愛行星》, Dante Lam 林超賢, 2002

To Be Number One《跛豪》, Man-Kit Poon 潘文傑, 1991

To Live《活着》, Zhang Yimou 張藝謀, 1994

To Live and Die in Tsimshatsui《新邊緣人》, Andrew Lau 劉偉強, 1994

To the Fore《破風》, Dante Lam 林超賢, 2015

Tom, Dick and Hairy《風塵三俠》, Chi-ngai Lee 李志毅 and Peter Chan 陳可辛, 1993

Tomorrow Is Another Day《黃金花》, Tai-Lee Chan 陳大利, 2017

Towards the River Glorious《打過長江去》, Oxide Pang 彭順, 2019

Tracey《翠詩》, Jun Lee 李駿碩, 2018

Triangle《鐵三角》, Johnnie To 杜琪峯, Ringo Lam 林嶺東 and Tsui Hark 徐克, 2007

Trivisa《樹大招風》, Frank Hui 許學文, Jevons Au 歐文傑 and Vicky Wong 黃偉傑, 2016

Troublesome Night 3《陰陽路之升棺發財》, Herman Yau 邱禮濤, 1998

True Women for Sale《性工作者2：我不賣身．我賣子宮》, Herman Yau 邱禮濤, 2008

Turning Point《Laughing Gor 之變節》, Herman Yau 邱禮濤, 2009

Turning Point 2《Laughing Gor 之潛罪犯》, Herman Yau 邱禮濤, 2011

The Twins Effect《千機變》, Dante Lam 林超賢, 2003

Unbeatable《激戰》, Dante Lam 林超賢, 2013

Undercover Hidden Dragon《至尊無賴》, Gordon Chan 陳嘉上 and Dante Lam 林超賢, 2006

The Untold Story《八仙飯店之人肉叉燒飽》, Herman Yau 邱禮濤, 1993

The Vanished Murderer《消失的兇手》, Chi-leung Lo 羅志良, 2015

Victim《目露凶光》, Ringo Lam 林嶺東, 1999

Victory《梅花》, Chia-chang Liu 劉家昌, 1976

The Viral Factor《逆戰》, Dante Lam 林超賢, 2012

The Volleyball Flower《排球之花》, Lu Jianhua 陸建華, 1980

Vulgaria《低俗喜劇》, Edmond Pang 彭浩翔, 2012

Walk In《奪舍》, Herman Yau 邱禮濤, 1997

The Wandering Earth《流浪地球》, Frant Gwo 郭帆, 2019

The War of Loong《龍之戰》, Gao Feng 高峰, 2017

The Warlords《投名狀》, Peter Chan 陳可辛 and Raymond Yip 葉偉民, 2007

The Way We Are《天水圍的日與夜》, Ann Hui 許鞍華, 2008

The Way We Dance《狂舞派》, Adam Wong 黃修平, 2013

We're Going to Eat You《地獄無門》, Tsui Hark 徐克, 1980

Weeds on Fire《點五步》, Steve Chi-fat Chan 陳志發, 2016

Wheels On Meals《快餐車》, Sammo Hung 洪金寶, 1984

When I Look Upon the Stars《天旋地戀》, Dante Lam 林超賢, 1999

Whispers and Moans《性工作者十日談》, Herman Yau 邱禮濤, 2007

The White-Haired Girl《白毛女》, Shui Hua 水華 and Wang Bin 王濱, 1950

The White Storm《掃毒》, Benny Chan 陳木勝, 2013

The White Storm 2: Drug Lords《掃毒2天地對決》, Herman Yau 邱禮濤, 2019

Who's the Woman, Who's the Man《金枝玉葉2》, Peter Chan 陳可辛, 1996

The Wicked City《妖獸都市》, Peter Mak 麥大傑, 1992

Wolf Warrior 2《戰狼2》, Wu Jing 吳京, 2017

Woman Basketball Player No. 5《女籃5號》, Xie Jin 謝晉, 1957

The Woman Knight of Mirror Lake《競雄女俠：秋瑾》, Herman Yau 邱禮濤, 2011

Yellow Earth《黃土地》, Chen Kaige 陳凱歌, 1984

Young and Dangerous《古惑仔之人在江湖》, Andrew Lau 劉偉強, 1996

Young and Dangerous 2《古惑仔2之猛龍過江》, Andrew Lau 劉偉強, 1996

Young and Dangerous 3《古惑仔3之隻手遮天》, Andrew Lau 劉偉強, 1996

Young and Dangerous 4《97古惑仔：戰無不勝》, Andrew Lau 劉偉強, 1997

Young and Dangerous V《98古惑仔：龍爭虎鬥》, Andrew Lau 劉偉強, 1998

Young and Dangerous: The Prequel《新古惑仔之少年激鬥篇》, Andrew Lau 劉偉強, 1998

Young Detective Dee: Rise of the Sea Dragon《狄仁傑之神都龍王》, Tsui Hark 徐克, 2013

The Young Dragons《鐵漢柔情》, John Woo 吳宇森, 1975

Yuppie Fantasia 《小男人周記》, Gordon Chan 陳嘉上, 1989

Z Storm 《Z風暴》, David Lam 林德祿, 2014

Zhou Enlai 《周恩來》, Ding Yinnan 丁蔭楠, 1992

Zodiac Killers 《極道追蹤》, Ann Hui 許鞍華, 1991

Zu: Warriors from the Magic Mountain 《蜀山》, Tsui Hark 徐克, 1983

Selected Hong Kong Directors' Main Melody Films in Mainland China (box-office return in RMB; available at <piaofang.maoyan.com>)

1911 《辛亥革命》 2011 Jackie Chan成龍40.67M

Bodyguards and Assassins 《十月圍城》 2009 Teddy Chan陳德森 213M

The Bravest 《烈火英雄》 2019 Tony Chan陳國輝1,706M

The Captain 《中國機長》 2019 Andrew Lau 劉偉強2,912M

Chasing the Dragon 《追龍》 2017 Jing Wong 王晶 and Jason Kwan 關智耀 577M

Chasing the Dragon II: Wild Wild Bunch 《追龍II：賊王》 2019 Jing Wong 王晶 and Jason Kwan 關智耀 309M

The Climbers 《攀登者》 2019 Daniel Lee 李仁港1,102M

The Crossings 《太平輪》 2014 John Woo 吳宇森195M (part 1) + 50.95M (part2)

Drug War 《毒戰》 2012 Johnnie To 杜琪峯146M

Extraordinary Mission 《非凡任務》 2017 Alan Mak 麥兆輝 and Anthony Pun 潘耀明 156M

The Founding of an Army 《建軍大業》 2017 Andrew Lau 劉偉強407M

God of War 《蕩寇風雲》 2017 Gordon Chan 陳嘉上65.13M

Healer Dealer 《毒誡》 2017 Lawrence Lau 劉國昌40.27M

Integrity 《廉政風雲：煙幕》 2019 Alan Mak 麥兆輝124M

L Storm 《L風暴》/《反貪風暴3》 2018 David Lam 林德祿442M

Leap 《奪冠》 2020 Peter Chan陳可辛836M

My War 《我的戰爭》 2016 Oxide Pang 彭順36.45M

Operation Mekong 《湄公河行動》 2016 Dante Lam 林超賢1,186M

Operation Red Sea 《紅海行動》 2018 Dante Lam 林超賢 3,650M

Our Time Will Come 《明月幾時有》 2018 Ann Hui 許鞍華63.49M

P Storm 《P風暴》/《反貪風暴4》 2019 David Lam 林德祿 799M

The Rescue 《緊急救援》 2020 Dante Lam 林超賢 485M

S Storm 《S風暴》/《反貪風暴2》 2016 David Lam 林德祿 208M

Shock Wave 《拆彈專家》 2017 Herman Yau 邱禮濤400M

Shock Wave 2 《拆彈專家2》 2020 Herman Yau 邱禮濤1,312M

The Taking of Tiger Mountain 3D 《智取威虎山》 2014 Tsui Hark 徐克883M

Towards the River Glorious 《打過長江去》 2019 Oxide Pang 彭順22.24M

The White Storm 2: Drug Lords 《掃毒2天地對決》 2019 Herman Yau 邱禮濤1,312M

The Woman Knight of Mirror Lake 《競雄女俠：秋瑾》 2011 Herman Yau 邱禮濤0.54M

Z Storm 《Z風暴》/《反貪風暴》 2014 David Lam 林德祿95.17M

Glossary

430 Space Shuttle 《430穿梭機》
Ah Sze 《阿詩》
Amazing China 《厲害了，我的國》
Anti-Corruption Pioneers 《廉政先鋒》
Ba, Jin 巴金
Bai, Liusu 白流蘇
Bai, Lydia 白浪
Bai, Michelle 白冰
Balguy Yuanye 鮑爾吉·原野
Below the Lion Rock 《獅子山下》
Bo Le 伯樂 ('person who is able to discover talents and understand their worth')
Boy 《少年》
Boy from Vietnam 《來客》
Chan, Benny 陳木勝
Chan, Chi-tak 陳智德
Chan, Danny 陳百強
Chan, Eason 陳奕迅
Chan, Gordon 陳嘉上
Chan, Hing-kar 陳慶嘉
Chan, Jackie 成龍
Chan, Jordan 陳小春
Chan, Joyce 陳韻文
Chan, Peter 陳可辛
Chan, Stephen Ching-kiu 陳清僑
Chan, Susan 陳淑賢
Chan, Teddy 陳德森
Chan, Tung-Man 陳銅民
Chan, William 陳偉霆
Chang, Eileen 張愛玲
Chang, Sylvia 張艾嘉
Chang, William 張叔平
Cheang, Pou-Soi 鄭保瑞

Chen, Edison 陳冠希
Chen, Kaige 陳凱歌
Chen, Zhaoti 陳招娣
Chen, Zhonghe 陳忠和
Cheng, Ekin 鄭伊健
Cheng, Matthew 鄭政恆
Cheung, Cecilia 張柏芝
Cheung, Jacky 張學友
Cheung, Kwok-Keung 張國強
Cheung, Leslie 張國榮
Cheung, Maggie 張曼玉
Cheung, Nick 張家輝
Chiang, David 姜大衛
Chin, Han 秦漢
China Film News 《中國電影報》
China Women's News 《中國女報》
Ching, Tony 程小東
Choi, Charlene 蔡卓妍
Choi, Si-won 崔始源
Chong, Felix 莊文強
Chong, John 莊澄
Chou, Jay 周杰倫
Chow, Stephen 周星馳
Chow, Yun-Fat 周潤發
CID: Murder 《CID：殺女案》
Cinema City 新藝城
'Creating Fate' 〈創造命運〉
dapian 大片 ('big-budget films')
'Dearest Love in My Life' 〈一生中最愛〉
Decision 《抉擇》
'Dedication movies' 獻禮片
Deng, Chao 鄧超
Deng, Xiaoping 鄧小平
Ding, Qiao 丁嶠
Dou, Shawn 竇驍
Dragon, Tiger, Panther 《龍虎豹》
Dung, Kai-Cheung 董啟章
'Dusk' 〈黃昏〉
'Emulate the Women Volleyball Team, Revitalize the Chinese Civilization: China Won'
    《學習女排，振興中華─中國贏了》
The Eternal Wave 《永不消逝的電波》
Fama 農夫
Fan, Liuyuan 范柳原

Fan, Mavis 范曉萱
Fang, Lan 方蘭
Feng, Xiaogang 馮小剛
'Fighting to Win' 〈愛拼才會贏〉
Film Unlimited Production 無限映畫
Flurry Girls 疾風少女
'Flurry Wind' (or 'Gusty Wind') 〈疾風〉
Fong, Alex 方力申
Fong, Henry 方平
Fong, Mona 方逸華
'Foreground main melody while encouraging diversity' 突出主旋律、堅持多樣化
Fung, Edmond 馮遠文
Fung, Stephen 馮德倫
Golden Dagger Romance 《金刀情俠》
Golden Harvest 嘉禾
Gong, Li 鞏俐
Gong, Xue 龔雪
Got, Eric 葛民輝
Guan, Hu 管虎
Guan, Yu 關羽
Gwo, Frant 郭帆
Hai, Yan 海岩
Han, Geng 韓庚
Ho, Kei-Ping 何冀平
'How Can I Let You Go?' 〈怎麼捨得你〉
Hu, King 胡金銓
Hu, Terry 胡茵夢
Huang, Bo 黃渤
Huang, Jianxin 黃建新
Huang, Lu 黃璐
Huang, Qunfei 黃群飛
Huang, Xiaoming 黃曉明
Huang, Xuan 黃軒
Huanzhu Louzhu 還珠樓主
Huaxia Film Company 華夏電影公司
Hui, Ann 許鞍華
Hui, Raman 許誠毅
Hui, Ruoqi 惠若琪
Hung, Samo 洪金寶
In the Dark 《暗算》
In the Name of the People 《人民的名義》
Ip, Deanie 葉德嫻
Ji, Mingkui 紀明貴

Ji, Yun 紀昀
jiang hu 江湖 ('river and lake')
Jiang, Ping 江平
Jiaozi 餃子
Jin, Yong 金庸
Jing, Boran 井柏然
jingju 京劇 ('Peking opera')
Juan, Ethan 阮經天
Kam, Ping-Hing 金炳興
Kaneshiro, Takeshi 金城武
Ko, Chun-Hsiung 柯俊雄
Koo, Louis 古天樂
Ku, Ming-Lun 谷名倫
Kwok, Aaron 郭富城
Kwok, Derek 郭子健
Lai, Gigi 黎姿
Lai, Leon 黎明
Lai, Yiu-Fai 黎耀輝
Lam, Dante 林超賢
Lam, George 林子祥
Lam, Gordon 林家棟
Lam, Jason 林紀陶
Lam, Ming-Kit 林明傑
Lam, Ringo 林嶺東
Lang, Ping 郎平
Lau, Andrew 劉偉強
Lau, Andy 劉德華
Lau, Jeffrey 劉鎮偉
Lau, Sean 劉青雲
Law, Kar 羅卡
'The Leading Group on Major Revolutionary and Historical Themes of Film and Television
    Creation' 重大革命歷史題材影視創作領導小組
Lee, Daniel 李仁港
Lee, Danny 李修賢
Lee, Rachel 李麗珍
Lee, Raymond 李惠民
Leung, Candy 梁鳳英
Leung, Elliot 梁皓一
Leung, Longman 梁樂民
Leung, Tony Chiu-wai 梁朝偉
Leung, Tony Ka-fai 梁家輝
Li, Jet 李連杰
Li, Kang-sheng 李康生

Li, Mei-ting 李薇婷
Li, Xuejian 李雪健
Liang Yusheng 梁羽生
Liew, Prudence 劉美君
Lin, Brigitte 林青霞
Lin, Gengxin 林更新
Lin, Xi 林夕
Liu, Changchun 劉長春
Liu, Heng 劉恆
Liu, Peiran 劉沛然
Liu, Ye 劉燁
Loo, Andrew 盧宏軒
Lord Hawk 座山雕
Lu, Han 鹿晗
luan si 亂世 ('turbulent time')
Lui, Tai-lok 呂大樂
Luk, Sunny 陸劍青
Luo, Dayou 羅大佑
Ma, Lunpeng 馬綸鵬
Ma, Wing-Shing 馬榮成
Mai, Jia 麥家
main melody 主旋律
Mak, Alan 麥兆輝
Mak, Heiward 麥曦欣
Maka, Karl 麥嘉
Man, Lim-Chung 文念中
Mao Dun 茅盾
Mella, Franco 甘浩望
Miao, Cora 繆騫人
Miao, Xiaotian 苗曉天
Miu, Michael 苗僑偉
Na, Ying 那英
'Need You Every Single Minute' 〈分分鐘需要你〉
Ngor, Peter 敖志君
Ning, Hao 寧浩
Ou, Oho 歐豪
Ow Man 牛佬
Pang, Edmond 彭浩翔
Pang, Oxide 彭順
Peng, Eddie 彭于晏
People's Daily 《人民日報》
'Pledged to Go into Knife Mountain' 〈誓要入刀山〉
Popular Movies 《大眾電影》

'Prelude to the Water Melody' 〈水調歌頭〉
Produce 101 《創造101》
Pu, Songling 蒲松齡
Pucheng 普城
Qi, Jiguang 戚繼光
Qian, Zhongsshu 錢鍾書
Qiu, Jin 秋瑾
Qiu, Jingwu 秋經武
Qu, Bo 曲波
Reunion 《團圓》
'River of Life' 〈生命之河〉
san tuchu 三突出 ('Theory of Three Prominences')
Sha Ou 沙鷗
Shang, Changrong 尚長榮
Shek, Dean 石天
Shek, Kei 石琪
Shi, Nansun 施南生
Shu, Kei 舒琪
Shu, Qi 舒淇
Siao, Josephine 蕭芳芳
Siqin, Gaowa 斯琴高娃
Siu Hak 小克
Social Worker 《北斗星》
Strange Tales from a Chinese Studio 《聊齋志異》
Su, Shi 蘇軾
Sun, Honglei 孫紅雷
Sun, Yat-sen 孫中山
Tam, Alan 譚詠麟
Tam, Helen 譚玉瑛
Teng, Jinxian 滕進賢
Teng, Teresa 鄧麗君
The Deepest Water Is Tears 《最深的水是淚水》
Tie, Ning 鐵凝
To, Chapman 杜汶澤
To, Johnnie 杜琪峯
Tong, David 佟大為
Tracks in the Snowy Forest 《林海雪原》
The Trading Floor 《東方華爾街》
Tsang, Derek 曾國祥
Tsang, Eric 曾志偉
Tse, Kwan-Ho 謝君豪
Tse, Nicholas 謝霆鋒
Tsoi, Terence 蔡國權

Tsui, Hark 徐克
Tsui, Po-Ko 徐步高
Tsui, Siu-Ming 徐小明
To, Johnnie 杜琪峯
Tong, Stanley 唐季禮
Wang, Hui-Ling 王蕙玲
Wei, Qiuyue 魏秋月
Wen, Muye 文牧野
Wind and Cloud (aka *Storm Rider*) 《風雲》
Wong, Ai-ling 黃愛玲
Wong, Anthony Chau-sang 黃秋生
Wong, Barbara 黃真真
Wong, Faye 王菲
Wong, Jing 王晶
Wong, Kar-Wai 王家衛
Wong, Manfred 文雋
Wong, Race 黃婉佩
Wong, Raymond 黃百鳴
Woo, John 吳宇森
Wu, Daniel 吳彥祖
Wu, David 吳大維
Wu, Jacklyn 吳倩蓮
Wu, Jing 吳京
Xi, Jinping 習近平
Xia, Meng 夏夢
Xiao, Hong 蕭紅
Xiao, Jun 蕭軍
Xie, Mian 謝冕
Xin, Zhilei 辛芷蕾
Xing, Jiadong 邢佳棟
Xu, Jiang 許江
Xu, Xilin 徐錫麟
Xu, Zheng 徐崢
Xue, Xiaolu 薛曉路
Yam, Simon 任達華
Yan, Su 閻肅
Yan, Yan 燕燕
yangbanxi 樣板戲 ('model works')
Yang, Elsa Yee-shan 楊漪珊
Yang, Kaihui 楊開慧
Yang, Kristy 楊恭如
Yang, Tony 楊祐寧
Yang, Yiwei 楊一威

Yang, Yu 楊宇
Yang, Zirong 楊子榮
Yau, Di 姚迪
Yau, Herman 邱禮濤
Ye, Daying 葉大鷹
Ye, Ting 葉挺
Ye, Xin 葉辛
Yee, Derek 爾冬陞
Yee, Jackson 易烊千璽
Yen, Donne 甄子丹
Yim, Ho 嚴浩
yinyang 陰陽
Yip, Raymond 葉偉民
Yip, Wilson 葉偉信
Yu, Dong 于冬
Yue, Shawn 余文樂
Yuen, Bun 元彬
Yuen, Woo-Ping 袁和平
Zhai, Jian 翟劍
Zhang, Changning 張常寧
Zhang, Hanyu 張涵予
Zhang, Hongsen 張宏森
Zhang, Lay 張藝興
Zhang, Ping 張平
Zhang, Yibai 張一白
Zhang, Yimou 張藝謀
Zhang, Yiwu 張頤武
Zhang, Ziyi 章子怡
Zhao, Ruheng 趙汝蘅
Zhao, Vincent 趙文卓
Zhao, Wei 趙薇
'Zhi Hu Zhe Ye' 〈之乎者也〉
Zhou, Xiaolan 周曉蘭
Zhou, Xun 周迅
Zhu, De 朱德
Zhu, Ting 朱婷
Zu, Feng 祖峰

Index

Page numbers in *italic* refer to tables.

1911 (2011), 15, 164, 189
1941 Hong Kong on Fire (1994), 112
2046 (2004), 101
29+1 (2017), *223*
77 Heartbreaks (2017), 165

Ab-Normal Beauty (2004), 201
absent presence concept, 179–82,
    183, 224, 226
Aces Go Places III (1984), 33
Aces Go Places IV (1986), 137
Against All (1990), 112, 114
The Age of Miracles (1996), 85
Ahmad, Aijaz, 70
Airport (1970), 126
*Alan and Eric Between Hello and
    Goodbye* (1991), 81, 83–4, 100,
    103
All About Women (2008), 29, 36
All the Wrong Clues (1981), 32
allegory, 69–70
All's Well, Ends Well Too 2010 (2010),
    175
Always Be With You (2017), 165, 169,
    170
Amazing China (2018), 12
American Dreams in China (2013), 19,
    82, *92*, 100, 103

American Flyers (1985), 145
And Now My Love (1975), 85
Anti-Corruption Pioneers (1981), 206
Anti-Corruption Pioneers II (1985),
    206
Applause Pictures, 81, 83, 89, 90, 201
Armageddon (1997), 137, 142
Armour of God (1987), 81, 111–12
Assembly (2007), 8, 189, 202
As the Light Goes Out (2013), 221
As Time Goes By (1997), 54
Au, Jevons, 223
Avatar (2009), 10
Azalea Mountain (1974), 38–9

Badham, John, 145
Badiou, Alain, 17, 66, 73
Baise Uprising (1989), 5
Bangkok Dangerous (1999), 201
Basic Pictures, 112, 115
Bay, Michael, 150, 152, 155, 157, 162n
Beast Cops (1998), 138, 139–40, 196,
    197
Beast Stalker (2008), 138, 139, 140–1
A Beautiful Life (2011), 113, 119
Beginning of the Great Revival (2011),
    10, 121, 123–4
Behind the Yellow Line (1984), 197

The Berlin File (2013), 225
Berry, Chris, 6, 12, 15, 38, 126, 151, 214
Berry, Michael, 30, 206
Best of the Best (1992), 175
Better Days (2019), 216, 217
A Better Tomorrow (1986), 33, 190, 191, 195
A Better Tomorrow II (1987), 190
Bettinson, Gary, 46, 105, 223
biopics, 126–7
The Birth of New China (1989), 5
Black Hawk Down (2001), 215
Black Mask 2: City of Masks (2002), 35
The Blade (1995), 34–5
blockbusters, 7–9, 10, 45, 89, 103, 163–4, 165, 169, 176, 208–9, 214
    commercial blockbusterisation, 12–17, 189–90, 214–15, 217–19
Blood Brothers (1972), 190
Blood Brothers (1979), 120
Boat People (1983), 55, 56, 57, 60, 61, 63, 67
BoB and Partners, 112, 113, 115
Bodyguards and Assassins (2009), 15, 17, 164, 166, 189, 218, 220–1
Bollywood, 214
Bona Film Group, 218
bookending, 42–3
Bordwell, David, 67, 170
Bound to Lead (1982), 11
The Boxer from Shantung (1972), 190
Boy from Vietnam (1978), 55, 57, 60
Braaten, Rachel, 63–7
The Bravest (2019), 16, 20, 207, 217
Breakfast at Tiffany's (1961), 85
Breaking Away (1979), 145–6
Broken Arrow (1996), 191

The Bugle from Gutian (2019), 16
Bullet in the Head (1990), 190, 195
The Butterfly Murders (1979), 32, 37

Call of Heroes (2016), 225–6
Cameron, James, 10
Cantopop, 3, 84, 85, 180, 221, 224
The Captain (2019), 16, 19, 113, 125–31, 157, 208, 215, 217, 218
catachresis, 47
censorship, 12, 14, 17, 42, 82, 96, 104, 167–8, 170, 182
Certeau, Michel de, 45, 170
Chairman Mao 1949 (2019), 16
Chan, Benny, 177, 205, 225–6
Chan, Chi-tak, 66–7
Chan, Gordon, 15, 137–8, 139, 140, 196–7
Chan, Jackie, 15, 34, 46–7, 80–1, 111–12, 137, 164, 189, 197, 228–9
Chan, Oliver Siu-Kuen, 223–4
Chan, Peter, 15, 16, 19, 80–110, 118, 119–20, 130, 140, 190, 201, 207, 222, 223
    awards, 81, 82, 86, 89–90
    box-office revenues, 92
    on censorship, 104
    and the Chinese film market, 88–93
    cross-border film co-production, 83
    diasporic themes, 84–7
    early life and career, 80–2
    flexible understanding of Hong Kong cinema, 81–2, 83, 103–4
    Hong Kong stories in films, 83–8
    sports films, 94–103
    transnational imagination, 86–7, 92–3

Chan, Stephen Ching-kiu, 220
Chan, Steve Chi-fat, 223
Chan, Tai-Lee, *223*
Chan, Teddy, 15, 164, 220
Chan, Tony, 16, 20, 207
Chang, Cheh, 120, 190
Chang, Eileen, 57–8, 59
Chang, Jing Jing, 66
Chang, William, 70
Chao, Shi-yan, 38, 39, 40–2, 223
Chasing the Dragon (2017), 14–15, 20, 176–7, 204, 205–6
Chasing the Dragon II: Wild Wild Bunch (2019), 205, 206
Cheang, Pou-Soi, 143–4
Chen, Guofu, 8
Chen, Guoxing, 6
Chen Jialin, 5
Chen, Kaige, 4, 47, 101, 221
Chen, Li, 16
Chen, Xiaomei, 12
Cheng, Clement, 142
Cheng, Matthew, 16
Cheuk, Pak Tong, 57, 65
Cheung, Alex, 116
Cheung, Leslie, 7
Cheung, Mabel, 15
Cheung, Matthew, 69
Cheung, Nick, 121, 140–3, 144, 150
Chiang, David, 3
Chin, Man-Kei, 112
China, popular culture, 2
China Daily, 152, 154–5
China Film Group Corporation, 9, 201–3
China Film News, 71
Chinese Box (1997), 101
Chinese Communist Party (CCP), 1, 5, 6, 12, 31, 43, 64, 123–4

Chinese Doctors (2021), 131
A Chinese Ghost Story (1987, 1990, 1991), 33, 46
Chinese Women's Volleyball (2020) (renamed *Leap*), 94
Chineseness, 72–3, 86, 87, 128
Ching, Tony, 33, 34
Chong, Felix, 198–9, 203
Chong, John, 147, 218
Chow, Rey, 4, 44, 47, 86, 128, 221–2
Chow, Stephen, 14, 101, 125, 137, 163, 164, 179–80, 197, 224
Chow, Yiu Fai, 116
Chow, Yun-Fat, 34, 196
Chu, Yingchi, 88
Chua, Ben-huat, 89
Chung, Billy, 207
Chungking Express (1994), 112
Cinema City, 32, 33, 111, 137, 191
Cinema Popular, 81–2
City Cop 2 (1995), 175
City on Fire (1987), 112
CJ 7 (2008), 180
Clark, Paul, 10, 38
The Climbers (2019), 16, 125, 126, 208, 217
Close Economic Partnership Arrangement (CEPA), 3, 8, 14, 38, 224
Cold War 2 (2016), 203
Cold War, Firestorm (2012), 203
Comrades, Almost a Love Story (1996), 83, 85–7, 90, 92–3, 100, 119
Confession of Pain (2006), 112, 118, 198
Confucianism, 168
Confucius (2010), 10
Conspirators (2013), 201
copyright, 96, 97, 168
'Creating Fate' (song), 3

The Creation of a World (1991), 5
crime thrillers/(anti-) crime thrillers,
    174–9, 203–6
    anti-corruption themes, 204, 205–7
    anti-drug themes, 204, 205–6
The Crossing (2014), 20, 193, 194–5,
    215
The Crossing II (2015), 194–5
Crouching Tiger, Hidden Dragon (2000),
    36
Curse of the Golden Flower (2006),
    101
Curtin, Michael, 87

Daisy (2006), 112–13
Dangerous Encounters of the First Kind
    (1980), 29, 30
dapian, 7, 8, 9
Darabont, Frank, 225
Davis, Darrell, 7, 9, 103–4
Days of Being Wild (1990), 112
Dealer Healer (2017), 177–8, 205
The Dearest (2014), 82, *92*, 93, 103
Decisive Engagement trilogy
    (1991–1992), 5
Deiji (Daisy) (2006), 118
The Demon Within, 156
Denby, David, 33
Deng, Xiaoping, 4
Denton, Kirk, 39
The Departed (2006), 112, 117
Derrida, Jacques, 226
Desser, David, 34
The Detective (2007), 201
The Detective 2 (2011), 201
Detective Dee and the Mystery of the
    Phantom Flame (2010), 36, 38,
    40, 46
Detective Gui (2015), 201
diasporic themes, 84–7
Ding, Qiao, 5

Dirlik, Arif, 6, 228
disaster films, 126–9, 131, 154–7,
    190
Don't Fool Me! (1991), 175
Doyle, Christopher, 112
Dragon (2011), 82, 91, *92*, 119,
    120–1
Dragon Blade (2015), 208
DreamWorks, 81, 88
The Drive to Win (1981), 95, 98
Drug War (2012), 16, 20, 40, 44,
    176, 205
Duara, Presenjit, 88
dubbing, 68, 180
The Duel (2000), 112
Dung, Kai-Cheung, 62–3

Eastwood, Clint, 128, 129
Ebola Syndrome (1993), 169, 170, 173
Edney, Kingsley, 11
Edwards, Louis, 167
Eight Hundred Heroes (1975), 123
Eighteen Springs (1997), 56, 57–8,
    61, 68, 71
Election (2005), 89
Emergency Landing (1999), 131
The Emperor and the Assassin (1998),
    101
Emperor Motion Pictures, 142
EntGroup, 14
Erens, Patricia, 65
Eros: The Hand (2004), 101
Eternal Wave (2017), 207
Extraordinary Mission (2017), 16, 20,
    149, 199–200
The Eye (2002–2005), 89, 200, 201

Face/Off (1997), 191
Fall in Love Like a Star (2015), 207
Farewell My Concubine (1993), 101
Fascination Armour (1999), 170, 173

Fatal Decision (2000), 206

Feel 100% (1996), 112

Feng, Xiaoning, 6–7, 8, 189

The Fiery Years (1974), 4

Fight Back to School (1991), 137, 197

Fight Back to School II (1992), 197

Fight Hard: The Champion's Story of Chinese Women's Volleyball Team (1982), 95

film directors

and commercial blockbusterisation, 12–17, 217–19

and erasure of styles, 219

Hong Kong model of filmmaking, 222–4

and main(land melody), 18–21

Film Foundation, World Cinema Project, 214

film titles, 68–9

Film Workshop Co., 33

The Final Option (1994), 197

Fire of Conscience (2010), 138, 141

The First Incense Burner (2021), 71

First Option (1996), 197

First Shot (1993), 206

Flag of the Republic (1999), 6

flashbacks, 65

Flirting Scholar (1993), 101

The Flock (2007), 112–13, 118

The Flowers of War (2011), 202

The Flying Guillotine (1975), 119

The Flying Scotsman (2006), 145

Flying Swords of Dragon Gate (2011), 36

Fong, Henry, 14

Fong, Karen, 73

food scenes, 66–7

Found in Transition (Chu), 2, 3

The Founding of a Republic (2009), 9–10, 13, 121, 123–4, 167

The Founding of an Army (2017), 15, 16, 19, 113, 121–5, 127, 131–2, 147, 218, 219

The Four (2012–2014), 197

From the Queen to the Chief Executive (2001), 169, 171

From Rags to Riches (1980), 191

From Where We've Fallen (2017), 183

Fu, Chaowu, 4

Fu, Poshek, 34, 228

Full Alert (1997), 141

The Fury of King Boxer (1972), 166–7

G Affairs (2018), 165, 183, 224

Gallants (2010), 142

gangster films, 114–17, 121, 137–8, 139–42, 175

Gao, Feng, 124

Gao, Qunshu, 8

Ghost Lantern (1993), 112

Give Me One Day (2021), 183

Give Them a Chance (2003), 169

Global Times, 31, 148, 150, 154, 179, 203–4

God of Gamblers II: Back to Shanghai (1991), 101

God of War (2017), 197

Golden Chicken (2002), 88

Golden Dagger Romance (1978), 32

The Golden Era (2015), 55, 56, 60, 62–3, 64, 65, 69, 71

Golden Harvest, 32, 80, 81, 111, 191

Gong, Li, 37, 100, 101–2

The Grandmaster (2013), 174, 218

Grossberg, Lawrence, 228, 229

Guillerman, John, 126

The Guillotines (2012), 113, 119–21, 122

Gwo, Frant, 215

Han, Sanping, 9, 10, 121
Han, Yan, 156
Hannibal Rising (2007), 101
Hao, Guang, 5
Hao, Jian, 190, 200
Hard Boiled (1992), 190, 191, 192, 195
Hard Target (1993), 191
He Ain't Heavy, He's My Brother (1993), 84–5
Heat Team (2004), 138
Heaven Can Help (1984), 3
Heidegger, Martin, 226
Helios (2015), 203
Hello, Late Comers (1978), 191
Hero (2002), 7–8
Heroes Shed No Tears (1986), 80, 191
He's a Woman, He's a Man (1994), 85
The High and Mighty (1954), 126
Hit Team (2001), 140
Ho, Elaine Yee-lin, 72–3
Ho, Kei-Ping, 68
Ho, Meng-hwa, 119
Ho, Sam, 36
Hollywood, 7, 8, 10, 30, 34–5, 81, 88, 104, 117–18
    influence on Chinese cinema, 214–16
Home with a View (2019), 165
Hong Kong
    and Ann Hui, 57–60
    cinema, trace of, 224–7
    cultural studies/culture, 2–3, 219–20, 228–9
    Hong Kong New Wave, 32, 54
    identity, 60, 116–17
    model of filmmaking, 222–4
    northbound imaginary, 219–22
Hong Kong directors *see* film directors
Hou, Yong, 95

Hu, King, 34, 41
Hu, Mei, 10
Huang, Bo, 99, 102
Huang, Jianxin, 9, 10, 16, 31, 38, 81, 121
Huang, Qunfei, 218
Huayi Brothers, 213
Hui, Ann, 18–19, 54–79, 84, 181, 207, 218, 219
    allegory, use of, 69–70
    awards, 54–5, 60, 62, 71, 73
    in China, 60–3
    Chineseness, 72–3
    contributions to cinema and Hong Kong, 70–1
    controversies, 67–9
    early life and career, 55–6
    films about ordinary people, 63–7, 71–2
    food scenes, 66
    juxtaposition of past and present, 65–6
    TV works, 56–7
    works related to Hong Kong, 57–60
Hui, Frank, 223
Hung, Sammo, 80, 111

I Corrupt All Cops (2009), 207
identity, 60, 116–17, 119, 122
In the Name of the People (2017), 206
Infernal Affairs trilogy (2002–2003), 19, 115–17, 119, 120, 122, 129, 130, 138, 149, 179, 198, 199
Initial D (2005), 112, 118, 198
An Inspector Calls (2015), 170, 175
Integrity (2019), 20, 207
Internal Affairs (2002–2003), 112
Ip, Deanie, 68–9
Ip Man: The Final Flight (2013), 169, 171, 172–4, 184

Jade Goddess of Mercy (2003), 56, 61, 62
Jameson, Fredric, 70
Jenkins, Mark, 119
Jenkins, Patty, 157
Jia, Zhangke, 47
Jiang Hu: the Triad Zone (2000), 140
jiang hu themes, 30, 34, 35, 37
Jiang, Ping, 8
Jiang, Zemin, 6
Jin, Yong, 19, 34, 38, 61
Jing, Mukui, 5
Ju Dou (1990), 101
Jules and Jim (1962), 83

Kagemusha (1980), 193
Kam, Ping-Hing, 59
Keep Rolling (documentary), 67
Kiang, Jessica, 148–9
The Killer (1989), 190, 195
Kloet, Jeroen de, 116
Kokas, Aynne, 215
Koo, Louis, 177, 178
Kung Fu Monster (2018), 113, 124, 125
The Kunlun Column (1988), 5
Kurosawa, Akira, 193
Kwok, Derek, 142, 221

Lam, Dante, 16, 19–20, 95–6, 125, 137–62, 190, 196, 199, 207, 218, 223
  awards, 139, 140, 148
  early life and career, 137–9
  police and gangster films, 139–42, 144–5
  sports films, 142–3, 145–6
  success as a director, 154
  war films, 147–54
Lam, David, 20, 190, 206–7
Lam, Jason, 46

Lam, Ringo, 35, 112, 137, 141, 191
Lang, Ping, 97, 98–102
Last Flight (2014), 131
The Last Samurai (2003), 120
Lau, Andrew, 16, 19, 111–36, 147, 157, 190, 198, 207, 217, 218, 219, 223
  awards, 115–16
  in China, 117–21
  disaster film, *The Captain*, 125–31
  early life and career, 111–13
  films for younger people, 113–17, 121–2
  gangster films, 114–17, 121
  and identity, 116–17, 119, 122
Lau, Andy, 137, 175, 176, 177, 178
Lau, Kar-Leung, 111
Lau, Lawrence, 177–8, 205
Lau, Ricky, 111
Laughing Time (1980), 32, 191
Law, Kar, 54, 72
Leading Group on Major Revolutionary and Historical Themes of Film and Television Creation, 5
The Leakers (2018), 165
Leap (2020), 19, 96–102, 103, 104, 218
Lee, Ang, 193
Lee, Bono, 14–15
Lee, Cheuk-Pan, 183, 224
Lee, Chi-ngai, 84–5, 140
Lee, Daniel, 16, 126, 208, 217
Lee, Erica, 178, 183
Lee, Jun, *223*
Lee, Leo Ou-fan, 59
Lee, Raymond, 34
Lee Rock/Lee Rock II (1991), 112, 205–6
  0, 177

The Legend is Born: Ip Man (2010), 173
Legend of the Fist: The Return of Chen Zhen (2010), 118
The Legend of Zu (2001), 30, 35–6
Legendary Weapons of China (1982), 111
Lei, Xianhe, 6
Lelouch, Claude, 85
Leth, Jørgen, 145
Leung, Candy, 147–8, 153
Leung, Helen Hok-sze, 119
Leung, Longman, 203
Leung, Tony Ka-Fei, 67, 116
Li, Cheuk-to, 70–1
Li, Hanjun, 95
Li, Jet, 34
Li, Jie, 151
Li, Jun, 5
Li, Mei-Ting, 72
Li Na (2019), 94, 102
Li, Qiankuan, 5
Li, Xiepu, 5
Lin, Gengxin, 17
Line Walker (2016), 203
Line Walker 2 (2019), 203
A Little Red Flower (2020), 156
Liu, Chia-chang, 123
Liu, Heng, 202
To Live (1994), 101
To Live and Die in Tsimshatsui (1994), 114, 116
Lo, Chi-leung, 224–5
Lo, Kwai-Cheung, 86–7, 115, 118, 192, 220–1
Long Live Youth (1959), 94
Loo, Andrew, 121
Look for a Star (2009), 118
The Lost Bladesman (2011), 198, 200
Lost in Transition (Chu), 2, 222
Louie, Kam, 2

Love in a Fallen City (1984), 57–60, 63, 64, 65, 66–7, 71, 84
Love in the Rocks (2004), 140
The Love Letter (1999), 81, 88
Lover of the Last Empress (1995), 112
Lover's Grief Over the Yellow River (1999), 6–7
Lu, Jianhua, 95
luan si themes, 34, 35, 37
Lui, Tai-lok, 181, 222–3
Luk, Sunny, 203

Ma, Lunpeng, 167
Ma, Ringo, 112
Mackinnon, Douglas, 145
Mad World (2017), 223
main melody films
  blockbusterisation, 12–17, 189–90, 214–15, 217–19
  categories, 6, 218
  commercial values, 12
  commercialisation, 189–90
  definition of, 4–5, 200
  international popularity, 10–11, 13
  notion of, 163
  production quality, 9–10
  quasi-main melody, 7, 163, 165, 169, 178, 184, 184n, 203–7, 204
  repackaging as genre films, 208, 218–19
  and/as soft power, 8–12, 15, 18
  transformations of, 3–8
Mak, Alan, 16, 20, 112, 115, 116, 118, 149, 190, 198–9, 203, 207
Mak, Heiward, 224
Mak, Peter, 29
Man on the Brink (1981), 116
Man, Wai-Hung, 203
Manhunt (1976), 196

Mao Dun, 64, 69
Marchetti, Gina, 65, 116
Master of the Flying Guillotine (1976), 119
Master Q 2001 (2001), 35
Mean Street Story (1995), 112, 114
Mean Streets (1973), 117
MediaCorp Raintree Pictures, 201
Mei, Qian, 166
Memoirs of a Geisha (2005), 101
The Mermaid (2016), 14, 125, 180, 224
The Mermaid 2 (2019), 181
The Message (2009), 8, 198
Miami Vice (2006), 101
Miao, Xiaotian, 13
The Midnight After (2014), 145
The Millionaire's Express (1986), 111
Missing (2008), 36
Mission: Impossible 2 (2000), 191
Mr Vampire (1985), 111
The Mobfathers (2016), 165, 175
Money Crazy (1977), 191
The Monkey King (2014), 144
Morton, Lisa, 35
motoring films, 143–4
Motorway (2012), 143–4
Mural (2011), 197
My American Grandson (1991), 56, 61
My Intimate Partners (1960), 85
My People, My Country (2019), 16, 125, 208, 217
My War (2016), 16, 20, 200, 201–2, 204
Mysterious Buddha (1981), 4

Naked Ambition (2003), 140
To, Nathan, 40
national rejuvenation, 1–3, 11, 30
Ne Zha (2019), 215

Neame, Ronald, 126
Nessun Dorma (2016), 165
New King of Comedy (2019), 164, 165, 169, 179–81
News Attack (1989), 81
Ngor, Peter, 111
Night and Fog (2009), 57, 71
Ning, Haiqiang, 16
No Regret (1987), 164, 170, 171
Nochimson, Martha, 114
noir/neo-noir, 141, 145
northbound imaginary concept, 219–22
Nye, Joseph, 11, 12

Olympia (1936), 94
On Fire series, 141
On the Edge (2006), 169, 173, 175
Once Upon a Time in China series, 33–4, 46
The One Man Olympics (2008), 95
Operation Mekong (2016), 16, 17, 19, 137, 139, 147–50, 199, 200, 204, 215
Operation Red Sea (2018), 16–17, 20, 95–6, 125, 137, 139, 148, 150–4, 155–6
The Opium War (1997), 6
Option Zero (1997), 137–8, 139
Ordinary Heroes (1999), 54, 60, 63, 64–5, 67, 68, 71
Orientalism, 128, 221–2
Our Time Will Come (2017), 16, 17, 19, 56, 60, 63–4, 65–6, 67–9, 70, 71–3, 218, 219
Out of Inferno (2013), 190, 201
Overheard trilogy (2009–2014), 198–9, 203
The Oxford History of World Cinema, 214

Painted Skin (2008), 196–7

pan-Asian cinema, 81, 89, 90, 92, 104, 105n, 142, 201

Pang, Danny, 200–1

Pang, Kearen, *223*

Pang, Laikwan, 155

Pang, Oxide, 16, 20, 190, 200–3

patriotism, 6–7, 11, 126, 148, 150–1, 152, 167

Paycheck (2003), 192, 193

Peking Opera Blues (1986), 33, 37

Peng, Eddie, 17, 146, 150, 156

Peng, Kan, 82

People's Daily, 98, 148

People's Liberation Army (PLA), 40, 113, 121, 122, 124, 147, 150–1, 203

Perhaps Love (2005), 19, 81, 82, 89–90, *92*, 103, 104, 222

period dramas, 197

poetry, 68, 73

Polybona Films, 128

Port of Call (2015), 41, 173, 223

The Poseidon Adventure (1972), 126

positive energy concept, 9, 11, 12

The Postmodern Life of My Aunt (2006), 54, 56, 61–2

Powerful Four (1992), 206

Princess Chang Ping (1976), 191

Princess Fragrance (1987), 19, 61

Project Gutenberg (2018), 203, 204

propaganda, 3–4, 5, 12, 17, 18, 94, 95, 96, 147, 152–3, 203

The Protector (1985), 81

Pun, Anthony, 16, 20, 149, 199–200

Qian, Zhongshu, 144

Qiu, Jin, 165, 166–7

Qiu Jin: A Revolutionary (1983), 166, 167

Qiu Jin and Xu Xilin (1948), 166

Qiu, Jingwu, 166

Queen of Sports (1934), 94

The Raid (1991), 45, 46

Raise the Red Lantern (1991), 101, 151

Rambo (2008), 215

Ran (1985), 193

Rancière, Jacques, 124, 157

Raped by an Angel (1993), 112

Red Cliff (2008), 192, 193

The Red Detachment of Women (1961), 4, 38–9

red poetics, 38–9

Reign of Assassins (2010), 193

The Rescue (2020), 20, 154–7

Revenge of the Green Dragons (2014), 121

Roaring Across the Horizon (1999), 6

Rocky Balboa (2006), 142

Roman Holiday (1953), 85

The Romance of Book and Sword (1987), 18–19, 54, 56, 60–1

Rosen, Stanley, 8, 11

Runaway (2001), 141

Ryoo, Seung-wan, 225

Said, Edward, 47

Sara (2014), 169, 171, 172, 184

Scorsese, Martin, 112, 117, 121, 214

Seaton, George, 126

The Secret (1979), 55, 57

The Secret of China (2019), 16

Seven Swords (2005), 36

Sha, Ou, 95

Shanghai Blues (1984), 33, 37

Shanghai Triad (1995), 101

Shaw Brothers, 58, 111, 197

Shawshank Redemption (1994), 225

Shek, Kei, 139

Shen, Jie, 95
Shi, Nansun, 31, 33
Shin, Thomas, 84
Shock Wave (2017), 20, 165, 169, 170, 175–6, 179, 203
Shock Wave 2 (2020), 156, 176, 179
Shu, Kei, 85
Shui, Hua, 4
Siao, Josephine, 70
The Silent War (2012), 198–9
A Simple Life (2012), 55, 56, 62, 66, 71, 218
Siu, Hak, 221
The Sleep Curse (2017), 165, 170, 173
The Sniper (2009), 140
soft power, 8–12, 15, 18, 95, 151, 193, 221
Song of the Exile (1990), 72
songs, 3, 64, 84, 86–7, 97, 180, 224
The Soong Sisters (1997), 15
Sparkling Red Star (2007), 140
Special Administrative Regions (SARs), 1, 3
special effects, 32–3, 35–6, 41, 120
Spielberg, Steven, 123
Spiridon, Monica, 44
Spivak, Gayatri, 47, 224, 226, 227
The Spooky Bunch (1980), 55, 70
sports films, 94–103, 142–3, 145–6, 190
Starry is the Night (1988), 60, 64, 65, 68, 84
State Administration of Radio, Film and Television (SAPPRFT), 7, 24n, 41
Still Human (2018), 224
Stokes, Lisa Odham, 63
The Stool Pigeon (2010), 19, 138, 140, 141

Storm Rider Clash of the Evils (2008), 140
The Storm Riders (1998), 112, 115, 123
Storm series (2014–2019), 20, 204, 206–7, 208, 217–18
The Story of Qiu Ju (1991), 101, 102
The Story of Woo Viet (1981), 55, 57, 63
Stuckey, G. Andrew, 90
Su, Chao-pin, 193
Su, Shi, 54, 68
Su, Wendy, 7
Sully (2016), 128, 129, 215
Summer Snow (1996), 55, 62, 67
Sun, Yongping, 4
Sun, Yu, 94
A Sunday in Hell (1976), 145
Swordsman series, 33–4
Szeman, Imre, 70
Szeto, Elyssa, 192
Szeto, Mirana, 66

Takakura, Ken, 196
The Taking of Tiger Mountain 3D (2014), 13, 16, 17, 18, 29, 30, 64, 67, 150, 167, 195, 200, 218
  bookending, 42–3
  director's strategies, 37–42, 45
  heroic positioning, 39–40
  narrative framing, 40–1, 44
  political aspects, 42–5
  popularity, 31, 41, 44
Taking Tiger Mountain by Strategy (opera), 30, 31, 38–9, 42
Tan, See Kam, 37, 44
Tang, Billy, 205
Taxi Driver (1993), 173
As Tears Go By (1988), 112, 117
Temptress Moon (1996), 101
Ten Years (2015), 41

Teng, Jinxian, 4
Teng, Teresa, 86–7
Teo, Stephen, 34, 90, 141, 193
A Terra-Cotta Warrior (1990), 37
That Demon Within (2014), 19, 138, 144–5
Theory of Ambitions (delayed), 207
Those Were the Days (1995), 205
Three (2002), 81, 89
three prominences theory, 39–40
Thunderbolt (1995), 137, 142, 197
Tie Ren (2009), 9
Time Raiders (2016), 208
A Time to Remember (1999), 6–7
Ting, Shan-Hsi, 123, 166
Tiramasu (2002), 140
Titanic (1997), 193, 194, 195, 215
To, Chapman, 172, 183
To, Johnnie, 16, 20, 89, 176, 179, 183, 205
To Be Number One (1991), 177, 205
To the Fore (2015), 19, 95, 139, 145–6
Tom, Dick and Hairy (1993), 84, 84–5, 139–40
Tomorrow is Another Day (2017), 223
Towards the River Glorious (2019), 203
The Towering Inferno (1974), 126
Tracey (2018), 223
Tracks in the Snowy Forest (film, 1960), 39–40, 46
transnational imagination, 86, 92–3
Triangle (2007), 36
Trivisa (2016), 223, 224
Troublesome Night series (1997–2017), 169
True Women for Sale (2008), 164, 169, 171, 173
Truffaut, François, 83

Tsang, Derek, 16
Tsang, Eric, 81
Tsui, Hark, 13, 15, 16, 17, 18, 29–53, 54, 64, 82, 124, 150, 164, 167, 191, 195, 200, 202, 207, 218, 223
   awards, 31, 32, 36, 41
   film career, 32–7
   in Hollywood, 34–5
   mixing of genres, 37–8, 41, 45–6
   political aspects of *Tiger Mountain*, 42–5
   strategies for *The Taking of Tiger Mountain 3D* (2014), 37–42, 45
Turning Point (2009), 173, 175
Turning Point 2 (2011), 175

The Twins Effect (2003), 138, 141, 142

Umbrella Movement, 44, 52n, 69, 145
Unbeatable (2013), 19, 138, 141, 142–3, 145, 156, 180
Undercover Hidden Dragon (2006), 138, 140, 196
United Filmmakers Organization (UFO), 81, 83, 87
The Untold Story (1993), 169, 170, 173

Van Damme, Jean-Claude, 35, 191
The Vanished Murderer (2015), 224–5
Veg, Sebastian, 171, 224
From Vegas to Macau III (2016), 121
Victim (1999), 141
Victory (1976), 123
The Viral Factor (2012), 138, 142
The Volleyball Flower (1980), 95
Vulgaria (2012), 172

The Wandering Earth (2019), 208, 215
Wang, Baoqiang, 180
Wang, Bin, 4
Wang, Feifei, 183
Wang, Hui-Ling, 193
Wang, Jimmy, 119
Wang, Jixing, 6, 16
Wang, Ning, 11
Wang, Wayne, 101
war films, 15, 16, 19, 113, 121–5,
    127, 131–2, 147–54, 191, 198,
    201–3
The War of Loong (2017), 124
The Warlords (2007), 19, 82, 90–1,
    92, 103, 120, 222
The Way We Are (2009), 57, 66, 67, 71
The Way We Dance (2013), 180
We Pictures, 81, 83, 94
Weeds on Fire (2016), 180, 223
Wellman, William A., 126
Wheels on Meals (1984), 80–1
When I look Upon the Stars (1999),
    140
Whispers and Moans (2007), 169,
    171–2
The White-Haired Girl (1950), 4
The White Storm (2013), 177, 205
The White Storm 2: Drug Lords (2019),
    20, 169, 176, 177–9, 179, 205,
    217
Who is Running (1997), 201
Who's the Woman, Who's the Man
    (1996), 85
The Wicked City (1992), 29, 30
Williams, Tony, 141, 196
Windtalkers (2002), 191, 192–3
Wolf Warrior (2015), 148, 149, 154,
    215
Wolf Warrior 2 (2017), 15, 17, 124,
    149, 151–2, 208, 215

Woman Basketball Player No. 5
    (1957), 94
The Woman Knight of Mirror Lake
    (2011), 20, 96, 164, 165–9, 173,
    176, 189
Wonder Woman 1984 (2020), 157
Wong, Ai-ling, 60–1
Wong, Anthony Chau-sang, 173
Wong, Chun, 223
Wong, Jing, 14, 20, 112, 113, 121,
    130, 176–7, 190, 205–6, 207
Wong, Kar-Wai, 35, 101, 112, 117,
    130, 172–3, 174, 181
Wong, Kin-yuen, 36
Wong, Manfred, 112, 113
Wong, Peter, 219
Wong, Raymond, 170
Wong, Vicky, 223
Woo, John, 20, 32, 33, 35, 80, 82,
    189, 190–6, 203
Wu, Daniel, 144
Wu, Jing, 124, 218
wuxia movies, 29–30, 31, 32, 34, 35,
    36, 37–8, 40, 82, 91, 119–20,
    121, 125, 193, 218

Xi, Jinping, 1, 3, 11, 12–13, 30
Xia, Meng, 60
xiao (filial piety), 168
Xiao, Guiyun, 5
Xiao, Hong, 62–3
Xie, Jin, 4, 6, 45, 166–7
Xie, Mian, 5
Xie, Wendy, 31
Xinhai Revolution, 15, 163–4, 165,
    189

Yang, Yiwei, 38
Yang, Yu, 215
Yates, Peter, 145

Yau, Edward, 219
Yau, Esther, 14–15, 141, 224, 226–7
Yau, Herman, 20, 35, 96, 156, 163–88,
    189, 203, 205, 224
  (anti-) crime thrillers, 174–9
  and Anthony Wong, 173–4
  awards, 169–70, 176
  and censorship, 168, 170, 182
  commitment to Hong Kong, 172
  co-productions, views on, 182,
    184
  making-do spirit, 170, 181
  prostitution themes, 171–2
  reputation, 169–70, 181
  self-effacing character, 179–82,
    183
  versatility and productivity, 164–5,
    170, 181–2
  and *The Woman Knight of Mirror
    Lake* (2011), 165–9, 189
Yau, Ka-Fei, 63
Yau, Shuk-ting Kinnia, 17, 71
Ye, Daying, 6–7, 123
Yee, Derek, 227
Yeh, Emilie Yueh-yu, 38, 39, 40–2,
    103–4, 223
Yellow Earth (1984), 4
Yen, Donnie, 172, 173
Yeung, Jessica Siu-Yin, 69–70
Yin, Li, 9
Young and Dangerous (1996–2000),
    19, 112, 113, 114–15, 116, 119,
    120, 130

*Young Detective Dee: Rise of the Sea
    Dragon 3D* (2013), 36
The Young Dragons (1975), 190
Youngs, Tim, 149, 200
Yu, Benzheng, 206
Yu, Dong, 8–9, 31, 128, 129, 218,
    221
Yu, Hongmei, 6, 7
Yu, Zhongying, 4
Yuan, Dengyu, 150
Yuen, Alan, 203
Yung, Philip, 173, 207, 223
Yuppie Fantasia (1989), 197

Zhang, Hongsen, 1, 8, 15
Zhang, Huaxun, 4
Zhang, Jianya, 131
Zhang, Jingwu, 9
Zhang, Nuanxin, 95
Zhang, Rui, 5
Zhang, Xudong, 4
Zhang, Yimou, 4, 7, 47, 101, 151,
    202, 221
Zhang, Yitong, 95
Zhang, Yiwu, 5
Zhou, Vincent, 131
Zhou, Xun, 68
Zhu, Ying, 8, 11
Žižek, Slavoj, 208–9
Zodiac Killers (1991), 57
Zu: Warriors from the Magic Mountain,
    32–3, 41, 46
Zwick, Edward M., 120